Fodor's First Edition

S0-AKE-375

Cuba

The complete guide, thoroughly up-to-date

Packed with details that will make your trip

The must-see sights, off and on the beaten path

What to see, what to skip

Vacation itineraries, walking tours, day trips

Smart lodging and dining options

Essential local do's and taboos

Transportation tips

Key contacts, savvy travel advice

When to go, what to pack

Clear, accurate, easy-to-use maps

Background essay

Fodor's Cuba

EDITORS: Laura M. Kidder, Christine Swiac

Editorial Contributors: Deb Carroll, David Dudenhoefer, Amy Karafin, John Marino, George Semler

Editorial Production: Rebecca Zeiler

Maps: David Lindroth, *cartographer;* Mapping Specialists Ltd., *cartographers;* Rebecca Baer and Bob Blake, *map editors*

Design: Fabrizio La Rocca, *creative director;* Guido Caroti, *art director;* Jolie Novak, *photo editor*

Cover Design: Pentagram

Production/Manufacturing: Mike Costa

Cover Photo: Jan Butchofsky-Houser

Copyright

First Edition

ISBN 0–679–00455–6

ISSN 1091–4749

Special Sales

Fodor's Travel Publications are available at special discounts for bulk purchases for sales promotions or premiums. Special editions, including personalized covers, excerpts of existing guides, and corporate imprints, can be created in large quantities for special needs. For more information, contact your local bookseller or write to Special Markets, Fodor's Travel Publications, 201 East 50th Street, New York, NY 10022. Inquiries from Canada should be directed to your local Canadian bookseller or sent to Random House of Canada, Ltd., Marketing Department, 2775 Matheson Boulevard East, Mississauga, Ontario L4W 4P7. Inquiries from the United Kingdom should be sent to Fodor's Travel Publications, 20 Vauxhall Bridge Road, London SW1V 2SA, England.

PRINTED IN THE UNITED STATES OF AMERICA

10 9 8 7 6 5 4 3 2 1

Important Tip

Although all prices, opening times, and other details in this book are based on information supplied to us at press time, changes occur all the time in the travel world, and Fodor's cannot accept responsibility for facts that become outdated or for inadvertent errors or omissions. So **always confirm information when it matters,** especially if you're making a detour to visit a specific place.

CONTENTS

ON THE ROAD WITH FODOR'S

THE TRIPS YOU TAKE this year and next are going to be significant trips, if only because they'll be your first in the new millennium. Acutely aware of that fact, we've pulled out all stops in preparing *Fodor's Cuba*. To guide you in putting together your Cuban experience, we've created multiday itineraries and neighborhood walks. And to direct you to the places that are truly worth your time and money in these important years, we've rallied the team of endearingly picky know-it-alls we're pleased to call our writers. Having seen all corners of the regions they cover for us, they're real experts. If you knew them, you'd poll them for tips yourself.

Freelance journalist and travel hack **David Dudenhoefer** spent most of the 1990s writing about things Latin American from his base in San José, Costa Rica. In addition to writing the central Cuba chapter, he has worked on five Fodor's guides and contributed articles and photos to dozens of newspapers and magazines published on both sides of the Rio Grande. Though his heart remains in Latin America, David currently resides in Chicago.

John Marino, who covered eastern Cuba and researched the information for Smart Travel Tips A to Z, has written frequently about Puerto Rico and the Caribbean for Reuters news service, the *New York Times, Newsday,* and other publications. He has also published two books on travel and myth in the region. He lives in San Juan, Puerto Rico, with his wife and son.

Barcelona-based journalist **George Semler,** who covered Havana and western Cuba, has been writing about Spain, France, and North Africa since the early '70s. Author of books on Madrid and Barcelona, George has reported on gastronomy, music, theater, poetry, fly-fishing, and baseball in both English and Spanish for the *Los Angeles Times, Saveur, Sky, Forbes FYI, The International Herald Tribune,* and *El Pais.* He's presently writing a book on the Pyrénées.

Don't Forget to Write

Keeping a travel guide fresh and up-to-date is a big job. So we love your feedback—positive and negative—and follow up on all suggestions. Contact the Cuba editor at editors@fodors.com or c/o Fodor's, 201 East 50th Street, New York, New York 10022. And have a wonderful trip!

Karen Cure
Editorial Director

The Caribbean

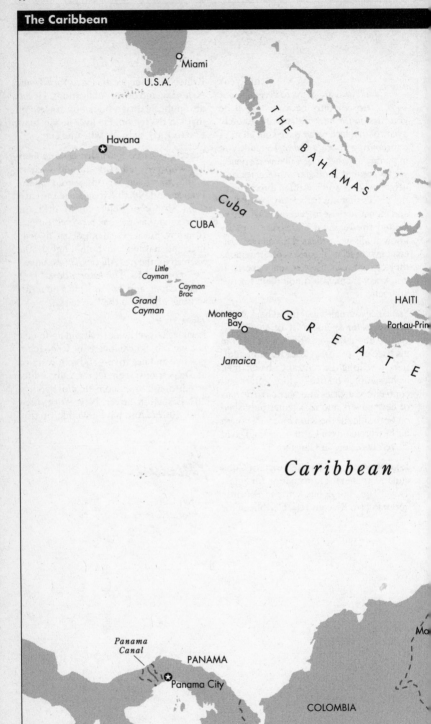

Miami

U.S.A.

THE BAHAMAS

Havana

Cuba

CUBA

Little Cayman

Cayman Brac

Grand Cayman

Montego Bay

HAITI

Port-au-Prin

G R E A T E

Jamaica

Caribbean

Panama Canal

PANAMA

Panama City

Ma

COLOMBIA

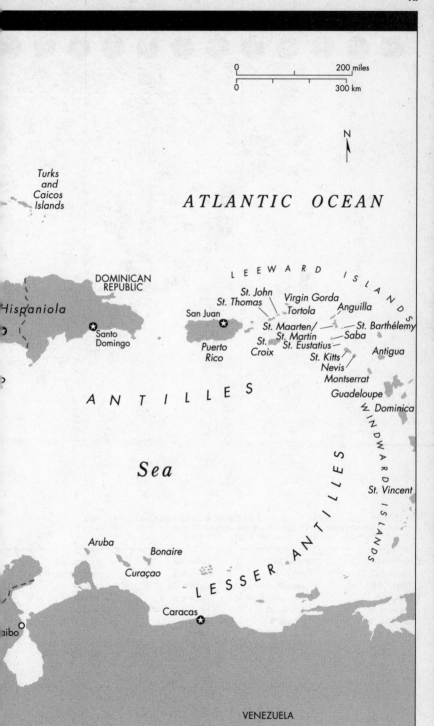

0   200 miles

0   300 km

N

Turks and Caicos Islands

ATLANTIC OCEAN

L E E W A R D   I S L A N D S

DOMINICAN REPUBLIC

Hispaniola

☆ Santo Domingo

San Juan ☆

Puerto Rico

St. John

St. Thomas

Virgin Gorda

Tortola

Anguilla

St. Maarten/ St. Martin

St. Barthélemy

Saba

St. Eustatius

St. Croix

St. Kitts

Nevis

Montserrat

Antigua

Guadeloupe

Dominica

W I N D W A R D   I S L A N D S

A N T I L L E S

Sea

St. Vincent

Aruba

Bonaire

Curaçao

L E S S E R   A N T I L L E S

Caracas ☆

aibo ○

VENEZUELA

World Time Zones

MONDAY
SUNDAY

International Date Line

+12 +13

-9

-10

+11

+12

-11

-10

-7

+11   +12 -   -11   -10   -9   -8   -7   -6   -5   -4   -3   -2

Numbers below vertical bands relate each zone to Greenwich Mean Time (0 hrs.).
Local times frequently differ from these general indications,
as indicated by light-face numbers on map.

Algiers, **29**	Berlin, **34**	Delhi, **48**	Jerusalem, **42**
Anchorage, **3**	Bogotá, **19**	Denver, **8**	Johannesburg, **44**
Athens, **41**	Budapest, **37**	Dublin, **26**	Lima, **20**
Auckland, **1**	Buenos Aires, **24**	Edmonton, **7**	Lisbon, **28**
Baghdad, **46**	Caracas, **22**	Hong Kong, **56**	London
Bangkok, **50**	Chicago, **9**	Honolulu, **2**	(Greenwich), **27**
Beijing, **54**	Copenhagen, **33**	Istanbul, **40**	Los Angeles, **6**
	Dallas, **10**	Jakarta, **53**	Madrid, **38**
			Manila, **57**

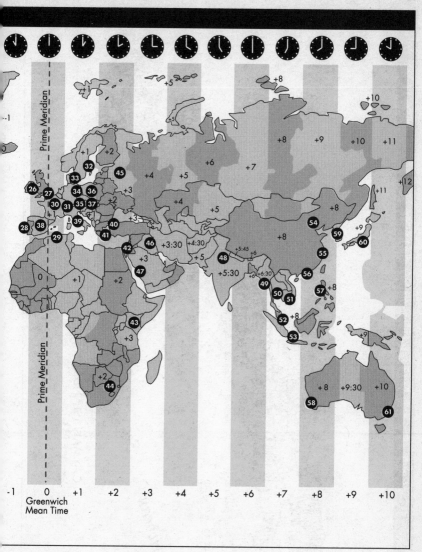

Mecca, **47**
Mexico City, **12**
Miami, **18**
Montréal, **15**
Moscow, **45**
Nairobi, **43**
New Orleans, **11**
New York City, **16**

Ottawa, **14**
Paris, **30**
Perth, **58**
Reykjavík, **25**
Rio de Janeiro, **23**
Rome, **39**
Saigon (Ho Chi Minh City), **51**

San Francisco, **5**
Santiago, **21**
Seoul, **59**
Shanghai, **55**
Singapore, **52**
Stockholm, **32**
Sydney, **61**
Tokyo, **60**

Toronto, **13**
Vancouver, **4**
Vienna, **35**
Warsaw, **36**
Washington, D.C., **17**
Yangon, **49**
Zürich, **31**

Cuba

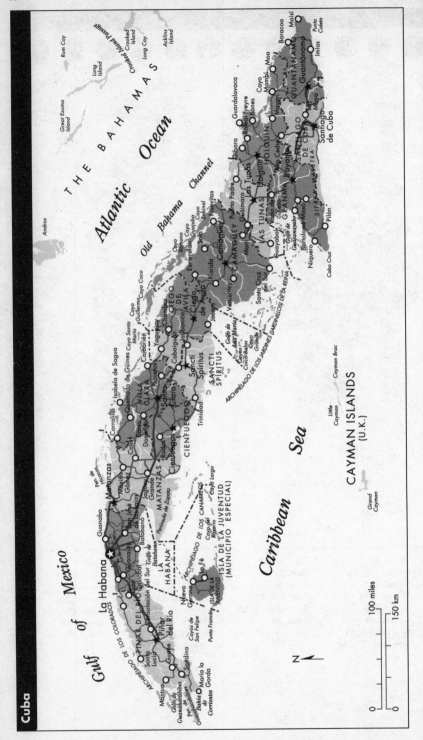

SMART TRAVEL TIPS A TO Z

Basic Information on Traveling in Cuba, Savvy Tips to Make Your Trip a Breeze, and Companies and Organizations to Contact

ADDRESSES

Addresses are frequently cited as street names with numbers and/or locations, as in: "Calle Concordia, e/Calle Gervasio y Calle Escobar" or "Calle de los Oficios 53, esquina de Obrapía". It's helpful to know the following terms and abbreviations: "e/" is *entre* (between); *esquina de* (sometimes seen as "esq. de") is "corner of"; and *y* is "and". Some streets have pre- and postrevolutionary names; both are often cited on local maps and on maps and in text throughout this guide.

AIR TRAVEL

Dozens of international airlines now serve Cuba, although air travel to the island is still dominated by charter flights. Many of these originate in Canada, Mexico, and Europe and are part of package deals that include stays in one of Cuba's burgeoning number of all-inclusive resorts. Flying within Cuba is extremely affordable by North American and European standards, and routes connect most major cities in the country.

Although there's still no regular, commercial service from the United States to Cuba (Americans touting the embargo often fly to the island from elsewhere in the Caribbean or from Canada or Mexico), new rules have cleared the way for more direct, charter flights between the two nations. Note that U.S. citizens still require special permission from the Treasury Department to travel to the island (☞ Americans and Cuba, *below*).

AIRPORTS

In addition to its main hub, Aeropuerto Internacional José Martí in Havana, Cuba has five international airports and several smaller, regional hubs. For details, *see* Arriving and Departing by Airplane *in* the A to Z section at the end of each chapter.

BOOKING YOUR FLIGHT

When you book **look for nonstop flights** and **remember that "direct" flights stop at least once.** Try to avoid connecting flights, which require a change of plane.

CARRIERS

Cubana, the national carrier, has both domestic and international flights on mostly Russian-built aircraft. Service is adequate but somewhat below North American and European standards. The airline offers direct service between Havana and just about anywhere in the world (except the United States) and between Santiago de Cuba and Madrid, Spain; Paris, France; and Frankfurt, Germany. Domestic service includes daily flights between Havana and Santiago de Cuba and Havana and Holguín. (Note that it's illegal for U.S. citizens to fly on Cubana, as it constitutes a cash payment to the Cuban government—a trade embargo no-no.)

Several major foreign carriers, which are undoubtedly more comfortable than Cubana, also serve the island. These include British Airways, which has weekly flights (on Saturday) from Gatwick to Nassau, Bahamas, and on to Havana, and Iberia, which flies nonstop from Madrid to Havana daily.

You can get the best rates to Cuba, particularly from Canada (Toronto handles most of the traffic), by booking a charter flight—whether you opt only to purchase seats on a plane or to buy a complete package that includes airfare, hotel, and transfers to and from the airport. From Canada, companies that offer such packages include Air Canada Vacations (a division of Air Canada, with several flights a week to Havana, Varadero, and Santiago de Cuba) and Air Transat (with service between Toronto and Havana, Varadero, Cienfuegos, and Santiago de Cuba).

Also, consider booking through a tour operator that specializes in travel to Cuba (☞ Tour Operators, *below*).

Mirazul Tours—which has been running charters to and from the United States to Cuba since 1979—offers weekly flights to Havana from Miami and, as of December 1999, from New York and Los Angeles. Note that only certain Americans qualify for licensed travel to Cuba (☞ Americans and Cuba, *below*).

➤ AIRLINES/CHARTERS FROM CANADA: **Air Canada Vacations** (☎ 514/422–5788 in Montréal). **Air Transat** (☎ 416/485–3377 in Toronto). **Bel-Air Inc.** (☎ 514/871–8330 in Montréal). **Cubana** (☎ 416/676–4723 in Toronto). **Cubanácan Canada International** (☎ 514/861–4444 in Montréal). **Regent Holidays** (☎ 416/673–3343 in Toronto). **Travel Deals** (☎ 416/236–0125 in Toronto). **Wings of the World** (☎ 416/482–1223 in Toronto).

➤ AIRLINES/CHARTERS FROM THE CARIBBEAN AND LATIN AMERICA: **Aeromexico** (☎ 5/207–6311 in Mexico City). **Aeropostal** (☎ 509–3666 in Caracas). **Cubana** (☎ 5/255–3776 in Mexico City; 809/549–0345 in Santo Domingo, Dominican Republic; 289–3548 in Caracas). **Divermex** (☎ 98/842325 in Cancún). **Mexicana** (☎ 5/325–0990 in Mexico City). **Sunholiday Tours** (☎ 809/952–5629 in Jamaica; 800/433–2920 in the United States). **Yucatán Tours** (☎ 299/282582 in Mérida).

➤ AIRLINES FROM EUROPE: **British Airways**(☎ 0345/222111 in London). **Cubana** (☎ 020/7734–1165 in London). **Iberia** (☎ 904/400500 in Madrid).

➤ CHARTERS FROM THE U.S: **Mirazul Tours** (✉ 771 NW 37 Ave., Miami, FL 33125, ☎ 305/559–3616; ✉ Tower Plaza Mall, 4100 Park Ave., Weehawken, NJ 07087, ☎ 201/319–9670).

CHECK-IN & BOARDING

Assuming that not everyone with a ticket will show up, airlines routinely overbook planes. When that happens, airlines ask for volunteers to give up their seats. In return these volunteers usually get a certificate for a free flight and are rebooked on the next flight out. If there are not enough volunteers, the airline must choose who will be denied boarding. The first to get bumped are passengers who checked in late and those flying on discounted tickets, so **get to the gate and check in as early as possible,** especially during peak periods.

Always **bring a government-issued photo ID to the airport.** You may be asked to show it before you are allowed to check in.

CUTTING COSTS

The least-expensive airfares to Cuba must usually be purchased in advance and are non-refundable. It's smart to **call a number of airlines, and when you are quoted a good price, book it on the spot**—the same fare may not be available the next day. Always **check different routings** and look into using different airports. Travel agents, especially low-fare specialists (☞ Discounts & Deals, *below*), are helpful.

ENJOYING THE FLIGHT

For more legroom **request an emergency-aisle seat.** Don't sit in the row in front of the emergency aisle or in front of a bulkhead, where seats may not recline. If you have dietary concerns, **ask for special meals when booking.** These can be vegetarian, low-cholesterol, or kosher, for example. On long flights, try to maintain a normal routine, to help fight jet lag. At night **get some sleep.** By day **eat light meals, drink water** (not alcohol), and **move around the cabin** to stretch your legs.

HOW TO COMPLAIN

If your baggage goes astray or your flight goes awry, complain right away. Most carriers require that you **file a claim immediately.**

AMERICANS AND CUBA

Although there are restrictions in place owing to the U.S. trade embargo, technically, it's not illegal for Americans to travel to Cuba; what *is* illegal is spending money in the country. American companies cannot conduct business with companies in

Cuba, and neither can individual Americans. Hence, credit cards issued by U.S. companies and insurance policies provided by U.S. insurers are not valid here; American airlines do not fly directly to Cuba (though there is charter-flight service from New York, Miami, and Los Angeles); and American tour operators and travel agents do not offer packages directly to the island.

Restrictions on individuals and businesses are contained within the Cuban Assets Control Regulations, first enacted in 1963 under the Trading with the Enemy Act, but revised through the years. For complete details on the latest regulations and on licenses for travel to Cuba contact the U.S. Department of the Treasury's Office of Foreign Assets Control (OFAC; the department also has a helpful Web site). In an effort to help explain the restrictions further, the U.S. State Department has also developed a useful Web site.

LICENSED TRAVEL TO CUBA

For official travel to Cuba, **look into OFAC general and specific licenses.** Those who qualify for a general license need not inform the OFAC in advance of their visit nor obtain a written OFAC license. Specific licenses are more complicated: if you qualify, you must obtain a written license by writing to the OFAC stating your name and title, when you plan to travel, and the length and purpose of your visit; you must also provide details on your background. Travel with either type of license allows you to spend up to $187 a day on hotels, meals, ground transportation, and other basics. You can also return to the United States with Cuban products whose value totals no more than $100 (educational and informational material, film, CDs, and books are exempt). **Save your receipts,** as a Cuban stamp in your passport will no doubt raise red flags with U.S. Customs officials.

The following U.S. travelers qualify for an OFAC general license: government personnel on official business, journalists and their support staff who are employed full time by a publication or broadcast company (such travelers should have a company ID with a photograph, business cards, and a letter—on company letterhead—verifying full-time employment), fully hosted travelers (☞ *below*), and individuals visiting close relatives (such trips are limited to once a year, though exceptions are made—via a specific license—for humanitarian reasons).

The following Americans can apply for a specific license: those involved in business, academic, international-relations, and human-rights research; people visiting close relatives more than once in a 12-month period for extreme humanitarian reasons; freelance journalists; graduate students; professors who will be lecturing at educational institutions; athletes who will be competing in events; and artists and performers who will be participating in exhibitions or concerts. Those accompanying licensed humanitarian donations (as specified by the U.S. Department of Commerce's Office of Export Administrations) also qualify for a specific license.

Licenses are also available for individuals or establishments affiliated with a U.S.-based religious organization. Such licenses must be renewed every two years. Travelers associated with a licensed organization are free to travel to Cuba as long as they carry a letter from the organization stating its license number and that the individual is affiliated with the organization and is traveling for the purpose of religious activity in Cuba under the organization's auspices.

FULLY HOSTED TRAVELERS

Fully hosted travelers are defined as those who spend no money on their Cuba trip as they're guests of a non-U.S. entity. Although such people qualify for travel under a general license, the guidelines and restrictions for such trips are more complex. Further, the $100 Cuban-goods import allowance does not apply, and you may be required to provide proof supporting your claim to being fully hosted. The OFAC warns that fully hosted travelers will be under intense scrutiny by State Department, Treasury Department, Customs, and

THE GOLD GUIDE / SMART TRAVEL TIPS

THE GOLD GUIDE / SMART TRAVEL TIPS

Immigration officials. If you're planning a fully hosted trip to Cuba, **be sure that you meet all the requirements and have all the necessary documentation.**

UNLICENSED TRAVEL TO CUBA

Cuba's romantic history, culture, and people have left an indelible imprint on the American psyche, making the idea of a leisure junket to the island very tempting. Many U.S. citizens visit Cuba by going through third countries such as Canada, Mexico, and the Bahamas (often using third-country tour operators and travel agents to arrange their trips) and by asking Cuban officials to stamp separate pieces of paper rather than their passports upon arrival on the island. Although there has been talk of easing restrictions (and no one has been prosecuted for violating the restrictions currently in place), **be aware that there are still penalties for unlicensed travel to Cuba.** The fines can be severe: for businesses, they're as much as $1 million, for individuals, up to $250,000. In certain circumstances, penalties include up to 10 years in jail.

➤ INFORMATION: **U.S. Department of the Treasury, Office of Foreign Assets Control** (☎ 202/622–2520 in Washington, D.C.; ☎ 305/810–5140 in Miami, FL; www.treas.gov/ofac). **U.S. State Department** (www.state.gov/www/regions/wha/cuba/index.html).

BOAT & FERRY TRAVEL

There's boat and ferry service from the Cuban mainland to several offshore keys. For details on such service, *see* Getting Around by Boat *in* the A to Z section at the end of each chapter.

BUS TRAVEL

Cubans rely a great deal on an unreliable bus system—one with crowded, badly maintained vehicles (even long-distance buses, called *especiales,* are well below North American and European standards), and slow service. Demand for service is so great and seats (and fuel) so scarce that not only are old farm trucks pressed into public-transport service but state trucks, by law, must pick up Cuban citizens hitching rides. For these reasons, public buses aren't really a viable option for most visitors. If you still dare catch a bus note that most cities have two types of terminal: the *terminal de omnibus nacional* serves especiales and the *terminal de omnibus intermunicipales* serves intercity buses.

Shuttle and tour buses that cater to visitors are your best options. They're economical, comfortable, and convenient. And there are tours of and trips to just about everywhere. Most can be booked through your hotel or at local offices of Havanatur and other state travel agencies. For details on companies and agencies that arrange bus travel, *see* Tour Operators and Travel Agencies *in* the A to Z section at the end of each chapter.

PAYING

Public buses accept only pesos. Tour operators that arrange shuttle and tour bus trips accept dollars and non-U.S. credit cards.

RESERVATIONS

Advance reservations are required for long-distance trips on public buses or on tour-operated vehicles. It's best to reserve at least a week ahead of time, though tour operators might not need quite so much notice.

BUSINESS HOURS

Banks and offices are usually open weekdays 8–noon and 1–5. Museums are generally open weekdays 9–5, with slightly shorter hours on weekends (e.g., 10–4 or simply an afternoon or morning off); some close on Monday. Most shops have hours Monday–Saturday 9–6, though some may close for an hour at lunchtime. Gas stations are open 24 hours.

CAMERAS & PHOTOGRAPHY

Cuba, with its unusual cityscapes and its majestic landscapes, is a photographer's dream. Cubans seem amenable to having picture-taking tourists in their midst, but you should always **ask permission before photographing individuals.** If you're bashful about approaching strangers, **photograph people with whom you interact:** your waiter, your desk clerk, the vendor selling you crafts. Even better, have a traveling companion or a passerby photograph you *with* them. Many Cubans will ask you to mail copies of the photos back to them, and, out of courtesy, you should do your absolute best to comply. You should also comply with the government's ban on photographing military or police installations or personnel and harbor, rail, or airport facilities. Note that there's often a charge for taking pictures and shooting video at museums and other sights.

Frothy waves in a turquoise sea and palm-lined crescents of beach are relatively easy to capture on film if you **don't let the brightness of the sun on sand and water fool your light meter.** You'll need to compensate or else work early or late in the day when the light isn't as brilliant and contrast isn't such a problem. Try to **capture expansive views** of waterfront, beach, or village scenes; consider shooting down onto the shore from a clearing on a hillside or from a rock on the beach. Or **zoom in on something colorful,** such as a delicate tropical flower or a craftsman at work.

Bring high-speed film to compensate for low light under the tree canopy on jungle or forest trips. **Invest in a telephoto lens to photograph wildlife:** even standard zoom lenses of the 35–88 range won't capture a satisfying amount of detail. Casual photographers should **consider using inexpensive disposable cameras** to reduce the risks inherent in traveling with sophisticated equipment. One-use cameras with panoramic or underwater functions can also be nice supplements to a standard camera and its gear.

➤ PHOTO HELP: **Kodak Information Center** (☎ 800/242–2424). *Kodak Guide to Shooting Great Travel Pictures,* available in bookstores or from Fodor's Travel Publications (☎ 800/533–6478; $16.50 plus $4 shipping).

EQUIPMENT PRECAUTIONS

Always **keep your film and tape out of the sun.** Carry an extra supply of batteries, and **be prepared to turn on your camera or camcorder** to prove to security personnel that the device is real. Always **ask for hand inspection** of film, which becomes clouded after successive exposures to airport X-ray machines, and **keep videotapes away from metal detectors.**

FILM & DEVELOPING

There are film labs in every city, but it's best to **process film back home.** Developing it here is expensive and time-consuming, and you may not want to trust your prize photos to the island's poorly equipped labs. Although the government-owned Photo Service chain sells film and basic camera gear, supplies of everything are limited. Bring more film and videotapes than you expect to use as well as extra batteries and other equipment.

CAR TRAVEL

Renting a car is an expensive proposition: gas prices are high, and rental rates are $45–$60 a day, not including insurance. If you're on a tight budget, consider traveling longer distances by tour bus and/or picking one city as a base from which to make short side trips by cab. If you do decide to rent a car, the good news is that most main roads are well maintained, and once you're out of the cities traffic is light. The bad news is that signage is very poor; it's easy to get lost, so **get good road maps.** If your arsenal of maps and the directions in this guide aren't enough to get you where you're going, **be a bold and artful traveler: use the time-honored method of asking a local for directions** (pointing to maps and gesturing if need be).

Before setting out, **check the car carefully for defects,** and **make sure your car has a jack and spare tire.** As roadside assistance is handled primarily through car rental companies, be sure to **ask your rental agent for the most up-to-date emergency number.** The two main agencies are Havanautos and Transautos. It's a good idea to use them because they have the most branches (which means that should you have car problems, they can get another vehicle to you fairly quickly) and the widest selections of autos.

➤ LOCAL AGENCIES: **Havanautos** (☎ 7/33–2369 in Havana, FAX 7/33–1416 in Havana). **Transautos** (☎ 7/33–5532 in Havana, FAX 33–4507).

THE GOLD GUIDE / SMART TRAVEL TIPS

CUTTING COSTS

Rates are pretty much set by the island's two major car rental companies, so shopping around for a better deal isn't an option. Still, remember to **ask about required deposits, cancellation penalties, and drop-off charges** if you're planning to pick up the car in one city and leave it in another. If you're traveling during a holiday period, **make sure that a confirmed reservation guarantees you a car.**

GASOLINE

Gas costs about $1 a liter (roughly $4 a gallon). There are state-run Servi-Cupet stations spread out along major routes; many are open 24 hours a day. Nonetheless, it's best to start a long journey with a full tank. These stations, which only accept payment in dollars, also sell food and beverages.

INSURANCE

When driving a rented car you are generally responsible for any damage to or loss of the vehicle as well as for any property damage or personal injury that you may cause. If you're a visitor from anywhere but the United States, see what coverage your personal auto-insurance policy and credit cards already provide before you rent. U.S. visitors should definitely purchase auto insurance locally.

PARKING

Parking is easy in most Cuban cities. On-street spaces are plentiful, and many hotels have large lots. (For guests, hotel parking is generally free; non-guests will have to pay a nominal fee.)

RENTAL SURCHARGES

Before you pick up a car in one city and leave it in another **ask about drop-off charges or one-way service fees,** which can be substantial. Note, too, that some rental agencies charge extra if you return the car before the time specified in your contract. Note that in Cuba you often pay for whatever gas is in the tank upon renting the car, and you're not necessarily expected to bring the tank back full or pay a hefty refueling fee if you fail to do so.

REQUIREMENTS & RESTRICTIONS

You must be 21 years old and have a valid national driver's license or an international driver's license to rent an automobile.

ROAD CONDITIONS

Most roads are well maintained, and once out of the cities traffic is light. The country's main artery, the six-lane Autopista Nacional, runs from Havana to Ciego de Ávila before hitting the two-lane Carretera Central, which runs to El Oriente, the island's eastern portion. The Autopista Nacional also runs westward from Havana into Pinar del Río. Cuba has tolls on some routes; a trip on the Matanzas–Varadero Expressway, for example, costs $2.

RULES OF THE ROAD

Driving is on the right side of the road. Speed limits range from 40 kph (25 mph) around schools to 100 kph (60 mph) on main highways. As anywhere, **avoid drinking and driving.** Cuba's police force is efficient by Caribbean and Latin American standards; you're likely to get caught if you break any laws. Note that any fines you incur for traffic violations will be deducted from your rental car deposit.

Although it's illegal in some parts of the world, hitchhiking is a main mode of transportation in Cuba. Although you should exercise caution about picking people up, note that most hitchhikers are ordinary folk, simply trying to get to work or pay a visit to relatives. Sharing the ride with them will put you in greater touch with the country and get you some much-needed navigational assistance.

CHILDREN IN CUBA

It's quite safe to travel the island with your kids. What's more, Cubans love children and will shower attention on them, so you may find yourselves interacting with locals a great deal.

Let older children join in on planning as you outline your trip. **Scout your library for picture books, storybooks, and maps about places you'll be going.** Try to **explain the concept of foreign language;** some kids, who may have just learned to talk, are thrown when they can't understand strangers and strangers can't understand them. On sightseeing days try to **schedule activities of special interest to your children.** If you're renting a car don't forget to **arrange for a car seat** when you reserve.

FLYING

If your children are two or older **ask about children's airfares.** As a rule, infants under two not occupying a seat fly at greatly reduced fares or even for free. (On Cuban national airlines children under 2 fly free; those under 12 fly at reduced rates.) When booking, **confirm carry-on allowances** if you're traveling with infants. In general, for babies charged 10% of the adult fare, you're allowed one carry-on bag and a collapsible stroller; if the flight is full the stroller may have to be checked or you may be limited to less.

Experts agree that it's a good idea to use safety seats aloft for children weighing less than 40 pounds. Airlines set their own policies: U.S. carriers usually require that the child be ticketed, even if he or she is young enough to ride free, since the seats must be strapped into regular seats. Do **check your airline's policy about using safety seats during takeoff and landing.** And since safety seats aren't allowed just everywhere in the plane, get your seat assignments early.

When reserving, **request children's meals or a freestanding bassinet** if you need them. But note that bulkhead seats, where you must sit to use the bassinet, may lack an overhead bin or storage space on the floor.

LODGING

Most major Cuban hotels allow children under 2 to stay in their parents' room at no extra charge (they're also given free meals). There are also often reduced rates available for children under 12. Still, when booking be sure to **find out the cutoff age for children's discounts.**

PRECAUTIONS

Children should have all their inoculations up to date before leaving home. Make sure that health precautions, such as what to drink and eat,

are applied to the whole family. Not cramming too much into each day will keep the whole family healthier while on the road.

SIGHTS & ATTRACTIONS

Places that are especially good for children are indicated by a rubber duckie icon in the margin.

SUPPLIES & EQUIPMENT

Pack things to keep your children busy while traveling. For children of reading age, **bring books from home;** locally, literature for kids in English is hard to find.

It's a good idea to **pack first-aid supplies and a few basic over-the-counter children's medicines.** Obviously, you should also bring an ample supply of any prescription medicines your child may be taking. Although Cuban diapers are available at reasonable prices (less than 50¢ each), they're shabbily made and may not offer the absorbancy you are used to; you may find other supplies lacking—in both quantity and quality. If you're traveling with an infant, **bring diapers, formula, and all other essential gear.**

COMPUTERS ON THE ROAD

If you're traveling with a laptop, fill out a declaration form for it upon entering Cuba. Carry a spare battery, extra disks, a universal adapter plug, and a converter if your computer isn't dual voltage. **Ask about blackouts and electrical surges** before plugging in your computer. **Keep your disks out of the sun** and **avoid excessive heat for both your computer and disks.**

Because the telecommunications system isn't as advanced as those in Europe and North America, Internet access isn't widely available. If you do find a place to tap into the Web, be prepared for your surfing expedition to be expensive and bumpy.

CRUISE TRAVEL

The trade embargo bars U.S. lines from offering cruises to Cuba. Since the mid-1990s, however, some European lines have been stopping in Havana and/or Santiago de Cuba as part of itineraries that also include stops in Jamaica, Grand Cayman, and the Dominican Republic.

THE GOLD GUIDE / SMART TRAVEL TIPS

CUSTOMS & DUTIES

When shopping, **keep receipts** for all purchases. Upon reentering the country, **be ready to show customs officials what you've bought.** If you feel a duty is incorrect or object to the way your clearance was handled, note the inspector's badge number and ask to see a supervisor. If the problem isn't resolved, write to the appropriate authorities, beginning with the port director at your point of entry.

IN CUBA

Expect X-ray machines and a thorough search by officials in military fatigues or blue uniforms upon your arrival. You many enter Cuba with three bottles of liquor, a carton of cigarettes, 50 cigars, gifts totaling no more than $100 in value, and prescription medicines (for personal consumption) either in their original bottles or in other bottles accompanied by a doctor's prescription. Be sure to register valuable items (such as a laptop) in your home country and declare them and large amounts of foreign currency upon entering Cuba.

Firearms aren't allowed, and Cuban authorities may confiscate written or visual material viewed either as "pornographic" or "counterrevolutionary." Don't even think of bringing illegal drugs into Cuba, which is remarkably drug-free and has among the region's stiffest penalties for offenders.

IN AUSTRALIA

Australian residents who are 18 or older may bring home $A400 worth of souvenirs and gifts (including jewelry), 250 cigarettes or 250 grams of tobacco, and 1,125 ml of alcohol (including wine, beer, and spirits). Residents under 18 may bring back $A200 worth of goods. Prohibited items include meat products. Seeds, plants, and fruits need to be declared upon arrival.

➤ INFORMATION: **Australian Customs Service** (Regional Director, ✉ Box 8, Sydney, NSW 2001, ☎ 02/9213–2000, FAX 02/9213–4000).

IN CANADA

Canadian residents who have been out of Canada for at least 7 days may bring home C$500 worth of goods duty-free. If you've been away less than 7 days but more than 48 hours, the duty-free allowance drops to C$200; if your trip lasts 24–48 hours, the allowance is C$50. You may not pool allowances with family members. Goods claimed under the C$500 exemption may follow you by mail; those claimed under the lesser exemptions must accompany you. Alcohol and tobacco products may be included in the 7-day and 48-hour exemptions but not in the 24-hour exemption. If you meet the age requirements of the province or territory through which you reenter Canada, you may bring in, duty-free, 1.14 liters (40 imperial ounces) of wine or liquor *or* 24 12-ounce cans or bottles of beer or ale. If you are 16 or older you may bring in, duty-free, 200 cigarettes and 50 cigars. Check ahead of time with Revenue Canada or the Department of Agriculture for policies regarding meat products, seeds, plants, and fruits.

You may send an unlimited number of gifts worth up to C$60 each duty-free to Canada. Label the package UNSOLICITED GIFT—VALUE UNDER $60. Alcohol and tobacco are excluded.

➤ INFORMATION: **Revenue Canada** (✉ 2265 St. Laurent Blvd. S, Ottawa, Ontario K1G 4K3, ☎ 613/993–0534; 800/461–9999 in Canada).

IN NEW ZEALAND

Homeward-bound residents 17 or older may bring back $700 worth of souvenirs and gifts. Your duty-free allowance also includes 4.5 liters of wine or beer; one 1,125-ml bottle of spirits; and either 200 cigarettes, 250 grams of tobacco, 50 cigars, or a combination of the three up to 250 grams. Prohibited items include meat products, seeds, plants, and fruits.

➤ INFORMATION: **New Zealand Customs** (Custom House, ✉ 50 Anzac Ave., Box 29, Auckland, New Zealand, ☎ 09/359–6655, FAX 09/359–6732).

IN THE UNITED KINGDOM

From countries outside the EU, including Cuba, you may bring home, duty-free, 200 cigarettes or 50 cigars; 1 liter of spirits or 2 liters of fortified or sparkling wine or liqueurs; 2 liters of still table wine; 60 ml of perfume; 250 ml of toilet water; plus £136 worth of other goods, including gifts and souvenirs. If returning from outside the EU, prohibited items include meat products, seeds, plants, and fruits.

➤ INFORMATION: **HM Customs and Excise** (✉ Dorset House, Stamford St., Bromley Kent BR1 1XX, ☎ 020/7202–4227).

IN THE UNITED STATES

Normally U.S. residents who have been out of the country for at least 48 hours (and who have not used the $400 allowance or any part of it in the past 30 days) may bring home $400 worth of foreign goods duty-free. With Cuba, however, all these bets are off. Licensed travelers (☞ Americans and Cuba, *above*) are limited to a total of $100 worth of Cuban products. Unlicensed travelers caught bringing Cuban items into the country should be prepared to have the goods confiscated and to face possible fines and/or other penalties.

➤ INFORMATION: **U.S. Customs Service** (inquiries, ✉ 1300 Pennsylvania Ave. NW, Washington, DC 20229, ☎ 202/927–6724; complaints, ✉ Office of Regulations and Rulings, 1300 Pennsylvania Ave. NW, Washington, DC 20229; registration of equipment, ✉ Registration Information, 1300 Pennsylvania Ave. NW, Washington, DC 20229, ☎ 202/927–0540).

DINING

Forty years of socialism, isolation, and hard economic times have taken their toll, often leaving Cuban food (and service in restaurants) uninspired and uninspiring. (Even Castro has remarked about the bad service given by Cuban waiters and waitresses.) Many of the country's best chefs and restaurateurs followed their upper- and middle-class clients into exile after the Revolution, and even local *comida criolla* (creole cuisine) isn't as good as the Cuban food served in the exile communities of Miami, New York, or Puerto Rico.

As the economy has become increasingly reliant on tourism, the government has made efforts to improve the quality of both the service and the food in state-run restaurants. Foreign management of hotels and their restaurants, through joint ventures with the Cuban government, is also helping matters.

Most hotel restaurants serve buffet-style breakfasts from 7 AM to 10 AM and dinners from 7 PM to 10 PM. The best meals, however, are those served in the *paladares*. These privately owned establishments are, by law, only allowed a maximum of 12 seats and can only be staffed by families. Many people—even professionals—have transformed their homes into these establishments, eager for the chance to supplement their meager peso incomes with dollars. Although there are restrictions on what can be served (lobster and shrimp, for example, are officially forbidden at paladares), the food that is served is usually fresh, authentic, and inexpensive (you can get a large meal for as little as $10). The overall experience of a meal in a paladar is certainly much more fulfilling than that offered by many state restaurants.

The restaurants (all of which are indicated by ✕) we list are the cream of the crop in each price category. Properties indicated by ✕🏠 are lodging establishments whose restaurant warrants a special trip.

CATEGORY	COST*
$$$$	over $35
$$$	$25–$35
$$	$15–$25
$	under $15

*per person for an appetizer, entrée, and dessert, excluding tip and beverages

PAYING

Dollars are almost always required in places frequented by tourists. In local establishments, which generally only take pesos (but will often accept your dollars and give you change in pesos), have small denominations on hand. Credit cards not issued by U.S. companies are accepted at government establishments but not in paladares.

RESERVATIONS & DRESS

Cuban meals are relaxed, and reservations are rarely required; we mention them only when they're essential or aren't accepted. Book as far ahead as you can, and reconfirm as soon as you arrive. Note that some restaurants frown on shorts for men and women both; beach attire is usually only acceptable on the beach. We mention dress requirements only when men are required to wear a jacket or a jacket and tie.

DISABILITIES & ACCESSIBILITY

Cuba has only recently—since the tourist boom of the 1990s—begun taking the needs of travelers with disabilities into account. Hence its infrastructure is dismal, with few ramps, curb dips, or wide doorways capable of accommodating wheelchairs; few realistic transportation options; and many cobblestone streets that can make getting around difficult. Your best bet for arranging a trip to Cuba is to work closely with a tour operator or travel agent who specializes in trips for people with disabilities.

LODGING

When discussing accessibility with an operator or reservations agent **ask hard questions.** Are there any stairs, inside *or* out? Are there grab bars next to the toilet *and* in the shower/tub? How wide is the doorway to the room? To the bathroom? For the most extensive facilities meeting the latest legal specifications **opt for newer accommodations.**

DISCOUNTS & DEALS

The most inexpensive way to visit Cuba is with a package that puts you in an all-inclusive beach hotel. (Don't confuse packages and guided tours: when you buy a package, you travel on your own, just as though you had planned the trip yourself.) Such establishments, however, may make you feel as if you were anywhere in the Caribbean rather than truly in Cuba. Further, you don't have much flexibility to get out and really explore the country. **Ask your travel agent about split stays** between two or more hotels in different areas. You may be able to get bottom-line package rates, yet still experience the island and its people.

Be a smart shopper and **compare all your options** before making decisions.

A plane ticket bought with a promotional coupon from travel clubs, coupon books, and direct-mail offers may not be cheaper than the least expensive fare from a discount ticket agency. And always keep in mind that what you get is just as important as what you save. To save money **look into discount-reservations services** with toll-free numbers, which use their buying power to get a better price on hotels, airline tickets, even car rentals.

ECOTOURISM

The government's general record on the environment isn't good, as the nation's smoke-clogged city streets testify. Cuba has, however, set aside large tracts of virgin mountains, tropical forests, and beachfronts as nature reserves. And much of the country is still bucolic, with rolling farmland that stretches from one mountain range to the next. Bird-watching paradises and cave systems dot the island; it also has several fabulous dive areas and fantastic fresh- and saltwater fishing opportunities, with annual competitions for marlin, swordfish, and other big-game fish. The state-run company Gaviota specializes in ecotourism, offering everything from white-water rafting excursions to hiking treks. For details on Gaviota branches, *see* Tour Operators and Travel Agents *in* the A to Z section at the end of each chapter.

ELECTRICITY

Cuba uses the North American system of 110 volts, 60 cycles, though some hotels operate with both this system and the 220-volt European system. North American–style plugs are the norm here. If your appliances are dual-voltage (as many laptop computers are) you'll need only an adapter. **Consider buying a universal adapter;** the Swiss Army knife of adapters, it has several types of plugs in one handy unit.

Although things have improved since the early 1990s, Castro's belt-tightening Special Period remains in effect; blackouts are still quite frequent. Most hotels have a backup power system, but these are designed to keep electricity flowing only to lights in lounges and hallways and to emergency lamps in guest rooms. Still, in an effort to ease the inconvenience, blackouts are often confined only to electrical grids that extend no more than a few city blocks. Power to various grids is shut off at different times, so only some, rather than all, establishments are affected by any given blackout.

EMBASSIES

➤ IN CANADA: **Cuban Embassy** (✉ 388 Main St., Ottawa, Ontario, K1S 1E3, ☎ 613/563–0141).

➤ IN CUBA: **British Embassy** (✉ Calle 34, No. 708, Miramar, Havana, ☎ 7/33–1771). **Canadian Embassy** (✉ Calle 30, No. 518, Miramar, Havana, ☎ 7/33–2516). **U.S. Special Interests Section** (✉ c/o Swiss Embassy; Calle Calzada, e/Calle L y Calle M, Vedado, Havana, ☎ 7/32–0550 or 7/32–0551).

➤ IN THE UNITED STATES: **Cuban Interests Section** (✉ 2630 16th St. NW, Washington, DC 20009, ☎ 202/797–8518 or 202/797–8522).

EMERGENCIES

In large cities and tourist areas, you'll find 24-hour *clinicas internacionales* (international clinics) with an on-duty doctor and nurse and a pharmacy. They're rarely crowded, and the pharmacy is apt to have the best supply of medicines you're likely to find anywhere. (Local pharmacies are often short of medicines and sometimes can only offer herbal remedies.) A visit with a doctor at the clinic costs about $25; house calls can sometimes be made for an extra $25. In addition, some large hotels have 24-hour medical service, with a doctor and a nurse.

Traveler's assistance is available through Asistur, which can help you with everything from providing tourist maps to arranging financial transactions to sorting out both medical and legal problems.

➤ CONTACTS: **Asistur** (✉ 254 Paseo Martí/Prado, Centro, Havana, ☎ 7/33–8527, ℻ 7/33–8087; 101 Calle 31, Varadero, ☎ 8/33–7276; ✉ Hotel Jagua, Calle 37, No. 1, Cienfuegos, ☎ 432/3021; ✉ Below Hotel Casa Granda, Parque Céspedes, Santiago de Cuba, ☎ 226/63–8284).

ENGLISH-LANGUAGE MEDIA

Outside of a few Havana bookshops and some hotel stores, it can be nearly impossible to find English-language books and international publications. (Note that markup on international newspapers and periodicals can be as much as four times the cover price.) Hotels and tourist offices throughout the country have bimonthly, monthly, and weekly publications with current information in English on arts events, movies, television, and other entertainment. *Business Tips on Cuba,* available at airports and hotels, is filled with useful information. *Prisma* is a bimonthly magazine that covers general subjects on Cuba, the Caribbean, and Latin America. It also has a travel section. *Granma,* the official Communist Party newspaper, is the nation's most important daily. Although laced with socialist propaganda, it also offers an interesting Cuban perspective on international news and issues. A weekly edition, *Granma Internacional,* is published in English, French, German, Portuguese, and Spanish.

Guest rooms in many hotels have cable TV, and CNN (in Spanish and English), similar European-based news programs, and a channel highlighting tourist attractions are always among the offerings. If your Spanish is good you might want to check out one of Cuba's five national stations; in some areas, you can tune into programming from Florida and Jamaica. International radio programs—from the BBC to the U.S.-based, anti-Castro broadcasts (started under President Reagan) of Radio Martí—can also be heard. Radio Taíno is geared to tourists.

GAY & LESBIAN TRAVEL

Although reports of police harassment persist, Cuba's tolerance of gays and lesbians has improved tremendously since the 1960s, when gays were rounded up and jailed. Most gays and lesbians remain in the closet, but formal and informal meeting places for them have begun popping up in Havana and other cosmopolitan areas. Nevertheless gay and lesbian travelers should be discreet about public displays of affection.

THE GOLD GUIDE / SMART TRAVEL TIPS

HEALTH

DIVERS' ALERT

Divers take note: **don't fly within 24 hours of scuba diving.** Neophyte divers should have a complete physical exam before undertaking a dive. If you have travel insurance, **make sure your policy applies to scuba-related injuries,** as not all companies provide this coverage.

FOOD & DRINK

In Cuba the major health risk is traveler's diarrhea, caused by eating contaminated fruit or vegetables or drinking contaminated water. So **watch what you eat.** Stay away from ice, uncooked food, and unpasteurized milk and milk products, and **drink only bottled water,** which is in good supply, or water that has been boiled for at least 20 minutes, even when you're brushing your teeth. (To be on the safe side, you could ask your doctor for a prescription for antibiotics and fill it before you leave. This may sound extreme, but if you have terrible stomach cramps in a tiny Cuban town, you'll be happy to be prepared.)

Drink plenty of purified water or tea—chamomile (*camomila*) is a good folk remedy. In severe cases, rehydrate yourself with a salt-sugar solution: ½ teaspoon salt (*sal*) and 4 tablespoons sugar (*azúcar*) per quart of water (*agua*).

MEDICAL PLANS

No one plans to get sick while traveling, but it happens, so **consider signing up with a medical-assistance company.** Members get doctor referrals, emergency evacuation or repatriation, hot lines for medical consultation, cash for emergencies, and other assistance.

➤ MEDICAL-ASSISTANCE COMPANIES: **AEA International SOS** (⊠ 8 Neshaminy Interplex, Suite 207, Trevose, PA 19053, ☎ 215/245–4707 or 800/523–6586, ℻ 215/244–9617; ⊠ 12 Chemin Riantbosson, 1217 Meyrin 1, Geneva, Switzerland, ☎ 4122/785–6464, ℻ 4122/785–6424; ⊠ 331 N. Bridge Rd., 17-00, Odeon Towers, Singapore 188720, ☎ 65/338–7800, ℻ 65/338–7611).

OVER-THE-COUNTER AND PRESCRIPTION REMEDIES

Since medical supplies in Cuba are short, **pack a small first-aid kit/medicine bag** with basic bandages and topical ointments as well as sunscreen; insect repellent; and your favorite brands of over-the-counter allergy, cold, headache, and stomach/diarrhea medicine. **Bring enough prescription medications to last the entire trip.**

PESTS & OTHER HAZARDS

There's some risk of contracting Hepatitis A, Hepatitis B, or the mosquito-carried dengue fever, though incidents of all three diseases are rare, and practically nonexistent in tourist zones. Visitors with allergies take note: the air quality in cities can be horrible, particularly in summer, when the thick, smoky exhaust from aging Eastern European trucks and buses mixes with choking dust and lingers in the humid air.

Tourism-related prostitution is flourishing, and there have been reports that AIDS is on the rise. Local condoms are of poor quality so bring your own supply from home.

➤ HEALTH WARNINGS: **National Centers for Disease Control** (CDC, National Center for Infectious Diseases, Division of Quarantine, Traveler's Health Section, ⊠ 1600 Clifton Rd. NE, M/S E-03, Atlanta, GA 30333, ☎ 888/232–3228, ℻ 888/232–3299).

HOLIDAYS

There are 15 national holidays, all celebrating revolutionary events or heroes. The two largest are May Day (International Workers Day on May 1, which is celebrated throughout Cuba with parades and other activities) and National Revolution Day (on July 26, honoring the attack on Moncada Barracks in Santiago, which proved the spark for the Revolution). In addition, since Pope John Paul's visit to Cuba in 1998, Castro has allowed Cubans to openly celebrate Christmas.

Other national holidays are: January 1–2 (liberation and victory days), January 28 (José Martí), February 24 (Second War of Independence),

March 8 (Women's/Mother's Day), March 13 (Students Attack), April 19 (Bay of Pigs Victory), July 30 (Martyrs of the Revolution), October 8 (Che Guevara), October 10 (First War of Independence), October 28 (Camilio Cienfuegos), December 2 (*Granma* landing), and December 7 (Antonio Maceo).

INSURANCE

The most useful travel insurance plan is a comprehensive policy that includes coverage for trip cancellation and interruption, default, trip delay, and medical expenses (with a waiver for preexisting conditions).

Without insurance you will lose all or most of your money if you cancel your trip, regardless of the reason. Default insurance covers you if your tour operator, airline, or cruise line goes out of business. Trip-delay covers expenses that arise because of bad weather or mechanical delays. Study the fine print when comparing policies.

If you're traveling internationally, a key component of travel insurance is coverage for medical bills incurred if you get sick on the road. Such expenses are not generally covered by private policies (particularly if you're a U.S. citizen traveling in Cuba). U.K. residents can buy a travel-insurance policy valid for most vacations taken during the year in which it's purchased (but check pre-existing-condition coverage). British and Australian citizens need extra medical coverage when traveling overseas.

Always **buy travel policies directly from the insurance company**; if you buy it from a cruise line, airline, or tour operator that goes out of business you probably won't be covered for the agency or operator's default, a major risk. Before you make any purchase **review your existing health and home-owner's policies** to find what they cover away from home.

➤ TRAVEL INSURERS: In Canada, **Voyager Insurance** (✉ 44 Peel Center Dr., Brampton, Ontario L6T 4M8, ☎ 905/791–8700; 800/668–4342 in Canada).

➤ INSURANCE INFORMATION: In the United Kingdom, the **Association of** **British Insurers** (✉ 51–55 Gresham St., London EC2V 7HQ, ☎ 020/7600–3333, FAX 020/7696–8999). In Australia, the **Insurance Council of Australia** (☎ 03/9614–1077, FAX 03/9614–7924).

LANGUAGE, CULTURE, & ETIQUETTE

Spanish is the official, and by far the most widely spoken, language. Many hotel personnel speak some English; German, Portuguese, Italian, and French are also often spoken at resorts. Outside of hotels and beyond cities, having a few rudimentary Spanish phrases in your repertoire will be very helpful.

Cubans are an open, gregarious people. Despite the United States government restrictions on its citizens traveling to the island, Cubans receive Americans just like all other foreigners: with open arms. Although Cubans will talk about the current political and economic situations, they generally do so only in vague terms. It's probably best to avoid talking politics with locals unless they bring up the subject.

LANGUAGES FOR TRAVELERS

A phrase book and language-tape set can help get you started. But if languages are your thing, you could take a Spanish course during your stay. In Havana, the José Martí School for Foreigners and the Mercadu SA offer courses that vary in length from one week to four months. Package trips can be arranged in the United States through Global Exchange.

➤ PHRASE BOOKS, LANGUAGE-TAPE SETS, &, COURSES: *Fodor's Spanish for Travelers* (☎ 800/733–3000 in the United States; 800/668–4247 in Canada; $7 for phrase book, $16.95 for audio set). **Global Exchange** (✉ 2017 Mission St., Suite 303, San Francisco, CA 94110; ☎ 800/497–1994). **Jose Martí School for Foreigners** (✉ Calle 16, No. 109, Miramar, Havana, 7/33–1697). **Mercadu SA** (Calle 13 951, esquina de Av. 8, Vedado, Havana, ☎ 7/33–3893).

LODGING

The construction of new hotels that gained momentum in the 1990s is

SMART TRAVEL TIPS / THE GOLD GUIDE

continuing well into the new millennium (the island has almost 50,000 rooms and counting). Accommodations include large, modern hotels; smaller, restored, colonial classics; and low-key beach resorts. Further, to improve its tourist infrastructure, the island has been entering into joint ventures with such foreign hoteliers as Spain's Sol Meliá. Local hotel operators include Cubanácan, with many traditional tourist properties; Gaviota, which offers more specialized or out-of-the-way accommodations; and Islazul, whose properties cater mostly to local tourists. To get the best deal, **book your room in advance.**

Assume that hotels operate on the European Plan (**EP,** with no meals) unless we specify that they're **all-inclusive** (including all meals and most activities) or use the Continental Plan (**CP,** with a Continental breakfast daily), Breakfast Plan (**BP,** with a full breakfast daily), or Modified American Plan (**MAP,** with breakfast and dinner daily).

The lodgings (all of which are indicated by 🏠) we list are the cream of the crop in each price category. We always list the facilities that are available—but we don't specify whether they cost extra: when pricing accommodations, always ask what's included and what costs extra. Properties indicated by an ✕🏠 are lodging establishments whose restaurant warrants a special trip.

CATEGORY	COST*
$$$$	over $150
$$$	$100–$150
$$	$50–$100
$	under $50

for a double room in high season

CASAS PARTICULARES

Since 1996, Cubans have been allowed to rent out rooms to visitors. The rates are excellent (as little as $25 daily, always payable in cash dollars only), and many of these *casas particulares* are absolutely charming. Some were mansions in their heyday and still have the power to impress; some even have such conveniences as air-conditioning and satellite TV. And Cuban home cooking often puts the institutional buffets at bigger resorts to shame.

Quality varies widely from one casa to the next, and you can't make reservations to stay in one through a tour operator. A good strategy is to **book a few nights at a tourist hotel, and then investigate area casas particulares.** Don't be shy; **ask locals for recommendations** and **ask to see the rooms before booking.** Just beware of recommendations from street hustlers; their desire to take you to a casa particular could be based only on the commission they hope to get.

HOSTELS

Although Cuba doesn't have a hostel network per se, international hostel organizations should be able to refer members to similar lodging options—in university dormitories—on the island. Membership in Hostelling International (HI), the umbrella group for a number of national youth-hostel associations, is open to travelers of all ages (one-year membership is about $25 for adults).

➤ ORGANIZATIONS: **Australian Youth Hostel Association** (✉ 10 Mallett St., Camperdown, NSW 2050, ☎ 02/9565–1699, 📠 02/9565–1325). **Hostelling International—American Youth Hostels** (✉ 733 15th St. NW, Suite 840, Washington, DC 20005, ☎ 202/783–6161, 📠 202/783–6171). **Hostelling International—Canada** (✉ 400–205 Catherine St., Ottawa, Ontario K2P 1C3, ☎ 613/237–7884, 📠 613/237–7868). **Youth Hostel Association of England and Wales** (✉ Trevelyan House, 8 St. Stephen's Hill, St. Albans, Hertfordshire AL1 2DY, ☎ 01727/855215 or 01727/845047, 📠 01727/844126). **Youth Hostels Association of New Zealand** (✉ Box 436, Christchurch, New Zealand, ☎ 03/379–9970, 📠 03/365–4476). Membership in the United States $25, in Canada C$26.75, in the United Kingdom £9.30, in Australia $44, in New Zealand $24.

HOTELS

Most new hotels and resorts are up to North American and European standards. Resorts offer an array of services, from day tours to organized sport and entertainment events to baby-sitting and children's programs. Rooms often have air-conditioners, refrigerators, cable TV, and other modern conveniences. All hotels listed have private baths unless otherwise noted.

MAIL & SHIPPING

Cuban mail is so slow that it can hardly be called reliable, but rates are fairly reasonable. A postcard sent to anywhere in the Americas or Europe will cost no more than 50¢, a letter 75¢. There have been reports of mail censorship; if you want your card to eventually reach its destination, consider choosing your words carefully.

DHL Express is the international air courier service with the biggest presence in Cuba. It has desks at some major hotels and offices in Havana, Camagüey, Cienfuegos, Holguín, Pinar del Río, Santiago de Cuba, and Varadero. The company offers package and letter delivery to international points within 24 hours, but it will cost you dearly.

➤ COURIER SERVICE: **DHL** (✉ Main office, Av. 1 y Calle 42, Miramar, Havana, ☎ 7/33–1578, FAX 7/33–1578).

MONEY MATTERS

Although the official *moneda nacional* (national money or currency) is the peso, the state has authorized the use of the U.S. dollar as legal tender. The government has also begun issuing a so-called convertible peso, which is on par with a dollar and which you can freely exchange back into dollars upon leaving.

Local establishments (buses, street vendors, paladares, casas particulares, and the like), generally accept only pesos, though many can take dollars (small denominations) and give you change in the local currency. When looking at price tags, remember that one line through the letter "S" is the symbol for pesos; two lines through it is the symbol for dollars (hence, that salad or street-fair trinket that may appear to cost a shocking $100 may actually cost 100 pesos or $1).

Prices throughout this guide are given for adults. Substantially reduced fees are almost always available for children, students, and senior citizens.

BANKS & ATMS

The major Cuban banks are Banco Nacional de Cuba, Banco Financiero Internacional SA, and Banco Internacional de Comercio. There are some automatic teller machines, particularly in urban areas, that accept international bank cards not issued through U.S. banks.

CREDIT CARDS & TRAVELER'S CHECKS

Traveler's checks and credit cards— such as Visa and MasterCard—not affiliated with U.S. banks or companies are honored at government hotels, restaurants, and stores. Several other European and Latin American credit cards are also accepted.

Throughout this guide, the following abbreviations are used: MC, Master-Card and V, Visa.

TAXES

The departure tax is $15 (it's payable in U.S. dollars before you board the plane home, so keep some cash on hand). No taxes are levied on goods and services. If, however, you buy artwork, you need to get a $10 export permit (☞ Shopping, *below*).

TIPPING

In hotel restaurants with buffet-style meals, tip the wait staff $2–$5, depending on the extent of service and the number of people in your party. Elsewhere, tip waiters and waitresses 10%–20% of the check. Tip hotel maids 50¢–$1 a day and porters 50¢–$1 a bag. Tips ($1 is usually enough) should also be given to museum docents, tour guides, taxi drivers, and anyone who keeps an eye on your rental car for you. Cubans who work in the service industry rely heavily on tips to merely subsist; therefore, you may feel better if you err on the generous side.

TRAVELER'S CHECKS

Do you need traveler's checks? It depends on where you're headed. If you're going to rural areas and small towns, go with cash; traveler's checks are best used in cities. Lost or stolen checks can usually be replaced within 24 hours. To ensure a speedy refund, buy your own traveler's checks—don't let someone else pay for them: irregularities like this can cause delays. The person who bought the checks should make the call to request a refund.

OUTDOORS & SPORTS

BICYCLING

Since the collapse of the Soviet Union, cycling has become a main means of transport in Cuba, and you'll see lovers out on a date, grandmothers with groceries, and farmers hauling crops from the fields on bicycles. Cuban tour operators offer everything from short trips to island-wide treks. You'll find bicycle rental shops—well-stocked with spare parts and supplies—in all major cities and tourist centers. Still, as country roads are rough (and can take you miles from the nearest shop), it's wise to bring your own emergency repair supplies.

Most airlines accommodate bikes as luggage, provided they are dismantled and boxed. For bike boxes, often free at bike shops, you'll pay about $5 (at least $100 for bike bags) from airlines. International travelers can sometimes substitute a bike for a piece of checked luggage at no charge; otherwise, the cost is about $100. Domestic and Canadian airlines charge $25–$50.

DIVING

Cuba offers some of the Caribbean's best diving. Its waters feature unexplored wrecks, attractive temperatures and visibility, abundant marine life, and miles of coral reefs. Particularly good sites are off the shores of the Isla de Juventud and Cayo Largo; the waters around the northern keys, such as Jardines del Rey (Gardens of the King); and the waters of the less accessible southern archipelago, known as the Jardines de la Reina (Gardens of the Queen). Cuba has several hyperbaric chambers in case of a diving accident.

PACKING

For sightseeing, casual lightweight clothing and good walking shoes are appropriate; most restaurants don't require very formal attire. For beach vacations, you'll need lightweight sportswear, a bathing suit, a sun hat, and lots of really good sunscreen. A sarong or a light cotton blanket makes a handy beach towel, picnic blanket, and cushion for hard seats, among other things.

Travel in forest areas will require long-sleeve shirts, long pants, socks, sneakers and/or hiking boots, a hat, a light waterproof jacket, a bathing suit, and plenty of insect repellent. Other useful items include a screw-top water container that you can fill with bottled water, a money pouch, a travel flashlight and extra batteries, a Swiss Army knife with a bottle opener, a medical kit (with first-aid supplies and basic over-the-counter remedies), binoculars, and lots of extra film.

In your carry-on luggage **bring an extra pair of eyeglasses or contact lenses** and **pack enough of any medication you take** to last the entire trip. In luggage to be checked, **never pack prescription drugs or valuables.** To avoid customs delays, carry medications in their original packaging. And don't forget to copy down and **carry addresses of offices that handle refunds of lost traveler's checks and credit cards.**

CHECKING LUGGAGE

How many carry-on bags you can bring with you is up to the airline. Most allow two, but not always, so make sure that everything you carry aboard will fit under your seat, and get to the gate early. Note that if you have a seat at the back of the plane, you'll probably board first, while the overhead bins are still empty.

International baggage allowances may be determined not by piece but by weight—generally 88 pounds (40 kilograms) in first class, 66 pounds (30 kilograms) in business class, and 44 pounds (20 kilograms) in economy.

Airline liability for baggage is limited to $1,250 per person on flights within the United States. On international flights it amounts to $9.07 per pound or $20 per kilogram for checked baggage (roughly $640 per 70-pound bag) and $400 per passenger for unchecked baggage. You can buy additional coverage at check-in for about $10 per $1,000 of coverage, but it excludes a rather extensive list of items, shown on your airline ticket.

Before departure **itemize your bags' contents** and their worth, and label the bags with your name, address, and phone number. (If you use your home address, cover it so that potential thieves can't see it readily.) Inside each bag **pack a copy of your itinerary.** At check-in **make sure that each bag is correctly tagged** with the destination airport's three-letter code. If your bags arrive damaged or fail to arrive at all, file a written report with the airline before leaving the airport.

PASSPORTS & VISAS

When traveling internationally **carry a passport even if you don't need one** (it's always the best form of ID), and **make two photocopies of the data page** (one for someone at home and another for you, carried separately from your passport). If you lose your passport promptly call the nearest embassy or consulate and the local police.

ENTERING CUBA

All foreigners must have passports to enter Cuba. Beyond that, in most cases, tourist cards ($20), rather than visas, are all that's required, and sometimes even this requirement is waved. Most tourist cards are good for 30 days, but in some cases are valid for up to three months. Regardless, renewing such a card for an additional 30 days is easy to do (for an additional $25).

Visas are required of business travelers, working journalists, and some other visitors. They cost $25 and are valid for 30 days. You must apply for them at your nearest Cuban embassy or consulate, and they can take up to three weeks to process. You may extend your visa for stays of up to six months.

PASSPORT OFFICES

The best time to apply for a passport or to renew is during the fall and winter. Before any trip, check your passport's expiration date (some countries don't accept passports due to expire within six months from your date of entry into the country), and, if necessary, renew it as soon as possible.

➤ AUSTRALIAN CITIZENS: **Australian Passport Office** (☎ 131–232).

➤ CANADIAN CITIZENS: **Passport Office** (☎ 819/994–3500 or 800/567–6868).

➤ NEW ZEALAND CITIZENS: **New Zealand Passport Office** (☎ 04/494–0700 for information on how to apply; 04/474–8000 or 0800/225–050 in New Zealand for information on applications already submitted).

➤ U.K. CITIZENS: **London Passport Office** (☎ 0990/210410) for fees and documentation requirements and to request an emergency passport.

➤ U.S. CITIZENS: **National Passport Information Center** (☎ 900/225–5674; calls are 35¢ per minute for automated service, $1.05 per minute for operator service).

REST ROOMS

All major public areas, from hotels to airports, have clean, private facilities. The words for "rest room" are *servicio* and *baño*. "Men" is *caballeros*; "women" is *mujeres* or *damas*.

SAFETY

There have been mixed reports on crime in Cuba. Some of them say that crime against tourists is on the rise, particularly in cities. Take the same precautions you would elsewhere in South America or the Caribbean; **keep a close eye on personal belongings, avoid adorning yourself with expensive jewelry,** and **follow local advice about where it's safe to walk,** particularly at night.

There are increasing numbers of panhandlers, looking for anything from cash to clothing to soap; *jineteros* (hustlers), wanting to serve as your guide or refer you to a casa particular or paladar; and *jineteras* (prostitutes). It's best to decline their services. If you consider the local economic conditions, it shouldn't be hard to remain polite and still keep confrontation to a minimum; on rare occasions, you may need to be more assertive.

THE GOLD GUIDE / SMART TRAVEL TIPS

WOMEN IN CUBA

You should avoid wearing revealing clothing—such as short shorts or skirts and halter tops—especially in the cities. Women traveling alone more often than not say that Cuban men treat them with great respect. But be aware that Cuban men—like Cuban women—may be on the prowl for foreign mates. Unless you're truly interested, it's best to avoid lengthy eye contact with the opposite sex.

SHOPPING

Most people buy rum and cigars and for good reason—Cuban versions of these products are among the world's finest. But there's much more here: artwork, crafts, CDs, and such traditional offerings as the men's dress shirt, the *guayabera*. ARTEX stores sell all these items and more, and there's one in practically every Cuban town. (Look for freestanding ARTEX stores as well as small booths near major sights and shops in Infotur centers and large hotels.)

Cuba also has other small stores (including gift shops in hotels and at museums and other sights), formal art galleries, and markets and streets where artists and craftsmen sell their wares from small stands. (If you buy a work of art, you need either an export permit or an official receipt from a government store or the work is subject to confiscation upon departure from Cuba. A permit costs $10 and is usually available from the artist. The National Registry of Cultural Goods also sells permits.) Bargaining with street vendors is acceptable, but the prices are so low that you might be ashamed to haggle.

The Diplotiendas, once the exclusive domain of foreign diplomats and tourists but now open to Cubans with dollars, sell consumer products popular in North America and Europe—from electronic equipment to clothing to personal-hygiene items. Even more abundant are the Tiendas Panamericanos, which sell the same type of merchandise. Most branches of both stores are open weekdays 10–10; they accept only U.S. dollars.

➤ EXPORT PERMITS: **National Registry of Cultural Goods** (✉ Calle 17, No. 1009, Vedado, Havana, ☏ no phone).

SIGHTSEEING TOURS

Most packages include a city tour as well as transfers to and from your hotel. You can also sign up for tours of all types through local tourist offices, branches of state travel agencies, or your hotel. City tours usually run about three hours and cost roughly $15.

STUDENTS IN CUBA

Several Cuban state agencies run foreign language and Cuban culture classes; the organization Global Exchange is a good source of information on such programs (☞ Language, Culture, and Etiquette, *above*). Additionally, several Cuban universities offer courses for foreigners or welcome them into their courses.

➤ STUDENT IDs & SERVICES: **Council on International Educational Exchange** (CIEE, ✉ 205 E. 42nd St., 14th fl., New York, NY 10017, ☎ 212/822–2600 or 888/268–6245, ℻ 212/822–2699) for mail orders only, in the United States. **Travel Cuts** (✉ 187 College St., Toronto, Ontario M5T 1P7, ☎ 416/979–2406 or 800/667–2887) in Canada.

TAXIS

Modern, well-maintained tourist taxis, which charge in dollars, congregate in front of hotels, transportation hubs, and major sights. Rates are affordable by North American and European standards. Metered cabs charge about $2 for every 10 km (6 mi) traveled; verify the rate with the driver before setting off, though, to avoid any misunderstandings.

You can hire unmetered *taxis particulares*, private (gypsy) cabs with yellow plates, for a day of driving around town for about $25 (be sure to establish the fare before you set off, however). Many of them are vintage cars—1958 Chevy Bel-Airs and 1959 Cadillacs—which adds to the fun.

TELEPHONES

Since 1992 Cuban phone service has been improving, thanks to a partial privatization and to joint ventures with foreign investors. But delays in placing calls, frequent service outages, and a limited supply of working public phones continue to be realities, making it best to place calls from phone centers or your hotel. Like many places in the world, phone numbers here continue to change as telecommunications upgrades are made—you may need the help of someone who speaks Spanish to get directory assistance.

Most hotels offer fax services to guests and, sometimes, nonguests. Although E-mail service and the Internet have become realities in Cuba, computers aren't widely available and service is irregular and costly.

COUNTRY & AREA CODES

Cuba's country code is 53, and there's direct-dial service to the country from North America and Europe. Within the country, city or area codes vary in length from one to three digits; the lengths of local numbers vary as well. Some of the more useful codes are: Bayamo, 24; Camagüey, 322 or 32; Cienfuegos, 432; Guantánamo, 21; Havana, 7; Holguín, 23 or 24; Matanzas, 52; Pinar del Río, 82; Santa Clara, 422; Santiago de Cuba, 226; Trinidad, 419; and Varadero, 8. You can also make direct-dial international calls from Cuba. The country codes are: 1 for the United States and Canada, 61 for Australia, 64 for New Zealand, and 44 for the United Kingdom.

DIRECTORY & OPERATOR INFORMATION

You get the operator by dialing 0 or 119. For information, dial 113. Note, however, that English-speaking operators are rare.

INTERNATIONAL CALLS

All major hotels have international phone service; just be sure to check the price of such calls beforehand. Also, if you experience a long delay in reaching your party, hang up and try again; you may be charged for the time spent waiting for the call to go through. International calls to North America average $2.50 per minute while to Europe and other international points, the cost jumps to $5.50 a minute.

LOCAL AND LONG-DISTANCE CALLS

To make a long-distance call within Cuba, dial 0, the area code, then the number. To make an international call, dial 88 from hotel rooms or 119 from other phones; wait for the dial tone; and then dial the country code, area code, and number.

PHONE CARDS AND PUBLIC PHONES

You can buy cards in denominations from $10 to $50 at *telecorreos* (phone centers); some, called *centros de llamadas internacionales,* specialize in international calls. Many phone offices are open 24 hours a day.

WIRELESS PHONES

Cubacel has been offering wireless phone service since 1993 through a joint venture with foreign investors (note that it has agreements with Telcel and Portatel in Mexico, Telecom Personal and TCP in Argentina, Telefonica Moviles in Spain, and Bell Mobility and Telus Mobility in Canada). The network extends to all but the most remote areas and allows for the use of AMPS cell phones (American norm).

Cubacel may be able to activate your own wireless phone for use within Cuba or you can rent one of theirs—an expensive proposition. Security deposits run several hundred dollars (depending on the length of usage), and rental fees are about $7 a day plus a one-time activation fee of about $140. International calls cost about 90 cents a minute (plus long-distance charges); calls within Cuba run 60 cents a minute.

➤ WIRELESS COMPANY: Cubacel (⊠ Calle 28, No. 510 e/Calle 5 y Calle 7, Miramar, Havana ☎ 7/80–2222; ⊠ Aeropuerto Internacional José Martí, ☎ 7/80–0043).

TIME

Havana is in the same time zone as Miami and New York and is 5 hours behind Britain, 3 hours ahead of Los Angeles, and 14 hours behind Melbourne, Australia. The island switches to daylight-savings time from April through October, when it's only 4 hours behind Greenwich mean time.

TOURS & PACKAGES

On a prepackaged tour or independent vacation everything is prearranged so you'll spend less time planning—and often get it all at a good price.

A variety of tour companies offer everything from conventional beach holidays to adventure getaways to theme trips. Foreign volunteers are welcome to lend the Revolution a hand for 20-day stints; assignments are handled through the Cuban Institute of Friendship. Vencremos Brigade and Brigada Antonio Maceo can also help place volunteers in Cuba and make travel arrangements. American Friends Service Committee offers student exchange (☞ *also* Airlines/Charters *under* Air Travel *and* Language, Culture, and Etiquette, *above*).

BOOKING WITH AN AGENT

Travel agents are excellent resources. But it's a good idea to collect brochures from several agencies because some agents' suggestions may be influenced by relationships with tour and package firms that reward them for volume sales. If you have a special interest **find an agent with expertise in that area**; ASTA (☞ Travel Agencies, *below*) has a database of specialists worldwide.

Make sure your travel agent knows the accommodations and other services of the place they're recommending. Ask about the hotel's location, room size, beds, and whether it has a pool, room service, or programs for children, if you care about these. Has your agent been there in person or sent others whom you can contact?

Do some homework on your own, too: local tourism boards can provide information about lesser-known and small-niche operators, some of which may sell only direct.

BUYER BEWARE

Each year consumers are stranded or lose their money when tour operators—even large ones with excellent reputations—go out of business. So **check out the operator.** Ask several travel agents about its reputation, and try to **book with a company that has a consumer-protection program.**

Remember that the more your package or tour includes the better you can predict the ultimate cost of your vacation. Make sure you know exactly what is covered, and **beware of hidden costs.** Are taxes, tips, and transfers included? Entertainment and excursions? These can add up.

➤ TOUR-OPERATOR RECOMMENDATIONS: **American Society of Travel Agents** (☞ Travel Agencies, *below*). **National Tour Association** (NTA, ✉ 546 E. Main St., Lexington, KY 40508, ☎ 606/226–4444 or 800/682–8886). **United States Tour Operators Association** (USTOA, ✉ 342 Madison Ave., Suite 1522, New York, NY 10173, ☎ 212/599–6599 or 800/468–7862, FAX 212/599–6744).

➤ OPERATORS, AGENCIES, & ORGANIZATIONS: **American Friends Service Committee** (✉ 1501 Cherry St., Philadelphia, PA 92102, ☎ 215/241–7000). **Brigada Antonio Maceo** (✉ Box 248829, Miami, FL, 33124, ☎ no phone). **Caribe Tours** (✉ 11414 Old Riber School Rd., Downey, CA 90241, ☎ 562/928–7383). **Caribic Vacations** (✉ 69 Gloucester Ave., Montego Bay, Jamaica, ☎ 809/979–0322). **Cubanacán UK** (✉ Skylines, Suite 49, Limeharbor, Docklands, London, United Kingdom, ☎ 020/7537–7907). **Cuba Tours Network, Inc.** (✉ 11401 SW 40 St., No. 334, Miami, FL 33165, ☎ 305/228–1808). **Emely Tours** (✉ Av. Tiradentes y Roberto Pastoriza, Plaza JR, 2nd floor, Ensanche Naco, Santo Domingo, Dominican Republic, ☎ 809/566–4545). **Havanatur UK** (✉ Interchange House, 27 Stafford Rd., Croydon, Surrey, United Kingdom, CRO 4NG, ☎ 020/8681–3613). **Instituto Cubano de Amistad** (Cuban Institute of Friendship; ✉ Calle 17, No. 301, Vedado, Havana, Cuba, ☎ 7/32–8017). **Latin American Travel** (✉ 7 Buckingham Gate, London, United Kingdom, SW1E 6JX, ☎ 020/7630–0070). **Magna Tours** (✉ 61 Alness St., Suite 203, Downview, Toronto, Ontario, M34J 2H2, ☎ 416/665–7330). **Regent Holidays** (✉ 15 John St., Bristol, United Kingdom, BS1 2HR, ☎ 02720/211711). **Sol del Caribe** (✉ 11865 SW 26 St., No. B9, Miami, FL 33175, ☎ 305/221–7100). **Sunholiday** (✉ Box 531, St. James, Montego Bay, Jamaica, ☎ 809/952–5629).

Vencremos Brigade (✉ Box 7071, Oakland, CA 94601, ☎ 510/267–0606). **Wings of the World Travel** (✉ 1200 William St., No. 706, Buffalo, NY 14240, ☎ 800/465–8687).

TRAIN TRAVEL

Cuba has the Caribbean's only comprehensive, passenger rail system. An *especial* tourist train (with air-conditioning, comfortable reclining chairs, and a food car) stops at major cities from Havana to Santiago including: Las Tunas, Camagüey, Ciego de Avila, Santa Clara, and Matanzas. The trip takes about 15 hours and runs daily in both directions. Although such trains have food cars, you may want to bring along some of your own provisions, including water.

Most stations are near a city's historic center and are open 8–4 daily. Although you can buy tickets at station counters up to an hour before departure, it's best to reserve them ahead of time. Ladis is the agency in charge of selling tickets to tourists. Fares are reasonable; the 15-hour, overnight Havana–Santiago train, for example, costs $40 one way.

➤ CONTACTS: **Ladis** (☎ 7/62–1770 main ticket office in Havana).

TRAVEL AGENCIES

A good travel agent puts your needs first. Look for an agency that has been in business at least five years, emphasizes customer service, and has someone on staff who specializes in your destination. In addition **make sure the agency belongs to a professional trade organization.** The American Society of Travel Agents (ASTA), with 27,000 agents in some 170 countries, is the largest and most influential in the field. Operating under the motto "Integrity in Travel," it maintains and enforces a strict code of ethics and will step in to help mediate any agent-client disputes if necessary. ASTA also maintains a Web site that includes a directory of agents. Note that if a travel agency is also acting as your tour operator, *see* Buyer Beware *in* Tours & Packages, *above.*

➤ LOCAL AGENT REFERRALS: **American Society of Travel Agents** (ASTA, ☎ 800/965–2782 24-hr hot line, FAX

703/684–8319, www.astanet.com). **Association of British Travel Agents** (✉ 68–271 Newman St., London W1P 4AH, ☎ 020/7637–2444, FAX 020/7637–0713). **Association of Canadian Travel Agents** (✉ 1729 Bank St., Suite 201, Ottawa, Ontario K1V 7Z5, ☎ 613/521–0474, FAX 613/521–0805). **Australian Federation of Travel Agents** (✉ Level 3, 309 Pitt St., Sydney 2000, ☎ 02/9264–3299, FAX 02/9264–1085). **Travel Agents' Association of New Zealand** (✉ Box 1888, Wellington 10033, ☎ 04/499–0104, FAX 04/499–0786).

VISITOR INFORMATION

On the island, you can get information at the offices and booths of Infotur and many state-operated tour and travel agencies throughout the country. Most major hotels have tour desks that can help you arrange flights, tours, and rental cars. *See* Visitor Information *in* the A to Z section at the end of each chapter for more details.

Internationally, Cuba is usually represented by Cubatur; international branches of other state-owned companies—such as Havanatur (a tour operator), Cubanacán (a hotel operation), or Cubana (a national airline)—can also be helpful. Because the Cuban government has no tourist offices in the United States, one of the best sources of information there is the Center for Cuban Studies, which publishes the bimonthly *Cuba Update.*

➤ TOURIST INFORMATION: **Center for Cuban Studies** (✉ 124 W. 23rd St., New York, NY 10011, ☎ 212/242–0559). **Cubanacán** (☎ 416/601–0343 in Toronto, FAX 416/601–0346 in Toronto; ☎ 020/7537–7909 in London, FAX 020/7537–7747 in London; ☎ 010/45–38–31–14 in Paris, FAX 01/43–58–89–68 in Paris). **Cuban Tourist Board** (✉ 55 Queens St. East, Suite 705, Toronto, Ontario M5C 1R6, ☎ 416/362–0700; ✉ Blvd. Rene Levesque West, Montréal, Québec, H2Z 1V7, ☎ 514/875–8004; ✉ 421 Insurgentes Sur, Complejo Aristos, Edificio 5, Local 310, Mexico City, DF 06100, ☎ 5/574–9454.

➤ U.S. GOVERNMENT ADVISORIES: **U.S. Department of State** (✉ Overseas Citizens Services Office, Room 4811

N.S., 2201 C St. NW, Washington, DC 20520; ☎ 202/647–5225 for interactive hot line; 301/946–4400 for computer bulletin board; FAX 202/647–3000 for interactive hot line); enclose a self-addressed, stamped, business-size envelope.

WEB SITES

Do **check out the World Wide Web** when you're planning. You'll find everything from up-to-date weather forecasts to virtual tours of famous cities. Fodor's Web site, www.fodors.com, is a great place to start your online travels. For more information specifically on Cuba, visit: historyofcuba.com, a fun time line of Cuban history with wonderful sidebars; the Cuba Solidarity Site (www.igc.apc.org/cubasoli), which supports the end of U.S. trade embargo against Cuba; and cubaweb.com, an English-language site with information on Cuban history and culture as well as links to sites with details on legislation, foreign policy, business issues, and other topics related to Cuba.

Americans interested in travel to Cuba should check out the U.S. State Department's Cuba site (www.state.gov/www/regions/wha/cuba/index.html) and the U.S. Treasury Department's site (www.treas.gov/ofac), which fully explains who can travel to Cuba.

WHEN TO GO

The best time to visit, December through April, is also the most popular time. Cuba's weather is at its coolest and driest during these months, yet it's still far warmer than North America and Europe.

In the spring and fall, things slow down. At off-the-track destinations and even some beach resorts, these off-seasons can mean fewer hotel amenities; some hotels may be closed entirely for repairs. There are, however, benefits to traveling in the off-seasons: lack of crowds, prices that tumble by up to 25%, and special events (such as Santiago's Carnaval in late July) are among them.

CLIMATE

Average temperatures range from 19°C (67°F) in January to 27°C (81°F) in July. Average humidity is about 80%, but much of the island is blessed by cooling trade winds. The central mountains are probably the coolest regions; temperatures here can dip down to 40°F at night during "cold spells." El Oriente, the country's easternmost portion, broils, especially in summer. In some urban areas, summer heat and humidity mixed with vehicular pollution is an irritating combination—especially for allergy sufferers.

The rainy season runs from May to November; the dry season, from December to April. About 52 inches (132 centimeters) of rain fall on Cuba each year. The north Atlantic coast and the central mountains are wetter than the south coast. Hurricane season runs from June to November, though most hurricanes hit between August and October.

➤ FORECASTS: **Weather Channel Connection** (☎ 900/932–8437), 95¢ per minute from a Touch-Tone phone.

1 DESTINATION: CUBA

CUBA: A ROMANTIC DRAMA

EVER SINCE Christopher Columbus called the largest of the Antilles "The most beautiful thing human eyes ever beheld," everyone who has known Cuba has fallen hopelessly in love with the place. Graham Greene, Ernest Hemingway, Ava Gardner, Winston Churchill, King Edward VIII . . . Cuba has had many passionate admirers. Novelists, in particular, have found Cuba fertile hunting grounds for comedy, tragedy, and, above all perhaps, for *poiesis*—the production of art and emotion. Cuba is consistently moving in a poetic way.

At once the most Spanish country in the Americas and the most Americanized of the Hispanic countries in the New World, Cuba is on the cusp of all things: New World and Old, Atlantic and Caribbean, Gulf of Mexico and Straits of Florida, Uncle Sam and Latin America, animism and Catholicism, Africa and Spain, east and west, and—for the last 40 years—individualism and collectivism, capitalism and socialism. Cuba is romantic and irresistible, it would seem, precisely because it's so conflicted, so paradoxical, so relentlessly ripe with irony, so impossible.

The list of Cuba's contradictions is long. One of the most fertile islands in the world, it has historically been plagued by extreme poverty and food shortages, first as a result of sugarcane that dominated the countryside for the enrichment of Spanish, Cuban, and American landowners; then as a result of trade with the Soviet Union; and, today, as a result of the island's own Soviet-style state apparatus. Education is easy to acquire, yet many well-educated people work as hotel doormen because it pays better than the profession for which they trained. Cuba's corps of physicians is among the best in the world, though treatment of patients can be erratic owing to the scarcity of medical supplies (partly as a result of the U.S. embargo) and gasoline.

In one area there is no contradiction: the island's natural beauty is matched by the beauty of its people, a tonic blend of indigenous Arawak cultures, former Spanish colonial masters, and West African slaves. A museum of slavery in the Valle de los Ingenios (Valley of the Sugar Mills) celebrates the resilience and courage of Afro-Cubans, just as the mountain camps of *cimarrons* (runaway slaves) are maintained as monuments to the heroic Afro-Cuban resistance during Cuba's independence movements. Cuba—which once was so racially segregated that dictator Fulgencio Batista was denied admittance to Havana's exclusive country and yacht club as a result of his cosmopolitan bloodlines—now claims its Afro-Cuban heritage as one of its proudest assets.

Nowhere is the island's heritage better reflected than in its music. Fernando Ortiz, the late, eminent Cuban ethnomusicologist, put it this way: "Cuba's history lies in the aroma of its tobacco and the sweetness of its sugar, but also in the lasciviousness of its music. And in tobacco, sugar and music, black and white have coexisted in the same creative effervescence since the 16th century. . . . White, sugar, and guitar; black, tobacco, and drums." To experience the island's many rhythms—*son, chachacha, guajira, mambo,* to name a few—is to understand Cuba and its people. As Norman Mailer chided President Kennedy after the Bay of Pigs: "Wasn't there anyone around to give you the lecture on Cuba? Don't you sense the enormity of your mistake—you invade a country without understanding its music!" The tiniest trio in the least famous bar is apt to hit that sweet musical spot that suddenly creates, or releases, emotion. Whether they're performing or listening to jazz tunes, folk songs, or Handel and Prokofiev, Cubans communicate in a way that is moving; it's a sharing of sweetness, an unconditional surrender to what the German philosopher and mathematician Gottfried Wilhelm Leibniz termed "the secret arithmetic of the soul."

Cuba—the real Cuba, not the tourist circuit—and its people will, sooner or later get a grip on your heart. The rank-and-file citizens are gracious and dignified; the children—in national school uniforms having been sworn in as "pioneers of socialism" at age six—happy and beautiful;

the dancers and musicians joyful and sensual; even the mobs of hitchhikers awaiting transport along the Autopista Central seem peaceful and cheerful. Despite the hustlers and *jiniteras* around tourist hotels, Che Guevara's ideal of the New Man seems to have had an effect: most Cubans seem more interested in sharing something with you than getting something from you. Despite all their problems and penuries, Cubans generally seem happier in their crumbling environment than citizens of many more affluent societies. How the island came to exist in this manner is a drama that is still unfolding.

The Plots and the Players

For 400 years Spain ruthlessly exploited its "Pearl of the Antilles." Trade monopolies, slavery, and lack of political autonomy caused many to suffer financially, physically, and emotionally. Although Cuba saw several skirmishes for greater freedom (including slave rebellions in 1812, 1841, and 1862), its first great flirtation with independence (and with America) began, ironically, when its economy burgeoned in the 19th century. Though talk of independence was often framed in high-minded principals such as self-rule and freedom for all men, it was also linked, in certain quarters, to self-serving issues—including maintaining the system of slavery that was key to Cuba's plantation economy.

Act I: The Ten Years War

Napoléon's 1808 conquest of the Iberian Peninsula sparked many independence movements in Spain's far-flung colonies. Initially Cuba's landed aristocracy hesitated to take such bold steps, fearful of losing Spanish support in the event of a major slave revolt such as those that occurred on Sainte-Domingue (Haiti) in the late 18th century. Further, many *peninsulares* (Spaniards) had emigrated to Cuba during the Napoleonic Wars, strengthening the bonds with the motherland. In 1817, however, the British began encouraging Spain to abolish its slave trade. Fearful of losing their labor source and their way of life, some land-owning *criollos* (creoles; Cuban-born people of Spanish descent) began to look at the United States as a possible benefactor. Between 1822 and 1861 there were several Cuban missions to America, seeking U.S. support if not outright annexation. (The United States expressed interest in acquiring the island as early as 1808, when President Jefferson tried to buy it from Spain. Subsequent purchase attempts by presidents Monroe, Polk, Pierce, and Buchanan brought the price up to $130 million, but Spain wouldn't sell.) It wasn't until the South lost the American Civil War and slavery was abolished in the United States that Cuban interest in American assistance dissolved. The criollos, once again, turned to Spain for reforms.

The independence movement reached its first nexus in 1868, when Carlos Manuel de Céspedes freed the slaves on his plantation and read his Grito de Yara (a Cuban Declaration of Independence). The Ten Years' War ensued, and with it two of Cuba's great military leaders—the Dominican-born Máximo Gómez and the Cuban mulatto Antonio Maceo—made their names. In February 1878 the Spanish and the Cuban rebels accepted the Peace of El Zanjón. The treaty seemed only to acknowledge that both sides were exhausted, their resources depleted. Its terms were unsatisfactory to many (including Maceo, who fought for another year); the island seemed far from achieving true local autonomy; and although steps were taken to gradually abolish slavery, its complete abolition—a goal for many revolutionaries—had not been realized.

Act II: The Second War of Independence

In 1895, a new independence movement was launched, with the great Cuban writer and patriot José Martí (1853–95) as its chief ideologue and Maceo and Gómez as its top generals. Martí, Cuba's foremost martyr and hero, was first a lyric poet, author of romantic verses such as *El corazón es un loco / Que no sabe de un color / O es su amor de dos colores / O dice que no es amor* (The heart is a madman / Who doesn't know one color / Either his love is of two colors / Or he says it isn't love) and such patriotic lines as *Muro de cuatro siglos, tiranía / Cada vez mas atrás para ir al frente / Bandera de cien años, cada día / mas y mas alta / para alzar la frente* (Wall of four centuries, tyranny / Ever farther back to move ahead / Flag of a hundred years, day by day, ever taller / to stand proud). He also contributed moving lyrics to the ubiquitous song "Guantanamera":

Yo *quiero cuando me muera / con patria pero sin amo / poner a mi losa un ramo / de flores, y una bandera* (I want, when I die / with a country but without a master / on my stone a bouquet / of flowers, and a flag).

Martí's long struggle for Cuba's freedom from Spain began with his imprisonment for publishing treasonous material at age 16 and ended with his death in 1895 (he was one of the first to fall in the Second War of Independence). In between, Martí studied law in Madrid; published books of poetry; wrote essays on the future of Latin America; and worked as a journalist in New York and as a reader in a cigar factory in Tampa, Florida, where he launched Cuba's definitive independence movement. Martí was wary of becoming too closely allied with the United States. The quote of his most often heard today is: "I know the Monster, because I have lived in his lair."

Cuba seemed on the verge of achieving its independence in 1898 when the United States, in a display of military prowess, sent the battleship *Maine* to the island. While in Havana Harbor, the ship was blown up. The flames of public opinion, fanned by Joseph Pulitzer's *New York World* and William Randolph Hearst's *New York Journal,* blamed the Spanish and demanded war with the cry, "Remember the *Maine,* to hell with Spain!" (Spanish and Cuban history texts maintain that the *Maine* was blown up by U.S. agents to provide a pretext for entering the war. Proponents of this version cite the facts that the explosion blew the hull out, not in, and that there were no officers on board at the time of the blast. The U.S. Navy has since claimed that a defective boiler caused the explosion.) On April 25, 1898, the United States declared war on Spain. American forces took Guam, Puerto Rico, and the Philippines in one day; the Spanish held on to Cuba till July 17. Down came the Spanish flag and up went . . . the Stars and Stripes.

Since its earlier purchase attempts, the United States had made little secret of its interest in acquiring "the key to the New World," a prize of enormous strategic and economic value. As Cuba's Second War of Independence drew to a close, the moment had arrived for the United States to make its move. General Gómez tried to

avoid U.S. intervention by asking for arms and ammunition instead of troops. However, the *mambises* (from the Congolese word meaning "despicable"), as the Spanish called the Cuban freedom fighters, could only watch helplessly as their liberation movement was stolen out from under them. In the end, the mambises, after losing more than 300,000 fighters in the struggle begun in 1868, were ordered to turn in their arms and were excluded from the victory parade staged by the triumphant U.S. military leaders.

Act III: The Way to Revolution

Martí's fears that the United States would subsume Cuba should the two nations become politically linked proved uncannily prophetic. In 1899, the island became an independent republic under U.S. protection. The 1901 Platt Amendment—accepted begrudgingly by Cuba—stipulated that America could intervene in Cuban affairs if the island's stability was at risk. It also allowed the United States to buy or lease Cuban land on which to build a military outpost (hence, the Guantánamo Naval Base). U.S. military occupation ended in 1902, but U.S. meddling did not. The Platt Amendment was invoked twice during the next 15 years, and U.S. diplomats whispered instructions into the ears of many a Cuban leader right up until Fidel Castro's Revolution in the 1950s. The United States was also heavily involved in the island's economics. By 1958, Wall Street controlled 90% of the Cuban nickel and copper mines; 90% of the sugar, tobacco, and coffee plantations; 80% of the public services; and 50% of the railroads. In addition, Standard Oil's annual profits were greater than all U.S. aid to Latin America combined while, for good measure, North American sugar markets bought Cuban sugar at abusively low prices.

By the 1950s, average Cubans were in no better shape economically than many of their forebears had been at the beginning of the Wars of Independence. In addition, the American mafia had made Havana its headquarters (Cuba was notorious as the brothel of North America, a free port for gambling, prostitution, and all the pleasures that were illegal 120 miles north). Years of political corruption, civil unrest, and such greedy dictators as Gerardo Machado and Fulgencio

Batista had taken their toll. The country was ready for Fidel Castro Ruz and his message.

The early Castro, a romantic Robin Hood figure, miraculously survived the 1953 attack on the Moncada Barracks in eastern Cuba and his subsequent trial and capture. Upon being released from prison, he went to Mexico in exile. In 1956, he and 81 rebels left Mexico aboard the yacht *Granma*. He lost most of his men after being ambushed by Batista forces in a landing described by Che Guevara as a shipwreck. Castro then organized an improbable guerrilla resistance movement in the highland jungle sanctuary of the Sierra Maestra. He took Havana in January 1959 after dictator Batista fled the country with much of the treasury. During his triumphal address, a white dove landed on his shoulder, an apparently spontaneous event that convinced Cuba's Santería worshippers of Castro's divine right to rule. Now well into his 70s, El Comandante is the planet's last governing socialist, head of a Soviet-style totalitarian regime short on civil liberties but justly proud of successes in health, education, and culture.

Ernesto "Che" Guevara, an Argentine born into a leftist bourgeois family in 1928, met Castro in Mexico in 1955 and joined the Cuban revolutionary movement. Described by Jean-Paul Sartre as "the most complete human being of our age," Che (the nickname comes from Argentine slang for "pal") was trained as a physician but proved to be an outstanding field commander. Poet, idealist, and philosopher, he seemed the perfect complement for the ever-pragmatic Fidel. The two revolutionaries parted ways only when Castro (for practical reasons) allied Cuba with the Soviet Union, which Guevara considered an imperialist force no less voracious than America. Obsessively opposed to capitalism, Che believed in the perfectibility of man and strove to create El Hombre Nuevo (The New Man), the true socialist who would work for the common good instead of for personal gain. After his break with the Cuban revolution, Che took up fights in the Congo and Bolivia. On October 9, 1967, he was ambushed, wounded, captured, and executed by Bolivian Army Rangers (allegedly on orders from the CIA). Castro has made his former comrade into a cult figure. Che's likeness is everywhere, from the huge sculpture in Havana's Plaza de la Revolución to the three-peso coin peddled (counter to Che's guiding beliefs) for dollars on the streets. The motto of the Young Pioneers, the national youth movement, is "Seremos como Che" ("We will be like Che").

In an effort to protect its interests since the Revolution, the United States has compiled a somewhat embarrassing record vis-a-vis Cuba. The 1961 Bay of Pigs Invasion was an outstanding example of American interventionism. As the Cold War drama unfolded, so did the naval blockade, the Cuban missile crisis, the trade embargo, and numerous alleged attempts to assassinate Castro. Though the Cold War has ended, relations between the two countries have hardly warmed up as evidenced by the 1996 Helms-Burton Act (proposing to penalize businesses and travelers from third countries for trading with or visiting Cuba).

Act IV: Today and Tomorrow

Today, Cuba maintains a precarious balance between state-controlled economy, expression, and movement, and the beginnings of such free-market phenomena as the legalization of the dollar and the heavily taxed private restaurants known as *paladares*. That the almighty dollar should be regarded as the salvation of one of the world's last bastions of socialism is yet another Cuban irony.

The lifting of the 40-year blockade, the pacification of the radical right-wing anti-Castro Cubans, and a transition to some form of government acceptable to all sides are urgent priorities as the new millennium begins and Fidel Castro starts his fifth decade of increasingly autocratic rule. "Our project," said a prominent Cuban statesman recently, "is to preserve the basic triumphs of the Revolution—our sovereignty, independence, health care, and education. Everything else is negotiable."

This view is shared by many Cubans and Cubanophiles who, perhaps utopistically, hope for the best of all worlds in a peaceful future: guaranteed medicine, education, and subsistence in an increasingly democratic society. A difficult act to balance, but for Cuba, master of the impossible, it could all fall into place.

—by George Semler

WHAT'S WHERE

Havana

Slightly more than 2 million people call the nation's capital, set on Cuba's northwestern coast, home. The city is surrounded by the Straits of Florida and Havana Province. It's also divided into 15 municipalities, which themselves often contain various neighborhoods. Some 145 km (90 mi) from Key West (which Cubans call Cayo Hueso, literally Bone Key), Havana is very nearly Cuba's closest point to the United States.

Western Cuba

Western Cuba includes the three provinces of Matanzas, La Habana, and Pinar del Río as well as the Municipio Especial (Special Municipality) of the Isla de la Juventud. Here you'll find everything from wetlands, such as the Ciénaga de Zapata, to the finest tobacco country, such as that in Pinar del Río. The diversity continues with the peaks of the central Cordillera de Guaniguanico, the scrubby woodlands of the Península de Guanahacabibes, and the sandy beaches along miles of coast.

Central Cuba

Set between the lowlands east of Havana and the mountainous eastern provinces, central Cuba is connected to the rest of the country by a highway that runs the length of the island. Heading east, that highway first skirts Cienfuegos, a small province surrounding the 19th-century city and deep bay of the same name, and then enters the larger Villa Clara Province near its capital, Santa Clara. Those two provinces, together with Sancti Spíritus, just to the east, surround the dark green Escambray Mountains, though they largely consist of flat or rolling lowlands covered with sugarcane, tobacco, and pasture. In Sancti Spíritus, the colonial city of Trinidad is nestled between the mountains and the sea, near the pale beaches of the Península de Ancón. Ciego de Ávila, the next province to the east, is known for the beaches of Cayo Coco and Cayo Guillermo, two cays off its north shore. The province of Camagüey, still farther east, has a large colonial capital set in a vast agricultural plain, to the northeast of which is the beach resort of Santa Lucia.

Eastern Cuba

The cradle of revolution, anvil-shaped eastern Cuba includes the provinces of Granma, Holguín, Santiago, and Guantánamo. Together with Las Tunas, they once comprised the single province of El Oriente. Santiago de Cuba, the region's most important city, lies on the southern coast of the province that shares its name. Far removed from Havana, Santiago has, throughout its history, been influenced by its Caribbean neighbors, as well as by French settlers and Afro-Cuban denizens. Though miles of farmland cover the region, it is also blessed with fabulous beaches, the majestic Sierra Maestra, and the forests surrounding Baracoa.

NEW AND NOTEWORTHY

In Havana, the Cuban government–sponsored company Habaguanex (the name of a Taíno Indian chief, the origin of the capital's name) and the Oficina del Historiador (Office of the City Historian) are restoring La Habana Vieja (Old Havana) with the help of UNESCO and private capital from Spain. This has led to the opening of several new hotels, many in renovated historic structures, and restaurants. The goal of the Habaguanex project is to have 1,425 hotel rooms in La Habana Vieja by 2004.

The Ministry of Tourism is attuned to the increasing interest in adventure and ecological tourism. There are many new packages on offer that allow visitors to explore nearly pristine wetlands and other remote areas such as the Sierra del Rosario, the Ciénaga de Zapata, and the Península de Guanahacabibes. Fishing, diving, and hiking trips are among the options.

Central Cuba's northern cays, called the Jardines del Rey (Gardens of the King), are the focus of some ambitious tourism development. Cayos Coco and Guillermo, in the province of Ciego de Ávila, now have half a dozen resort hotels with several more under construction. The beaches on these cays are gorgeous, and the country needs the revenue. Come quickly before development disrupts the delicate coastal ecosystems or frightens away the thousands of flamingos that nest here.

The eastern Cuba beach resort of Marea del Portillo is now more accessible than ever from Santiago de Cuba thanks to the fact that the southern coastal road, running west from Santiago into Granma Province, is now completely paved. This beautiful route runs between the Sierra Maestra and a coast lined by the sparkling blue Caribbean waters that lap dark-sand beaches. At press time, improvements to a road from Guardalavarca to Baracoa were also under way.

PLEASURES AND PASTIMES

Beaches

Cuba's 3,735 km (2,319 mi) of coast is washed by the waters of the Atlantic Ocean to the north, the Caribbean Sea to the south and east, and the Gulf of Mexico's Yucatán Channel to the west. Just 20 km (12 mi) east of Havana are the famous Playas del Este, whose white sands frequently fill up with *Habaneros,* as the city's residents are called. In the western provinces, you'll also find everything from the lively resort strip of Varadero to the wild, unspoiled Playa María la Gorda. Central Cuba's northern keys (Cayo las Brujas, Cayo Coco, and Cayo Guillermo) have beautiful sandy stretches as well as outstanding fishing and dive sites. El Oriente is blessed with a dark-sand coastline in southwest Granma Province, resort towns along Holguín's northern coast, and isolated coastal enclaves surrounding Baracoa in the far reaches of Guantánamo Province. Water sports are also abundant throughout the eastern region.

Dining

A standard Havana wisecrack credits the Revolution's three great triumphs—health, education, and culture—as having been achieved at the expense of breakfast, lunch, and dinner. Food conversations here turn repeatedly to the vicissitudes of supply: 100 heads of garlic for 100 pesos ($5) is a true bargain opportunity; friends in from the country with a load of *frijoles negros tiernos* (tender black beans) is an event to recount—albeit in whispers as these are black-market black beans. *Res* (beef) and *pernil* (ham) are dollar-store items, until recently off limits to Cubans and now merely cripplingly expensive. Without a doubt, the combination of food shortages and state-run restaurants has produced some remarkably undistinguished cooking over the past 40 years. But the legalization of the dollar and the opening of privately owned paladares have sparked a renaissance of authentic *cocina criollo,* traditional Cuban home cooking that truly ennobles lowly ingredients.

Pollo (chicken), *puerco* (pork), *camarones* (shrimp), *langosta* (lobster), *pescado* (fish), and to a lesser degree, beef and *cordero* (lamb) are the meat and seafood staples. *Frijoles negros* (black beans), *arroz* (rice), *yuca* (cassava or manioc), *malanga* (sweet potato), *boniato* (yam), and *plátanos* (plantains) are the leading legumes and starches. *Salsa criolla* (onion, tomato, pepper, garlic, salt, and oil), *ajiaco* (aji—a hot, red pepper—yucca, malanga, turnips, and herbs) and *mojo* (garlic, tomato, and pepper) are the main sauces.

The plantain alone has 1,001 preparations in the Cuban kitchen. When ripe, it may be cut diagonally and fried. When green, it can be sliced into *lascas* (thin wafers), fried, and salted to create *mariquitas,* or chopped into thick wedges, pounded, and fried as *plátanos a puñetazos* (punched plantains). Green or mature it may be boiled, mashed with a fork, dressed with olive oil and crisped pork rinds to create *fufú,* or mashed and mixed with *picadillo* (ground meat) and melted cheese for a *pastel de plátano* (plantain pudding)—tropical shepherd's pie.

Moros y cristianos ("Moors and Christians" or "blacks and whites") is a combination of black beans and rice. *Ropa vieja* (literally, "old clothes") or *aporreado de res* is shredded beef recooked in a criolla sauce. *Arroz congrí* is white rice "with gray," that is, with frijoles negros *dormidos* (literally "put to sleep"—cooked and allowed to stand overnight). *La caldosa,* a universal favorite, is a soup or stew of chicken, onions, garlic, oregano, plantain, squash, yams, carrots, potatoes, malanga, butter, and ham—all left to simmer slowly. Other standard dishes include cordero *estofado con vegetales* (lamb stew made with malanga, boniato, carrots, onions, garlic, and turnips), *chicharrones de puerco* (pork crisps), and *masas de cerdo* (morsels of pork, often served in mojo criollo).

8

REVOLUTIONARY RECIPES

POLLO AL BLOQUEO (chicken à la blockade) is a popular recipe from the Special Period (the belt-tightening period called by Castro after trade with and support from the Soviet Union ceased).

Day 1: Skin a chicken, boil it, and make soup from the stock, adding *viandas* (potatoes, tomatoes, carrots, yuca, boniato, tamale, and maybe some pasta, corn, or rice). Day 2: Brown the pieces and parts of the chicken, and serve it in a salsa criolla (onion, tomato, pepper, garlic, salt, and oil). Day 3: Sauté the chicken until it's crackly hard; serve with white rice. Day 4: Crack the chicken bones and suck out the marrow.

In the colonial city of Trinidad, the *pargo* (red snapper) run in the Gulf of Mexico just in time for Mother's Day. Sons and grandsons emerge from restaurants all over town carrying large platters home for a feast of *pargo a la criolla*.

Step 1: Marinate pargo in lemon, onion, garlic, and salt. Step 2: Place in earthenware vessel with a small amount of butter spread over the bottom. Step 3: Cook for three minutes on low heat, turning quickly several times. Step 4: Cover casserole and allow pargo to simmer until done. Step 5: Serve to mother with an exuberant "*felicidades!*" ("congratulations!")

On the island's eastern end, dishes are more Caribbean and less Spanish; they're prepared with more spices and are typically cooked in coconut oil and *lechita* (coconut milk). Eastern dishes include *congrí oriental* (rice and red kidney beans), *bacón* (a plantain tortilla filled with spicy pork), and *tetí* (a small, orange fish caught in the river estuaries between August and December.) Rice is yellow not from saffron but from annatto seeds, also used to color butter. "Indian bananas" are boiled in their salmon-colored skins and dressed with garlic and lime juice.

Desserts include specialties such as *guayaba* (guava paste) or *mermelada de mango* (mango jelly), both often served *con queso* (with cheese). The eastern treat, *cucurucho*, is made of coconut, sweet orange, papaya, and honey. Of course the island's love affair with sugarcane led to its *ron* (rum) industry. While you're here, be sure to have a *mojito* (light rum, sugar, mint, and soda; from the verb "mojar," meaning "to moisten, to wet" as in "to whet your whistle") or the classic *daiquiri* (blended light rum, lime, and ice). If you'd like the sugar experience without the kick, have a *guarapo* (cane juice; thought to be an aphrodisiac). Cuba also has several fine beers ranging from light lagers such as Cristal to dark varieties like Hatuey and Mayabe.

Music

Your Cuban journey will no doubt be accompanied by a veritable soundtrack of island music. There are countless genres, from classical to Latin jazz to such hybrids of European and African sounds as *salsa, timba, conga, rumba, bolero, son, danzón, guájira, mambo, nueva,* and *vieja trova.* And every community seems to have some sort of weekly musical event. On a typical Sunday night in Trinidad (where two music havens—La Casa de la Musica and La Casa de la Trova—are steps from each other), for example, you might encounter a septet led by a man of 70-odd years playing for a crowd of 50. Men and women of all ages will no doubt dance with confidence and aplomb.

For another type of experience, try to catch a performance of the Cuban National Symphony in Havana's Amadeu Roldan concert hall. Don't let the youth of the musicians or their seemingly casual attire (white shirts and black bow ties as opposed to the white tie and tail of European symphonies) fool you. These are professional, well-directed musicians who open their hearts and truly communicate with music.

FODOR'S CHOICE

Cigar Sights

⋆ **Fábrica de Tabacos Partagás, Havana.** A look inside this cigar factory is a must. The store has more than $1 million of tobacco on sale. You can smoke, sip coffee or a mojito, or tour the upstairs factory, where 500 people roll cigars for eight hours a day Monday through Saturday.

⋆ **Vuelta Abajo, Western Cuba.** The finest-quality tobacco leaves come from this region west and south of Pinar del Río. Some 80,000 acres of tobacco are planted annually in the province, and the best of it is found around San Luis and San Juan y Martínez.

Comforts

⋆ **Hotel Nacional, Havana.** The memorabilia-filled Nacional, Cuba's great national treasure, retains its glitter no matter how bad times may get (and they're getting better). *$$$$*

⋆ **Las Américas, Varadero, Western Cuba.** Once the Du Pont mansion, this hotel offers a taste of what Varadero was like before the Revolution. *$$$—$$$$*

⋆ **Cuatro Vientos, Playa Santa Lucía, Central Cuba.** This rambling hotel has comfortable rooms that overlook tropical gardens or a gorgeous beach washed by the aquamarine Caribbean. *$$$*

⋆ **Hotel Moka, Las Terrazas, Western Cuba.** Ecology is the theme at this modern hotel, where a large tree grows up through the center of the reception area and the bar and restaurant seem perched over the valley. *$$$*

⋆ **Hotel Casa Granda, Santiago, Eastern Cuba.** This classic property—with a gracious patio bar, an elegant dining room, and antiques-filled guest rooms—is set right on Parque Céspedes in Santiago's historic district. *$$—$$$*.

⋆ **Faro Luna, Playa Rancho Luna, Central Cuba.** Set on a rocky point near the public beach, this hotel has bright, spacious, ocean-view rooms and a dive center whose staffers help you discover just what's in that shimmering sea. *$$*

⋆ **Hostal Valencia, Havana.** This hotel is set in a lovingly restored 18th-century La Habana Vieja mansion. Although the gracious patio is more reminiscent of Seville and Andalusia, each of the guest rooms is named for a Valencian village, and the restaurant specializes in paella. *$$*

⋆ **Convento de Santa Clara, Havana.** This former Clarist convent has very few rooms, but if you can get one you'll be sleeping in one of Havana's most picturesque and historic spots. *$—$$*

⋆ **Hotel Castillo, Baracoa, Eastern Cuba.** Set in a fort dating from the 18th-century, this hotel offers comfortable rooms that mix antiques with modern facilities and afford views of the town and El Yunque. *$*

⋆ **Hotel Mascotte, Remedios, Central Cuba.** Dating from the late 19th century, this small hotel on an historic plaza offers tranquil, charming accommodations in an equally enchanting town. *$*

Flavors

⋆ **El Floridita, Havana.** On everyone's short list as one of Havana's greatest spots, El Floridita lives up to the advance billing splendidly. The bar is better than the restaurant. *$$$$*

⋆ **Rumayor, Pinar del Río, Western Cuba.** Though state-owned, this restaurant is filled with Afro-Cuban crafts that give it great personality; it turns into a disco at night. *$$$—$$$$*

⋆ **Antigüedades, Varadero, Western Cuba.** With an intimate, antiques-filled dining room and only the freshest of seafood dishes, this restaurant is considered by many to be the best on the Península de Hicacos. *$$$*

⋆ **El Aljibe, Havana.** The breezy Miramar pavilion takes top honors in the criollo cuisine stakes. Leaving Havana without a taste of *pollo Aljibe* is almost as serious an offense as not dancing or smoking a Havana cigar. *$$—$$$*

★ **La Maison, Santiago, Eastern Cuba.** Dinner at this elegant establishment in the charming Vista Alegre neighborhood is often accompanied by a fashion show. Lunch in the patio and browsing in the on-site boutique are also options. $$–$$$

★ **Palacio de Valle, Cienfuegos, Central Cuba.** Surrounded by this 19th-century mansion's elegant marble columns and sculpted Moorish arches, you can feast on langosta. $$–$$$

★ **Casa de Don Tomás, Viñales, Western Cuba.** If you have to pick a place to go out of your way for, this spot—known for both its fine food and its good music—is it. $$

★ **La Guarida, Havana.** This funky paladar run by Enrique Nuñez and his wife, Odeysis, is a delight for the decor, the cuisine, and the gracious owners. $$

★ **Restaurant Zun Zún, Santiago, Eastern Cuba.** The dishes at this eatery have won culinary awards, the wine list is extensive, and the elegant decor reflects the tastes of the Arab merchant who once owned the house in which it's set. $$

★ **Sol y Son, Trinidad, Central Cuba.** This intimate restaurant in the garden patio of a private home is one of the region's best paladares, serving an inventive, eclectic selection of dishes. $

★ **La Campana de Toledo, Camagüey, Central Cuba.** Housed in an 18th-century building on Camagüey's timeless Plaza de San Juan, this small restaurant serves food to match its ambience—authentic Cuban. $

Museums and Monuments

★ **Antiguo Cuartel Moncada, Santiago, Eastern Cuba.** The former army barracks that Castro and his rebels attacked during Carnaval of 1956 is now a museum with comprehensive exhibits on the Revolution.

★ **Casa Natal de José Martí, Havana.** Cuba's *padre de la patria* (father of the nation) was born of Spanish parents in this humble La Habana Vieja house on January 28, 1853. The moving displays here convey the esteem in which this poet-patriot is held by Cubans.

★ **Monumento Che Guevara, Santa Clara, Central Cuba.** It wasn't until 1997 that the remains of Cuba's great revolutionary were identified; it took another year for them to arrive in Cuba from Bolivia for burial at this monument.

★ **Museo Bacardí, Santiago, Eastern Cuba.** Founded in 1898 by the rum-making Bacardí family, Cuba's oldest museum contains a fascinating collection of indigenous artifacts, colonial items, and 19th- and 20th-century works of art.

★ **Museo Histórico, Trinidad, Central Cuba.** It's no accident that UNESCO designated Trinidad a world heritage site; a stroll through the city's rambling historic center feels like a trip into the 18th century. The history museum traces the city's development from its founding by Diego Velázquez to the early years of the Revolution.

★ **Museo de la Revolución, Havana.** Set in what was once Batista's Palacio Presidencial, the displays in this museum tell the tale of Cuba's Revolution. The Cretin's Corner has some familiar faces.

Natural Wonders

★ **Caleta Buena, Western Cuba.** East of Playa Girón is this exquisite limestone *cenote* (sinkhole) and coral cove.

★ **Cayo Coco and Cayo Guillermo, Central Cuba.** The white-sand beaches and turquoise sea of these two islands are alone enough to make them major destinations, but the cays are also near an array of legendary fishing and diving spots, and they're home to an abundance of birds.

★ **Cueva Punta del Este, Western Cuba.** This group of caves on the Isla de la Juventud has aboriginal paintings of stunning color and originality.

★ **Parque Nacional Turquino, Eastern Cuba.** A short hike through the lush vegetation of this national park in the Sierra Maestra brings you to Castro's camp and headquarters during the Revolution.

★ **Playa Santa Lucía, Central Cuba.** Its sands are pale and lovely, and the ocean that washes against them affords excellent diving opportunities.

★ **Valle de Viñales, Western Cuba.** With its limestone *mogotes* (hillocks) and verdant valleys, this area has some of Cuba's most unique landscapes.

Sacred Spots

★ **El Convento Menor de San Francisco de Asis, Havana.** This lovely church has many irresistible features, from its facade and bell tower to its cloister and interior patios. The artwork displayed in the permanent and itinerant collections is excellent.

★ **Iglesia del Santo Cristo del Bien Viaje, Havana.** A miniaturesque-yet-weighty character gives this church universal appeal. The square around it and the richly vegetated churchyard all form a compact esthetic unit.

★ **Necrópolis Cristóbal Colón, Havana.** Founded in 1868, the Christopher Columbus Cemetery is a veritable pantheon of monuments commemorating poets, novelists, musicians, soldiers, statesmen, and rank-and-file citizens. It's also a place full of legend.

Time-Honored Places and Spaces

★ **Castillo de Jagua, Cienfuegos, Central Cuba.** Set above the Bahía de Cienfuegos, this fort was built in 1745 to discourage pirates from trading with locals. It has been completely refurbished (even the drawbridge works) and has an historical museum, a bar, and a restaurant.

★ **Castillo de San Carlos de la Cabaña, Havana.** Every night at 9 sharp, the ceremony of the cannon draws Cubans and visitors alike to this fort. This not-to-miss event is even more enjoyable when followed by dinner at one of the restaurants in the Morro fortress area.

★ **Parque Céspedes, Santiago, Eastern Cuba.** Santigueros love to congregate in this historic square, where life continuously unfolds and music always fills the air.

★ **Plaza de Armas, Havana.** The most fundamental of Havana squares is surrounded by fascinating buildings, from the Castillo de la Real Fuerza to the Palacio del Segundo Cabo and the Palacio de los Capitanes Generales.

★ **Plaza de la Catedral, Havana.** The baroque facade of the Havana Cathedral is very possibly the most powerful sight in the city. The square in which it sits is ringed with other important palaces; the restaurant El Patio has tables in the square, and the Bodeguita del Medio is right around the corner.

★ **Plaza de San Juan de Dios, Camagüey, Central Cuba.** This splendid cobbled square—surrounded by 18th- and 19th-century buildings—has been declared a national monument. It is part of the historic district in the friendly city of Camagüey—Cuba's third largest community but one that's still off the tourist track.

★ **Plaza Vieja, Havana.** Plaza Vieja and the buildings around it—particularly the Casa de los Condes de Jaruco, the Casa del Conde de Lombillo, and the Casa de la Hermanas Cárdenas—are all knockouts.

FESTIVALS AND SEASONAL EVENTS

➤ DEC.: Havana's **Festival Internacional de Cine Latinoamericano** (International Festival of Latin American Film) held in mid-December, has become one of the hemisphere's great film festivals—blockade or no. The December 17th **Procesión de los Milagros** (Procession of the Miracles) features penitents dragging stones or themselves through the streets of Rincón (outside Havana, near Santiago de las Vegas) to the Santuario de San Lázaro to give thanks to the Santería *orisha* (god) Babalu Aye, patron of lepers, medicine, and the harvest.

➤ JAN.: Havana's **Cabildos Festival** on January 6 features people in costumes dancing through the streets. During Trinidad's (central Cuba)**Cultural Festival,** held the second week of the month, there are music, dance, and theater performances as well as art exhibitions.

➤ FEB.: In Havana, February sees the **Festival Nacional de Teatro** (National Theater Festival). **Carnaval,** centered in La Habana Vieja, is a three-week blowout that seems headed for eventual equity with Rio de Janeiro's

famous fête. The mid-month **Santa Lucía Festival** in central Cuba includes carnival-style parades, concerts, and other events.

➤ MARCH: Cárdenas, in western Cuba, celebrates a **Semana de la Cultura** (Culture Week) in early March honoring the founding of the city.

➤ APR.: You can get your chops at the **Havana Jazz Festival.** During the first week of April, Baracoa (eastern Cuba) hosts **Semana de la Cultura** (Culture Week).

➤ MAY: Havana's impressive **May Day** celebration, on the first of the month, features a procession of more than a million Cubans filing by El Comandante on his reviewing stand in the Plaza de la Revolución.

➤ JUNE: The central Cuban city of Trinidad holds a **religious procesion** on June 13. The lively **Trinidad Carnaval** happens June 24–29.

➤ JULY: July sees a **Guitar Festival** in Havana. Early in the month, Santiago hosts the **Festival of Caribbean Culture,** organized by the Casa del Caribe, which features musical and cultural events involving local artists and those from throughout the Caribbean. In western Cuba, mid-July is the time for the **Varadero Carnaval.** Eastern Cuba's biggest annual event is **Santiago's Carnaval,** which takes place in late July. The streets are filled with costumed dancers, musicians, floats, and revelers. In the middle of the month, Cienfuegos in central Cuba holds its **Fiesta de los Amigos del Mar** (Friends of the Sea Festival) with a variety of boating competitions and plenty of partying on land.

➤ SEPT.: The **Festival Internacional de Teatro de la Habana** (Havana International Theater Festival) takes place in September.

➤ OCT.: October sees Havana's **International Ballet Festival.**

➤ NOV.: In November, head to Havana for the **Contemporary Music Festival.**

2 HAVANA

In this cosmopolitan seaport, classic American cars clatter along streets lined with Spanish architecture and alive with Caribbean rhythms. The old city's baroque facades, colonial palaces, and lush patios whisper tales of the past while Vedado's 20th-century skyscrapers shout dreams of the future. Everywhere Spanish, African, Caribbean, and American flavors are blended into an irresistibly romantic brew.

By George
Semler

I F I GET LOST, LOOK FOR ME IN CUBA. . . "** wrote the Spanish poet Federico García Lorca. If you visit Havana, you'll soon find out why. Part Cádiz, part Miami, the city is an intoxicating mixture of opulence and decay; Old World and New; socialism and capitalism; Europe, Africa, and America. The Spanish baroque architecture of the 16th- and 17th-century colonial period, the neoclassical dome of the Capitolio (built in 1929 and modeled on the U.S. Capitol), and the modern glass-and-steel skyscrapers: each has a story to tell.

You'll discover still more tales in buildings that crumble behind Corinthian columns and in 1950s Chevrolets and Oldsmobiles traveling beside Soviet-made Volgas and Ladas, tiny motor scooter–powered *coco-taxis,* and *ciclo-taxis* (bicycle rickshaws) for two. Modern hotel and apartment blocks tower garishly over streets choked with roaring trucks that spew black smoke. Slogans printed in block letters on government buildings loom alongside bars and cafés where red-hot salsa combos play. The air is almost asphyxiating, the heat is relentless, and most things are in disrepair. Yet all this only strengthens Havana's allure. Graham Greene and Ernest Hemingway drank deeply of it and were inspired; Ava Gardner and Winston Churchill—to name a few—also imbibed and were enchanted.

One of the oldest cities in the Americas, Havana was founded on Cuba's southern coast as San Cristóbal de la Habana in the early 16th century. In 1519 it was moved to its present northwestern location, where a natural harbor, one of the Caribbean's best, made it an ideal maritime hub. For almost 250 years, however, Havana was little more than a staging area for Spanish convoys loaded with New World treasures and bound for Europe. The captain-general governed Cuba from here, but ultimately reported to the powerful Spanish vice-royalty in Mexico. In 1750, Cuba's population numbered only about 150,000, half of whom lived in Havana or in other towns such as Matanzas, Trinidad, Sancti Spiritus, and Santiago de Cuba. The island had a handful of aristocratic, *criollo* (Spanish settler) families but few plantations, and hence, few slaves. (Indeed, about ⅓ of Havana's population consisted of freed blacks, owing to laws that allowed slaves to buy their freedom.) Trade with foreigners for the island's few resources was officially banned (though there was smuggling), making Cuba seem isolated. In 12 years, all this would change, and Havana, with its great port, would be transformed.

In 1762, Britain's Lord Albemarle conquered Havana during the Seven Years War. Under his yearlong administration, British merchants flocked to the city. They sold foodstuffs, cloth, horses, agricultural equipment, and thousands of slaves. Though the island was turned back over to the Spanish in 1763 (under the Treaty of Paris and in exchange for Florida), the ties to British markets were already strong. The ports were flung open to trade, and the interior was flung open to development. Before the British arrived, Havana saw half a dozen ships a year, and the average size of Cuba's few plantations was 300 acres; after the British left, about 200 ships called annually in Havana, and the island's increasing number of plantations consisted of 700 acres on average. By the 19th century Havana was the Western Hemisphere's busiest commercial center, made fabulously rich by sugar, tobacco, coffee, and rum. Behind such exports was a plantation society run by criollos for their benefit and that of the *peninsulares* in Spain. It also relied heavily upon vast numbers of West African slaves, whose culture, traditions, and blood often mixed with that of the criollos to create a truly Cuban people and heritage.

Cuba's flirtation with independence began in the 19th century as well, and Havana, as the capital, was often in the eye of the storm. During the Ten Years War (1868–78), Cuba's first attempt at independence, the city was a haven for conservatives loyal to Spain. It later became a hotbed of liberalism and a hub of yet another independence movement—spawned by its native son, the eloquent revolutionary José Martí—which led to the Second War of Independence (1892). In 1898, it was the last port of call for the *Maine,* a U.S. military vessel, whose explosion led to the Spanish-American War, the end of Spanish sovereignty, and the beginning of heavy U.S. involvement in island affairs. And though the Revolution of the 1950s—against dictator Fulgencio Batista—was fought elsewhere on the island, Fidel Castro's most victorious moment came when he arrived in Havana in January of 1959.

Castro's Soviet-style regime improved the quality of life for most Cubans, especially in the areas of education and medicine. But the 1990 collapse of the Soviet Union combined with the long-standing U.S. blockade have caused severe shortages of goods throughout the island. However, an increase in visitors from Canada and Europe (and increasingly, though not always legally, from America) and the state authorization of the U.S. dollar as legal tender have helped to improve matters slightly.

Havana is a work in progress, rough and real, caught in its own history and struggling toward an uncertain future. Although nearly 150 of its colonial buildings have been preserved, they need so much more than just another coat of paint. Across from the imposing Capitolio, apartment dwellers use pulleys to hoist water buckets up from the street because their buildings' pipes no longer function. Ornate entryways are festooned with spiderwebs of loose wires. Impeccably uniformed *pioneros* (schoolchildren) pour from the one-time luxury hotels that are now their families' homes. The determination and openheartedness of the Cuban people have given present-day Havana an undeniable poetic power. Add rum, baseball, tobacco, Caribbean rhythms, and American *carros* (cars) to the mix, and you have a city that truly enchants and inspires.

Pleasures and Pastimes

Architecture

Havana has many outstanding examples of Spanish colonial architecture, particularly those done in the exuberant, early baroque style known as *churrigueresque,* named for Spanish architect José Benito Churriguera. (His highly textured and dramatically sculpted facades, or copies of them, are found throughout the Americas.) Eusebio Leal, the Historiador de la Ciudad (City Historian) and the man in charge of restoration, has become one of Havana's most powerful figures. The UNESCO restoration project that is currently underway will, over the next decade, transform La Habana Vieja (Old Havana)—a World Heritage Site—into a virtual museum of colonial architecture. Until then, you may need to content yourself with the fascinating contrasts and ironies that history and circumstances have wrought in the city's structures. Dubbed "city of columns" by Nobel Prize–winning Cuban novelist Alejo Carpentier, Havana has many, often poor, neighborhoods filled with crumbling houses that peer from behind ornate Corinthian columns. In contrast, the mansions of the Miramar district are reminiscent of those in such posh American communities as Palm Beach or Newport.

Beaches

Habaneros (residents of Havana) catch their rays on the Playas del Este, a string of white-sand beaches 20 km (12 mi) east of Havana on the

Straits of Florida. The strands themselves are fine, shoaling off into brilliant aquamarine waters over coral reefs; the resorts, however, may disappoint. The western beaches of El Mégano and Santa María del Mar are the most popular, and the Hotel Tropicoco is the hub.

Music

In Havana's bars and clubs, dozens of sounds and rhythms pulsate around the clock: salsa, *guaguancó* (Afro-Cuban percussion), *son* (a style of music usually performed by a trio of singer, guitarist, and percussionist), *timba* (a hot, fast mambo), *la nueva trova* (guitar-accompanied ballads) are but a few of them. All Havana seems to turn out for these *bailables* (literally, "danceables"), and they come to *move*. In addition, Afro-Cuban music is often performed at the Union de Escritores y Artistas de Cuba and in the Callejón de Hamel. Don't miss a chance to hear the Sinfónica Nacional—a brilliant, young symphony orchestra directed by the equally brilliant and young Iván del Prado—perform in the Teatro Amadeo Roldán.

Dining

Shortages of foodstuffs combined with a lackadaisical approach to food preparation and service in state-owned restaurants often add up to mediocre meals (there are a few exceptions; the famous El Floridita bar-restaurant is one). Although you'll find some international dishes, home-style criollo cuisine is much more common. For a good meal, your best bets are the privately run *paladares* (literally "palates"; the name was cribbed from a popular Brazilian soap opera in which the heroine makes her fortune with a roadside restaurant named "El Paladar de Raquel"). In the *comedores obreros* (workers' dining rooms), you can have a criollo meal for less than a penny.

Pork and chicken dishes are common, but *res* (beef) is scarce and generally not of high quality. Lobster, shrimp, porgy, and sea bass are frequent seafood offerings, and bananas, plantains, potatoes, yams, and yucca (also known as cassava or manioc) are staples. Standard criollo dishes include *frijoles negros con arroz* (black beans with rice); *pollo asado en salsa criolla* (grilled chicken in a sauce of tomato, onion, and *ají*—a hot, red pepper); *pierna de puerco asado en su jugo* (roast leg of pork in its own gravy); *aporreado de res* or *ropa vieja* (shredded beef in salsa criollo); *yuca con mojo* (cassava in salsa criolla), *chicharrones de plátano* (finely sliced and salted plantain chips); and *plátanos a puñetazos* (literally, "punched plantains"; banana or plantain half cooked, taken out, placed under a cloth and hammered flat with a fist before being placed back in the pan to finish browning).

Wine is expensive and frequently of poor to average quality (the quality is often made worse by improper storage—acclimatized wine cellars are few and far between). Even so, a vintage Rioja shows up from time to time. Rum and beer are better options. *Mojitos* (light rum, sugar, mint, and soda) and *daiquiris* (blended light rum, lime, and ice) are the most famous rum drinks. Cuban beer includes the standard, light Cristal; the slightly more full-bodied Lagarto; the still darker Bucanero (which also comes in a light version); and the darkest brews of all, Hatuey and Mayabe.

Lodging

The most exciting and esthetically pleasing place to stay is La Habana Vieja. Several hotels and hostels presently offer lodging in this neighborhood, and more are opening up all the time. Many hotels are concentrated in the Vedado district, where the Hotel Nacional and the Hotel Habana Libre reign supreme. (The traditional, elegant Nacional is probably the city's best hotel, but it's an hour's walk or a 10-minute taxi ride from La Habana Vieja.)

You can save from $75 to $100 a night by staying in someone's home. The opportunity to directly help individual Cubans with U.S. dollars as well as the chance to live like a native make this an attractive alternative. Specific private accommodations are difficult to recommend (people go into and out of business rapidly as a result of ferocious taxation), but rest assured that arriving in Havana without a reservation and finding acceptable private lodging *in situ* is a sure thing.

EXPLORING HAVANA

Set in Havana Province and edged by the Straits of Florida to the north, the city of Havana is officially divided into 15 municipalities, which themselves often contain various neighborhoods. For the purposes of touring the city, it's best to divide it into six main areas. Moving from east to west (and, roughly, from old to new) you'll find La Habana Vieja, with its many historical charms; Centro, with the sight-laden Paseo de Martí (Prado), the Capitolio, and the 7-km (4-mi) seaside Malécon; Vedado, which is reminiscent of both Manhattan and Miami; and Miramar, with its grand manses. Across Havana Harbor are the fortresses— El Morro and La Cabaña—and the Cristo de la Habana statue as well as the municipality known as Regla and other sights in Eastern Havana.

To see La Habana Vieja and its many colonial palaces and baroque churches at their best, plan to tour on foot. Although you could spend days here, you can see the highlights of this municipality's southern half on one day, and visit its northern portion on another. It's best to make the fortresses across the bay a side trip from here, and save the sights farther east and/or the Playas del Este for another day. Centro Habana also has many historic sights. A tour of it can begin and end at El Malécon, which you should also set aside time to fully explore— perhaps as part of a tour of Vedado. This district sprawls all the way from Calzada de Infanta to the Río Almendares (Almendares River). It's difficult to fully explore on foot, although the area around the Hotel Nacional, the Habana Libre, and the Universidad de la Habana is filled with stately town houses and leafy side streets. Miramar, which stretches southwest across the Río Almendares, was the residential area for wealthy Habaneros and foreigners before the Revolution. A tour of its wide, tree-lined avenues is best made by car. A 20-minute drive farther southwest is the Marina Hemingway yacht harbor. (Note that pre- and postrevolutionary street names are often used in the older parts of the city; addresses contain both throughout this chapter).

Great Itineraries

IF YOU HAVE 3 DAYS

In **La Habana Vieja,** do a whirlwind tour of Plaza Vieja, Plaza de la Catedral, and Plaza de Armas, with a stop at La Bodeguita del Medio for a mojito. Take a taxi through the harbor tunnel to the **fortresses.** Have dinner at XII Apóstoles restaurant before heading to the Castillo de San Carlos de la Cabaña for the 9 PM cannon blast. On day two, explore **Centro Habana**; visit the Capitolio, the Fábrica de Tabacos Partagás, and the Parque Central before having a daiquirí at El Floridita. In the afternoon, stroll along the Paseo del Prado and/or the Malecón. On day three, visit the Universidad de la Habana and the Necrópolis Cristóbal Colón before touring **Vedado**'s impressive town houses and the mansions of Miramar. Dine at El Aljibe, and then head for the Tropicana cabaret.

IF YOU HAVE 5 DAYS

On the first day, explore the many sights in **La Habana Vieja**'s southern half, starting at the Casa Natal de José Martí and ending at the Plaza

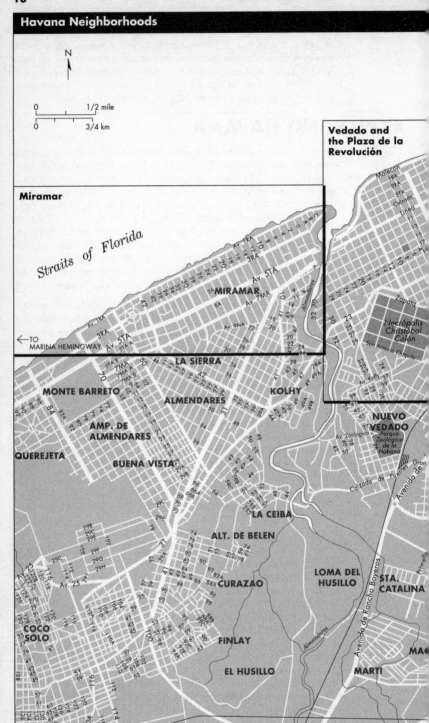

N

| 0 | | 1/2 mile |
| 0 | | 3/4 km |

Miramar

Vedado and the Plaza de la Revolución

Straits of Florida

←TO
MARINA HEMINGWAY

MIRAMAR

Av. 5TA

Av. 7NA

Av. 9NA

Malecón
1RA
3RA
5TA
Calzada
Línea

Zapata

Necrópolis
Christóbal
Colón

San Antonio Chiquito

LA SIERRA

MONTE BARRETO

ALMENDARES

KOLHY

Av. Kohly

AMP. DE ALMENDARES

NUEVO VEDADO

Parque
Zoológico
de la
Habana

Av. Zoológico

QUEREJETA

BUENA VISTA

Calzada de Puentes

Avenida de

LA CEIBA

ALT. DE BELEN

LOMA DEL HUSILLO

STA. CATALINA

Av. 25

Av. 25

CURAZAO

Almendares

Avenida de Rancho Boyeros

Primell

COCO SOLO

FINLAY

MA●

EL HUSILLO

MARTI

LOS ANGELES

Straits of Florida

La Habana Vieja, Centro Habana, and The Fortresses

VEDADO

Av. de los Presidentes (G)

ZMA Malecon

Linea

23

Calzada de Infanta

Caleta de San Lázaro

Malecon

LA HABANA VIEJA

CENTRO

Via Monumental
TO
PLAYAS DEL ESTE,
REGLA, GUANABACOA

Canal de Entrada

Av. del Puerto

Parque de los Mártires

Paseo de Martí (Prado)

Parque Cespedes

Parque Central

Zapata

Zanja

Zanja

Av. Salvador Allende (Carlos III)

Feria de la Juventud

Padre Varela (Belascoain)

Av. Simón Bolívar (Reina)

Dragones

Zapata

Avenida Carlos M. de Céspedes

Plaza de la Revolución

Avenida Rancho Boyeros

Aranguren

Calzada de Ayesterán

Av. Manglar

Gómez (Monte)

Egido

Destamparado

Bahía de la Habana

Independencia

Máximo

Calzada de Infanta

Ensenada de Atarés

CERRO

Calzada del Cerro

Via Blanca

Lagunas

PALATINO

Calz. de Palatino

General Lacret

STA. SUAREZ (Dolores)

Calzada del 10 de Octubre

LUYANO

Calzada de Luyanó

Via Blanca

Central

Via Blanca

Mayia Rodríguez

Av. Santa Catalina

Av. Porvenir

Calz. de San Miguel del Padrón

JUANELO

Calzada de Vento

Av. Acosta

VIBORA

Camaguey Andres (San Miguel)

JACOMINO

Calzada de Güines

General Lacret (Dolores)

LAWTON

Av. de Acosta

Av. Porvenir

MA. CRISTINA

SEVILLANO

Vieja. On day two, take in the Plaza de la Catedral and the Plaza de Armas before wandering along Calle de los Oficios, with its many art galleries. In the early evening, taxi through the harbor tunnel to the **fortresses.** Visit the Museo del Che and the Museo de la Cabaña in the Castillo de San Carlos de la Cabaña, have dinner at XII Apóstoles restaurant, and return to La Cabaña for the nine o'clock cannon blast.

On the third day, head for **Centro Habana** to see the Capitolio, the Fábrica de Tabacos Partagás, and the Parque Central. On day four, explore the campus of the Universidad de la Habana, and visit the Callejón de Hamel, UNEAC (for an Afro-Cuban performance), and the Necropolis de Colón. On the fifth day, stroll the Paseo del Prado or the Malecón in the morning, and then take a taxi tour of **Vedado**'s elegant town houses and the mansions of Miramar. Have dinner at El Aljibe, and then take in the floor show at the Tropicana.

IF YOU HAVE 7 DAYS

Follow the five-day itinerary. On the sixth day, check out the water-front crafts market before visiting the Plaza de la Revolución. From here, drive to **Eastern Havana,** stopping at the fishing village of Cojí-mar—for lunch at Las Terrazas—and visiting Hemingway's Finca Vigía. Continue to the **Playas del Este.** Stay overnight and spend the morning on the beach before returning to Havana on the seventh day.

When to Tour

December through May is high season, and temperatures are more mod-erate than at other times of the year. February is Cuba's coolest month, with temperatures in the 24°C to 26°C (75°F to 79°F) range. Don't rule out a visit during May through October; although this is rainy sea-son, there are fewer tourists and generally lower rates.

La Habana Vieja

La Habana Vieja is a thick concentration of colonial architecture and humanity—a wedge of restoration work and contemporary squalor. In the 17th–19th centuries, Havana was such an important city that it was dubbed "The Key to the New World." The tremendous wealth of this era is reflected in the plazas and mansions sprinkled through-out the old city. They also bear witness to the social inequities that led to the Revolution, which, in turn, resulted in the unusual conditions that make the place so moving today.

More than half this municipality is surrounded by the Bahía de la Ha-bana (Havana Bay). It has a dozen north-south streets that are inter-sected by about 20 east-west arteries, forming more than 100 surprisingly symmetrical blocks. Innumerable mansions and palaces, nearly two dozen cultural centers and museums, six churches, and five convents are crowded into this 1½-sq-mi municipality. Calle Brasil (Teniente Rey) roughly divides La Habana Vieja into a southern sector, built (for the most part) in the 17th and 18th centuries, and a northern area, developed in the 18th and 19th centuries.

La Habana Vieja Sur

The southern portion of La Habana Vieja is more heart-rending and less monumental than its northern section; it's also explored by fewer visi-tors, making it the ideal place to see how Habaneros truly live. This walk begins at the railroad station and passes some of Havana's oldest (17th-century) structures, some of them brilliantly restored, some of them under repair, and some of them still in desperate need of attention.

Numbers in the text correspond to numbers in the margin and on the Habana Vieja and Centro Habana map.

A GOOD WALK

Directly across from the Estación Centrál (Central Railway Station) is the **Casa Natal de José Martí** ①, the birthplace of Cuba's poet-patriot and of this tour. Follow Calle Leonor Pérez (Paula) east toward the bay and the **Iglesia y Convento de la Merced** ②, just up from the corner of Calle de Cuba. The **Antigua Iglesia de San Francisco de Paula** ③ stands almost catercorner to La Merced, at the end of Calle de Cuba. From this church, follow Calle Desamparado (San Pedro/Av. Carlos Manuel de Céspedes/Av. del Puerto) along the harbor, and turn left onto Calle Acosta. Follow it to Calle de Cuba to reach the **Iglesia del Espíritu Santo** ④, Havana's oldest church. From here walk north on Calle de Cuba; on your left, in the block between Calle Luz and Calle Sol, you'll see the lovely **Convento de Santa Clara** ⑤. Return to Calle Luz, turn right and walk to the **Antigua Iglesia y Convento de Nuestra Señora de Belén** ⑥, which is between Calle Picota and Calle Compostela.

From Nuestra Señora de Belén, take Compostela north for four blocks to the intersection with Calle Brasil (Teniente Rey) and the art nouveau **Droguería Sarrá** ⑦. Follow Calle Brasil east to the intersection with Calle de Cuba. Notice the ornate facades and balconies here. Have a look inside the comedor obrero. For less than a penny, people wash great portions of *yuca con mojo* (manioc in garlic sauce) down with water or raw rum. Continue along Brasil to Calle San Ignacio and the **Plaza Vieja** ⑧, one of the city's great squares. After exploring this plaza, backtrack along Calle Brasil, take a right onto Calle de Cuba, and follow it to the **Museo Histórico de las Ciencias Carlos J. Finlay** ⑨. After learning a little more about the life and work of a great scientist, follow Calle Amagura west for five blocks to the **Iglesia Santo Cristo del Buen Viaje** ⑩.

TIMING

You can march through this walk in about three hours, though you need a full day to truly do it justice. (Wear cool clothing and very comfortable shoes.) If you're short on time, the Casa Natal de José Martí, the Plaza Vieja, and the Iglesia Santo Cristo del Buen Viaje are the must-see sights.

SIGHTS TO SEE

❻ **Antigua Iglesia y Convento de Nuestra Señora de Belén.** Havana's first baroque church (1712–18) was originally conceived as a convalescent hospital. The founding Belenistas (members of the Order of Bethlehem) were replaced in 1842 by the Jesuits, who established a school here in 1856. The niche over the main door contains a nativity scene under a fluted conch shell; it's beautifully illuminated from behind by an amber reflector, which throws extra light on the heads of the saints. (The lighting here is the work of electrical engineer Félix de Noval, who has illuminated many of Havana's monuments.) The convent's Arco de Belén, at the corner of Acosta and Compostela, has long been identified with the neighborhood's Jewish community (after their 1492 expulsion from Spain, the Sephardic diaspora spread throughout the Mediterranean and the New World). ⊠ *Calle Compostela y Calle Luz,* ☎ *7/63–7814.* ☑ *$2.* ☉ *Mon.–Sat. 9–5, Sun. 9–1.*

❸ **Antigua Iglesia de San Francisco de Paula.** What's left of the once lovely old San Francisco de Paula church stands in a plaza at the edge of the harbor. Built between 1730 and 1745 as part of what was then a hospital for women, its facade is described as "pre-churrigueresque," meaning that it was done prior to the popular exuberant baroque style for which Spanish architect José Benito Churriguera is known. The church, which is undergoing restoration, fell into disrepair in the 20th century when the adjoining hospital was moved far from the uproar-

22

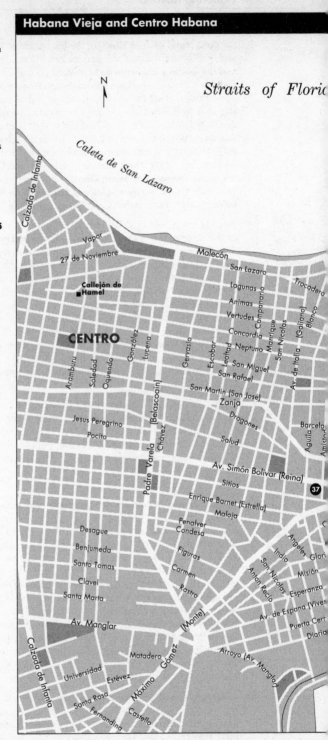

Habana Vieja and Centro Habana

N

Straits of Florida

Caleta de San Lázaro

Calzada de Infanta

Vapor

27 de Noviembre

Malecón

San Lazaro

Callejón de Hamel

Lagunas

Trocadero

Animas

Vertudes

Concordia

Neptuno

Campanario

Manrique

San Nicolas

Blanco

(Galiano)

Av. de Italia

CENTRO

González

Lucena

Gervasio

Escobar

Lealtad

San Miguel

San Rafael

Aramburu

Soledad

Oquendo

San Martin (San José)

Zanja

Dragones

Barcelo

Aguila

Jesus Peregrino

Pocito

[Belascoain]

Chávez

Salud

Amistad

Av. Simón Bolívar (Reina)

Sitios

Padre Varela

Enrique Barnet (Estrella)

Maloja

37

Penalver

Condesa

Desague

Benjumeda

Santo Tomas

Clavel

Santa Marta

Figuras

Carmen

Rastro

Angeles

Indio

San Nicolas

Anton Recio

Gloria

Misión

Esperanza

Av. Manglar

[Monte]

Av. de España (Vives)

Puerta Cerr

Diaria

Calzada de Infanta

Matadero

Gómez

Arroyo (Av. Manglar)

Universidad

Estévez

Máximo

Santa Rosa

Fernandina

Castello

ious port. ⊠ *Plazuela de Paula, esquina de Calle San Ignacio,* ☎ *no phone.* 🎟 *Free.*

★ ❶ **Casa Natal de José Martí.** On January 28, 1853, Cuba's *padre de la patria* (father of the nation), José Martí, was born of Spanish parents in this humble house. As a child he prophetically announced "Five generations of slaves must be followed by a generation of màrtyrs." At age 16 he wrote a newspaper piece judged treasonous by the Spanish governors, and he was exiled to Spain, where he later studied law. Martí then spent 14 years in the United States, working as a newspaper reporter. Three volumes of poetry and several books of essays established him as the most brilliant Latin American writer and political analyst of his day.

Martí's words stirred both moral and financial support for Cuban independence. In mid-April 1895, as part of a revolutionary plan that was months in the making, Martí joined General Máximo Gómez on Santo Domingo (Dominican Republic). The two set out for eastern Cuba, where General Antonio Maceo awaited them. A month later, Martí became one of the Second War of Independence's first casualties when he charged, allegedly on a white steed, into Spanish lines during a battle at Dos Ríos. His lyrics in "Guantanamera," are premonitory: *"Que no me entierran en lo oscuro / a morir como un traidor / yo soy bueno y como bueno / moriré de cara al sol."* ("May they not bury me in darkness / to die like a traitor / I am good, and as a good man / I will die facing the sun.")

The moving memorabilia in this museum conveys the esteem in which this poet-patriot is held by the Cuban people. You'll find locks of his hair as a four-year-old; his letters, books, and poetry; his spurs and ammunition belt; and a rare 1893 photograph of him with Gómez in New York. ⊠ *Calle Leonor Perez (Paula) 314,* ☎ *7/61–3778.* 🎟 *$3.* ☉ *Mon.– Sat. 9–5, Sun. 9–1.*

❺ **Convento de Santa Clara.** It is hard to miss Havana's oldest convent (c. 1638–44) as it is painted a bright, rich yellow and occupies an entire block. It now houses the Centro Nacional de Conservación, Restauración, y Museología (National Center for Conservation, Restoration, and Museum Science) as well as the Residencia Académica (Academic Residence), where small groups and some individuals can stay (☞ Lodging, *below*). It once housed hundreds of nuns and was a refuge for young women with problems that ranged from the routine broken heart to unwanted pregnancies and dowries insufficient for marriage. The *mudéjar* wood-beamed ceilings and the lush courtyard are extraordinary, as is the Salón Plenario, the marble-floored hall used for seminars. The convent regularly hosts art exhibits and concerts and has a small bar and restaurant. ⊠ *Calle de Cuba 610,* ☎ *7/66–9327.* 🎟 *$2.* ☉ *Weekdays 9–5.*

❼ **Droguería Sarrà.** This art nouveau pharmacy is short on drugs but long on design. Founded by a Catalan apothecary in 1874, it was built in the elaborate modernist style curiously favored by pharmacies. The carved wooden racks and shelves backed by murals painted on glass are especially ornate, and the ceramic apothecary jars, though probably empty, are colorfully painted. Also known as La Reunión (note the inscription on the wall behind the counter), this pharmacy was a famous meeting place, a sort of informal neighborhood clubhouse. ⊠ *Calle Brasil (Teniente Rey) 251, esquina de Calle Compostela,* ☎ *7/ 61–0069.* 🎟 *Free.* ☉ *Weekdays 9–5.*

❷ **Iglesia y Convento de la Merced.** Although it was begun in 1755, this church and convent complex wasn't completed until the 19th century.

Hence you can clearly see a progression of architectural styles, particularly in the facade, with its six starchy-white pillars and its combination of late-baroque and early neoclassical elements. Inside are numerous works by 19th-century Cuban painters. ⊠ *Calle de Cuba 806, esquina de Calle de la Merced,* ☎ *7/63–8873.* 🎟 *Free.* ⊙ *Mon.–Sat. 9–5, Sun. 9–1.*

❹ Iglesia del Espíritu Santo. Havana's oldest church (c. 1638) was built by Afro-Cubans who were brought to the island as slaves but who later bought their freedom, a common phenomenon in Cuba. Fittingly, today it's the only church in the city authorized to grant political asylum. Its interior has several notable paintings; notice especially the representation of a seated, post-Crucifixion Christ on the right wall. The crypt under the left of the altar contains catacombs, which you can visit with the custodian-guide, who speaks a little English (a $1 tip is appreciated). The three-story belfry to the left of the church is one of La Habana Vieja's tallest towers. ⊠ *Calle Acosta 161, at Calle de Cuba,* ☎ *7/62–3410.* 🎟 *Free.* ⊙ *Mon.–Sat. 9–5, Sun. 9–1.*

★ ❿ Iglesia Santo Cristo del Buen Viaje. Although it was originally founded in 1640 as the Ermita de Nuestra Señora del Buen Viaje, the present church was built in 1755. The advocation to the *buen viaje* (good voyage) was a result of its popularity among seafarers much in need of a special patron and a place to pray for protection. The baroque facade is notable for the simplicity of its twin hexagonal towers and the deep flaring arch in its entryway. The interior has a wood-beamed ceiling redolent of a schooner's hold. Traditionally the final stop on the Vía Crucis (Way of the Cross) held during Lent, the church and its plaza have an undeniably informal and transient quality, possibly because some of the surrounding buildings seem to crumble as you watch. This is the plaza where Graham Greene's character, Wormold (the vacuum-cleaner salesman/secret agent), is "swallowed up among the pimps and lottery sellers of the Havana noon" in *Our Man in Havana.* Don't miss the view from the corner of Amargura: you can see straight down Villegas to the dome of the old Palacio Presidencial (Presidential Palace). ⊠ *Plaza del Cristo,* ☎ *7/63–1767.* 🎟 *Free.* ⊙ *During Masses.*

| NEED A BREAK? | From the Iglesia Santo Cristo del Buen Viaje, it's a short walk southwest to the **Hanoi** restaurant, a great place for an eclectic criollo-Vietnamese meal (☞ Dining, *below*). |

❾ Museo Histórico de las Ciencias Carlos J. Finlay. This science museum is named in honor of Carlos Juan Finlay (1833–1915), the Cuban physician of Scottish and French descent whose life work on yellow fever conclusively proved, in 1882, that the mosquito of the genus *stegomyia* was the carrier of the disease. Trained at Jefferson Medical College in Philadelphia, Pennsylvania, Dr. Finlay spent his entire professional life in Havana and was Cuba's chief health officer from 1902 to 1909. The museum contains scientific and medical paraphernalia and Finlay memorabilia. ⊠ *Calle de Cuba 460,* ☎ *7/63–4823.* 🎟 *$2.* ⊙ *Weekdays 8:30–5, Sat. 9–3.*

★ ❽ Plaza Vieja. The Old Square was originally known as the Plaza del Mercado (Market Square) and was once the city's commercial hub. As with Madrid's Plaza Mayor, it was also the site of executions, processions, bullfights, and fiestas—all witnessed by the city's wealthiest citizens, who looked on from their balconies. The square had a stone fountain surrounded by four dolphins, until the 1930s, when President Gerardo Machado (1871–1939) built an underground parking lot here. Today, its surrounding structures vary wildly in condition, but several of them are noteworthy.

The impressive mansion in the square's southwestern corner is the **Casa de los Condes de Jaruco** (1733–37), the seat of the Fondo Cubano de Bienes Culturales (BFC; Cuba's version of the National Endowment for the Arts). Its lush main patio is surrounded by massive, yet delicate, pillars. Notice also the ceramic tiles along the main stairway and the second-floor stained-glass windows. You can linger in the tea room, the boutique, or at one of the art exhibitions frequently held here. To your left as you exit is the interesting 1762 Elias Durnford painting titled *A View of the Market Place in the City of the Havana* [sic].

On the square's southeastern corner, the **Palacio Viena Hotel** (also known as the Palacio Hotel Cueto) is a 1906, art-nouveau gem that was occupied by several dozen families after the Revolution. The intense floral relief sculpture and stained-glass windows are still intact, if a little sooty, on all five stories. The laundry hanging from these once-formal balconies makes for a tableau worthy of pause. Someday, with or without the clotheslines, this building will be an eye-popper.

On the square's western edge is the 1752 **Casa de Juan Rico de Mata** (Calle Mercaderes 307), now housing the Fototeca de Cuba (☞ Shopping, *below*). The building with the towers on the corner beyond it will soon be a magnificent hotel.The **Casa de las Hermanas Cárdenas** (Calle San Ignacio 307), on the square's eastern side, was once the seat of Havana's first Philharmonic society. Today it's home to the Centro de Desarrollo de Artes Visuales (Center for the Development of Visual Arts), which hosts temporary exhibits. In the 18th-century **Casa del Conde San Estéban de Cañongo** (Calle San Ignacio 356) you'll find the Artesanías para Turismo workshop, where you can watch artisans assemble crafts that are for sale. While wandering along San Ignacio, notice the faded VAPORES CUBA–ESPAÑA (STEAMBOATS CUBA–SPAIN) sign on the wall at the entryway of **No. 358**. The 18th-century **Casa del Conde de Lombillo** (Calle San Ignacio 364; not to be confused with the Conde de Lombillo house in the Plaza de la Catedral) has semi-restored murals. It also contains a shop where artisans make and sell folkloric items. (☞ Shopping, *below*).

La Habana Vieja Norte

This walk through the most popular and best restored of La Habana Vieja's sights stays close to the Bahía de la Habana and the harbor. For the most part, it also stays above Calle Brasil (Teniente Rey), which divides La Habana Vieja into its northern and southern sectors.

Numbers in the text correspond to numbers in the margin and on the Habana Vieja and Centro Habana map.

A GOOD WALK

Begin at the lovely **Iglesia y Convento Menor de San Francisco de Asis** ⑪, across from the Sierra Maestra boat terminal. From here, walk north along Calle de los Oficios to the **Plaza de Armas** ⑫. After browsing through some bookstalls, you can visit several important structures that ring the plaza, including the **Palacio de los Capitanes Generales** ⑬, **El Templete** ⑭, and the **Castillo de la Real Fuerza** ⑮. From the Plaza de Armas follow Calle Obispo one block west to the **Hotel Ambos Mundos** ⑯, where Ernest Hemingway once lived. Cross Calle O'Reilly and proceed to the **Plaza de la Catedral** ⑰, where you'll find not only the **Catedral de la Habana** ⑱ but also several other noteworthy buildings. If you feel like shopping, head for the Mercado de Arte y de Artesanía (☞ Shopping, *below*), a crafts market near the cathedral on Calle Empedrado.

From the Plaza de la Catedral, take Calle San Ignacio to the **Centro Wilfredo Lam** ⑲, an arts center in the Casa del Obispo Peñalver. From here head west on Calle Empedrado and turn left onto Calle de Cuba.

Four blocks north, in the Plazuela de la Maestranza, is the Palacio de la Artesanía (☞ Shopping, *below*), formerly called the Palacio Pedrosa (c. 1780), whose graceful patio has two excellent bars, a state-run cigar store, and a shop with a vast selection of Cuban music. From here follow Calle Tacón to the **Museo de la Música** ⑳, in the elaborate, early 20th-century Casa Pérez de la Riva.

TIMING

This walk will take several hours (or days, if you have them), particularly if you linger in the museums and galleries along the way. If your feet tire, taxis are readily available along the northern (harbor) edge of the old city, a block above the Plaza de la Catedral.

SIGHTS TO SEE

♨ ⑮ **Castillo de la Real Fuerza.** Constructed in 1558 by order of Spanish King Felipe II three years after an earlier fortress was destroyed by the French pirate Jacques de Sores, this classic, moat-enclosed fortress was the residence of the local military commanders until 1762. The tower, added in 1632, is topped by the famous Giraldilla (Weathervane), a nod to the one atop the Giralda minaret in Seville, the city whose Casa de Contratación (House of Trade) oversaw financial and shipping operations between Spain and its territories in the Americas. Havana's favorite symbol—it's even on the Havana Club rum label—the Giraldilla honors Doña Inés de Bobadilla, Cuba's lone woman governor, who replaced her husband, Hernando de Soto, when he left to conquer Florida (and search for the Fountain of Youth) in 1539. De Soto and his expedition went on to explore much of North America and were among the first white men to cross the Mississippi River. He died in 1542, but Doña Inés spent years scanning the horizon, awaiting his return. The current Giraldilla is a copy of an earlier bronze one toppled by a hurricane and now on display in the Museo de la Ciudad de La Habana (☞ Palacio de los Capitanes Generales, *below*). In addition to absorbing the fort's historical ambience, you can visit its museum devoted to ceramics, shop in its gift store, or have a drink in its El Globo bar. ⊠ *Plaza de Armas, e/Calle O'Reilly y Av. Carlos Manuel de Céspedes (Puerto),* ☎ *7/61–6130.* ☞ *$2.* ☉ *Weekdays 9–5.*

★ ⑱ **Catedral de la Habana.** Cuba's Nobel Prize–winning novelist, Alejo Carpentier, may have borrowed from St. Augustine when he described the city's cathedral as "music made into stone", but the words—like the bells in the structure they describe—ring true and clear. Work on the church was begun by the Jesuits in 1748, who weren't around to see it finished in 1777 (King Carlos III of Spain expelled them from Cuba in 1767). The facade is simultaneously intimate and imposing, and one of the two towers is visibly larger, lending an asymmetry that seems totally natural. The two bells in the taller, thicker tower are said to have been cast with gold and silver mixed into the bronze, thus giving them their sweet tone. In *Our Man in Havana,* Graham Greene describes the statue of Columbus that once stood in the square as looking "as though it had been formed through the centuries under water, like a coral reef, by the action of insects." This is, in fact, exactly the case: coral, cut and hauled from the edge of the sea by slaves, was used to build many of Havana's churches. Look carefully and you'll see the shapes of marine flora and fauna fossilized into the cathedral. ⊠ *Plaza de la Catedral,* ☎ *7/61–5213.* ☉ *Weekdays 9–11 and 2:30–6; Mass Tues. and Thurs. at 8 AM, Sun. at 10:30 AM.*

⑲ **Centro Wilfredo Lam.** Dedicated to and named for a great Cuban surrealist painter, this gallery and museum is just behind the Catedral de la Habana in the elegant, 18th-century Casa del Obispo Peñalver. Along with a permanent exhibit of Lam's lithographs and etchings, the center hosts temporary shows with works by contemporary Cuban and South American artists. Lam, born in 1902, studied in Spain and fought with the Republic against Franco's military uprising. He later fled to France, where he was influenced by the painters Pablo Picasso and Georges Braque and the poet André Breton, among others. He returned to Cuba to support the Revolution, and later returned to Paris, where he died in 1982. ⊠ *Calle San Ignacio 22, esquina de Calle Empedrado,* ☎ *7/61–2096.* ⊑ *$3.* ⊙ *Mon.–Sat. 10–5.*

⓰ Hotel Ambos Mundos. Ernest Hemingway stayed here in 1928 on his first trip to Havana (allegedly made only because of an unscheduled boat layover). It went on to become his haunt and residence, before Martha Gellhorn made him buy Finca Vigía and move to the suburbs. Room 511 is kept as it was in 1938, when Hemingway lived here while writing *For Whom the Bell Tolls*. Esperanza García (ask for her at the reception desk), an excellent guide, knows nearly everything about Hemingway and gives a fascinating tour ($3) of his room. In one of the magazine articles collected here, you can read Hemingway's description of the sun rising over eastern Havana and shining through the window, "to wake you up fresh, no matter where you've been the night before." ⊠ *Calle Obispo 153,* ☎ *7/66–9530.*

NEED A BREAK? From the Hotel Ambos Mundos, follow Obispo to the corner of Calle San Ignacio and the **Café Paris,** which is open around the clock and often has live music performances (☞ Nightlife and the Arts, *below*).

★ ⓫ Iglesia y Convento Menor de San Francisco de Asís. The Latin inscription over the main door of this church and convent dedicated to St. Francis reads: NON EST IN TOTO SANCTIOR ORBE LOCUS (THERE IS NO HOLIER PLACE ON EARTH). As it is now a museum and concert hall, it may no longer be earth's holiest place, but it certainly is one of the loveliest. Built in the 16th century, in 1730 it was restored in a baroque style, resulting in a richly adorned facade with fluted conchlike tympanums over the doors and windows. Just inside the door you'll see tombs beneath a glass floor panel. (Churches were used as cemeteries until Bishop Espada founded what is now the Necrópolis Cristóbal Colón in 1868, a detail all Cubans seem to know and cherish). Note also the 19th-century grandfather clock made by Tiffany. The rooms to the right of the nave house archaeological finds and art exhibits.

Precisely 117 steps lead to the top of the 141-m (463-ft) tower, the tallest in Havana. Your climb (and your well-spent payment of an extra dollar) are rewarded by an excellent view of La Habana Vieja and the harbor. You can also get a close-up look at the fossilized imprints in the *arrecife* (reef coral) stone used to build this and many other Havana churches. On your way down, notice the vaulted archway over the last set of stairs. Concerts are usually held in the main nave at 6 PM on Saturday and 11 AM on Sunday (check the schedule at the entrance). In the summer of 1999, the Philadelphia Boys Choir—directed by Dr. Robert Hamilton—performed here, filling the church with admirers. One of them, Grupo Moncada leader Jorge Gomez, later confessed that "the tears just kept coming. I couldn't stop!" ⊠ *Plaza de San Francisco,* ☎ *7/61–3312.* ⊑ *$3 (not including bell-tower fee).* ⊙ *Weekdays 9–12:30 and 5–8.*

⓴ Museo de la Música. This museum is housed in the early 19th-century Casa de Pérez de la Riva, a white, ornately decorated structure overlooking the harbor. You can browse through its collection of Cuban musical instruments, especially drums, as well as the sheet music and recordings for sale in its store. ⊠ *Calle Capdevila (Cárcel) 1.* ☎ *7/61–9846.* ⊑ *$2.* ⊙ *Tues.–Sat. 9–5, Sun. 8–noon.*

⑬ Palacio de los Capitanes Generales. On the western end of the ☞ **Plaza de Armas** is the former residence of the men who governed Cuba. A succession of some five dozen Spanish captain-generals (also called governors) lived here until 1898, and the U.S. governor called it home prior to the Revolution. The wooden "paving" on the plaza in front of it was installed on the orders of a 17th-century captain-general, who wanted to muffle the clatter of horses and carriages so he could enjoy his naps undisturbed. Today, the palace contains the **Museo de la Ciudad de la Habana,** with such unique treasures as a throne room built for the King of Spain (but never used); the original Giraldilla, which once topped the tower of the Castillo de la Real Fuerza (☞ *above*); and a cannon made of leather. Groups of pioneros often gather in the gallery here for art history classes, and you can buy art books in the on-site shop. Concerts are often held in the bougainvillea-draped, palm-shaded patio. Inside it and to the right is a plaque dated 1557; it commemorates the death of Doña Maria de Cepeda y Nieto, who was felled by a stray shot while praying in what was then Parroquia Mayor, Havana's main parish church. The tomb in the pit to the left holds the remains of several graves discovered in the church cemetery. ✉ *Plaza de Armas, Calle Tacón e/Obispo y O'Reilly,* ☎ *7/61–5779.* 🎫 *$3.* ⊙ *Tues.–Sat. 9:30–6:30, Sun. 9–1.*

★ **⑫ Plaza de Armas.** So called for its use as a drill field by colonial troops, this plaza was the city's administrative center and command post almost from the beginning. The statue in the center is of Manuel de Céspedes, hero of the Ten Years War, Cuba's first struggle for independence from Spain. Today, this is the city's most literary square; an army of erudite secondhand booksellers encircles it during the day.

As home to the UNESCO Cultural Library and the Instituto Cubano del Libro (Cuban Book Institute), the **Palacio del Segundo Cabo** (☎ 7/62–8091), on the square's northwestern corner, is a haven for literati of every spot and stripe. They come for lectures and readings, to buy books in the on-site shops, and to see films and art exhibitions. Nearby is the ☞ **Palacio de los Capitanes Generales** across from which are ☞ **El Templete** and the ☞ **Castillo de la Real Fuerza.** Note that there are often concerts in the plaza on Sunday evenings—events not to be missed.

★ **⑰ Plaza de la Catedral.** The square that surrounds and is named for the ☞ **Catedral de la Habana** is one of La Habana Vieja's most beautiful spots. In addition to the cathedral, you'll find several elegant mansions that once housed the city's aristocrats.

The **Casa de los Marqueses de Aguas Claras** (1751–75), in the square's northwestern corner, was built by Antonio Ponce de León, the first Marquis of Aguas Claras and the descendent of the discoverer of Florida, Juan de Ponce de León. Today, the building contains El Patio (☞ Dining, *below*), a restaurant whose tables fill a verdant interior courtyard as well as the upper floors. On the square's western edge is the 19th-century **Casa de Baños** (Bath House), which was built on the spot where an *aljibe* (cistern) was constructed in 1587. It served as the main municipal water supply as well as a public bathing house. The narrow cul-de-sac next to the Casa de Baños is the Callejón del Chorro (Alley of the Water Fountain), named for an aqueduct that ended here in Havana's early days.

Directly across the square from the cathedral is the **Museo de Arte Colonial** (✉ Calle San Ignacio 61, ☎ 7/62–6440), with its rich collection of colonial items ranging from violins to chamber pots. It's in the Casa de Luis Chacón—also known as Casa del Conde de Bayona after the son-in-law of the original owner—which dates from the 17th century and which saw its first restoration in 1720. A small theater here, La Salita, often has plays and monologues. The museum is open Tuesday–Saturday 10–6 and Sunday 9–1; admission is $3. Wander along the square's eastern edge for a look at the early 18th-century **Casa de Lombillo,** the site of Cuba's first post office. A letter drop in the shape of a Greek tragedy mask grimaces from the wall to the right of the main door. Its inscriptions reads: CORRESPONDENCIA INTERIOR Y PENINSULAR. In the old days, it seems, you could plop both local and international ("peninsular" mail was being sent to the Iberian Peninsula or Spain) letters in one slot. The building is now home to an education museum, with displays honoring a 1961 campaign in which students and teachers took to the hills to spread literacy.

NEED A BREAK?	You can refresh yourself at **El Patio,** a restaurant right in the Plaza de la Catedral, or head just out of the plaza to **La Bodeguita del Medio,** where you can sip a mojito and take in the Hemingway vibe (☞ Dining, *below*).

🕚 **El Templete.** This neoclassical, faux-Doric temple was built in 1828 on the site where the city's first Mass and its first *cabildo* (city council) meeting were held. The cabildo took place under a massive *ceiba* (kapok) tree, which was felled by a 19th-century hurricane. The present tree—planted in the little patio in front of El Templete in 1959, the year of the Revolution—is honored each November 19, the day celebrating Havana's founding. It's said that if you walk three times around the tree and toss a coin toward it, you'll be granted a wish—provided, of course, that you keep your wish secret. El Templete is also the site of a triptych by French painter Jean-Baptiste Vermay portraying the first Mass, the first cabildo, and the municipal personalities who participated in the building's opening ceremonies. It's also home to the ashes of the painter and his wife, who—along with 8,000 other Habaneros—were victims of the 1833 cholera epidemic. ⊠ *Plaza de Armas,* ☎ *7/62–1021.* ☉ *Weekdays 9–11 and 2:30–6.*

The Fortresses and Monuments

Havana's great *fortalezas* (fortresses; also referred to as *castillos,* or castles) are reminders of Spain's mighty presence. Monuments testifying to Cuba's struggles for independence surround these forts, and museums have long replaced barracks within their massive, time-worn walls. Sunsets and the *cañonazo de las nueve* (9 PM cannon blast) at the Castillo de San Carlos de la Cabaña are timeless events beloved by Cubans. You can join them and then enjoy a meal at the nearby XII Apóstoles or La Divina Pastora restaurants. Locals also like to picnic and party in the park around El Cristo de la Habana.

Numbers in the text correspond to numbers in the margin and on the Habana Vieja and Centro Habana map.

A Good Tour

Begin at the remnants of the **Cárcel de la Habana** ㉑, just off the Paseo de Martí (Prado) and across from the **Monumento Máximo Gómez** ㉒, honoring the great military hero of Cuba's wars of independence. North along the paseo is another monument, the **Estudiantes de Medicina** ㉓, commemorating the execution of a group of medical students by the Spanish in 1871 (one of many events leading to the Ten Years War). Just across Avenida Carlos Manuel de Céspedes (del Puerto), at the beginning of the Malecón, is the 16th-century **Castillo de San Salvador de la Punta** ㉔, a stalwart reminder of Spain's control of the island. From here, take a taxi through the tunnel to the other side of the bay and the mighty **Castillo de los Tres Reyes del Morro** ㉕, or El Morro. From here head east to the **Castillo de San Carlos de la Cabaña** ㉖. A ways beyond this fort is **El Cristo de la Habana** ㉗, a giant statue of Christ overlooking the harbor.

TIMING

Touring the monuments and fortresses on both sides of the harbor can easily fill an afternoon. Although ferries regularly cross the bay to the eastern Havana municipalities of Regla and Casa Blanca, the lines for them are long. If you haven't rented a car, your best bet is to hire a taxi for the duration of the tour. Just be sure to agree upon a price before setting off.

Sights to See

㉑ **Cárcel de la Habana.** A fragment of this 19th-century jail has been preserved as the Cárcel José Martí, commemorating the national hero's 1869–70 incarceration here as an adolescent advocate and activist for independence. It contains four cells and a chapel presently used for concerts and art exhibits. ⊠ *Av. de los Estudiantes, e/Paseo de Martí (Prado) y Agramonte (Zulueta),* ☎ *no phone.* ☞ *$2.* ☉ *Tues.–Sat. 10–6, Sun. 9–1.*

★ ☙ ㉖ **Castillo de San Carlos de la Cabaña (La Cabaña).** In 1762 Lord Albemarle took El Morro for the English after a 44-day siege. A year later, Carlos III recovered Cuba in exchange for Florida and promptly ordered the construction of what was then the largest fort in the Americas. Sprawling across the hill east of El Morro, the fortress was named for the Spanish king and for the typical Cuban cabanas or *bohíos* (cabins) that once occupied the site. With the capacity to house 1,000 troops, this immense bastion was said to be so big that Carlos was given a telescope with which to admire it from Madrid.

The infamous Foso de los Laureles (Graveyard of the Laurels) was the execution wall described by one Cuban historian as the place where "hundreds and hundreds of defenders of justice and of national sovereignty were deprived of life" during the wars of independence. The 9 PM *ceremonia del cañonazo* (ceremony of the cannon shot) is a must-see event filled with nostalgia and mystery. First, a lamplighter lights the gas lanterns. Then, a crier (a recruit with a voice so good he's been signed on permanently even though his military service ended two years ago) begins an eery plainsong chant that reverberates throughout the fortress and, when the wind is right, across the bay to La Punta: *"Silencio; ha llegado la noche / Las luces están encendidas / Nuestro cañon se llama Capitolino / A las nueve sonará"* ("Silence; night has fallen / The lanterns are lit / Our cannon is named Capitolino / At nine it will sound"). Finally, a detail of some half-dozen soldiers dressed in scarlet, 18th-century uniforms marches in and loads and fires the cannon, which makes a deafening noise (cover your ears).

La Cabaña's two museums are both excellent. The **Museo de la Cabaña** documents Cuba's military history, and the **Museo del Che** is dedicated to the life of Ernesto "Che" Guevara, who ranks equally with José Martí for the honor of national martyr. ⊠ *Carretera de la Cabaña,* ☎ *7/62–4092.* ☞ *$3.* ☉ *Daily 10–10.*

☙ ㉔ **Castillo de San Salvador de la Punta (La Punta).** On a point (hence, the name) directly across from El Morro, La Punta took 11 years to build (1589–1600), under the supervision of the same Italian military engineer—Juan Bautista Antonelli—responsible for its sister fortress. The two forts are so close, it's said that voice communication is possible in calm weather. In the early 17th century a heavy chain was stretched between them, sealing the port at night and during attacks. Today the fortress has an even more romantic role in the city's unfolding drama: it's a favorite spot for lovers. ⊠ *Paseo de Martí (Prado) y Av. Carlos Manuel de Céspedes (del Puerto),* ☎ *no phone.* 🎟 *Free.* ☉ *Daily 10–10.*

★ ℭ ㉕ **Castillo de los Tres Reyes del Morro (El Morro).** Begun in 1589, Havana's landmark fort is named for the Reyes Magos—the Magi or Three Kings of Bethlehem, who are the patrons of its chapel—and for the fact that it occupies a *morro* (promontory) at the harbor entrance. It and its sister fort across the way, La Punta, made Havana the safest port in the Americas at a time when both pirates and imperialists helped themselves to whatever could be had. Built into cliffs, El Morro was endowed with a battery of 12 cannons christened La Batería de los Doce Apóstoles (The Battery of the Twelve Apostles) facing the sea and another dozen, called Las Pastoras (The Shepherdesses) nearer the ramparts. The active lighthouse flashes its beam over Havana every 15 seconds. Inside the castle, across a moat and drawbridge, are stables, the chapel, dungeons, and a wine cellar. You'll also find the fortified vaults, which contain the **Museo del Morro,** with displays on the fortress itself; the **Museo de la Navegación,** with navigation and seafaring artifacts; and the **Museo de Piratas,** with exhibits and bits of folklore on pirates. The armory displays weapons from around the world. ⊠ *Carretera de la Cabaña,* ☎ *7/62–0617.* 🎟 *$3.* ☉ *Tues.–Sat. 10–6, Sun. 9–1.*

ℭ ㉗ **El Cristo de La Habana.** Sometimes referred to as El Cristo de Casa Blanca for the eastern Havana municipality above which it stands, the 18-m (59-ft), Carrara-marble colossus by Cuban sculptress Jilma Madera is said to be the largest open-air sculpture ever built by a woman. It was unveiled in 1958, a year before the Revolution and a year after the student assault on Fulgencio Batista's Palacio Presidencial. It's said that Batista's wife, praying for her husband to escape the shoot-out alive, vowed to erect a statue of Christ like that in Rio de Janeiro, Brazil, if her prayers were answered. Batista survived, and the statue was built while he tortured and murdered political opponents—especially students—with renewed brutality. For this reason, there's a certain official coldness toward the site. Certainly the sculpture itself is less interesting than the views (from its base) of the harbor and La Habana Vieja and the ambience of the park—a popular local picnic spot—that surrounds it. ⊠ *Carretera de Casa Blanca,* ☎ *no phone.* 🎟 *Free.* ☉ *Daily 10–10.*

㉓ **Estudiantes de Medicina.** This fragment of Havana's early ramparts commemorates the spot where eight medical students were unjustly executed for independence activism by the Spanish governors in 1871. At night, the monument is beautifully illuminated, the work of the electrical engineer, Félix de la Noval. You'll see amber light representing rifle fire; it can't, however, extinguish the white light (against the wall), which symbolizes the ideals of independence. ⊠ *Paseo de Martí (Prado) y Av. Carlos Manuel de Céspedes (del Puerto).*

㉒ **Monumento Máximo Gómez.** This bronze equestrian monument honors the great military leader of Cuba's 19th-century Wars of Independence. It was erected in 1935 in modern Havana's most pivotal location—in an important traffic circle and at the entrance to the tunnel leading to the fortresses across the harbor. The Dominican-born General Gómez led the *mambises* (a term used by the Spanish for Cuban rebels) in the Ten Years War, refused to surrender when an unsatisfactory treaty was signed in 1878, left the island, and returned with José Martí almost 20 years later to continue the fight in the 1895 Second War of Independence. Martí died in the opening battle; fellow gen-

eral Antonio Maceo fell in December of 1895, but Gómez survived.
⊠ *Av. Carlos Manuel de Céspedes (del Puerto), e/Agramonte (Zulueta)
y Av. de las Misiones.*

Centro Habana

The Centro Habana neighborhood has a little something for everyone.
History buffs will appreciate its eclectic mixture of monuments and
monumental architecture from the 17th through the 20th centuries.
Art lovers will enjoy its Museo Nacional de Bellas Artes. Connoisseurs
of all things Cuban will appreciate its offerings of cigars, rum, and Revolution.

*Numbers in the text correspond to numbers in the margin and on the
Habana Vieja and Centro Habana map.*

A Good Walk

Begin at the 17th-century **Iglesia del Santo Angel Custodio** ㉘. Across
Avenida de la Misiones (Bélgica/Edigio/Monserrate) is the former Palacio Presidencial, which now houses the **Museo de la Revolución** ㉙ on
Calle Refugio. Behind the museum to the south is the **Memorial
Granma** ㉚. From here you can follow Calle Agramonte (Zulueta)
south two blocks and take Calle Ánimas west one block to the **Paseo
de Martí (Prado)** and its attractions or you can stay on the tour, following Avenida de las Misiones south to the **Museo Nacional de Bellas Artes** ㉛ and the **Edificio Bacardí** ㉜.

From the Edificio Bacardí, follow Av. de la Bélgica (Misiones/Edi-
gio/Monserrate) south to the **Parque Central** ㉝. Follow Calle San
Martín (San José) southwest to the **Capitolio** ㉞. Behind it, on Calle Industria, is the **Fábrica de Tabacos Partagás** ㉟, where cigars are still
made by hand. Just south of here, at the **Parque de la Fraternidad Americana** ㊱, you can contemplate Latin America's independence from
Spain. Catercorner from the park and across Avenida Simón Bolívar
(Reina) is the **Palacio de Aldama** ㊲, once owned by a man who fought
specifically for Cuba's independence from Spain.

TIMING

Paseo de Martí (Prado) aside, you can walk this tour in 1½ hours. But
walking isn't all you'll be doing, so budget 5 to 6 hours. You can easily spend at least an hour each in the Museo de la Revolución, the Museo
Nacional de Bellas Artes, and the Fábrica de Tabacos Partagás. A
promenade slightly off the path and along the Paseo de Martí (Prado)
is a chance to take Havana's pulse—something you shouldn't rush.

Sights to See

㉞ **Capitolio.** Modeled after Washington, D.C.'s domed Capitol, Havana's
Capitolio was built in 1929 and is rich in iconography. The statue to
the left of the entrance stairway represents Work (considered a mas-
culine ethic); that on the right is of Virtue (a perceived feminine attribute).
Some 30 bas-reliefs on the main door depict events in Cuba's history.
The giant main hall is called the Salon de los Pasos Perdidos (Hall of
the Lost Steps), allegedly for the fading reverberations of footsteps. It's
dominated by the gigantic bronze statue of Minerva (once known as
La República). Set into the floor at her feet is a diamond (presently a
fake) from which all distances on the island are measured. The former
Senate Chamber is at the end of the right-hand corridor; the one-time
Chamber of Representatives is on the far left. The on-site restaurant
El Salón de los Escudos serves a reasonable lunch; the Café Mirador
offers lighter fare. ⊠ *Paseo de Martí (Prado),* ☎ *7/62–8504.* ⌨ *$3.*
☺ *Tues.–Sun. 10–5.*

㉜ Edificio Bacardí. Built in 1930, the former Bacardí rum headquarters (the family elected not to brave the Revolution and now makes rum in Puerto Rico) is an art-deco outburst best admired from the roof of the Hotel Plaza across the street. Its terra-cotta facade is covered with nymphs, sylphs, salamanders, and undines; its bell tower is capped with a brass, winged gargoyle you'll recognize from the Bacardí rum label. ⊠ *Calle San Juan de Dios 202, esquina de Av. de la Bélgica (Monserrate).*

★ **㉟ Fábrica de Tabacos Partagás.** Tobacco is a fundamental part of Cuban life and a look inside this cigar factory, which is also known as La Casa del Habano, is a must—despite the high entry fee and the pricey cigars. The store itself has more than $1 million of tobacco on sale and an inner sanctum sanctorum where you can smoke and sip coffee or a mojito. The upstairs factory has been in operation since 1845 and employs 500 people who roll cigars for eight hours a day Monday through Saturday. When the *lector* isn't entertaining these artisans by reading a newspaper or a novel, Cuban music is piped into the rooms and 500 voices sing along, often drowning out the speakers on the crescendoes.

The operation is divided into seven departments: *despalillo* (stripping the central nerve from the tobacco leaf), *liga* (mixing leaves into combinations appropriate for making a cigar), *la galera* or *departamento de torcido* (the gallery or rolling—literally, twisting—department, where some 260 workers actually craft cigars), *escogida* (choosing esthetically matching cigars for presentation in the box), *anillado* (placing the paper rings on the cigars), *adorno de caja* (decorating the cedar boxes), and *embalaje* (wrapping for shipping). Depending on the quality of the cigar, from the majestic Monte Cristo A down, each roller is expected to meet a daily quota of anywhere from 60 to 250 cigars (the average is about 170). Look for the older woman in the *liga* department who works with a giant stogy dangling from her lips. Seek out la galera's Alfredo Perez (he sits in the back row, in an aisle seat in front of the air shaft), the top gun who rolls three times his quota daily. ⊠ *Calle Industria 520,* ☎ *7/33–8060.* 🎫 *$10.* ☉ *Store: Mon.–Sat. 10– 5. Factory visits: 10 and 4.*

㉘ Iglesia del Santo Angel Custodio. This prim little white church is a required visit for literature buffs hot on the trail of scenes from the novel by Cirilo Villaverde (1812–1894), *Cecilia Valdés (o la Loma del Angel).* The novel's bloody denouement takes place on the steps here during a marriage scene straight out of Racine. (A plaque on a wall across from the church door lauds Villaverde's portrait of 19th-century life here.) The church is, indeed, set on La Loma del Angel (The Hillside of the Angel) and is—with a neo-Gothic design of pure, vertical lines— markedly different from La Habana Vieja's hulking baroque structures. Originally erected in 1690 and rebuilt in 1866, Santo Angel del Custodio was where Martí was baptized. Another hero to receive this sacrament here was Félix Varela, the priest, patriot, and educator credited with having "first taught Cubans to think." *Calle Compostela 1, esquina de Calle Cuarteles,* ☎ *no phone.* 🎫 *Free.* ☉ *Daily 10–10.*

★ ☝ **㉚ Memorial *Granma*.** A glass enclosure behind the Museo de la Revolución shelters the *Granma,* the yacht that transported Castro and 81 guerrillas back to Cuba from exile in Mexico in 1956. Bought from an American, the 38-ft craft designed to carry 25 (presumably unarmed) passengers nearly foundered during the weeklong crossing. It eventually ran aground at Oriente Province in eastern Cuba, but it was two days behind schedule. The saga gets worse: Castro's forces were ambushed and only 16 survived, including Fidel, Che, Raúl Castro, and Camilo Cienfuegos. The park around the yacht is filled with military curios: tanks, Jeeps, the delivery truck used in the 1957 assault on the

Palacio Presidencial, and a turbine from a U-2 spy plane allegedly downed during the 1962 Cuban Missile Crisis. ⊠ *Calle Colón, e/Av. de la Bélgica (Misiones/Edigio/Monserrate) y Calle Agramonte (Zulueta),* ☎ *7/ 62–4091.* 🎫 *$3 (for memorial and Museo de la Revolución).* ⊙ *Tues.– Sun. 10–5.*

㉛ Museo Nacional de Bellas Artes. Havana's fine arts museum, established in 1856, has an outstanding collection of Cuban paintings. The European collection is also worth a look with works by Joseph Turner, Sir Joshua Reynolds, Francisco José de Goya, Bartolomé Estaban Murillo, Peter Paul Rubens, and Diego Velázquez. The displays of Roman, Greek, and Egyptian ceramics and statuary are some of the best in Latin America. ⊠ *Calle Trocadero, e/Av. de la Bélgica (Misiones/Edigio/Monserrate) y Calle Agramonte (Zulueta),* ☎ *7/61– 1864.* 🎫 *$3.* ⊙ *Tues.–Sun. 9–5.*

★ **㉙ Museo de la Revolución.** Batista's Palacio Presidencial, unsuccessfully attacked by students on March 13, 1957, was converted into the Museum of the Revolution after Castro's 1959 victory. The Russian tank outside was used in the Bay of Pigs invasion of 1961. The marble staircase and the magnificent upstairs ceiling mural tell one story while galleries, with displays of items from colonial times to the present, tell another; the contrast is effective. Photographs of tortured revolutionaries, maps tracing the progress of the war, the bloodstained uniforms of rebels who fell in the 1953 Santiago de Cuba Moncada Barracks attack, and photos of Fidel and Che complete a comprehensive tour of the Revolution's history. Don't miss Cretin's Corner for a look at some familiar faces. ⊠ *Calle Refugio 1,* ☎ *7/62–4092.* 🎫 *$3 (for museum and Memorial Granma).* ⊙ *Tues.–Sun. 10–5.*

㊲ Palacio de Aldama. Just past the Parque de la Fraternidad Americana's southwest corner is this Italianate mansion, built in 1840 by the Spanish merchant Domingo de Aldama. His son, Miguel de Aldama, worked for Cuban autonomy from Spain until his palace was sacked by the Spanish authorities in 1869. Don Miguel fled to the United States where he continued his work as an activist for Cuban independence until his death in 1888. ⊠ *Av. Simón Bolívar (Reina) 1.*

㉝ Parque Central. Across from the Hotel de Inglaterra and the Gran Teatro de la Habana, this park has always been a hub of Havana social activity. Centered around a statue of (who else?) Martí and shaded by royal palms and almond trees, this is *the* place for heated debates on Cuba's national passion—baseball. The Hotel Plaza is on the park's northern end. On its southern end, notice the 1885 Centro Asturiano, now the People's Supreme Court, and the 1878 Teatro Payret, now a cinema.

NEED A
BREAK?

Centro is full of classic Havana haunts where you can rejuvenate your body and soul. If you're not staying at the **Hotel Inglaterra** (☞ *Dining and* Lodging, *below*), its rooftop terrace restaurant is a good excuse to stop by. A plaque to the right of the hotel commemorates victims of the wars of independence who traditionally rallied at the nearby Acera del Louvre (Sidewalk of the Louvre). The **Gran Café del Louvre,** in the ground floor of the Hotel Inglaterra and across from the Gran Teatro de La Habana, is a well-known saloon and café—long a Havana nerve center. Across the Parque Central on Avenida de la Bélgica (Misiones/Edigio/Monserrate) is the famous Hemingway haunt with the divine daiquiris, **El Floridita** (☞ *Dining, below*).

㊱ Parque de la Fraternidad Americana. South of the Capitolio, this park is centered around another sacred ceiba tree. This one was planted in 1928 with soil from all of the free countries of the Americas.

PASEO DE MARTÍ (PRADO) – The shady, tree-lined Paseo de Martí, generally known as Paseo del Prado, is favored by Habaneros for strolls and
encounters of all kinds. It is lined with 19th- and 20th-century architecture, such as the 1914 **Antiguo Casino Español** (No. 306, esquina de
Ánimas, ☎ 7/62–5781)—once a den of iniquity known worldwide and
now the Palacio de Matrimonios, where couples from all over Cuba
come to be married (and photographed) in elegant Old World–style
rooms. Wandering north toward the bay you'll see the **Prado 264** restaurant, between Ánimas and Trocadero; the **Hotel Sevilla** at Trocadero; the
Casa Jose Miguel Gómez across from the Sevilla; the **Hotel Caribbean** at
No. 164; and the **Casa Steinhardt** at No. 120. If you continue all the
way to the harbor, you'll come to **La Punta** (☞ The Fortresses and Monuments, *above*).

Vedado and Beyond

In colonial days this area was a hunting preserve, called a *vedado* (as
in "vetoed" or "forbidden"). The pristine landscape and the game have
long since been replaced by fast-moving traffic and wide streets, but
the name remains. Although a walk through this neighborhood won't
be as pleasant as one through La Habana Vieja, don't veto it entirely—
Vedado has plenty of leafy green side streets and noteworthy sights.

Vedado is a good area from which to wander west along the waterfront Malecón to the fortress-restaurant, Santa Dorotea de Luna de la
Chorrera, at the mouth of the Río Almendares. From here you can continue southwest on a drive through the Miramar district, with its beautiful mansions, famous hotels, good restaurants, and fantastic nightclubs.
Vedado is also a good jumping-off point for the Necrópolis Cristóbal
Colón, a cemetery full of heroes and legends, and the immense Plaza
de la Revolución—both to the south.

*Numbers in the text correspond to numbers in the margin and on the
Vedado and the Plaza de la Revolución map.*

A Good Tour

At the Plaza Mella, next to the Hotel Colina, climb the famous 100-
step Escalinata to the seated figure of Alma Mater at the **Universidad
de la Habana** ㊳ on La Colina (The Hill). From here, you can head northeast and slightly off the tour to the **Callejón de Hamel,** an Afro-Cuban
street project, or you can wander northwest through the shady university courtyard to the **Parque Coppelia** ㊴. From the park, take Calle
21 southwest three blocks, turn right onto Calle H, and follow it to
Calle 17 and the **Union Nacional de Escritores y Artistas de Cuba
(UNEAC)** ㊵. Afterward walk six blocks northeast on Calle 17 and turn
right onto Calle N. At Calle 21 turn right again and you'll soon come
to the Hotel Nacional, an excellent place for a swim or a mojito. From
here you have two choices: head west along **El Malecón** ㊶ on foot or
by taxi and then take a ride through **Miramar** ㊷, or hop a cab south
to the **Necrópolis Cristóbal Colón** ㊸. From the cemetery, it's a short taxi
ride east to the **Plaza de la Revolución** ㊹.

TIMING
You can follow the walk through Vedado in about three hours. Prom-
enading along the Malecón from La Punta to Santa Dorotea de Luna
de la Chorrera takes one to two hours. A car tour of Miramar can be
done in an hour if you don't make any stops. A visit to the Necrópolis Cristóbal Colón is at least a two-hour event, as is the exploration
of the Plaza de la Revolución.

Sights to See

OFF THE
BEATEN PATH

CALLEJÓN DE HAMEL – This neighborhood project, directed by and featuring the painting (note the vivid street murals) and sculpture of Salvador Gonzalez Escalona, is an ongoing Afro-Cuban educational and artistic event. There's always something happening here: a performance by the youth club on the third Saturday of each month, theatrical events on the fourth Thursday, music shows on the last Friday. The outstanding, Afro-Cuban music and theater ensemble, Clave y Guanguancó, regularly performs here. ⊠ *Off San Lázaro, e/Calle Ánimas and Calle Soledad,* ☎ *7/78–1661.* ⊙ *Daily 9 AM–midnight.*

⟲ ④ **El Malecón.** Havana's famous Malecón (Sea Wall) runs east for 14 km (8 mi) from La Punta (where it's also known as Avenida Antonio Maceo) and the harbor's entrance to the Santa Dorotea de Luna de la Chorrera fortress, near the mouth of the Río Almendares. Although it was designed in 1857 by a Cuban engineer, it wasn't built until 1902, thanks, in part, to the American capital that flowed to the island after the Spanish–American War. Once an opulent promenade flanked by brightly painted houses, the Malecón today is dark and dilapidated, the houses crumbling, and the wide limestone walkway broken and eroded. Yet it still has its charms. As it faces north, it offers spectacular views of both sunrise and sunset—perhaps accounting for the belief that there's not a single Habanero who hasn't professed love eternal here at one time or another. Crashing waves and the rainbows created from their spray and the sun adds to the Malecón's magic.

As you walk, look for rectangles carved into the stone. These were once sea baths, which filled at high tide and allowed people to splash about, safe from both currents and sharks. Just west of the Hotel Nacional you'll come to **Monumento al *Maine*** honoring the 260 American sailors killed in the 1898 explosion of that U.S. warship, which was visiting Havana in a show of American might. Although the Spanish did all they could to immediately help the seamen, American officials and the press accused them of destroying the vessel. Cuban and Spanish historians believe that the explosion was deliberately planned by the Americans to justify U.S. intervention in the ongoing Second War of Independence. The event did, indeed, lead to the Spanish–American War followed by a period of heavy U.S. involvement in Cuban affairs. A plaque dedicated by the Castro government here reads: TO THE VICTIMS OF THE *MAINE*, WHO WERE SACRIFICED BY IMPERIALIST VORACITY IN ITS EAGERNESS TO SEIZE THE ISLAND OF CUBA.

Farther along, where Calle L runs into the Malecón, is the **U.S. Interests Section**, the de facto embassy. A billboard facing it depicts a Cuban soldier shaking a rifle at Uncle Sam (who peers across from Florida), while shouting, *"Señores Imperialistas: No les tenemos absolutamente ningún miedo"* ("Señores Imperialists: We are not at all afraid of you"). When you reach the **Santa Dorotea de Luna de la Chorrera (La Chorrera)** fortress—built in 1643 and named for the wife of Governor Alvaro de Luna and for the Almendares River or *chorrera* (stream)— be sure to stop in its restaurant for a meal or a mojito.

④ **Miramar.** At the beginning of the 20th century, Cuban magnates and American businessmen built their houses in this neighborhood, which begins west of the tunnel under the Río Almendares and ends at the Río Jaimanitas. Unless you're eager for some long distance hiking, it's best to tour this part of town by rental car or taxi. Public transport here is scarce as indicated by the mobs of schoolchildren *pidiendo botellas* (hitchhiking; literally "asking for bottles," as in favors or baby bottles).

Vedado and the Plaza de la Revolución

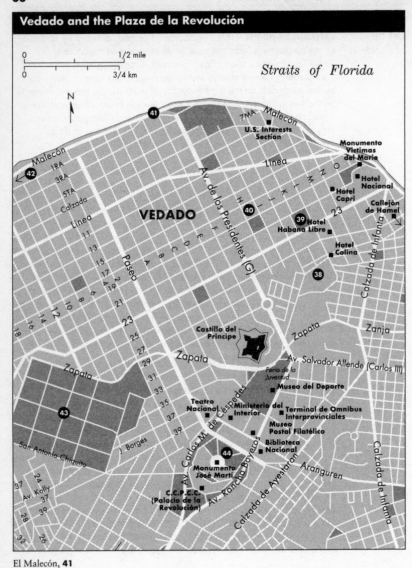

Straits of Florida

0 — 1/2 mile
0 — 3/4 km

N

Malecón
7MA. Malecón
U.S. Interests Section
Linea
Monumento Victimas del Maine
Hotel Nacional
Hotel Capri
Callejón de Hamel
VEDADO
Hotel Habana Libre
Hotel Colina
Calzada de Infanta
Zanja
Castillo del Principe
Zapata
Av. Salvador Allende (Carlos III)
Feria de la Juventud
Zapata
Museo del Deporte
Teatro Nacional
Ministerio del Interior
Terminal de Omnibus Interprovinciales
Museo Postal Filatélico
Biblioteca Nacional
San Antonio Chiquito
J. Borges
Monumento José Martí
C.C.P.C.C. (Palacio de la Revolución)
Av. Rancho Boyeros
Calzada de Ayestarán
Aranguren
Calzada de Infanta

1RA, 3RA, 5TA, Calzada, Linea
Paseo
Av. de los Presidentes (G)

In the **Museo del Ministerio del Interior** (✉ Av. 5 y Calle 14, ☎ 7/33–2112, 🎫 $3, ☉ Tues.–Fri. 8:30–5) you can see displays purporting 30 years of CIA efforts to eliminate Fidel Castro. The **Maqueta de La Habana** (✉ Calle 28, e/Av. 1 y Av. 3, ☎ 7/33–2661, 🎫 $3, ☉ Tues.–Sat. 2–6) is a 1:1,000 model of Havana. At the **Aquario Nacional** (✉ Calle 60 y Av. 1, ☎ 7/33–1321, 🎫 $3, ☉ Tues.–Sat. 2–6) you can learn about some of Cuba's marine life. The **Museo de la Alfabetización** (✉ Calle 31 y Av. 100, Marianao, ☎ 7/33–2001, 🎫 $3, ☉ Weekday 8–5) is a museum dedicated to the literacy crusade of 1961 during which students and teachers taught illiterate peasants around Cuba to read and write. Miramar ends at the **Marina Hemingway,** a yachting facility just across the Río Jaimanitas.

★ 🖐 ㊸ **Necrópolis Cristóbal Colón.** The Christopher Columbus Cemetery sprawls behind a huge ceremonial arch and is a repository for a great deal more than just the deceased. Founded in 1868 by Bishop Espada, it's a veritable pantheon of monuments commemorating poets, novelists, musicians, soldiers, statesmen, and rank-and-file citizens. Cuban novelist Cirilo Villaverde and Nobel-laureate Alejo Carpentier are here as are the martyrs of the *Granma* yacht landing and the students killed in the 1957 assault on the Palacio Presidencial. This is also a place full of extraordinary legends, some of them macabre. You can learn all about them on a guided tour (highly recommended; you can arrange for one in English for a $2 fee at the hut just inside the grounds to the right). Be sure to ask about the story of La Milagrosa (The Miraculous). ✉ *Calle Zapata y Calle 12,* ☎ *7/32–1050.* 🎫 *$2.* ☉ *Mon.–Sat. 9–5, Sun. 8–noon.*

🖐 ㊴ **Parque Coppelia.** Named for an 1870 ballet by the French composer Léo Délibes, this park and its ice cream emporium are Havana institutions. The Star Wars–type flying saucer in the middle of the square was the Revolution's answer to the many ice cream parlors, that, prior to 1959, were highly discriminatory. This state-owned establishment serves more than 25,000 customers daily—the only requirement is that they be Cuban. (Note that non-Cuban visitors not part of a tour group and possessing good Spanish-language skills have been known to secure one of the four-scoop bowls). The parlor once offered a legendary number of flavors, but after the Special Period (the national emergency declared upon the collapse of the Soviet Union, after which Cuba suffered severe shortages of everything from fuel to food; ☞ *also* "Cuba's Organic Revolution" box, *below*) supplies became scarce, and a flavor a day became the rule.

🖐 ㊹ **Plaza de la Revolución.** This plaza may seem grandiose and soulless, but it has several monuments with a lot of heart. Since the Revolutionary victory of 1959, it has been the official parade grounds for events ranging from the annual May Day celebration to the 1998 visit of Pope John Paul II. A political, administrative, and cultural hub, the square is surrounded by army, police, Communist Party, and other ministries. Castro's whereabouts, always a mystery, include visits to these government centers, though he's just as likely to be coaching the national baseball team, resting in one of his many secret Havana residences, or off fishing on the Península de Zapata. The highlight is the **Museo Memorial José Martí** in the plaza's center. It consists of a massive granite sculpture of the national hero—in a seated, contemplative pose—on a 30-m (98-ft) base and a 139-m (456-ft) tower constructed of marble from La Isla de la Juventud (where Castro was imprisoned for his attack on the Moncada Barracks). The museum contains first editions of Martí's works, drawings, maps, and other memorabilia. Also on display are the original plans for both the monument and the square. ✉ ☎ 7/82–

CUBA'S ORGANIC REVOLUTION

WHEN THE UNITED STATES blockaded Cuba in 1961, the Soviet Union was Castro's only trade-partner option. As the island's economy progressively fell apart, Soviet aid became Cuba's daily bread. In 1989, however, the Berlin Wall and the Soviet Union both collapsed. Cuba's economy went from bad to worse, and its shelves were left bare. Castro declared a "Special Period in Time of Peace" and called for belt-tightening austerity and Revolutionary sacrifice.

Life during the Special Period, especially after June 1992 when the supply of oil was ceased, has included electricity blackouts, stopped machinery, crops rotting in the fields, and hotel and restaurant closures. Once the only country in the Americas to have eliminated hunger, Cuba became malnourished.

For centuries, Cuba was reliant on food imports as the nation's agriculture was dominated by the export crop of sugarcane. After the 1959 Revolution, dependence on the Soviet Union led to mechanization and the use of chemical insecticides and fertilizers. Upon the collapse of the Soviet bloc, Cuba was left without either subsidies for agricultural chemicals or food shipments. To make matters worse, the years of insecticide use had caused a dearth of natural insect predators as well as the development of new "super-pests" resistent to chemicals. Further, the quality of the soil had deteriorated owing to over-irrigation and the heavy use of both pesticides and chemical fertilizers.

Over the last decade, Cuba has had a surprising agricultural revolution. The na-tion has turned to organic farming, using natural fertilizers and creative pest-management strategies and practicing such soil conservation techniques as crop rotation. The oxen you may see plowing the fields are actually a sign of progress, not penury.

More than 200 enterprises around Cuba are now run by university-educated agronomists. One of them, Julio Ortega, works at East Havana's Rotonda de Agricultura Organopónica, site of a thriving plantation of lettuce, chard, Chinese cabbage, celery, parsley, spinach, and spring onions. According to Ortega, year-round watering and the use of biofertilizers (animal manure, bat guano, and organic material created by the cultivation of earthworms) have replaced much needed nitrogen in the soil and enabled crops to grow more rapidly. Instead of using chemical fertilizers to combat plant pests, farmers now use other insects as well as bacteria and fungal diseases. Oxen are used for plowing because they provide natural fertilizer instead of petroleum-based air pollution.

Director Dr. Peter Rosset and his staff at California's Institute for Food and Development Policy (Food First) work with both the Cuban Association for Organic Farming and with the Advanced Institute for Agricultural Sciences of Havana. They're watching carefully as Cuban agronomists establish what may well be a world model for agriculture in the future. (Further reading: *The Greening of Cuba: A National Experiment in Organic Agriculture,* by Peter Rosset and Medea Benjamin.)

0906. ☎ $5 museum entry fee, $5 extra for photos, $5 entry fee to tower observation deck. ☉ Tues.–Sat. 10–6, Sun. 10–2.

It's hard to miss the giant etching of Che Guevara on the **Ministerio del Interior** (Ministry of the Interior) at the plaza's northwestern edge. It bears the words HASTA LA VICTORIA SIEMPRE (ALWAYS ONWARD TO VICTORY). Just east of Che, you'll find the outstanding **Museo Postal/Filatélico** (Postal Museum; ☎ 7/70–5193, ☎ $2, ☉ Weekdays 9–4) on the ground floor of the Ministerio de Comunicaciones (Communications Ministry). Still farther east of Che is the **Biblioteca Nacional José Martí**, which, with 2 million volumes, is Cuba's largest library. Two blocks up along Avenida de la Independencia (Rancho Boyos), you can get an interesting look at the achievements of Cuban athletes during the past 40 years in the **Museo del Deporte** (☎ 7/81–4696, ☎ $1, ☉ Tues.–Sun. 10–5). On the square's western edge, across Avenida Carlos Manual de Céspedes, is the **Teatro Nacional**, Cuba's most important theater.

㊵ Union Nacional de Escritores y Artistas de Cuba (UNEAC). Occupying what was once the Casa Juan Gelats, one of Vedado's finest early 20th-century mansions, the National Union of Writers and Artists is the site of cinematic events; lectures and prose and poetry readings; and, on Wednesday and Saturday, Afro-Cuban performances. The bar and restaurant serve good criollo fare. The building across Calle H from this one is an important UNEAC annex. ⊠ *Calle 17 y Calle H*, ☎ *7/32–2211.* ☎ *$3.* ☉ *Open daily 9 AM–midnight.*

NEED A BREAK?   Made famous in the days when Batista still ruled the nation and gangsters like Meyer Lansky ruled its casinos, the **Hotel Nacional** is still very much a center of activity. You can have a meal or a mojito in the outstanding Aguiar restaurant here or refresh yourself with a dip in the pool. (☞ Dining, Lodging *and* Outdoor Activities and Sports, *below*).

㊳ Universidad de la Habana. The University of Havana was originally founded in 1728 behind the Palacio de los Capitanes Generales on Calle Obispo. The present campus was built early in the 19th century and modeled after New York City's Columbia University. Its 100-step Escalinata leads to the Alma Mater, a statue that welcomes students to the halls of higher learning and has been a gathering spot for demonstrations and rallies ever since 1928, when student leader Julio Antonio Mella led uprisings against the brutal dictator, General Gerardo Machado. (The founder of Cuba's Communist Party, Mella, whose ashes rest in the monumental sculpture at the foot of the Escalinata, was assassinated by Machado agents in Mexico in 1929.) It was here that thousands—including Fidel, who gave a three-hour speech—welcomed the national baseball team back from the United States after their victory over the Baltimore Orioles in May 1999. The courtyard is generally a peaceful place, shaded by luxuriant *jagüé* trees, which are often referred to as "the trees that walk" or "the trees of a thousand feet," owing to their multiple trunks. The tank at the back of the courtyard was captured (for a while) by students in a pitched battle with Batista forces in the early 1950s.

Eastern Havana

Havana's eastern reaches have several interesting sights. The **Regla** neighborhood has strong Afro-Cuban traditions, and nearby **Guanabacoa** is known for its excellent museum dedicated to Santería, an Afro-Cuban religion. You can visit both municipalities as an extension of your tour of the fortresses or on a separate side trip. Transportation to and around them can be a combination of ferries or launches, taxis, trains, and walks.

Hemingway fans must include a trip to **Cojímar**—a small fishing village where Gregorio Fuentes, Hemingway's friend and boatman, still lives—and **Finca Vigía,** Hemingway's home. In six or seven hours you can drive along the Carreterra Central 13 km (8 mi) southeast of Havana to San Francisco de Paula, the village where Finca Vigía is located, and then drive up to Cojímar on the Circunvalación (Ring Road) for lunch in La Terraza and a look around town.

You could spend your life in the **Parque Lenin,** a sprawling, Soviet-style amusement park 20 km (12 mi) southeast of Havana. To drive out to it, have a look, and drive back is only a two-hour proposition. If your time is limited, this is one eastern excursion you can skip.

Sights to See

Cojímar. The fishing village Hemingway described in *The Old Man and the Sea* is modeled after this sleepy maritime hamlet where the author's wooden sportfishing craft, *El Pilar,* was berthed. At press time, Gregorio Fuentes—Hemingway's skipper and pal from 1935 to 1960—was still alive, still lucid, and still downing his share of whiskey and dining at La Terraza, the town's top restaurant. El Torreón, the small fortress built here after the English used Cojímar as a landing point in their 1762 attack on Havana, is the site of a Hemingway bust made of brass fittings, each donated by a Cojímar fisherman.

★ ☻ **Finca Vigía.** Even those convinced that they've outgrown their thirst for Hemingway will feel a flutter of romanticism on a visit to Finca Vigía (Lookout Farm), the American Nobel Prize–winner's home from 1939 to 1961. The excellent guides will show you his weight charts—faithfully kept on the bathroom wall and never varying much from 242.5 pounds—a first edition of Kenneth Tynan's *Bull Fever* by the toilet; the lizard preserved in formaldehyde and honored for having "died well" in a battle with one of Hemingway's five dozen cats; the pool where Ava Gardner swam naked; Hemingway's favorite chair (ask about what happened to people who dared sit in it); his sleek powerboat, *El Pilar;* and much, much more. ⊠ *San Francisco de Paula,* ☎ *7/91–0809.* ☞ *$3.* ☾ *Mon. and Wed.–Sat. 9–4, Sun. 9–noon.*

★ **Guanabacoa.** Once a small sugar and tobacco center, Guanabacoa is inhabited primarily by the descendents of slaves who worked the fields here. Though the town, which is full of colonial treasures, is now part of sprawling Havana, its old Afro-Cuban traditions and religions have been kept alive. The **Museo Histórico Municipal de Guanabacoa** (⊠ Calle Martí 108, ☎ 7/97–9117, ☞ $2, ☾ Mon. and Wed.–Sat. 8–6, Sun. 9–1) has comprehensive exhibits on Santería as well as on town history.

☻ **Parque Lenin.** This vast amusement park was popular with Cubans before the 1992 collapse of the Soviet Union. The penury of the Special Period, however, has caused the carousels and other fairground attractions to be shut down. Developed on what was once a farming estate 20 km (12 mi) southwest of Havana, the 745-hectare (1,841-acre) park contains rolling meadows, small lakes, and woodlands. Look for the Monumento Lenin, a mammoth granite sculpture of the Russian Revolutionary. The Monumento a Celia Sánchez has photographs and portraits of Cuba's unofficial First Lady (☞ box, *below*). The park's offerings also include art galleries, ceramics workshops, and a movie theater. Horseback riding, boating, and swimming are options here as well. You can have a good meal in Las Ruinas and stay overnight in the comfortable motel.

CELIA SÁNCHEZ

FIDEL CASTRO'S SECRETARY, confidante, and lover, Celia Manduley Sánchez was Cuba's unofficial First Lady and, as stated on her monument in Manzanillo, LA MAS HERMOSA Y AUTÓCTONA FLOR DE LA REVOLUCIÓN (THE MOST BEAUTIFUL AND INDIGENOUS FLOWER OF THE REVOLUTION). The two were inseparable from their meeting in 1957 till her death of cancer in 1980.

Before becoming involved in the resistance against Fulgencio Batista, Sánchez worked as a teacher. Ever the idealist, she was a José Martí disciple; in 1952, she climbed Pico Turquino to erect a bust of the national hero there. After joining the 26th of July Movement (named for the 1953 attack on Santiago's Moncada Barracks), Sánchez again climbed Cuba's highest mountain, this time with Castro and a CBS news crew for an interview with him next to Martí's bust.

Sánchez worked as Castro's logistics, propaganda, and espionage chief in the lowlands around Manzanillo while he held out in the Sierra Maestra. Later, she shared his command cabin on a ridge west of Pico Turqino. Without her efforts, it's difficult to imagine Castro's mountain-based guerrilla movement gaining political strength. Sánchez was El Commandante's "eyes and ears" and the only person who could tell him things he didn't like to hear. Her death deprived him of a link with reality—his own and Cuba's.

Regla. Although this fishing town has become increasingly industrialized, there's still a quiet intimacy in its streets. Regla is named for its lovely waterfront church built in 1810, the Iglesia de Nuestra Señora de Regla, famous for its black Madonna cradling a white infant. Identified with Yemayá—the Yoruban *orisha* (West African goddess) of the sea—the Black Virgin of Regla is the patron saint of sailors and seafarers. September 8th sees both Christian and Santería celebrations honoring her.

Many streets, notably Calle Calixto García, have tiny Santería shrines outside houses. The **Palacio de Turismo** (⊠ Calle Sanctuario 13, ☎ 7/ 90–0182), holds a Fiesta de los Orishas (Celebration of Yoruban Deities) every Tuesday at 8 PM. The **Museo Municipal de Regla** (⊠ Calle Martí 158, ☎ 7/97–6989, ⊠ $2 ⊙ Mon. and Wed.–Sat. 9:30–6, Sun. 9–1) has a complete exhibit on Regla's many Santería associations.

BEACHES

The Playas del Este (Eastern Beaches) are just 20–30 minutes from Havana on the coast road to Varadero. Full of sun worshippers and local flavor, these sands have an atmosphere like that of daytime disco by the sea. Although a morning of basking in the sun is conceivable, it's really more of a full day operation. Take Vía Monumental toward Cojímar; 1 km (½ mi) beyond the second Cojímar exit, Vía Blanca splits off to the beaches.

The first beach is **Bacuranao,** 18 km (11 mi) east of Havana. Beneath the waters off this small, white-sand cove are coral reefs and an 18th-century Spanish galleon, making this a popular scuba diving spot. Look for the Villa Bacuranao, a bustling bar-disco that also has inexpensive cabins to rent. Two kilometers (1 mile) east of Bacuranao is **Playa Tarará,** a small stretch of white sand that's home to the 50-berth Marina Tarará/Club Nautico, site of the Old Man and the Sea Fishing Tournament (☞ Outdoor Activities and Sports, *below*) every July. You can arrange boat rentals, yacht cruises, and diving or snorkeling excursions here.

Just 2 km (1 mi) farther east is **Playa El Mégano,** a quiet stretch of sand. El Mégano is really considered a western extension of the main beach, **Playa de Santa María,** which runs east to the mouth of the Río Itabo. This happening swath is home to the Hotel Tropicoco, which is action central. Just beyond the mouth of the Río Itabo is the dune-flanked **Playa Boca Ciega.** If you head still farther east, you'll come to **Playa Guanabo.** The least lovely of the Playas del Este is, nevertheless, popular with surfcasters and joggers.

Driving 10 km (6 mi), you'll reach Santa Cruz del Norte, an industrial town that's home to Cuba's greatest distillery, the Ronera Santa Cruz, where the ubiquitous Havana Club rum is made. Don't let the offshore oil rigs or the less than pristine waters here deter you from continuing. Just 3 km (2 mi) east of Santa Cruz is **Playa Jibacoa,** the best and least spoiled of all of the beaches near Havana. Nestled between headlands at the mouth of the Río Jibacoa, its white sands are backed by cliffs that overlook crystal clear, aquamarine waters. Divers will appreciate the coral reefs here; landlubbers can follow hiking trails from the beach into the back country.

DINING

Although Havana may not, for the moment, offer a head-spinning number of irresistible gastronomical choices, things are improving. And there *are* ways to have a good meal. Stick with the paladares as much as possible. These privately owned establishments are, by law, only allowed a maximum of 12 seats and can only be staffed by families. They offer the chance to interact with Cubans in their homes, *and* your dollars go directly to them. The food is usually fresh, authentic, and inexpensive. Although there are regulations on what can be served (lobster and shrimp, for example, are officially forbidden at paladares), the owners often find a way around such rules, lending a cozy, clandestine, speakeasy atmosphere. The Vedado district, especially inland from Parque Coppelia, and La Habana Vieja have many paladares.

As a rule, the government-owned establishments are not good. However, they are often in such spectacular settings that you may find them hard to resist despite their overpriced, fair-to-decent offerings. There are also some exceptions to the rule. El Floridita, though overpriced, serves fine, if not terrific, food; Miramar has some stand-out establishments; and those near the fortresses across the harbor are surprisingly good as well (they also have killer city views). Finally, the hotel restaurants (not the cafeterias or buffets) are often noteworthy, especially Aguiar in the Hotel Nacional. Two caveats: beware of elegant but empty establishments, and opt for simple criollo fare over sophisticated or "international" creations.

For the moment, consider the U.S. dollar the only reliable form of payment in Cuba. Credit cards *not* affiliated with U.S. banks or companies are accepted in government restaurants and hotels, though never in paladares. If your Spanish is good enough to create any doubt as to your nationality, you can use Cuban pesos in Cuban restaurants and dine relatively well for nearly nothing (though you may feel you're taking unfair advantage of the parallel economies). Don't be alarmed if a menu offers, say, a salad for what appears to be $100; one line through the letter "S" is the symbol for pesos, two lines through the letter is the symbol for U.S. dollars. Hence, that salad actually costs 100 pesos, or $1. For price categories, *see* Dining *in* Smart Travel Tips A to Z.

La Habana Vieja

$$$$ ✕ **Café del Oriente.** Try for the upstairs corner table, which overlooks the Plaza de San Francisco and has a view of the Sierra Maestra boat terminal, the Iglesia y Convento Menor de San Francisco de Asis, and the Lonja del Comercio (Commerce Exchange) across the way. At press time, the food was overpriced and only fair, but as the restaurant was still new, perhaps the criollo and international cuisine will improve with time. ✉ *Calle de los Oficios 112,* ☎ *7/66–6686. MC, V.*

$$$$ ✕ **Vuelta Abajo.** An elegant, intimate spot in the Hostal Conde de Villanueva (☞ Lodging, *below*), this restaurant specializes in dishes from Vuelta Abajo, Cuba's best tobacco-growing region. Try the *pollo yumurino* (chicken in a criollo sauce). ✉ *Calle Mercaderes 202,* ☎ *7/62–9682. MC, V.*

$$$ ✕ **La Bodeguita del Medio.** What may be Havana's best-known bar-restaurant is truly a required stop for a drink, even though the mojitos cost a steep $4. What the heck? Why not hoist one for Hemingway? The downstairs bar is always packed with tourists looking expectantly toward the door as if Papa himself were about to enter and belly up to the bar. The upstairs bar is usually empty despite being a good place to hang out. If you plan to dine here, ask for a seat on the upstairs terrace (the downstairs dining room is airless, ovenlike, and overcrowded). Note that the criollo fare is unjustifiably famous. Stay on the cheap end of the menu as the food doesn't improve as prices rise. Good bets are the *picadillo a la habanera* (ground beef with onions, garlic, tomatoes, and olives) and the *aporreado de tasajo* (shredded beef in criollo sauce). ✉ *Calle Empedrado 207,* ☎ *7/62–4498. MC, V.*

$$$ ✕ **Don Giovanni.** It's named not for the famous Italian Don Juan but rather for the military engineer, Juan Bautista Antonelli, responsible for Havana's 16th-century fortresses. The wait staff is amenable, as is the setting in a stately colonial mansion surrounding a leafy patio; the view from the upper floor is of the harbor and El Morro. The menu offers both passable Italian fare (the pizzas are noteworthy) and simple criollo dishes. ✉ *Calle Tacón 4,* ☎ *7/61–2183. MC, V.*

$$$ ✕ **Al Medina.** This restaurant is part of an Arabic cultural center with the city's only mosque and an oasis-like courtyard that hosts arts and crafts shows and sales. The eclectic menu offers both Moroccan and criollo fare, ranging from couscous and lamb dishes to criollo standards such as roast chicken or pork and black beans with rice. ✉ *Calle de los Oficios 12,* ☎ *7/63–0862. MC, V.*

$$$ ✕ **La Paella.** Set in the charming Hostal Valencia (☞ Lodging, *below*), this restaurant specializes in paella, just as its name suggests, and has won high praise for its Valencian dishes. In keeping with the cuisine, the large, airy dining room has a terra-cotta floor and traditional Spanish furnishings. ✉ *Calle de los Oficios 53, esquina de Calle Obrapía,* ☎ *7/57–103. MC, V. No dinner Sun.*

$$$ ✕ **El Patio.** It might be hard to pick a table at this restaurant. It's set ★ in a stunning colonial house, and your choices are out on the Plaza de la Catedral or in the namesake central patio, with its lovely fountain. The criollo menu is complete, and although the food and service fall short of the spectacular settings, the prices are reasonable and the quality is good. ✉ *Plaza de la Catedral 54,* ☎ *7/61–8504. MC, V.*

Straits of Florida

N

0   1/2 mile
0   3/4 km

MIRAMAR

LA SIERRA

KOLHY

ALMENDARES

MONTE BARRETO

NUEVO VEDADO

AMP. DE ALMENDARES

QUEREJETA

BUENA VISTA

LA CEIBA

ALT. DE BELEN

Necrópolis Christóbal Colón

Parque Zoológico de la Habana

Dining

Aguiar, **41**
El Aljibe, **50**
Amor, **33**
Bar la Tasca, **59**
El Bistrot, **44**
La Bodeguita del Medio, **14**
Café el Mercurio, **4**
Café del Oriente, **3**
Castillo del Farnés, **28**
Le Chansonnier, **37**
Chung Shan los Dos Dragones, **31**
La Divina Pastora, **58**
Doña Eutinia, **13**

Don Cangrejo, **49**
Don Giovanni, **16**
Dos Gardenias, **51**
XII Apóstoles, **57**
La Ferminia, **56**
El Floridita, **27**
El Gato Tuerto, **43**
La Guarida, **25**
Hanoi, **29**
Al Medina, **7**
La Moneda Cubana, **11**
La Optima Instancia, **34**
La Paella, **5**
El Patio, **15**
Ranchón, **47**

Restaurante Pacífico, **32**
La Roca, **38**
La Terraza, **26**
La Terraza Florentina, **40**
Tocororo, **48**
La Torre, **42**
Torre de Marfil, **8**
Vuelta Abajo, **2**

Lodging

Chateau Miramar, **53**
Convento de Santa Clara, **1**
Habana Riviera, **46**
Hostal El Comendador, **6**
Hostal Conde de Villanueva, **2**
Hostal San Miguel, **18**
Hostal del Tejadillo, **17**
Hostal Valencia, **5**
Hotel Ambos Mundos, **9**
Hotel Capri, **40**
Hotel Caribbean, **19**

Straits of Florida

LA HABANA VIEJA (See Below)

VEDADO

Caleta de San Lázaro

Malecón

Canal de Entrada

Vía Monumental

Bahía de la Habana

LA HABANA VIEJA

Canal de Entrada

El Parque de los Mártires

Parque Cépedes

Av. del Puerto

San Lázaro
Trocadero
Colón
Lagunas
Ánimas
Campanario
San Nicolás
Manrique
Galiano (Blanco)
Concordia
Vertudes
Neptuno
San Miguel
San Rafael
San Martín (San José)
Zanja
Dragones
Salud
Sitios

Av. de Italia
Av. de Bélgica (Monserrate)
Agramonte
Bernaza
Villegas
Aguacate
Compostela
Habana
Cuba
Aguiar
San Ignacio
Mercaderes
Oficios

Genios
Paseo de Martí (Prado)
Chacón
Tejadillo
Empedrado
Progreso
O'Reilly
Obispo
Obrapía
Lamparilla
Amargura
Basil (Teniente Rey)
Muralla
Sol
Santa Clara
Luz

Parque Central
Av. Simón Bolívar (Reina)
Dragones
Independencia
Zapata

Vía Blanca

LUYANÓ

Hotel Colina, **35**
Hotel Comodoro, **55**
Hotel Deauville, **20**
Hotel Florida, **10**
Hotel Habana Libre, **36**
Hotel Inglaterra, **26**
Hotel Itabo, **61**
Hotel Meliá Cohiba, **45**
Hotel Meliá Habana, **54**
Hotel Mirazul, **52**
Hotel Nacional, **41**
Hotel Plaza, **24**
Hotel Santa Isabel, **12**
Hotel Saratoga, **30**

Hotel Sevilla, **21**
Hotel Telégrafo, **22**
Hotel Tropicoco, **62**
Hotel Victoria, **39**
Parque Central, **23**
Villa Jibacoa Loma, **60**

$$ ✕ **Café el Mercurio.** If you're peckish before or around sunrise, this is a good place to come. It's named for Mercury—the god of commerce, whose likeness sits atop the Lonja del Comercio building in which it's set—and is open around the clock every day. Its specialties are unusual for Cuba: omelets, sandwiches, and salads. ⊠ *Plaza San Francisco de Asis,* ☎ *7/66–6188. MC, V.*

$$ ✕ **Torre de Marfil.** Eating Chinese food in Havana might seem strange, but when slavery in Cuba ended, thousands of Chinese came to this island as laborers, so there's a large community here. This spot has all the traditional trappings: lamps and lanterns, Chinese waiters, and tasty Chinese fare that's a nice change from all the international and criollo food. The prices are good, too. ⊠ *Calle Mercaderes 121,* ☎ *7/62–3466. MC, V.*

$ ✕ **Doña Eutinia.** Tucked away in the tiny Callejón del Chorro, this charming spot is little more than Doña Eutinia's kitchen and sitting room, and she and her crew serve you to the very best of their abilities. Although it's practically at the back door of the Bodeguita del Medio, no two establishments could be more dissimilar. ⊠ *Plaza de la Catedral 62,* ☎ *7/61–5163. No credit cards.*

$ ✕ **La Moneda Cubana.** The quarters at this friendly, inexpensive paladar—just a block east of Plaza de la Catedral—are tight, but that just adds to the charm. The criollo specialties include picadillo a la habanera, aporreado de tasajo, and *masas de puerco fritos* (fried pork cutlets). ⊠ *Calle San Ignacio 77,* ☎ *7/61–0401. No credit cards.*

The Fortresses

$$$ ✕ **La Divina Pastora.** Although prices are on the high side, the romantic
★   location makes them worth it. Tucked into the berth of the sailing ship *El Galeón* at the foot of El Morro, this restaurant offers splendid views over Havana and is a good spot for dinner after the cañonazo at La Cabaña. Your best bet is lobster; kept alive in an on-site tank, it's guaranteed to be fresh. ⊠ *Parque Historico Militar Morro–Cabaña,* ☎ *7/33–8341. MC, V.*

$$$ ✕ **XII Apóstoles.** Stationed at the base of El Morro, this restaurant offers marvelous views of Havana and better-than-average international and criollo fare. Opt for a meal of grilled fish, as this is one of the fishing fleet's first stops on the way back into the harbor. ⊠ *Parque Histórico Militar Morro–Cabaña,* ☎ *7/63–8295. MC, V.*

$$ ✕ **Bar la Tasca.** This little *bodega* (wine cellar) offers terrific city views and delicious seafood. Standard criollo dishes—platanos a puñetazos, arroz e frijoles negros, ropa vieja—are also available. Heavy wood beams and old weapons hung on the walls add to the traditional feel of the place. ⊠ *Parque Histórico Militar Morro–Cabaña,* ☎ *7/63–1329. MC, V.*

Centro Habana

$$$$ ✕ **El Floridita.** This famous bar-restaurant is everything it's cracked up
★   to be. The daiquiris are nonpareil however you choose to have them: with or without sugar, frozen, shaken, or stirred. The ever-present *mariquitas* (deep-fried plantain chips) are delicious, and the appetizers are excellent. Try the *crepas de espinacas* (spinach crêpes) or the frogs' legs soufflé. The bar has *marcha* (movement) and excitement, but in the restaurant beyond it, things slow down and prices go up. ⊠ *Calle Obispo 557,* ☎ *7/33–8856. MC, V.*

$$$ ✕ **Castillo del Farnés.** Notable as Fidel Castro's favorite hangout when he was a student and the place where he and Che celebrated victory on January 9, 1959, this modest bar-restaurant is a good choice for a meal or a drink. They charge a little extra for the historical rush (which seems

counterrevolutionary of them), but the shrimp dishes are good, and the Spanish and criollo cuisine is acceptable, if not brilliant. ✉ *Av. de la Bélgica (Misiones/Edigio/Monserrate) 361,* ☎ *7/63–1260. MC, V.*

$$$ ✕ **Restaurante Pacífico.** Both Fidel and Papa have dined at this Chinese establishment, giving it undeniable pre- and postrevolutionary chic. Not far from the Chinese market, which is held every day but Wednesday on Calle Cuchillo, the building is one of Chinatown's most interesting. It has restaurants on all its floors, but the main one is on the third floor (the one on the fifth floor is where Fidel reportedly still dines). ✉ *Calle San Nicolas y Calle Cuchillo,* ☎ *7/63–3243. MC, V.*

$$$ ✕ **La Terraza.** In the terrace grill-saloon of the Hotel Inglaterra (☞ Lodging, *below*), you can dine on criollo and international fare that's less pretentious and of a better quality than many of Havana's more opulent restaurants. Try the pollo en salsa criolla or, if it's available, the grilled lobster. The view of the Parque Central and the Prado is grand. ✉ *Paseo de Martí (Prado) 416,* ☎ *7/33–8593. MC, V. No lunch.*

$$ ✕ **La Guarida.** Enrique Nuñez and his stunning wife, Odeysis, have
★ made their paladar one of the city's best. Its 18th-century town house setting is so photogenic that scenes in *Fresa y Chocolate* (*Strawberry and Chocolate*), the Cuban film nominated for an Academy Award in 1995, were shot here. The three-floor climb up the wildly squalid stairway provokes an appetite-enhancing adrenaline. Everything— from the gazpacho to the grouper—is good here. The special of the day consists not of what the Nuñezes want to get rid of, but of what they think will make you happiest. ✉ *Calle Concordia 418, e/Calle Gervasio y Calle Escobar,* ☎ *7/62–4940. No credit cards.*

$$ ✕ **Hanoi.** Also known as Casa de la Parra (Grape Arbor House), this
★ restaurant specializes in criollo and Vietnamese food, an unlikely combination until you remember that any foe of Uncle Sam's is a friend of Fidel's. The varied menu includes such excellent dishes as *arroz Vietnamita* (rice with chicken, chorizo, and shrimp) and *boniato cocido* (boiled yam). The black bean soup and the *chicharrones* (pork crisps) are terrific, too, and the $1 mojitos and 85¢ beers make it easy to spend time getting to know this place better. ✉ *Calle Brasil (Teniente Rey) y Calle Bernaza,* ☎ *7/57–1029. MC, V.*

$ ✕ **Chung Shan los Dos Dragones.** This Chinatown restaurant is tucked
★ behind the Capitolio in the bottom floor of a crumbling building. Fresh vegetables and seafood and prices that (almost) make you plead to pay more make this place notable. ✉ *Calle Altos 311, e/Calle Rayo y Calle San Nicolas,* ☎ *7/63–3442. No credit cards.*

Vedado

$$$$ ✕ **Aguiar.** For decades, the elegant dining room in the Hotel Nacional (☞ Lodging, *below*) has been one of the city's premier establishments. Despite the table-side shrimp-and-rum flambé performances, which are always entertaining, the atmosphere is generally subdued—even when the place is full. The wine list is excellent, though pricey. ✉ *Calle O y Calle 21,* ☎ *7/33–3564. MC, V.*

$$$$ ✕ **La Torre.** At press time, this was *the* dining hot spot. Chef Frank Pecol,
★ a native of France who fell for Havana and never looked back, is known as one of Havana's hottest, most innovative young chefs. His bright restaurant has wonderful views of the Malecón from its 35th floor perch in the Focsá building. He somehow manages to rustle up decent ingredients and present superb creations, and his wine list is one of Havana's best. ✉ *Calle 17, e/Calle M y Calle N,* ☎ *7/55–3088. MC, V.*

$$$ ✕ **La Roca.** Don't let the setting in a dilapidated shack deter you; this restaurant actually offers good criollo (try the tasajo de res) and international dishes. The scandalous bar at the back is an incitement to licentiousness. ✉ *Calle 21 y Calle M,* ☎ *7/33–4501. No credit cards.*

$$-$$$ ✕ **Le Chansonnier.** Founded by a waiter from the original Paris Chan-
  ★   sonnier, this friendly paladar is very much like a French bistro. At one
       of only a few tables in the verdant patio, you can feast on such French
       staples as lamb chops and duck as well as criollo fare. ⊠ *Calle 15, e/Calle
       H y Calle I,* ☎ *7/32–3788. No credit cards.*

$$-$$$ ✕ **El Gato Tuerto.** This café-restaurant and cabaret is open until dawn
       and serves a great onion soup. The ropa vieja, presented elegantly on
       a huge plate with mint and parsley garnishes, is also excellent. The spe-
       cialty, however, is chef Miguel Magraner's *langosta Magraner,* lobster
       tail fried in batter with a sweet and sour sauce. Downstairs in the cabaret,
       performances continue until the sun rises over the Malecón. ⊠ *Calle
       O, e/Calle 17 y Calle 19,* ☎ *7/55–2696. MC, V.*

$$-$$$ ✕ **La Terraza Florentina.** The Italian restaurant in the Hotel Capri (☞
       Lodging, *below*) was probably what drew the mob to this Havana ad-
       dress in the first place. Lots of good pasta and other Italian special-
       ties—particularly the shrimp pasta in a garlic sauce—at more than
       acceptable prices make this 18th-floor dining room overlooking the
       Malecón hard to resist. The wine list has some excellent Italian vin-
       tages. ⊠ *Calle 21, e/Calle N y Calle O,* ☎ *7/33–3571. MC, V.*

  $ ✕ **Amor.** A creaky elevator takes you up to this charming paladar on
       the third floor of a lovely early 20th-century mansion. Just a 15-minute
       walk up Calle 23 (La Rampa) from Parque Coppelia, Amor is owned
       by the eponymous pop singer who has turned the family house into
       the family business. The decor, the Wedgwood china, the candelabras,
       and the embroidered tablecloths are all from an elegant bygone era.
       The food is good, if unremarkable; the service is caring and careful;
       and the prices are exceptional. ⊠ *Calle 23 (La Rampa), e/Calle B y
       Calle C,* ☎ *7/33–8150. No credit cards.*

  $ ✕ **El Bistrot.** Despite its Gallic name, this cozy little paladar serves very
       respectable criollo cuisine. The beer selection (Cristal, Lagarto, Bucanero)
       perfectly accompanies such local delicacies as *mixto cubano* (a mixed
       bag of Cuban dishes), platanos a puñetazos, and mariquitas. The ter-
       race offers dramatic views of waves crashing into the Malecón. ⊠ *Calle
       K, e/Calle 7 y Malecón,* ☎ *7/32–2708. No credit cards. No lunch.*

  $ ✕ **La Optima Instancia.** If you duck into the driveway just six blocks
       up Calle 23 (La Rampa) from the Parque Coppelia, you'll find a spi-
       ral staircase leading through a thicket of bougainvillea. Upon ascend-
       ing it, you'll enter the equally junglelike interior of a private house for
       an outstanding criollo meal. Menu choices include *masas de cerdo con
       mojo criollo* (pork morsels with criollo sauce) and *cordero estofado
       con vegetales* (lamb and vegetable stew). Try a typical criollo dessert
       of *casco de guayaba* (guava paste) or *mermelada de mango* (mango
       marmalade), both served *con queso* (with cheese). ⊠ *Calle D 557, e/Calle
       23 (La Rampa) y Calle 25,* ☎ *7/31–1007. No credit cards.*

Miramar

$$$-$$$$ ✕ **Ranchón.** This Miramar standby is noteworthy for its open-air
       atmosphere and its bargain-price specials. Chef Juan Luis Rosales's strong
       suits are grilled lobster and roast pork or chicken (occasionally he also
       finds some lamb). The wine list is only mediocre; stick with beer,
       which accompanies Cuban food extremely well. ⊠ *Av. 5, esquina de
       Calle 16,* ☎ *7/24–1185. MC, V.*

$$$-$$$$ ✕ **Tocororo.** Depending on who you read, this one-time winner is ei-
       ther the Caribbean's best restaurant or its worst. It may not be Euro-
       pean perfect, but it's Cuban pluperfect. Don't hesitate to come here
       for good, although somewhat overpriced, criollo fare. ⊠ *Calle 18 y
       Calle 3,* ☎ *7/24–2209. MC, V.*

$$$ ✕ **Don Cangrejo.** Shrimp, crab, lobster, grouper, snapper—every type
★ of seafood available in the Antilles seems to find its way through this
bustling kitchen. The ambience is relaxed, and the service is quick and
friendly. But what's the rush? With a location overlooking the Straits
of Florida, you can easily—and happily—while away an afternoon here.
⊠ *Av. 1, e/Calle 16 y Calle 18,* ☎ *7/24–4169. MC, V.*

$$–$$$ ✕ **El Aljibe.** The criollo fare here is beyond reproach; it is also reasonably
★ priced and served professionally and gracefully. The place is always filled
to the brim with clued-in diners who appear to be having the time of
their lives: a sure sign of a winner. The roast chicken served in a cit-
rus and meat sauce is the dish of choice, at once dark and tangy. The
accompanying *papas* (fried potatoes), mariquitas, and frijoles negros
are about as good as they can be. ⊠ *Av. 7, e/Calle 24 y Calle 26,* ☎
7/24–1584. MC, V.

$$–$$$ ✕ **La Ferminia.** The grilled prawns and the *pargo* (grouper) are staples
at this open-air restaurant. Members of the better-than-average staff serve
you at tables scattered about the patio and garden of a large private
house. ⊠ *Av. 5, e/Calle 182 y Calle 184,* ☎ *7/33–6786. MC, V.*

$–$$ ✕ **Dos Gardenias.** This restored colonial mansion is filled with various
★ restaurants, all of which offer solid international and criollo dishes at
reasonable prices. The downstairs Fonda de Maravillas, a garden enclave,
is particularly good. ⊠ *Av. 7 y Calle 26,* ☎ *7/33–2353. MC, V.*

LODGING

Let your interests dictate where you stay. If you love history, pick a hotel
in La Habana Vieja or Centro. If you like to play until the wee hours,
Vedado offers a midtown Manhattan atmosphere with plenty of nightlife.
If you seek peaceful sea breezes, consider staying in Miramar. If you
can't decide, head for the Hotel Nacional: it's set in an historical, early
20th-century Vedado enclave that's close to all the night-time action,
yet offers the peace and quiet of gardens and a waterfront location.

Lodging in private houses is highly recommended but difficult to arrange in advance. Any taxi driver can take you directly to a friend or
family member with rooms to rent, but you should check the place out
carefully before making a deal. Since laws in Cuba change overnight,
the rental of private rooms, now legal, could be illegal by tomorrow.
Ask at the airport hotel reservation desk.

Nearly all the government-operated hotels take credit cards as long as
they aren't affiliated with U.S. banks or companies. For price categories,
see Lodging *in* Smart Travel Tips A to Z.

La Habana Vieja

$$$$ 🏨 **Hotel Florida.** Joaquín Gómez, a wealthy merchant, built this man-
★ sion in 1835. It was later converted into a bank and has recently been
lavishly restored and transformed into a hotel under the supervision
of Habaguanex, the government consortium that's developing and
restoring Habana Vieja. Geared for business travelers, the guest rooms
and facilities (including the communications network) are outstanding. ⊠ *Calle Obispo 252,* ☎ *7/62–4127,* 𝔽𝔸𝕏 *7/62–4117. 21 rooms, 4
suites. Restaurant, bar, air-conditioning, minibars, meeting room, parking (fee). MC, V.*

$$$$ 🏨 **Hotel Santa Isabel.** This 17th-century building is so stately that the
★ Counts of Santovenia made it their home during the late 19th century.
Today, it's Habana Vieja's most charming hotel, whose guest rooms
all have Spanish colonial furniture and period accent pieces. A stay in
the east wing might get you a view of the port and El Morro; the west

wing looks out over the historic Plaza de Armas. As befits such a fine establishment, the staff is highly professional. ⊠ *Plaza de Armas, Calle Baratillo 9,* ☎ *7/33–8201,* FAX *7/33–8391. 27 rooms. Restaurant, bar, air-conditioning, minibars, pool. MC, V.*

$$$–$$$$ ★ 🏨 **Hostal El Comendador.** Before becoming the home of Don Pedro Regalado Pedroso y Zayas in 1801, this historic building—one of the earliest in the original town of San Cristóbal de La Habana—served as a cabildo, a jailhouse, a butcher shop, and then a fish market. It's now an intimate hotel hideaway overlooking Havana harbor. Rooms are tastefully restored and have many modern amenities. ⊠ *Calle Obrapía 55,* ☎ *7/57–1037,* FAX *7/33–5628. 14 rooms. Breakfast room, bar, snack bar, wine shop, air-conditioning, minibars, shop. MC, V.*

$$$–$$$$ 🏨 **Hostal Conde de Villanueva.** Set in a 19th-century house that once belonged to a Spanish financier, this is a far cry from your typical hostel. It was designed as a cigar-aficionado enclave (there's an on-site smoke shop and cigar club, with leather chairs, special lockers for important guests, and cigar-related information and memorabilia), and the theme throughout is a nod to the Vuelta Abajo, the western Cuba region where the world's finest leaves grow. The restaurant, Vuelta Abajo (☞ Dining, *above*), specializes in dishes from Pinar del Río and Viñales. Rooms are impeccable, comfortable, and spacious; the central Habana Vieja location is ideal. ⊠ *Calle Mercaderes 202,* ☎ *7/62–9293,* FAX *7/62–9294. 9 rooms. Restaurant, bar, air-conditioning, minibars. MC, V.*

$$$–$$$$ ★ 🏨 **Hostal San Miguel.** Carrara marble floors, intricate plaster carvings, and rich woodwork throughout make this hotel one of Habaguanex's best La Habana Vieja restoration projects. Built in the mid-19th century, the house was bought in 1923 by Antonio San Miguel, who financed some of the building's eclectic architectural features. The belle epoque–style decor, the creature comforts, and the modern facilities guarantee your stay here will be pleasant. ⊠ *Calle de Cuba 52,* ☎ *7/ 33–8694,* FAX *7/33–8697. 10 rooms. Breakfast room, bar, air-conditioning, minibars, library. MC, V.*

$$$–$$$$ ★ 🏨 **Hostal del Tejadillo.** Just a block from the harbor, a few steps from the cathedral, and very near La Bodeguita del Medio, this 18th-century mansion has an ideal location. Although rooms are equipped with many modern amenities, they're more like those in a private colonial estate than a hotel. Decorative details include Spanish ceramic tiles, wrought-iron grates, and lathed-wood trim. ⊠ *Calle Tejadillo 12,* ☎ *7/63–7283,* FAX *7/63–8830. 28 rooms, 2 suites, 2 minisuites. Breakfast room, snack bar, air-conditioning, minibars, shop. MC, V.*

$$$ ★ 🏨 **Hotel Ambos Mundos.** One of the first (and most successful) of Habaguanex's restoration projects, this charming establishment is just around the corner from the Plaza de Armas and the Palacio de los Capitanes Generales. Rooms are small but cozy, and the hotel is very well equipped for everything from business meetings to honeymoons. If you're a Hemingway fan, visit his corner room, No. 511, where an expert guide will tell you anything you want to know about Papa. ⊠ *Calle Obispo 153,* ☎ *7/66–9530,* FAX *7/66–9532. 52 rooms, 3 suites. Restaurant, bar, air-conditioning, minibars, baby-sitting, meeting rooms. MC, V.*

$$ ★ 🏨 **Hostal Valencia.** In a joint Spanish-Cuban effort, this 18th-century mansion has been lovingly restored. Although the bougainvillea-draped central patio is more reminiscent of Seville and Andalusia, the theme is Valencia, and each room is named for a Valencian village or town. (Request the Morella Room, which has a private rooftop patio). Ceiling fans keep the air moving, but the lack of air-conditioning can be a problem. Following the eastern Spanish theme, the on-site restaurant is known for (and named for) its paella (☞ Dining, *above*). ⊠ *Calle de los Oficios 53,* ☎ *7/62–3801,* FAX *7/33–5628. 12 rooms. Restaurant, bar, shop. MC, V.*

$–$$ ▣ **Convento de Santa Clara.** Although this beautiful 17th-century
★   building, a former convent, is officially a Residencia Académica for students, the management accepts other guests if there's space. Rooms,
some of which are dormitory style, all have wood-beam ceilings and
ceiling fans; the lack of air-conditioning, TVs, and other modern amenities is offset by the Habana Vieja location, the elegantly authentic
atmosphere, and the reasonable rates. As the convent is also a gallery,
its doors are patrolled at all hours. ⊠ *Calle Cuba 610,* ☎ *7/61–3335,*
FAX *7/33–5696. 9 rooms (2 doubles, 3 triples, 3 quadruples, and a
room for 6). Restaurant, bar. No credit cards.*

Centro Habana

$$$$ ▣ **Hotel Saratoga.** Constructed in 1879 to house shops, restaurants,
★   and living spaces, recent restoration work has transformed this building into an elegant hotel. The old and the new blend seamlessly here,
and there are plenty of comforts and services. The location is pivotal:
the 19th-century, neoclassical facade overlooks the Paseo del Prado,
El Capitolio, and the Parque de la Fraternidad. ⊠ *Paseo de Martí (Prado),
esquina de Calle Dragones,* ☎ *7/33–8694,* FAX *7/33–8697. 100 rooms.
2 restaurants, 2 bars, air-conditioning, minibars, pool, exercise room.
MC, V.*

$$$–$$$$ ▣ **Hotel Telégrafo.** This architectural hodgepodge built between 1886
★   and 1888 was once the home of the Helados de Paris ice cream par-
lor, the Café Continental, and the Hotel Americano. Recent renova-
tions have given the hotel modern, elegantly appointed rooms. The
location, on the border of La Habana Vieja and Centro Habana, is clas-
sic. ⊠ *Paseo de Martí (Prado) 408,* ☎ *7/33–8694,* FAX *7/33–8697. 4
rooms, 9 suites. Restaurant, snack bar, air-conditioning, minibars.
MC, V.*

$$$ ▣ **Hotel Inglaterra.** In 1958, when Graham Greene last visited Havana,
★   he stayed at this landmark hotel, the city's oldest. At first glance the
wood decor makes the place seem foreboding; give your eyes a chance
to adjust, however, as there's much to admire (note especially the
lobby's intricate Andalusian–Moorish tile work). Rooms are gloomy,
but they seem more "real" than those in the glass-and-steel high-rises
of today. The ground floor Gran Café del Louvre is a great people-watching spot, and the sights of Centro and La Habana Vieja are just a short
walk away. ⊠ *Paseo de Martí (Prado) 416,* ☎ *7/33–8593,* FAX *7/33–
8524. 83 rooms. Restaurant, bar, air-conditioning, shop, cabaret, parking (fee). MC, V.*

$$$ ▣ **Hotel Plaza.** There's something charming about the Plaza, despite
its cavernous, tourist-packed hallway. Although its rooms aren't very
distinguished, the early 20th-century Spanish architecture has inspir-
ing overtones of pre–Civil War Madrid. This hotel is no Madrid Ritz,
but, with its full range of services and facilities, it will do in early 21st-
century Havana. A stay here gets you pool privileges at the Hotel
Sevilla (☞ *below*). ⊠ *Calle Agramonte (Zulueta) 267,* ☎ *7/33–8583,*
FAX *7/33–8591. 188 rooms. Restaurant, bar, air-conditioning, billiards,
cabaret. MC, V.*

$$$ ▣ **Hotel Sevilla.** The setting for several episodes in Graham Greene's
Our Man in Havana, this hotel is right on the edge of La Habana Vieja.
Although it has a pleasant, clublike atmosphere and an appealing gar-
den surrounding its swimming pool, its rooms are small and disap-
pointing. The view from the rooftop restaurant is better than the food.
⊠ *Calle Trocadero 55,* ☎ *7/33–8560,* FAX *7/33–8582. 188 rooms.
Restaurant, bar, air-conditioning, minibars, pool. MC, V.*

$$$ 🏨 **Parque Central.** Part of the Dutch Golden Tulip chain, this hotel, which is right on the park for which it is named, offers creature comforts as well as a convenient location. Although more modern—and, hence, not as charming as other area hotels—it has generally spacious, well-equipped rooms. The pool area, bar, and restaurant are lively. If you like cigars, you'll appreciate the on-site cigar shop and club. ⊠ *Calle Neptuno, e/Paseo de Martí (Prado) y Calle Agramonte (Zulueta),* ☎ *7/66–6627,* FAX *7/66–6630. 281 rooms. Restaurant, bar, air-conditioning, minibars, pool. MC, V.*

$$ 🏨 **Hotel Deauville.** Most people agree that the building in which this hotel is set is Havana's second ugliest structure (the Russian Embassy, ironically, is considered the ugliest). A stay here, however, means you won't spend much time looking at it; indeed, the views (of the city and the Straits of Florida) *from* it are terrific. Further, as it's such a good deal, the clientele is usually an interesting collection of students, professors, and the occasional writer. ⊠ *Av. Italia (Galiano) 1,* ☎ *7/33–8148,* FAX *7/33–8213. 148 rooms. Restaurant, bar, air-conditioning, pool, cabaret. MC, V.*

$ 🏨 **Hotel Caribbean.** Don't expect too much from this budget option on the La Habana Vieja–Centro Habana border. Although it's no Shangri-la it does have recently (1997) renovated rooms with air-conditioning, TVs, and private baths. Top floor rooms are the best. ⊠ *Paseo de Martí (Prado) 164,* ☎ *7/33–8233,* FAX *7/33–8210. 40 rooms. Restaurant, coffee shop, air-conditioning. MC, V.*

Vedado

$$$$ 🏨 **Hotel Meliá Cohiba.** Part of the Spanish Meliá chain, this mammoth glass-and-steel hotel looms over the western end of the Malecón and has very little to do with the Havana of baroque churches and colonial palaces. It does a superb job of providing efficient service and support for executives on the move. The staff—from the bellhops and busboys to the receptionists and concierges—is highly professional, and everything in the place functions impeccably. ⊠ *Calle Paseo, e/Calle 1 y Calle 3,* ☎ *7/33–3636,* FAX *7/33–4555. 342 rooms, 120 suites. 4 restaurants, 3 bars, air-conditioning, room service, pool, shops, cabaret, parking (fee). MC, V.*

$$$$ 🏨 **Hotel Nacional.** Officially the Hotel Nacional de Cuba, this elegant
★   establishment elicits nostalgia for the bad old days. Filled with memorabilia of such famous (and infamous) guests as Winston Churchill, Ava Gardner, Frank Sinatra, and Meyer Lansky—who ran casinos here during the Batista regime—the Nacional still buzzes. Although guest rooms are disappointing, and the service is only fair, the Vista al Golfo (Gulf View) bar is a great place for a mojito, as is the patio with its gracious columns. Invariably there's a hot trio playing son, the perfect accompaniment to the movements of visitors from all over the world as they wander in and out of this national monument. ⊠ *Calle O y Calle 21,* ☎ *7/33–3562,* FAX *7/33–5054. 434 rooms, 16 suites. 2 restaurants, 2 bars, air-conditioning, minibars, 2 pools, cabaret, parking (fee). MC, V.*

$$$ 🏨 **Habana Riviera.** Although it's large, impersonal *and* inefficient, the Riviera is home to El Palacio de la Salsa, one of Havana's best music venues. The top groups all perform here, and the place goes disco the moment they stop. If you end up staying here, take comfort in the fact that Esther Williams and Ginger Rogers once splashed about the pool and the notion that your bed is crawling distance from the city's hottest dance floor. ⊠ *Calle Paseo y Malecón,,* ☎ *7/33–4051,* FAX *7/33–3739. 330 rooms. 2 restaurants, 2 bars, air-conditioning, minibars, pool, shops, dance club, parking (fee). MC, V.*

$$$ 🏨 **Hotel Capri.** At first glance, this high-rise doesn't seem very distinguished. But look again, and you'll understand why this was once the mob's favorite Havana hangout. Rooms are spacious and tastefully decorated, and the service is more personal than that at the Capri's more famous neighbors. You can bask in the afternoon sun beside the attractive rooftop pool; have a dinner of decent Italian fare at La Terraza Florentina (☞ Dining, *above*); and end the day dancing to hot salsa at the Salon Rojo disco. ⊠ *Calle 21, e/Calle N y Calle O*, ☎ 7/33–3747, ℻ 7/33–3750. *183 rooms, 12 suites, 10 triples, 10 duplexes. 2 restaurants, 2 bars, breakfast room, air-conditioning, minibars, pool, shops, dance club, parking (fee). MC, V.*

$$$ 🏨 **Hotel Habana Libre.** Originally the Havana Hilton, this high-rise monster is, at least, easy to find. Rooms are functional and modern; some offer panoramic sea views. The restaurants and bars are always abuzz, and some of Cuba's best musicians play at the rooftop Turqino disco (the vistas from here are stunning, especially at dawn). The location puts you in the municipal nerve center: Calle 23 (La Rampa) slopes right down to the Malecón, Parque Coppelia's ice cream emporium is just across the way, and the Universidad de la Habana is a five-minute walk east. ⊠ *Calle 23 (La Rampa) y Calle L*, ☎ 7/33–4011, ℻ 7/33–3141. *547 rooms. 3 restaurants, 3 bars, air-conditioning, minibars, pool, shops, dance club, parking (fee). MC, V.*

$$–$$$ 🏨 **Hotel Victoria.** Just a few blocks from the Malecón, this hotel may be modest but it has much to recommend it. It's one of Vedado's few intimate establishments. Its rooms are small but well equipped, it has a passable restaurant, and you can't help but make a new friend or two at its pocket-size swimming pool. The Victoria's clientele tends to return faithfully, so reserve well in advance. ⊠ *Calle 19 y Calle M*, ☎ 7/33–3510, ℻ 7/33–3109. *31 rooms. Restaurant, bar, air-conditioning, pool. No credit cards.*

$$ 🏨 **Hotel Colina.** Set on and named for the famous hill at the university, Colina has a semi-squalid, mid-century charm and a drop or two of student (read: revolutionary) chic that seems to attract a predominately French clientele. Rooms are small and humbly furnished, but you can't beat the atmosphere and convenient location. ⊠ *Calle L, No. 502, esquina de Calle 27*, ☎ 7/32–3535, ℻ 7/32–0317. *75 rooms. Restaurant, bar, air-conditioning. MC, V.*

Miramar

$$$$ 🏨 **Hotel Meliá Habana.** Despite this hotel's enormity, the staff succeeds in making you feel as if they know you're here and they care how you're getting along. The decor here is minimalist (bordering on the sterile), but rooms are clean and well maintained. The various swimming pools (the view of the Gulf of Mexico is terrific from the ocean-side pool) and the private beach make this a refreshing place to unwind after a few hours of sightseeing. ⊠ *Av. 3, e/Calle 76 y Calle 80*, ☎ 7/24–8500, ℻ 7/24–9505. *405 rooms, 4 suites. 3 restaurants, 2 bars, air-conditioning, minibars, 3 pools, beach, shops, cabaret, parking (fee). MC, V.*

$$$–$$$$ 🏨 **Chateau Miramar.** If you're looking for a small, intimate, Miramar hotel, this is a viable option. Although its rooms have a somewhat antiseptic decor, the place is so close to the Gulf of Mexico that sea spray reaches the windows; rooms on the Gulf side have wonderful terraces overlooking the water. ⊠ *Av. 1 y Calle 62*, ☎ 7/24–1951, ℻ 7/24–0224. *41 rooms, 9 suites. Restaurant, bar, air-conditioning, minibars, pool, parking (fee). MC, V.*

$$$–$$$$ 🏨 **Hotel Comodoro.** Although popular with package tours, the Comodoro isn't as impersonal as you might expect from a hotel with a thousand or so guests. Quarters here are in modern rooms or condo-

minium bungalows, and there's a private beach as well as a pool. Its amenities and location are both a blessing and a curse: you may be tempted to stay on the grounds—remaining cool, comfortable, and collected—rather than taking yet another taxi to Habana Vieja or Vedado. If that's your inclination, you might as well be in Miami or Acapulco. ✉ *Av. 1 y Calle 84,* ☎ *7/24–5551,* ℻ *7/24–2028. 257 rooms, 301 bungalows. 3 restaurants, 2 bars, air-conditioning, minibars, pool, beach, shops, dance club, parking (fee). MC, V.*

$$$ 🏨 **Hotel Mirazul.** "Mirazul" means "blue view," an appropriate name for this hotel. It's in a stately, blue, early 20th-century *palacete* (town house) once owned by the heirs of the Partagás cigar dynasty. Each room has a different shape and decor; all are equipped with everything from cable TV to air-conditioning. The bathrooms deserve rave reviews for their original design. Although this hotel is far from La Habana Vieja, its rates are reasonable for the level of comfort it offers. ✉ *Av. 5, e/Calle 36 y Calle 40,* ☎ *7/33–0088,* ℻ *7/33–0045. 45 rooms. Restaurant, bar, air-conditioning, minibars, pool. MC, V.*

Playas del Este

$$ 🏨 **Hotel Itabo.** Hidden away on the lagoon formed by the estuary of the Río Itabo, this is generally thought of as the best of the Playas del Este's generally mediocre hotels. Bungalows containing rooms are set around the well-regarded restaurant (a thatch-roof, bohío-style structure) and the large swimming pool. ✉ *Laguna Itabo, Playa Santa María del Mar y Playa Boca Ciega,* ☎ *7/97–1520,* ℻ *7/97–1519. 50 bungalows. Restaurant, bar, air-conditioning, pool, dance club. MC, V.*

$$ 🏨 **Hotel Tropicoco.** This Soviet-style concrete monolith is a rabbit warren of German and Italian tour groups whose members definitely haven't come to admire Havana's colonial architecture. Although it's adequately equipped, you should avoid the Tropicoco unless you're looking for a tropical frat-house-party experience. ✉ *Av. Sur y Av. de la Terrazas, Playa Santa María del Mar,* ☎ *7/33–8040,* ℻ *7/33–5158. 188 rooms. Restaurant, bar, air-conditioning, dance club. MC, V.*

$$ 🏨 **Villa Jibacoa Loma.** Set on a promontory overlooking the mouth of the Río Jibacoa and the beach, this hotel offers stone bungalows in various sizes and shapes. The views are excellent, and the prices are soothing. Some guest quarters have kitchens; all are well cared for and clean. ✉ *Playa Jibacoa (at bridge across from campground),* ☎ *7/83–3316,* ℻ *7/33–0045. 33 bungalows. 2 restaurants, pool, horseback riding, dance club. MC, V.*

NIGHTLIFE AND THE ARTS

Music is a Cuban passion rivaled only by baseball and the Revolution itself. *Everyone* here knows who El Médico de la Salsa (The Salsa Doctor) is and what type of music he plays. The Van Van, Beny Moré, and Compay Segundo are all celebrities on the order of Frank Sinatra, the Beatles, or Elvis. Caribbean, Spanish, African, and American rhythms have been combined to create more than three dozen musical styles, which are themselves evolving into still more varieties. To experience the music is to learn about it, and Havana offers plenty of opportunities for both. The city also has splashy cabaret revues as well as jazz haunts and cafés that offer quiet entertainment.

Dance performances—from traditional ballet to traditional Afro-Cuban—are also options. If your Spanish is good, you'll appreciate the active film, theater, and literary scene. You don't need any Spanish to enjoy the art exhibited in Havana's many galleries. Attire at theaters and other venues ranges from cocktail dresses and jackets and ties to blue jeans and shorts. Tickets are nearly always available (check with your hotel concierge) at box offices and are very inexpensive by European or North American standards.

Cartelera, a Spanish-English weekly published by the Instituto Cubano del Libro and usually available for free at major hotels, lists concerts, plays, and other artistic events. *Opciones* is another bilingual weekly publication with cultural listings. The *Programación Cultural,* published monthly in Spanish by the Oficina del Historiador de la Ciudad (Office of the City Historian), has what is probably the most complete schedule of events. Ask for a copy at Museo de la Ciudad in the Plaza de Armas.

Nightlife

Bars and Cafés

Bar Dos Hermanos (⊠ Av. Carlos Manuel de Céspedes/Av. del Puerto y Calle Sol, La Habana Vieja, ☎ 7/61–1221). At what was once a Hemingway haunt, you can drink with the locals and get the feel of life along the wharf.

Café Cantante "Mi Habana" (⊠ Calle Paseo y Calle 39, Vedado, ☎ 7/33–5713). On the upper edge of Vedado, near the Plaza de la Revolución, this café often has live music and dance or comedy shows.

Café Paris (⊠ Calle San Ignacio 22, esquina de Calle Obispo, La Habana Vieja), ☎ 7/62–0466). You're usually entertained by one of the city's excellent trios at this 24-hour standby. No matter how many times you have heard "Guantanamera," these performers always give it new meaning.

Café O'Reilly (⊠ Calle O'Reilly 203, e/Calle de Cuba y Calle San Ignacio, La Habana Vieja, ☎ 7/62–0613). Here you can take a seat on a New Orleans–like, wrought-iron balcony that overlooks the street for people-watching all day and all night.

Casa de las Infusiones (⊠ Calle Mercaderes 109, esquina de Calle Obispo, La Habana Vieja, ☎ 7/61–1614). This standard meeting place for Cubans and visitors alike is quiet despite being in the middle of everything and near the Plaza de Armas. It serves "infusions" of *aguardiente* (sugarcane liquor) around the clock.

El Gato Tuerto (⊠ Calle O, e/Calle 17 y Calle 19, Vedado, ☎ 7/55–2696). Just steps from the Hotel Nacional, the recently reopened Gato offers a variety of musical entertainment in its downstairs bar.

La Lluvia de Oro (⊠ Calle Obispo 316, esquina de Calle Aguiar, La Habana Vieja, ☎ 7/62–0613). Open around the clock, this bar-café often has live music and is always full of life. It's a good starting point for a night on the town.

Monserrate (⊠ Av. de la Bélgica/Misiones/Edigio/Monserrate, esquina de Calle Obrapía, La Habana Vieja, ☎ 7/63–1260). Just across from Fidel's student-days hangout, the Castillo del Farnés (☞ Dining, *above*), this place hops 24 hours a day. There's usually a trio playing.

El Patio (⊠ Plaza de la Catedral, Calle San Ignacio 54, La Habana Vieja, ☎ 7/61–8511). You'll be hard-pressed to avoid stopping here at least once during your stay. The flow of human scenery through the square is endless.

Piano Bar La Torre (⊠ Calle 17, e/Calle M y Calle N, Vedado, ☎ 7/32–5650). Come for the giddy views and the fabulous music. Depending on the crowd, you may want to stay till the wee hours—possibly even till sunrise.

El Polvorín (⊠ Castillo de los Tres Reyes del Morro, ☎ 7/63–8295). Set as it is next to El Morro, this is an excellent place to spend an evening away from the rush of downtown Havana.

Taberna del Galeón (⊠ Plaza de Armas, Calle Obispo y Calle Baratillo, La Habana Vieja, ☎ 7/33–8061). Just off the eastern corner of the Plaza de Armas is this store where you can sample shots of rum. Afterward, head to the upstairs bar for a *puñetazo* (a punch made with rum, coffee, and mint).

Cabarets

La Cecilia (⊠ Av. 5, e/Calle 110 y Calle 112, Miramar, ☎ 7/24–1562). Here, a feather-clad chorus dances to incandescent salsa. The place goes disco between and after performances.

Habana Café (⊠ Hotel Meliá Cohiba, Calle Paseo, e/Calle 1 y Calle 3, Miramar, ☎ 7/33–3636). The show in the Hotel Meliá Cohiba (☞ Lodging, *above*) is a torrid mix of live music and dance performances and red-hot dancing, with patrons and professional dancers joining the fray.

Parisien Café (⊠ Hotel Nacional, Calle O y Calle 21, Vedado, ☎ 7/33–3564). The Hotel Nacional (☞ Lodging, *above*) is always at the center of things, so it's no surprise that the nightly performance in its café is a winner. The wild show is followed by equally wild dancing on the part of the audience.

Tropicana (⊠ Calle 72, e/Calle 43 y 45, Marianao, ☎ 7/27–9147). Havana's most famous floor show is in a district just south of Miramar. Reserve a table (this place fills up fast), a bottle of Havana Club, and a bucket of ice, and you're set for the night. More than 200 gorgeous dancers picked from Cuba's many dance troupes are guaranteed to get your attention. The cover ($40–$60 per person, depending on seating and including a drink) is astronomical for Cuba, but the lush, outdoor venue is unforgettable. Shows are held Tuesday–Sunday at 9 PM, and when they finish, the place becomes a disco.

Dance Clubs

Palacio de la Salsa (⊠ Habana Riviera, Calle Paseo, Vedado, ☎ 7/33–4051). As its name suggests, this establishment in the Habana Riviera hotel (☞ Lodging, *above*) is *the* place for salsa. Big bands, from Los Van Van (they've been together for 30 odd years, and they're still hot) to the Grupo Moncada drive audiences mad here nightly. Don't let the steep (for Cuba) $20 cover charge prevent you from spending a night on the town here.

Salon Rojo (⊠ Hotel Capri, Calle 21, e/Calle N y Calle O, Vedado, ☎ 7/33–3571). At this hot spot in the Hotel Capri (☞ Lodging, *above*), live musical entertainment and spectacle alternates with disco and participation.

Jazz Club

La Zorra y el Cuervo Club de Jazz (⊠ Calle 23/La Rampa, e/Calle N y Calle O, Vedado, ☎ 7/66–2402). An Afro-Cuban hook makes the tunes at the city's premier jazz venue unique. Unlike most of Havana's music venues, the sounds here make you snap your fingers and shake your head instead of everything else.

The Arts

Dance, Music, and Theater

Live Cuban music and dance performances are regularly held in the city's many cultural centers. Some of these also host more traditional music and dance shows as well as literary events, plays, and art exhibits. At UNEAC (☞ Vedado and Beyond *in* Exploring, *above*), for example, you can find everything from lectures to performances of Santería rituals. The Palacio del Segundo Cabo in the Plaza de Armas (☞ La Habana Vieja *in* Exploring, *above*) is another literary and artistic hub.

If your Spanish is good, try to take in a play. These are held not only in theaters and cultural centers but also in such surprising venues as the Museo de la Ciudad in the Palacio de los Capitanes Generales, the Casa Natal de José Martí, and the Museo de Arte Colonial (☞ La Habana Vieja *in* Exploring, *above*).

Havana teems with dancers. Drop by the Escuela Provincial de Ballet (Provincial Ballet School) at Calle L and Calle 19 and have a look at the 220 little swans that Silvia María Rodriguez is training. Each year 45 of 800 nine-year-old applicants begin working here. After five years, some 15 of them (and those chosen from the six other provincial schools) make it to the Escuela Nacional de Ballet (National Ballet School), currently run by Cuba's prima ballerina, Alicia Alonso. Other large dance troupes include Christi Dominguez's Compañia de Ballet de la Television Cubana (Ballet Company of the Cuban Television Network), the Compañia de Dansa Contemporánea de Cuba (Cuban Contemporary Dance Company), and the Ballet Nacional Folklórico (National Folklore Ballet). Reinaldo Suarez's Danz-Art and Regla Salvent's Compañia de Dansa del Cuerpo Armónico are among the city's many small ensembles.

CULTURAL CENTERS

Casa de África (✉ Calle Obrapía 157, e/Calle Mercaderes y Calle San Ignacio, La Habana Vieja, ☎ 7/61–5798). As its name suggests, this center specializes in Afro-Cuban music.

Casa de la Amistad (✉ Calle Paseo 406, esquina de Calle 17, Vedado, ☎ 7/30–3114). Come here for groups that perform Afro-Cuban and other traditional music.

Casa de la Comedia (✉ Calle Justiz 18, esquina de Calle Baratillo, La Habana Vieja, ☎ 7/63–9282). This center has a full and ever-changing roster of events, including Cuban music shows, that take place weekdays from 9 to 1.

Casa de la Cultura Julián del Casal (✉ Calle Aguiar 509, e/Calle Amargura y Calle Brasil/Teniente Rey, La Habana Vieja, ☎ 7/63–4860). One of the most active and authentic of the ubiquitous Casas de Cultura hosts everything from big bands, to Cuban trios, to solo singer-songwriters.

Casa 10 de Octubre (✉ Calzada de Luyanó 361, Luyanó, ☎ 7/99–0653). Just south of La Habana Vieja, this center hosts authentic performances of trova and other types of traditional Cuban music.

Casa de la Trova (✉ Calle San Lázaro 661, e/Calle Gervasio y Calle Padre Varela/Belascoaín, Centro Habana, ☎ 7/79–3373). This is a good place to hear traditional Cuban music.

Delirio Habanero (✉ Calle Paseo y Calle 39, Vedado, ☎ 7/33–5713). Not many visitors know about this hot spot despite the fact that it's a great place to hear Cuban musicians work their magic.

Dos Gardenias (✉ Av. 7 y Calle 26, Mindanao, ☎ 7/24–2353). There's almost always some type of musical event at this complex. The Bar la Tarde is open from 8:30 to 11:30; Salon Boleros operates from 11:15 on; and Jardin del Humor Dos Gardenias has comedy shows Wednesday through Sunday.

THEATERS

Gran Teatro de la Habana (✉ Paseo de Martí/Prado 458, e/Calle San Rafael y Calle San Martín/San José, Centro Habana, ☎ 7/61–3078 or 7/61–3079). Also known as the Teatro García Lorca, this theater has a spectacular baroque facade with white marble angels dancing gracefully on its four corner towers. It's a beautiful place to see opera, jazz shows, symphony performances, and plays. In addition, the National Ballet performs here under the direction of Alicia Alonso, who is now in her 80s but is still considered Cuba's premier ballerina. There are two theaters here: the **Sala García Lorca** and the **Sala Antonin Artaud,** which is known for its avant-garde theater productions.

Teatro Amadeo Roldán (⌗ Calzada, e/Calle D y Calle E, Vedado, ☎ 7/32–1168). This is the home of the Sinfónica Nacional (National Symphony), which is currently directed by the young Iván del Prado and which is much better than the ages of the musicians (who look for all the world like a high school band) would suggest. Listen to them deal with with Handel's "Water Music" or Prokofiev's 7th, especially the allegro movements.

Teatro Nacional (⌗ Plaza de la Revolución, Calle Paseo y Av. Carlos Manuel de Céspedes/Puerto, ☎ 7/79–6011). Cuba's most important theater is used for classical music and ballet performances, as well as for contemporary theater and dance productions.

Teatro Julio Antonio Mella (⌗ Calle Línea/Calle 7, No. 657, esquina de Calle A, Vedado, ☎ 7/38–6961). The home of the Danza Contemporánea de Cuba is the standard venue for contemporary theater as well as for dance.

Teatro Trianon (⌗ Calle Línea/Calle 7, e/Calle Paseo y Calle A, Vedado, ☎ 7/31–3611). This theater stages plays by contemporary playwrights.

Film

For a small, blockaded country, Cuba has a surprisingly prestigious film industry. Camilo Vives, director of the Instituto Cubano de Arte e Industria Cinematográficos (ICAIC; Cuban Institute of Art and Cinematography) predicts that Cuban filmmakers will continue to coproduce (with countries such as Spain) four or five films a year. Cubans love the cinema, and if your Spanish is good, you can join them for a night at the movies. Cubans love American movies and somehow (pirated, smuggled, loaned), such films always get here, though they're nearly always dubbed in Spanish.

The **Casa de la Poesía** (⌗ Calle Muralla 63, La Habana Vieja, ☎ 7/62–1801) has films as well as lectures and poetry readings. The **Cine Charles Chaplin** (⌗ Calle 23/La Rampa, e/Calle 10 y Calle 12, Vedado, ☎ 7/31–1101) is an extremely large movie house that shows pictures at 5 PM and 8 PM every day but Tuesday. The **Cine Payret** (⌗ Paseo de Martí/Prado 513, Centro Habana, ☎ 7/63–3163) shows American films, nearly always Westerns, beginning at 12:30 PM. Near the Parque Coppelia and its famous ice cream shop, **Cine Yara** (⌗ Calle 23/La Rampa y Calle L, Vedado, ☎ 7/32–9430) is a great favorite. It opens its doors at 12:30 PM.

The **ICAIC** (⌗ Calle 23/La Rampa 1155, e/Calle 10 y Calle 12, ☎ 7/30–5041), next to the Charles Chaplin movie house (☞ *above*), is the the Cuban film industry's central nervous system and often shows advance screenings of new Cuban releases. **La Rampa** (⌗ Calle 23/La Rampa y Calle O, Vedado, ☎ 7/78–6146) starts showing movies at 4:30 PM. **La Riviera** (⌗ Calle 23/La Rampa y Calle H, Vedado, ☎ 7/30–9564) shows Cuban and international films starting at 4:30 PM.

Painting and Sculpture

Carmen Montilla (⌗ Calle de los Oficios 162, La Habana Vieja, ☎ 7/33–8768). A $3 admission gets you in to see this patio's sculptures and other objets d'art by Cuban and international artists. It's open Tuesday–Saturday 10–5 and Sunday 9–1.

Centro de Desarrollo de las Artes Visuales (⌗ Plaza Vieja, Calle San Ignacio 352, La Habana Vieja,☎ 7/62–6295). The emphasis here is on contemporary and conceptual art by Cuban and other Latin American artists. Admission is $3, and the center is open Tuesday–Saturday 10–5.

Galería–Estudio Yanes (⌗ Calle Obrapía y Calle San Ignacio, La Habana Vieja,☎ 7/62–6195). You can stop by Tuesday–Sunday 10–5 (admission is free) to see the permanent collection of works by resident artists Orlando Yanes and his wife, Casiguaya, as well as temporary exhibits of pieces by other Cubans.

Galería Haydee Santamaría (⊠ Calle G/Av. de Presidentes 69, Vedado, ☎ 7/32–4653). Named for a fallen heroine of the 1953 attack on the Moncada Barracks, this gallery shows prints, drawings, graphics, and photographs from Cuba and throughout Latin America. It's open Monday–Saturday 10–4; admission is free.

Galería Horacio Ruiz (⊠ Palacio del Segundo Cabo, Plaza de Armas, Calle Tacón 4, La Habana Vieja, ☎ 7/32–4653). You can drop by Monday–Saturday 10–4 to see (and, perhaps, buy) leather goods, glassware, drawings, and prints made by Cuban craftspeople and artists. Admission is free.

Galería los Oficios–Nelson Dominguez (⊠ Calle de los Oficios 166, La Habana Vieja, ☎ 7/33–9804). The sculptures and paintings of Nelson Dominguez and other artists are shown in a lovely 17th-century colonial mansion and patio weekdays 10–5 and Saturday 9–2. There's no admission fee.

Galería Roberto Diago. (⊠ Plaza Vieja, Calle Muralla 107, La Habana Vieja, ☎ 7/33–8005). The patio here is as fantastic as the Afro-Cuban art. It's open Monday–Saturday 10–5 and Sunday 9–2. Admission is $3.

Galería Victor Manuel (⊠ Plaza de la Catedral, Calle San Ignacio 56, La Habana Vieja, ☎ 7/61–2955). This gallery with works by Latin American artists is almost an inevitable stop on a trip to the Plaza de la Catedral. It's open daily 9–9, and a $2 admission fee is charged.

Taller Experimental de la Gráfica (⊠ Callejón del Chorro 62, La Habana Vieja,☎ 7/61–2955). If you find yourself in the Plaza de la Catedral on a weekday between 9 and 4, head for this gallery (there's no admission fee) in a nearby alleyway for a look at graphic works by a wide range of artists, all of them Cuban.

Terracota 4 Galería-Estudio (⊠ Calle Mercaderes 156, La Habana Vieja, ☎ 7/66–9417). This gallery specializes in ceramic and terra-cotta artwork and crafts. It's open daily 10–6; admission is free.

OUTDOOR ACTIVITIES AND SPORTS

Participant Sports

Boating, Fishing, and Scuba Diving

Marina Hemingway (⊠ Calle 248 y Av. 5, Santa Fé, Playa, ☎ 7/33–1150), home of the Ernest Hemingway International Marlin Tournament each May–June, can help you to arrange fishing, yachting, diving, and snorkeling trips—regardless of your level of skill or your budget. Scuba diving costs $30 per dive, (there are discounts if you book multiple dives), and snorkeling excursions go for $20. A four-hour, deep-sea fishing outing in the Gulf Stream will cost about $250 (per boat load). Yacht rentals range from $250–$300 a day to $2,000–$3,000 a week.

July sees the Old Man and the Sea Fishing Tournament. The staff at the **Marina Tarará/Club Naútica** (⊠ Calle 5, e/Calle 2 y Calle Cobre, Tarará, Playas del Este, ☎ 7/33–5499) can fill you in on this competition. They also charter boats and run diving, snorkeling, and deep-sea fishing excursions in the Gulf Stream. Costs are slightly lower than those at the Marina Hemingway (☞ above).

Golf

The **Club de Golf Habana** (⊠ Carretera de Vento, Km 8, ☎ 7/33–8919) is a 15-minute (and roughly $15) taxi ride south of downtown Havana. Though a little rough, the course offers a good walk in the sun, and the swimming pool and Hoyo 19 bar are both good places to relax after a round. Greens fees here are $20 for 9 holes, $30 for 18 holes.

A top set of clubs rents for $10, and caddies cost $3 for 9 holes, $6 for 18 holes. If you'd like to play, call ahead to be sure there's not a tournament on.

Hiking and Horseback Riding

Cubans favor the Parque Escaleras de Jaruco, 25 km (2 mi) east of La Habana, for hiking or horseback-riding outings. Well-marked trails of varying degrees of difficulty and length wind through the park's rolling hills and along its limestone cliffs, which are full of caves and underground streams. It makes a good day trip from the city, particularly if you stop at one of the Playas del Este on the way back. From Havana, take the Autopista Nacional 15 km (9 mi) east to the turnoff for Tapaste and Jaruco. The park is 6 km (4 mi) west of Jaruco village.

Running

Although the air quality can be poor, the Malecón is a picturesque place to jog, for the human as well as for the marine scenery. The **Estadio Juan Abrahantes** (⊠ Calle Zapata y Calle G/Av. de los Presidentes, Vedado, ☎ 7/78–6959), just south of the university, has a well-groomed track-and-field complex that's open to serious runners (call ahead for details). There are also places to run (there's a $2 locker fee) at the **Ciudad Deportivo** (⊠ Av. de la Independencia/Rancho Boyeros y Vía Blanca, Palatino, ☎ 7/40–3302).

Swimming

Pools are everywhere in Havana; even the elegant Hotel Nacional allows nonguests to use its two swimming pools for a $5 fee. The **Complejo Panamericano** (⊠ Km 4.5, Av. Monumental, Villa Panamericana, ☎ 7/97–4221), which is 2 km (1 mi) east of Havana on the road to Cojímar, has the city's best Olympic pool. You can swim here for a $5 fee.

Although you'll see residents swimming off the Malecón, it's not recommended that you join them: the water quality is poor to poisonous. If you really want a beach, stay at one of the Miramar hotels that has its own private stretch. Otherwise, head to the Playas del Este.

Tennis (And More)

Club Havana (⊠ Av. 5 y Calles 188–192, Flores, Playa, ☎ 7/24–5700) is the country club that was once so exclusive that even President Fulgencio Batista was denied membership (he didn't meet the racial standards). "The Club" is still private and exclusive, but if you're quiet and well mannered (and are carrying a copy of Fodor's) the management has promised to arrange a day pass. In addition to a match on one of the four tennis courts (both clay and hard courts are available), a game of squash, a swim in the pool, a windsurfing excursion along the private beach, a massage, or some time in a sauna are also possibilities. A pass costs $10 weekdays, $15 weekends; getting a massage, indulging in a sauna, or using the tennis and squash courts will cost you $2 (each) extra. Windsurfers rent for $5 an hour.

Spectator Sports

Baseball

Cuba, a recognized baseball power, has teams capable of beating Major League U.S. clubs, as the Cuban National Team's 12–5 victory over the Baltimore Orioles (in Baltimore) amply demonstrated in May 1999. To watch Cubans play baseball is to see poetry and passion in motion. Top league teams play from December through June in the 60,000-seat **Estadio Latinoamericano** (⊠ Calle Zequeira 312, Cerro, ☎ 7/70–6526). Games are usually held Tuesday–Thursday at 8 PM, Saturday at 1:30 and 8 and Sunday at 1:30. Tickets are cheap. You may also be able to catch a game at the university's **Estadio Juan Abrahantes** (⊠ Calle Zapata y Calle G/Av. de los Presidentes, Vedado, ☎ 7/78–6959).

Boxing

You can catch a boxing match at the **Sala Polivalente Kid Chocolate** (⊠ Paseo de Martí/Prado y Calle Brasil/Teniente Rey, La Habana Vieja, ☎ 7/62–8634).

Pelota

For Basque pelota in its various forms (*pala, remonte,* or jai-alai), the **Complejo de Canchas de Pelota Vasca y Patinódromo Raul Díaz Arguelles** (⊠ Av. 26 y Av. de la Independencia/Rancho Boyeros, Palatino, ☎ 7/81–9700) is the only game in town.

SHOPPING

Until very recently, shopping lists in Cuba were short: *puros habanos* (cigars) and rum. Since the Cuban government's decision to permit the free circulation of the U.S. dollar as legal tender, things have changed somewhat—such international chain stores as Benetton have even opened.

Look for *muñequitas,* little dolls representing orishas. Handmade goods—from wood and leather items to terra-cotta pieces—cinema posters and other graphics, musical instruments, and photographs of the Revolutionary period also make interesting buys. The light-cotton men's shirt known as the *guayabera* is Cuba's national garment, worn by everyone from taxi drivers to El Comandante himself. Practical (side pockets) and elegant (embroidered), the guayabera is worn loose (not tucked in) for coolness, and is considered flattering to middle-age figures.

The state agencies ARTEX and Fondo de Bienes Culturales have shops throughout Havana that sell postcards, books, cassettes, rum, cigars, and crafts. *La Habana: Touristic and Commercial Guide,* a booklet published by Infotur, lists the locations of the city's many Tiendas Panamericanas, which sell toiletries and other basic items.

Bargaining is expected, although unlike in other countries where this is true, Cubans ask very low prices to begin with and don't move far. It generally feels better to pay the extra dollar or two. At this juncture, it means a lot more in Cuban hands than in yours.

Note: owing to the trade embargo, if you're caught bringing Cuban goods into the United States, customs could confiscate them, and you could be subject to penalties. Even Americans who are visiting Cuba with either a general or specific licence (issued by the U.S. State Department's Office of Cuban Affairs) or on a fully hosted basis, are subject to strict limitations on the total amount they're allowed to spend daily—for hotels, meals, transportation, and Cuban goods—and customs officials may ask to see receipts. For more information, *see* Americans and Cuba *in* Smart Travel Tips A to Z.

Areas and Markets

The Plaza de Armas, the Plaza de Catedral, and the Plaza Vieja are rich in shops and vendors selling crafts. At the end of Calle Empedrado, near the Catedral de la Habana and along the Parque Luz Caballero, is the **Mercado de Arte y de Artesanía de la Catedral** (⊠ Calle Tacón), a street market choked with paintings and crafts. It's open Monday–Saturday 10–7. The **crafts market** on the Malécon in Vedado is open from 9 am to dusk.

Specialty Shops

Cigars

Cuba is, of course, *the* place for cigars. The best leaves are grown here, and the world's most skilled artisans roll them into the finest of stogies. In Havana, a box of Monte Cristo A's sells for $500; the same box costs roughly $700 in Canada and as much as $900 in, say, Belgium. Never buy from the many street *jineteros* (hustlers), whose cigars are invariably of inferior quality dressed up to look like top Cohibas or Romeo y Julietas.

The three locations of the **Casa del Tabaco** (⊠ Av. 5, No. 1407, Miramar, ☎ 7/29–4040; ⊠ Calle Obispo, esquina de Calle Bernaza, La Habana Vieja, ☎ 7/63–1242; ⊠ Marina Hemingway, Calle 248 y Av. 5, Jaimanitas, ☎ 7/33–1154) make shopping for tobacco convenient. At the fascinating **Fábrica de Tabacos Partagás** (⊠ Calle Industria 520, Centro, ☎ 7/33–8060), also known as the Casa del Habano, you can see how cigars are made by hand as well as shop for them. Note, however, that the tobacco sold here can be found elsewhere at better prices. The **Palacio del Tabaco** (⊠ Calle Agramonte/Zulueta 106, La Habana Vieja, ☎ 7/33–8389) is another good bet for cigars.

Clothing

For guayaberas check out hotel shops, open-air markets, and Cuban department stores (which price things in pesos, though they accept dollars) along Calles San Rafael or Avenida de Italia (Galiano). **Acuario** (⊠ Calle San Rafael 102, Centro Habana, ☎ 7/33–8431) has a good selection of guayaberas. For women's clothing, including lovely dresses by Verano, as well as guayaberas with the coveted Pepe Antonio label, head for **La Flora** (⊠ Av. 11, esquina de Calle 6, Mindanao, ☎ 7/22–3522).

At **La Maison** (⊠ Av. 7, esquina de Calle 16, Miramar, ☎ 7/33–1543) the evening fashion shows will knock your eyes out—more for the human display than for the textiles—and the luxury clothing is on sale duty free. **Salon Galiano** (⊠ Av. de Italia/Galiano 480, Centro Habana, ☎ 7/63–1861) has a good guayabera stock.

Graphics

Centro del Desarollo de los Artes Visuales (⊠ Casa de las Hermanas Cárdenas, Plaza Vieja, La Habana Vieja, ☎ 7/62–3533) sells posters and art books. In the Casa de Juan Rico de Mata, **Fototeca de Cuba** (⊠ Plaza Vieja, Calle dos Mercaderes 307, La Habana Vieja, ☎ 7/62–2876) purveys photographs from the Revolutionary period. **Galería Exposición** (⊠ Manzana de Gómez, Calle San Rafael, Centro Habana, ☎ 7/63–8364) has prints by Cuba's best artists, and famous Revolutionary pictures and posters.

Handicrafts

In the Plaza Vieja, behind the facade with the murals, is the **Casa del Conde de Lombillo** (⊠ Calle San Ignacio 364, La Habana Vieja, ☎ 7/33–1884), where you can watch artisans make muñequitas. **La Casona** (⊠ Plaza Vieja, Calle San Ignacio y Calle Muralla, La Habana Vieja, ☎ 7/33–8005) sells a variety of crafts. For tobacco, rum, Cuban music, and all manner of crafts, don't miss the **Palacio de la Artesanía** (⊠ Calle de Cuba 10, La Habana Vieja, ☎ 7/33–8072). In addition, the colonial architecture here is superb and the mojitos are first rate.

Rum

You'll find rum in the Casas del Ron at tourist attractions all over town—from the Castillo de la Real Fuerza to El Morro across the bay. The **Taverna del Galeón** (⊠ Calle Baratillo, esquina de Calle Obispo, La

Habana Vieja), ☏ 7/33–8476), at the eastern corner of Plaza de Armas, offers free tastings of everything from Pinar del Río's Guayabito to Caribbean Club's Ron Mulata. La Taverna stocks Cuban rums of every description and even "Cuban" wines such as the dry white San Cristobal made by Italian oenologists from Chilean grapes.

Musical Instruments

Music and musical instruments can be purchased at the **Casa de la Música** (✉ Calle 20, No. 3309, Vedado, ☏ 7/33–8311). As its name suggests, the **Musica e Instrumentos Musicales** (✉ Calle 18, No. 509, Vedado, ☏ 7/24–1212) also sells music and instruments.

HAVANA A TO Z

Arriving and Departing

By Airplane

The **Aeropuerto Internacional José Martí** (☏ 7/33–5786) is a simple little air station, redolent of military airfields, 17 km (10 mi) south of Havana (via the Plaza de la Revolución and Avenida de la Independencia/Avenida Rancho Boyeros). The nearby **Terminal Aerocaribbean** (☏ 7/45–3013) serves domestic flights and those throughout the Caribbean. The **Aeropuerto Nacional** (☏ 7/45–1853), 1 km (½ mi) south of the international airport, serves domestic flights only.

Principal international carriers serving José Martí include **Aerocaribbean** (☏ 7/33–5016), **Aeroflot** (☏ 7/70–6242), **Air Canada** (☏ 7/33–5257), **Cubana de Aviación** (☏ 7/33–4949), **Iberia** (☏ 7/33–5041), and **Mexicana** (☏ 7/33–3531).

FROM THE AIRPORT

Taxis or rented cars are currently the only means of transport to and from the airports. The fare from either airport to town is about $20.

Getting Around

The streets in La Habana Vieja and Centro have been, in European fashion, given such poetic names as Amargura (Bitterness), Esperanza (Hope), or Ánimas (Souls). Note that some streets have pre- and postrevolutionary names; both are often cited on maps and are always cited in this chapter. The Vedado and Miramar districts have a New York City–style grid plan with numbered and lettered intersecting streets and avenues. As the scheme of lettering and numbering varies in these two areas, addresses routinely include district names to help avoid confusion. Throughout the city, addresses are also frequently cited as street names with numbers and/or locations, as in: "Calle Concordia, e/Calle Gervasio y Calle Escobar" or "Calle de los Oficios 53, esquina de Obrapía". It's helpful to know the following terms and abbreviations: "e/" is *entre* (between); *esquina de* (sometimes seen as "esq. de") is "corner of"; and *y* is "and".

By Bus

Havana's famous *camellos* (so-named for their humped, camel-like shape) are little more than huge tractor trailers. Lines for these 300-passenger buses are often hundreds of people long, folks are packed onto them like sardines in a can, and on-board temperatures are all but life-threatening. In addition, you need exact change (10 céntimos) to board, and most Cubans tell tales (no doubt true) of pickpockets and lost watches and jewelry. If, however, you want to experience Cuba the way Cubans do, by all means, hop a camello.

By Car

Car rentals in Cuba are expensive ($500–$600 a week), and the car you reserve may or may not be available when you arrive to pick it up. Be prepared to leave a deposit of $500 or more.

Reliable rental agencies include: **Havanautos** (✉ Aeropuerto José Martí ☎ 7/33–2891), which has offices at the airport and major hotels; **Panautos** (✉ Calle Línea/Calle 7 y Malecón, Vedado, ☎ 7/55–3298), which has offices all over Havana; **Transautos** (✉ Hotel Capri, Calle 21, e/Calle N y Calle O, Vedado ☎ 7/24–5532); and **Trans-gaviota** (✉ Aeropuerto José Martí, ☎ 7/23–7000), which rents cars with or without a driver.

Gasoline prices are about double those in North America (though probably comparable to those in the United Kingdom). **ServiCupet** (Cuba-Petroleo; ✉ Calle Paseo y Malecón, Vedado; ✉ Calle L y Calle 17, Vedado; ✉ Calle 31 y Calle 18, Miramar; ✉ Calle 41 y Calle 72, next to Hotel Tropicana, Mindanao) stations are open 24 hours a day. Another chain is **Cubalse** (✉ Av. 7 y Calle 2, Miramar; ✉ Av. 5 y Calle 120, Coco Solo; ✉ Av. 13 y Calle 84, Almendares).

By Taxi

Taxis are inexpensive by European or North American standards, and you can grab them from in front of hotels, hail them on the streets, or call them. Although they have meters, a pre-trip negotiation of the fare is the norm. Official taxis are often Hyundais, Mercedes, or Russian-made Ladas. Around Parque Central, you may still find American-made, 1950s vehicles. *Cuentapropistas* (privateers) offer their services everywhere, especially along Calle 23 (La Rampa) in Vedado. Ciclo-taxis (bicycle rickshaws) are breezy, slow, offer a scenic ride, and cost about the same as auto taxis. Coco-taxis (motor scooter–powered conveyances) are another option. Always negotiate the price before you get in any type of cab. The fare from Vedado to La Habana Vieja is about $3; from Miramar it's about $5.

Official taxi companies include **Fenix** (☎ 7/63–9720), **Gaviota** (☎ 7/33–1730), **Micar** (☎ 7/24–2444), **Panataxi** (☎ 7/55–5555), **Taxis OK** (☎ 7/24–9518), and **Turistaxi** (☎ 7/33–5539).

Contacts and Resources

Embassies

Canada (✉ Calle 30, No. 518, Miramar, ☎ 7/33–2516). **Switzerland** (✉ Av. 5, No. 2005, Miramar, ☎ 7/33–2611). **United Kingdom** (✉ Calle 34, No. 708, Miramar, ☎ 7/33–1771).

Americans in serious trouble can contact the **U.S. Interests Section** (✉ Calzada, e/Calle L y Calle M, ☎ 7/32–0551), although given its mission in Cuba (to protect U.S. interests, not U.S. citizens flouting the embargo), don't expect them to roll out the carpet. Of course, all of this may change in the near future.

Emergencies

Ambulance: 40–5093. **Fire:** 81–1115. **Highway assistance: Cubalse** (☎ 7/33–6558). **Hospital: Clinica Central de Atención a Extranjeros Cira García** (✉ Calle 20, No. 4101, Mindanao, ☎ 7/24–2811), just across the Río Almendares and in a district near Miramar, is dedicated to medical care for foreigners. Considered the best hospital in Havana, the clinic handles emergencies expertly and pleasantly and expects payment in dollars. **Pharmacy: Servimed Internacional** (✉ Av. 41, esquina de Calle 20, Mindanao, ☎ 7/24–2051), part of the Clinica Cira García, is the pharmacy to use; it's open 24 hours a day. **Police:** 7/82–0116.

Asistur (✉ Paseo Martí/Prado 254, Centro Habana, ☎ 7/62–5519) specializes in helping tourists in trouble. They can handle anything from insurance claims and lost luggage to repatriation of the deceased.

Health and Safety

Locals call the *almacigo* tree the "tourist tree" owing to its red, peeling bark (and its bulging trunk), a nod to Cuba's greatest health risk: the Caribbean sun. Use plenty of sunscreen. Make sure that fruit is thoroughly washed and/or peeled before eating it. Although Cuban lobsters are beyond reproach, clams and mussels are suspect. Bottled water is a must outside of Havana.

Cuban physicians are well trained and numerous. Though health care is free for Cubans, visitors are required to pay (in dollars) for medicines and services.

Official figures on AIDS place Cuba among the world's least affected countries, but the recent boom in sexual tourism and prostitution makes Cuba a high-risk zone. Bring your own protection; Cuba's Chinese-made condoms are notoriously crude and cumbersome, and higher-quality imported condoms are sold at extortionist prices. Women traveling alone can expect to get plenty of attention, though no dangerous hassling. Even so, walking solo through unlit Centro Habana would be a bad idea. Muggings and petty crime are rare in Cuba, though not unheard of. Although official policies have eased up on the persecution of gays and lesbians, same-sex couples should still be extremely discreet in public.

Telephones and Mail

The area code for Havana is 7. Plan to have some problems communicating electronically with the outside world during your stay in Cuba. Direct-dial phones work well in most hotel rooms, but the rates are beyond scandalous (around $10 per minute for international calls). The cheapest way to make local and long-distance calls is from public phone booths using a prepaid $10 or $20 phone card. You can buy them in hotels, tourist shops, and at the Intertel booths around town (there's one at the corner of Calle 23/La Rampa and Calle N, about midway between the Hotel Habana Libre and the Hotel Nacional). Frequently, however, they're out of stock.

Post offices are scarce, though most hotels have letter boxes and sell stamps. Letters and postcards to North America and Europe cost less than $1. The best post office is in La Habana Vieja's Plaza San Francisco de Asis. In Vedado there's one at the corner of Calle 23 (La Rampa) and Calle 12. At press time, letters were known to take three to four weeks to reach destinations outside Cuba.

Tour Operators and Travel Agencies

Cubatur (✉ Calle F, No. 157, e/Calle 9 y Calzada, Vedado, ☎ 7/33–4155) is the island's most important travel agency. The very professional staff can help you make arrangements for anything from a guided tour to a table at the Tropicana. Cubatur's office in the Hotel Nacional is a good place to know about. The staff at **Havanatur** (✉ Calle 2, No. 17, e/Av. 1 y Av. 3, Miramar, ☎ 7/24–2161) does it all—from excursions to car rentals to plane tickets. Havanatur also has an office in the Hotel Habana Libre.

Paradiso (✉ Calle 19, No. 560, esquina de Calle C, Vedado, ☎ 7/32–9538) is a small company that offers guided tours and cultural trips of all kinds. The Vaivén is a tourist bus (with a guide) that passes Havana's most important sights, from El Morro to the Palacio de Convenciones. It circulates every 35 minutes, has 23 stops (including the

Hotel Nacional, the Hotel Habana Libre, El Capitolio, and the Necrópolis de Cristóbal Colón), and operates 8:45 AM–10 PM. You can buy tickets at **Rumbos Travel Agencies** (⊠ Calle 23/La Rampa y Calle P, Vedado, ☎ 7/33–4634 or 7/66–9713 to Vaivén for information).

Visitor Information

Cuba Autrement (⊠ Lonja del Comercio, Plaza San Francisco de Asis, La Habana Vieja ☎ FAX 7/66–9874) can recommend lodging in private homes and provide cultural and general information. **Infotur** (⊠ Calle Obispo 63 y Calle San Ignacio, La Habana Vieja, ☎ 7/63–6884; ⊠ Av. 5 y Calle 112, Miramar, ☎ 7/24–3977) has several convenient locations. It's a little far from the center of town, but the **Oficina de Turismo de La Habana/El Palacio del Turismo** (⊠ Calle 28, No. 303, e/Av. 3 y Av. 5, Miramar ☎ 7/24–0624) is a good place to get your bearings. Although **Roots & Culture** (⊠ Hotel Colina, Calle L, No. 502, esquina de Calle 27, Vedado, ☎ 7/55–4005) caters primarily to French tourists, the staff is eager to advise visitors from anywhere on private lodging options, paladares, and cultural events.

3 WESTERN CUBA

From the remote strands of María la Gorda at Cuba's western tip to the urban sprawl of Varadero's smooth white beaches, from the southern Archipiélago de los Canarreos to the vertebral Cordillera de Guaniguanico—western Cuba holds a wide range of geographical treasures. The Valle de Viñales and its limestone hillocks, Vuelta Abajo and its tobacco plantations, and the wetlands of the Península de Zapata are unforgettable Cuban nuggets to discover and explore.

By George
Semler

WESTERN CUBA'S THREE PROVINCES of Matanzas, Havana (outside the capital), and Pinar
del Río, along with the Municipio Especial
(Special Municipality) Isla de la Juventud, offer attractions that range
from the tobacco plantations of Viñales to the cosmopolitan beaches
of Varadero to the wilds of crocodile country on the Península de Zapata. In addition, pristine beaches and nonpareil diving opportunities
can be found off—among other spots—Cayo Levisa, the Península de
Guanahacabibes, and Cayo Largo.

Pinar del Río Province is Cuba's prime tobacco-growing country;
there's a cigar-rolling factory to visit, and there are numerous plantations to explore. The Valle de Viñales (Viñales Valley) and the curious
mogotes form some of Cuba's most spectacular countryside. These free-
standing limestone formations from the Jurassic era are surrounded
by *hoyos* (holes), valleys or depressions filled with rich red soil ideal
for the cultivation of tobacco. Far to the west, the Península de Guanahacabibes is a UNESCO-funded nature preserve on the Straits of Yucatán and a haven for nearly every kind of wildlife in the Antilles.

En route to Pinar del Río Province, the province of Havana offers little in the way of distraction. The pastel-columned town of Artemisa
and its Museo de Historia (featuring the two dozen Artemisa revolutionaries who died in the 1953 Moncada attack) are the more interesting sights, outside of the capital. Mariel, site of the 1980 boat lift
that sent 120,000 Cubans to Florida, is an industrial port dominated
by Cuba's largest cement factory.

Matanzas Province stretches east and south of its eponymous capital
city, which is often called the "Athens of Cuba" for its onetime artistic and literary prestige. Just west of the city, the Valle de Yumurí, drained
by the Río Yumurí (Yumurí River), is a rich basin of sugarcane plantations surrounded by rolling hills. To the east of the city is Cuba's premier beach resort—Varadero, a sandy sin city studded with about
two-thirds of Cuba's hotels. On the slender Península de Hicacos, Varadero has its own international airport, two yacht marinas, a golf course,
several torrid discotheques and cabarets, and miles of silver sands. The
town of Cárdenas, just east of Varadero, is known for its hundreds of
horse-drawn carriages.

The Isla de la Juventud is the largest island in the Archipiélago de los
Canarreos, south of the Cuban mainland. Known mainly for the diving off Punta Francés, it's the site of the Presidio Modelo (Model Jail),
where Castro penned his famous *La Historia me Absolverá* speech and
spent 18 months for his part in the 1953 attack on the Moncada Barracks (☞ Santiago de Cuba *in* Chapter 5).

Pleasures and Pastimes

Dining

Dining in the provincial capitals and towns is spotty; some places are
acceptable while others seem fortunate to be able to provide nourish-
ment at all. Varadero has several good restaurants, though the hotel
fare tends to be mediocre. Look for establishments that specialize in
local staples. Certain delicacies, such as crocodile tail (said to be an
aphrodisiac) at Guamá, roast suckling pig on the Isla de la Juventud,
and lobster at Cayo Levisa, are typical dishes.

Reservations aren't necessary, except in Varadero—especially at Las
Américas and Antigüedades. Tipping is important to Cubans, but a lit-

tle goes a long way; a dollar here or there is much appreciated. Five to ten percent of a restaurant bill is fine. Credit cards *not* affiliated with U.S. banks or companies are accepted in most government restaurants and hotels, though never in *paladares* (privately owned restaurants). For price categories, *see* Dining *in* Smart Travel Tips A to Z.

Lodging

Lodging varies widely, from the new luxury hotels of Varadero and Cayo Largo to the charming hotels around Viñales and the rudimentary housing of María la Gorda. In towns and cities outside Havana, rooms are available in private houses, some of them charming. Nearly all the government-operated hotels take credit cards as long as they aren't affiliated with U.S. banks or companies. For price categories, *see* Lodging *in* Smart Travel Tips A to Z.

Beaches

The beaches throughout Matanzas, Havana, and Pinar del Río provinces and on the Archipiélago de Canarreos vary from virtual outdoor discotheques to vast strands all but devoid of human life. Varadero has some of the most socially active beaches; Cayo Levisa, Playa María la Gorda, and the Isla de la Juventud's Playa Larga are among the wildest and least spoiled.

Diving and Snorkeling

Cuba is gaining recognition as one of the great diving and snorkeling destinations in the Caribbean, with sunken Spanish galleons and U-boats to explore as well as such subaquatic life as rays, barracuda, and triggerfish. The south coast is generally considered to have better diving than the north coast, although the latter also has some excellent spots, particularly along the 40-km-long (25-mi-long) reef off Santa Lucía. Other top diving destinations include the Archipiélago de los Colorados, the Isla de la Juventud, and María la Gorda.

Exploring Western Cuba

Caves, beaches, mountain waterfalls, underwater reefs and galleons, and flora and fauna—from hummingbirds to whale sharks—are all present in western Cuba. Pinar del Río's *vegas* (tobacco fields), the mogotes of Viñales, the Robinson Crusoe-esque simplicity of Cayo Levisa's virgin beaches, the faded glory of the city of Matanzas, and Varadero's long strand are all worlds unto themselves. The swampy Península de Zapata, with its crabs and crocodiles, and the dive sites near María la Gorda and the Isla de la Juventud offer even more variety.

Numbers in the text correspond to numbers in the margin and the Western Cuba map.

Great Itineraries

IF YOU HAVE 3 DAYS

Head west from Havana to **Pinar del Río** ⑨, stopping briefly at the cigar factory for a look at this unique Cuban craft. Continue on to the **Valle de Viñales** ⑧ for a night at the panoramic Hotel Los Jazmines or the equally scenic La Ermita. On Day 2, after exploring the caves and the tobacco fields around Viñales, tour the northern coast from **Cayo Levisa** ⑥ back to Havana, continuing on through **Matanzas** ⑮ to **Varadero** ⑯ for an evening *mojito* (a Cuban cocktail of rum, mint, sugar, and soda) at Las Américas, the old Du Pont mansion. On Day 3, drive through **Cárdenas** ⑰ over to the **Península de Zapata** ⑱ for a visit to the crocodile farm at **La Boca de Guamá** and on to Playa Girón and the **Bahía de Cochinos** ⑲ for a look through the Museo Playa Girón's display on the Bay of Pigs Invasion. Either spend the third night at Playa Larga's Villa Playa Larga hotel or motor two hours back to Havana along the Autopista Nacional.

IF YOU HAVE 5 DAYS
Follow the first day of the itinerary above. On Day 2, after exploring the caves and the tobacco fields around Viñales, tour the northern shore from **Cayo Levisa** ⑥ through the tiny port of Santa Lucía and the pretty town of Mantua to **María la Gorda** ⑪ for a night at Villa María la Gorda on the Bahía de Corrientes, famed for its clear waters and marine life. On Day 3, after exploring the Península de Guanahacabibes, drive back through Pinar del Río along the central Autopista Nacional for a night at the excellent Hotel Moka near **Soroa** ③. On Day 4, drive east past Havana for a stop at **Matanzas** ⑮ and on to **Varadero** ⑯ for an evening mojito at Las Américas, the old Du Pont mansion. On the fifth day, follow Day 3 of the itinerary above, driving through **Cárdenas** ⑰ to the **Península de Zapata** ⑱ for a look at the crocodile farm, and on to Playa Girón and the **Bahía de Cochinos** ⑲ to see the Museo Playa Girón.

IF YOU HAVE 7 DAYS
Follow the five-day tour above and then hop out to the **Isla de la Juventud** ⑫–⑬ for first-rate diving at Punto Francés, and then to the beaches of **Cayo Largo** ⑭. If you plan to fly to the Isla de la Juventud after Day 5, head back to Havana for the night so that you can catch the 7 AM flight on Day 6. If you choose to take the ferry or the hydrofoil from the boat landing at Surgidero de Batabanó, you can sleep at Playa Larga's Villa Playa Larga and drive to Batabanó in the morning. (The lodging at Batabanó ranks somewhere between mediocre and depressing.) You can book Cayo Largo as a day trip from Havana or as a side trip from the Isla de la Juventud.

When to Tour Western Cuba

La Seca is the February–April dry period in Cuba's western and central zones; with temperatures down to 25°–27°C (77°–81°F) and rains scarce, this is a good time to go. Peak vacation times in spots such as Cayo Largo and Varadero fall during Christmas and Easter breaks, when package-tour groups fly in from all over the world. If wild parties are what you're looking for, this is the time to come. If not, visit in November, early December, or early May. Reservations for the Easter and Christmas periods are best made as far in advance as possible.

PINAR DEL RÍO PROVINCE

Settled during the early 18th century (relatively late in the Spanish colonial era) and dubbed "La Cenicienta," or Cinderella, for its reputation as a newcomer and for its poverty and good-heartedness, the province forms either the head of the crocodile or the tail of the shark, depending on which view of the Cuban mainland's shape you prefer. Once the home of the Guanahatabey aboriginal people, the region was taken by the Ciboney Indians in their flight from the Taíno civilization, which eventually reigned prior to the arrival of the Spanish.

Tobacco, sugar, and coffee plantations have been rival influences in what traditionally has been one of Cuba's most backward regions. Famous as the producer of the world's finest tobacco leaves, the typical Pinareño (native of Pinar del Río) is the straw-hatted, oxen-driving *guajiro* (peasant) with a drooping home-rolled cigar clenched between his teeth. In general, however, Pinareños are known as noble and simple citizens with an extraordinary capacity for hard work and generosity. Be prepared to be invited into private homes for anything from sweet black coffee to black beans and rice.

Western Cuba

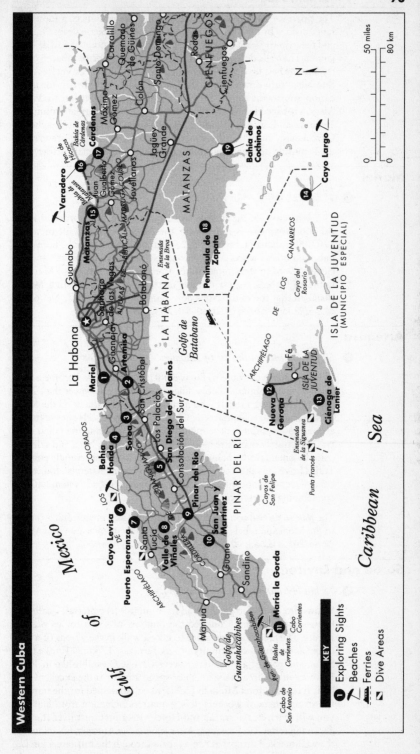

KEY

🔴1 Exploring Sights

⚓ Beaches

⛴ Ferries

◪ Dive Areas

The province's spine is the Cordillera de Guaniguanico, a mountain range divided by the Río San Diego into the western Sierra de los Órganos and the eastern Sierra del Rosario, with its highest point at Pan de Guajaibón. The Valle de Viñales is Pinar del Río's most scenic tobacco country, but the best leaves are grown in the county known as Vuelta Abajo (literally, "turn down"—so called, according to one theory, for its location southwest of the provincial capital). In addition to Vuelta Abajo's tobacco farms, the pine-forested mountain retreat around Las Terrazas and Soroa, the hillocked Valle de Viñales, the beaches at Cayo Levisa and Playa María la Gorda, and the nature preserve on the Península de Guanahacabibes are the province's main attractions.

Mariel

❶ *45 km (28 mi) west of Havana.*

This port city—in the province of Havana, near the border of Pinar del Río Province—is famous for the April 1980 boat lift in which 120,000 Cubans fled to Florida. (That included criminals, homosexuals, and others who Castro viewed as "antisocial elements" and decided to send to the United States along with the refugees.) Mariel is home to Cuba's largest cement factory and an interesting **Museo Histórico** that traces the city's development. ✉ *Calle 132, No. 6926,* ☎ *63/92554.* ✉ *$3.* ☉ *Tues.–Sat. 8–5, Sun. 8–noon.*

Artemisa

❷ *60 km (37 mi) southwest of Havana.*

This little town en route to Pinar del Río Province has become an enclave of revolutionary history since contributing no fewer than 24 of the original Castro rebels who mounted the 1953 attack on the Moncada Barracks (☞ Santiago de Cuba *in* Chapter 5). Plaques scattered around town and a bronze monument commemorate the fallen martyrs. The stately main street—with its faded yellow, blue, and salmon-color colonial facades behind ornate columns—is surprisingly elegant. Trains leave Havana's central railroad station for Artemisa four times a day—a good opportunity to try the Cuban railroad system without condemning yourself to a long trip.

The **Museo de Historia** displays photographs and memorabilia related to the Moncada rebels and the Wars of Independence. ✉ *Calle Martí,* ☎ *63/2412.* ✉ *$3.* ☉ *Tues.–Sat. 8–5, Sun. 8–noon.*

Soroa and Environs

❸ *75 km (47 mi) southwest of Havana.*

Known for its orchid garden and its 30-m (99-ft) waterfall—called El Salto—Soroa has been dubbed the rainbow of Cuba for its pristine beauty. The area is a good place to take a walk in the woods or a tour of the agricultural community of Las Terrazas, 17 km (11 mi) east of Soroa and part of a biosphere reserve UNESCO established in 1985. If you're in the area, have lunch or spend a night at the excellent ecological retreat Hotel Moka in Las Terrazas (so named for the terraced forests and tiers of workers' living quarters). Coming from Havana, you will reach Las Terrazas and Hotel Moka first, just over the border in Pinar del Río Province. After leaving the Autopista Nacional at the well-marked turnoff at Km 51, pass through the toll gate 4 km (2½ mi) north and continue into the park, which originally was used as coffee plantations by French settlers who had come from Haiti at the end of the 18th century. Soroa can be reached via the mountain road through the reserve or from the autopista turnoff at Km 80. Guided tours of Soroa's orchid garden, the **Orquideario Soroa,** are available 10–5:30 daily, except Fridays, and cost $3 (not including tips for tour guides).

Dining and Lodging

$$–$$$ ✕ **El Castillo de las Nubes.** Overlooking the village of Soroa and the palm-canopied valley, this restaurant—appropriately christened "Castle in the Clouds"—occupies an unusual stone, Spanish-style structure. It specializes in standard Cuban chicken and meat dishes, but the views far exceed the fare; on clear days, you can see the Isla de la Juventud more than 100 km (62 mi) to the south. ✉ *Soroa–Autopista Rd.,* ☎ *85/1531. No credit cards.*

$$ ✕ **El Salto.** More apt to be open than El Castillo de las Nubes, though without the nonpareil views, this simple spot 250 m (825 ft) above Soroa's waterfall serves simple Cuban fare and always has a good trio playing wonderful boleros and *son* (a versatile dance rhythm that originated in the eastern cities). ✉ *Soroa–Autopista Rd.,* ☎ *85/1350. No credit cards.*

$$$ ✕🏨 **Hotel Moka.** The comfortable all-but-outdoor rooms with floor-
★ to-ceiling glass doors that lead to terraces, the fine restaurant, and the well-designed ecological theme make this hotel well worth seeking out. An immense tree stands in the reception area, escaping overhead through four skylights. The bar and restaurant seem suspended over the edge of the valley. The *aporreado de res* (shredded beef in criollo sauce) and the *masas de cerdo* (pork fillets) are excellent. The wine list also is quite respectable, if pricey. ✉ *Las Terrazas,* ☎ *85/2921. 26 rooms. Restaurant, bar, pool, free parking. MC, V.*

Outdoor Activities and Sports

Exploring the Sierra del Rosario can provide a day or two of exercise and fresh air between Soroa and Las Terrazas. Guides are available for **nature hikes** ($3 per hour per person, three people maximum). From Las Terrazas, the trails called La Delicias and La Serafina are the two most beautiful hikes, each about 4 km (2½ mi) or two hours long. El Salto, the waterfall, is accessed from Soroa via a concrete stairway leading down from the well-marked Bar Edén. The so-called Baños Romanos (Roman Baths) are below the falls. Guides can be arranged in Las Terrazas at **Hotel Moka** or in Soroa at **Villa Soroa** (✉ Carretera de Soroa, Km 8; ☎ 82/2122).

Shopping

The village community center of Las Terrazas has several crafts stores to visit. Handcrafted hardwood spoons and ladles are the specialty of the **Taller de Alberto** (Alberto Workshop). At the **Taller de Fibras,** a women's cooperative, you can buy straw hats, baskets, and other items. There are also several artists' studios with works generally related to natural themes.

Bahía Honda

❹ *65 km (40 mi) west of Havana.*

At the head of the picturesque bay of the same name, this town is a handy way station if you're traveling the Circuito Norte (the northern circuit) around western Cuba.

Lodging

$$ 🏨 **Motel Punta de Piedra.** This rudimentary lodging just north of town offers spectacular views over the bay, but little else beyond the basics. ✉ *Circuito Norte, Km 65,* ☎ *86/341 or 86/208. 16 rooms. Restaurant, bar, pool, free parking. No credit cards.*

San Diego de los Baños

❺ *120 km (74 mi) southwest of Havana.*

The German scholar and explorer Alexander von Humboldt, heralded as "Cuba's second discoverer," was an early enthusiast of the spa waters in this little town named "de los Baños" (of the baths) for thermal springs that reportedly cured everything from arthritis to eczema. Once well known in the United States as "the Saratoga of the tropics," these waters attracted the ailing—and the malingering—wealthy from all over the world, including Napoléon's private physician. The Templado springs here are rich in magnesium, calcides, and sulphur, and maintain a constant temperature just under 40°C (104°F). The spa offers whirlpool baths, massages, and acupuncture for $10–$20.

Lodging

$$–$$$ 🏨 **Hotel El Mirador.** This beautiful complex includes terraced, landscaped grounds and spacious rooms with floral motifs and rattan furniture. Equipped with all the modern amenities, it's worth keeping in mind if you're road-weary and looking for a comfortable spot in the Sierra del Rosario. ✉ *Carretera de La Guira s/n,* ☎ *8/5410 (7/33–2658 for booking in Havana),* 📠 *7/33–1630. 30 rooms. Restaurant, bar, air-conditioning, pool, free parking. MC, V.*

Cayo Levisa

❻ *110 km (68 mi) west of Havana, 52 km (32 mi) north of Viñales.*

The Archipiélago de los Colorados that runs along Cuba's northern coast begins at Cayo Paraíso just west of Las Pozas and continues to the island's western tip. Cayo Paraíso was a famous Hemingway haunt, a spot he visited with his yacht-fishing boat *El Pilar.* A plaque erected near the wooden dock at Cayo Paraíso by the provincial authorities on what would have been the novelist's 90th birthday immortalizes Hemingway's predilection for this pristine spot. Cayo Levisa is the next key. Easily visible a little more than a mile offshore, Cayo Levisa is ringed by white-sand beaches and offers some fantastic diving. Lobsters and black coral are the main aquatic attractions. The boat (for which, for some mysterious reason, you need a passport) leaves at 11 AM and 5 PM from the coast guard station at Palma Rubia; it costs $10 per passenger (one way) and returns to the mainland at 3 PM and 7 PM. To get to the boat landing, turn north off the northern-coast circuit just after the town of Las Cadenas.

Dining and Lodging

$$ ✕🏨 **Villa Cayo Levisa.** This tourist resort and dive center offers cabins on the beach and water sports for every taste and level of expertise. The buffet restaurant serves passable Cuban specialties, fresh-caught lobsters foremost among them. The bar is a lively spot after hours, and you probably will meet a full range of fellow guests; Spain and Italy are especially well represented during the summer months. The boutique—the only emporium on the key—sells handmade wicker crafts and cotton dresses and vests. ✉ *Cayo Levisa,* ☎ *8/66–6075. 20 bungalows. Restaurant, bar, air-conditioning, beach, dive shop, dock, snorkeling, surfing, windsurfing, boating, waterskiing, shop. MC, V.*

Puerto Esperanza

❼ *200 km (124 mi) west of Havana, 52 km (32 mi) north of Pinar del Río.*

This tiny fishing village north of Viñales is known mostly as a base from which to explore the port of Santa Lucía, the Bahía de Santa Lucía, and Cayo Jutía—all remote and, so far, untouched by tourism.

Dining and Lodging

$$ **★** **X 🏨 Villa Rosario.** This colonial mansion, 4 km (2½ mi) east of Puerto Esperanza, has a decent restaurant that serves boiled lobster about as fresh as it can be. Once the house of a wealthy landowner, Villa Rosario became the Casa del Partido (Communist Party Headquarters and Clubhouse) after the Revolution. A hotel and restaurant since 1990, it is an excellent base for exploring a part of Cuba most visitors never see. Reserve as far in advance as possible; this is the only lodging for miles around. ⊠ *El Rosario,* ☎ *8/93828, 4 rooms. Restaurant. No credit cards.*

Valle de Viñales

⑧ *26 km (16 mi) north of Pinar del Río, 212 km (131 mi) southwest of Havana.*

The valley is justly ranked among Cuba's most beautiful landscapes, an expanse of lush green studded with the famous mogotes—free-standing, flat-topped, sheer-sided rock formations. Don't fail to stop at the Hotel Los Jazmines (☞ Dining and Lodging, *below*) for a breath-taking view over the valley, the immense mogotes towering over deep green *vegas* (plantations) and stretching into the distance backed by the Sierra de los Órganos (so called for the peaks' resemblance to the pipes of an organ). The mogotes are the remains of the limestone *meseta,* or plateau, that rose from the sea during the Jurassic era some 160 million years ago to form the Guaniguanico Mountains. Subsequent erosion left a classic karstic terrain replete with sinks, ravines, underground streams, and hoyos—rich depressions of red soil ideal for cultivating tobacco. The hidden canyons and the natural tunnels leading into them provided shelter for pre-Columbian peoples and later for communities of *cimarrones* (runaway slaves).

The valley's flora and fauna include many unique treasures: the underbrush, ferns, and rare cork palms on the mogotes; the silk-cotton tree, *Ceiba pentandra*; the royal palm; the caiman oak; and the mariposa, Cuba's national flower. Fauna includes the world's smallest hummingbird, the *zunzuncito,* as well as various snails native to the mogotes.

The town of Viñales itself is a national monument, a charming rural collection of small houses shaded by pine trees. The de rigueur José Martí monument in the main square is surrounded by graceful wooden houses. The **Museo Municipal Adela Azcuy** displays objects and photographs on local history, including a bronze bust of Captain Adela Azcuy herself—a top-ranked woman warrior who fought for Cuba's independence. ⊠ *Calle Salvador Cisnero s/n,* ☎ *8/1029.* 🎫 *$3.* ☉ *Tues.– Sat. 8–5, Sun. 8–noon.*

La Casa del Veguero, just south of Viñales and well marked, is a typical tobacco farmer's bungalow and drying shed with a restaurant and souvenir store. **Cuevas de Viñales,** a grotto 4 km (2½ mi) north of Viñales, doubles as a disco at night. The 140-m (462-ft) tunnel piercing the mogote opens onto a replica of a cimarron campsite and the outdoor *bohío*-style (hut-style) restaurant El Palanque de los Cimarrones. The **Cueva del Indio,** about 6 km (4 mi) north of Viñales, is named for the Guanahatabey aboriginals who once lived here. The cave has a 1½-km (1-mi) underground river, a third of which is electrically illuminated. After a 255-m (842-ft) walk through the high-ceilinged grotto, a small boat takes you another 300 m (990 ft) through stalagmites shaped like a champagne bottle, a skull, a crocodile, a sea horse, and the *Niña, Pinta,* and *Santa María.* Admission to the cave, open daily 9–5, is $3.

Half a kilometer north of Cueva del Indio, you'll find yourself at the edge of the sparsely populated but stunningly beautiful Valle de Ancón.

At the Dos Hermanas Mogote, 5 km (3 mi) west of Viñales, Diego Rivera disciple Leovigildo González (or the 25 farmers he directed) painted the immense **Mural de la Prehistoria**—200 m by 300 m (660 ft by 990 ft)—between 1959 and 1962. Commissioned by Fidel Castro, the painting depicts the evolutionary process in the Sierra de los Órganos. Admission is $1, daily 9–5. The on-site restaurant serves *cerdo asado Viñales*—roast pig Viñales style, macerated for 24 hours in bitter orange, cumin, garlic, oregano, salt, and pepper and cooked slowly over coals—which is worth the trip on its own.

Dining and Lodging

$$ ✕ **Casa de Don Tomás.** The excellent local cuisine, cheerful and charm-
★ ing service, and hot-as-a-pistol trio singing old favorites such as "Guan-
tanamera" so well it can be hard to swallow your lunch make this a
place not to miss anytime you're near Viñales. Located in the oldest
house in Viñales (built in 1822), this little spot enjoys well-deserved
fame as one of Cuba's most pleasant restaurants. The *delicias de Don
Tomás* (a concoction of ham, pork, chicken, lobster, and sausage) is a
house favorite, as is the *tasajo a lo guajiro* (shredded beef in a criollo
sauce). ⊠ *Calle Salvador Cisneros 141,* ☎ *8/93114. MC, V.*

$$$–$$$$ ✕🏨 **La Ermita.** The terrace restaurant, with its panoramic views of the
★ valley and reliable country cooking, is worth a visit even if you're not
staying in the hotel. If you are staying here, get a room overlooking
the valley (not the pool), if one is available. Be warned: once settled in
here, leaving may be difficult. ⊠ *Carretera La Ermita, Km 2,* ☎ *8/
93204,* 🆕 *8/94974. 64 rooms. Restaurant, bar, air-conditioning, pool,
free parking. MC, V.*

$$$–$$$$ ✕🏨 **Hotel Los Jazmines.** The views from this hotel are spectacular. The
★ rooms are tastefully decorated with rattan furniture and floral prints.
The best are in the old part of the hotel, near the pool—an Olympic-
size expanse on the edge of the terrace over the valley. The restaurant
is better than average, and the management offers day hikes and ex-
cursions throughout western Cuba. ⊠ *Carretera de Viñales, Km 25,*
☎ *8/93265,* 🆕 *8/93265. 14 rooms, 16 bungalows. Restaurant, bar,
pool, free parking. MC, V.*

Pinar del Río

❾ *178 km (110 mi) southwest of Havana.*

Named for the stands of autochthonous pine trees that once shaded the banks of the Río Guamá, this has been Cuba's tobacco city since its first land grants were allocated in 1544. Viñales and Vuelta Abajo were the island's great tobacco plantations, and Pinar del Río pros-pered as the tobacco market town and manufacturing center, even after the rest of the island turned almost exclusively to the cultivation and export of sugarcane.

Today, the city (population 125,000) is distinguished by little more than its cigar factory, a distillery that produces *guayabita* (a brandy-like liqueur made from sugarcane and guava), and its many fluted-columned and pillared porches in pastels that seem to reflect the red soil of the vegas in the surrounding area. Pinar del Río doesn't have the atmosphere of Viñales, but a short layover here would provide a sampling of life in what is probably the most provincial of Cuba's provincial cities. There are several acceptable restaurants to choose from, and the very absence of tourism makes this an interesting opportunity to drop in on Cuba au naturel.

The **Francisco Donatien cigar factory** offers a more intimate cigar-factory visit than some of the major Havana works. You might even hear the *lector* (reader) entertain the cigar rollers with newspaper articles from *Granma* or novels. ⊠ *Calle Antonio Maceo 157,* ☎ *82/3424.* ☞ *$3.* ⊘ *Weekdays 7–5, Sat. 8–noon.*

The **Fábrica de Bebidas Guayabita** offers tours and tastes of the traditional rum-and-guava brew made from wild berries that grow exclusively in Pinar del Río Province. ⊠ *Calle Isabel Rubio 189,* ☎ *82/2966.* ☞ *$3.* ⊘ *Weekdays 9–5.*

Pinar del Río has its own **Museo Histórico Provincial,** tracing its local history. ⊠ *Calle Martí 58,* ☎ *82/4300.* ☞ *$3.* ⊘ *Mon.–Sat. 9–5, Sun. 9–1.*

Pinar del Río's **Casa de Cultura** is open during concerts and other events, usually in the evening. ⊠ *Calle Máximo Gomez 108,* ☎ *82/9923.* ☞ *$3.*

Dining and Lodging

$$$–$$$$ ✕ **Palacio de la Artesanía.** This restaurant and crafts shop near the railroad station on the La Coloma road out of Pinar del Río is known to have the best food in town. Try the aporreado de res or the excellent *pollo criollo* (chicken in criollo sauce). ⊠ *Carretera de la Coloma, Casa 1890, esquina de Sol y Coloma,* ☎ *82/8263. No credit cards.*

$$$–$$$$ ✕ **Rumayor.** Though state-owned and -run, this Afro-Cuban crafts center and restaurant just outside of town is highly acclaimed. The decor at the restaurant—which is famed for its pollo *ahumado* (smoked)— is basic bohío style, with wood beams and a cane roof. The bar and cabaret double as the city's top nightspot. ⊠ *Carretera Viñales, Km 2,* ☎ *82/3507. MC, V.*

$$–$$$ ✕🏠 **Hotel Pinar del Río.** Despite its modern and none-too-charming structure, this is the city's prime hotel, with a pleasant staff and all the basic comforts to get you through a night or two. ⊠ *Calle Martí y Autopista Nacional,* ☎ *82/5071,* 🖷 *82/0224. 149 rooms. Restaurant, bar, pool, free parking. MC, V.*

San Juan y Martínez

⑩ *23 km (14 mi) southwest of Pinar del Río, 209 km (130 mi) southwest of Havana.*

The finest-quality tobacco leaves come from Vuelta Abajo—the region southwest of Pinar del Río city—thanks to a combination of abundant rainfall throughout the year (except for during the growing season). And although the countryside here is relatively drab, it's the mecca *puro* (cigar) purists must visit. Some 80,000 acres of tobacco are planted annually in the province, and the best of it is found around San Luis and San Juan y Martínez.

The main street in San Juan y Martínez is lined with the provincial pastel-color, columned houses typical throughout Cuba. Other than a café or two and the odd paladar, this sleepy tobacco town has little to offer. A visit to a tobacco farm is the main reason for lingering in Vuelta Abajo. Drop in at any plantation and the farmers will show you the crops, techniques, and drying barns, and possibly invite you for lunch.

María la Gorda and the Península de Guanahacabibes

⑪ *150 km (93 mi) west of Pinar del Río, 328 km (203 mi) southwest of Havana.*

Named for a voluptuous young woman who was allegedly captured by pirates and returned to this westernmost Cuban point only to set

CIGAR SOCIETY

EARLY CHRONICLES tell us that Taíno Indians were found puffing on twisted bunches of what they called *cohiba* (tobacco) when Christopher Columbus came ashore in early December 1492. Five hundred years later, some 60 million cigars, known as *habanos* or *puros*, are consumed annually worldwide; Cubans are estimated to smoke some 250 million domestically. International journals and magazines such as *Cigar Aficionado* and *European Cigar Cult Journal* keep the faithful informed on every aspect of the Cuban cigar, and conventions such as early 1999's Habanos 2000 bring together eminent cigar lovers, merchants, and producers from around the world.

Tobacco was found to have narcotic or soothing qualities from the start and became popular in Spain by the late 16th century. By 1717, cigars made with Cuban tobacco were manufactured in Sevilla; the British and French brought the habit home from the Peninsular campaign of the early 19th century. By the middle of that century, tobacco was Cuba's main export, with more than 1,000 cigar factories on the island.

Cigars come in a bewildering range of brands, lengths, widths (ring gauges), and shapes. The Cohiba brand is generally understood to be the best cigar in the world, though Upmann, Partagás, Romeo y Julieta, and Montecristo are among the elite brands. The newest addition to this group, Vegas Robaina, honors nonpareil *veguero* (tobacco grower) Don Alejandro Robaina.

The worldwide fascination with Cuban cigars is difficult to calibrate or comprehend. Every detail of the growing and rolling process is of vital interest to cigar worshippers—from soil composition in the Vuelta Abajo region of Pinar del Río Province and the amount and timing of the rainfall to the training and selection of cigar rollers, or *torcedores*, in the top cigar factories of Havana. Though legend has it that the national treasure was "rolled on the dusky thighs of Cuban maidens," the fact is that, although women sorted the leaves holding the bunches across their laps, only men were employed to roll cigars until after the Revolution.

Ideally, the story of a cigar begins in the *vegas* (fields) of Vuelta Abajo, 200 km (124 mi) southwest of Havana—preferably those of Don Alejandro Robaina, now nearly 80 years old, a veguero whose tobacco leaves have been identified by connoisseurs as the best in the world. Planted in late October and harvested by hand 120 days later, tobacco leaves are hung to dry in sheds for 45 to 60 days. Sorted, selected, and left to ferment for up to three months, they are then fermented again to remove more tar and nicotine before being sent to cigar factories. There the leaves may be left to mature for as long as two years before passing through the factory's six stages: *despalillo* (stripping out veins), *liga* (bunching filler, wrapper, and binder leaves), *galera* (the "galley," where artisans roll the cigars), *escogida* (selecting uniformly colored cigars), *anillado* (placing on of paper rings), and *adorno de caja* (boxing).

Cigar factories are a fundamental part of Cuban life. One of the best to visit is the Partagás factory (☞ Exploring *in* Chapter 2). It houses hundreds of workers, most of them seated in long rows at old-fashioned wooden school benches in the galera section. When lectors aren't reading to the workers from newspapers or novels, Cuban music soothes and entertains these artisans as they concentrate on their craft, the windows rattling as dozens of singing voices drown out the recording on the crescendos.

up a brothel, María la Gorda is on the Bahía de Corrientes, 2½–3 hours from Pinar del Río over difficult road. The small, quiet beaches and clear water make the trip worthwhile, as does the chance to encounter a wide range of fauna, from wild boar and deer to crocodiles and wildcats—though you're more likely to see Cuba's ubiquitous land-crab population headed for the seashore to lay eggs.

The flat and scrub-forested Península de Guanahacabibes was the final refuge for Cuba's Ciboney aboriginals fleeing first the Taíno Indians and then the Spanish conquerors of the late 15th and 16th centuries. The Bahía de Corrientes has some excellent virgin beaches, and the 90-km-long (56-mi-long), 30-km-wide (19-mi-wide) peninsula is known for certain species of birds found only here—notably, the tiny zunzuncito and the similar *torcaza*.

At the end of the road from Pinar del Río, the village of La Bajada lies at the junction of the roads left to Playa María la Gorda (14 km, or 9 mi, south) and right into the Parque Nacional Península de Guanahacabibes. Permits ($10 per person) to enter the park, a UNESCO Biosphere Reserve, must be obtained at Villa María la Gorda in order to clear the military checkpoint at La Bajada. The drive out to Cuba's western tip at Cabo de San Antonio 54 km (33 mi) over a rough dirt track is a long haul to undertake, unless you're happy exploring the wilderness. If you go, a cooler and a few sandwiches are advised.

Dining and Lodging

$$ ✕⊡ **Villa María la Gorda.** This lone beachside hotel may suffer somewhat from the lack of competition. Although the fare is only mediocre, the cabins and rooms are acceptably comfortable and the Villa María la Gorda organizes some of the best diving and fishing excursions from the island. The hotel doubles as bar, disco, dive school, and general headquarters for the entire Península de Guanahacabibes. Permits for the Parque Nacional Península de Guanahacabibes must be obtained here before driving the 2½ hours out to Cuba's western tip. ⊠ *Bahía de Corrientes,* ☎ *84/3121,* 𝖥𝖠𝖷 *84/2024. 40 rooms and cabins. Restaurant, bar, air-conditioning, pool, beach, dive shop, dock, snorkeling, windsurfing, boating, waterskiing, free parking. MC, V.*

Outdoor Activities and Sports

Scuba diving (including night dives), snorkeling, and fishing trips are all on the menu at the **María la Gorda International Dive Center** (⊠ Bahía de Corrientes, ☎ 84/3121). Run by Villa María la Gorda management, the center has half a dozen dive masters and packages ranging from a $15 initiation dive to $200 for a 10-dive package.

ARCHIPIÉLAGO DE LOS CANARREOS

Of Cuba's 4,000 islands, most of them specks known as *cayos* (keys), the largest is the main island in the Archipiélago de Canarreos, the Isla de la Juventud (Isle of Youth)—so called for the more than 20,000 Third World students who once studied and worked here. Nearly due south of Havana in the Golfo de Batabanó, the Isla de la Juventud previously was called La Isla de los Pinos (The Isle of Pines) for the native pine forest that once covered the roughly circular, 49½-km-diameter (31-mi-diameter) island. Fidel Castro was imprisoned here for 18 months for the 1953 assault on the Moncada Barracks. After the Revolution, he undertook the international socialist experiment in education and field work known as the Youth Brigades and accordingly renamed the island.

A special municipality (as opposed to a full-fledged province), the island has little to offer outside of abundant grapefruit orchards, its quirky nature, and excellent dive opportunities; sunken Spanish galleons virtually line the bottom of the Ensenada de la Siguanea, or Bay of Siguanea. Nueva Gerona, the administrative center of the archipelago and the only important town, is where some 30,000 of the archipelago's 70,000 residents live.

Isla de la Juventud

Flat, scrubby, and—except for its subaquatic marvels—geographically undistinguished, the island was a pirate refuge for centuries after Columbus discovered it in 1494. In the 19th century, after the pirates, this is where the Spanish sent exiles. In the late 19th century, emigrants from the Cayman Islands started a British colony here, leaving some native English-speakers even today around the town of Cocodrilo on the south coast. Americans colonized the island in the early 20th century, thinking it could become another state; the Mafia considered making it an insular gambling paradise in the 1940s. Finally, after the Revolution, Castro established his experimental, international student community—a plan to combine work and study and, in the process, convert the island into a citrus power. The experiment fell apart during the Special Period; most of the boarding schools are now in ruins.

Nueva Gerona

⑫ *170 km (105 mi) south of Havana.*

This sleepy town barely merits a browse, though its pillars and columns and horses and buggies make it seem refreshingly stuck in the flow of history. The main street, Calle 39 (Calle Martí), will take you past the restaurants El Cochinito and El Corderito—"the piglet" and "the lamb," respectively. If you walk to Nueva Gerona's ferry terminal (✉ Calle 31, e/Calle 22 y Calle 24, ☎ 61/22324) on the Río Las Casas, you can see *El Pinero,* the boat that ferried Castro to freedom in 1955 after his prison sojourn.

At the **Museo de la Lucha Clandestina** (Museum of the Clandestine Struggle), you can view exhibits relating to the Movimiento 26 de Julio—the date of the attack, in 1953, on the Moncada Barracks and the name of Castro's revolutionary movement. ✉ *Calle 45, esquina de Calle 24,* ☎ *61/2400.* ✆ *$2.* ◷ *Tues.–Sat. 9–5, Sun. 8–noon.*

Five kilometers east of Nueva Gerona is the area's most popular sight, the **Presidio Modelo** (Model Prison), built in 1926–31 by the dictator Machado. Modeled on the infamous penitentiary in Joliet, Illinois, the presidio facilitated constant surveillance of up to 6,000 prisoners. The doorless cells in the four circular, five-tiered buildings were crammed with inmates and overseen from central watchtowers. The fifth block, where prisoners weren't allowed to speak, housed the dining hall, known as *el comedor de tres mil silencios* (the dining hall of 3,000 silences). German and Japanese prisoners of war were held here during World War II and, most famously, Fidel Castro, his brother Raúl, and 24 fellow rebels were jailed here from October 1953 to May 1955 after the attack on the Moncada Barracks. Celebrity inmates, Castro and company were housed in the prison infirmary; their bunks are still in place, with photographs of each prisoner on the wall over the bed. Castro penned his now famous *La Historia me Absolverá* ("History Will Absolve Me")—his defense speech for his trial for the Moncada attack and a manifesto of the cause against the dictator Fulgencio Batista—at the Presidio Modelo, which has been a museum since 1967. ✉ *Carretera Playa Bibijagua (Calle 32 leaving Nueva Gerona), Km 5,* ☎ *61/7564.* ✆ *$2.* ◷ *Tues.–Sat. 9–5, Sun. 9–1.*

$$-$$$ ✕ **El Corderito.** As the name implies, *cordero* (lamb) is the specialty in
★ this unpretentious little spot near the very center of Nueva Gerona. Try
the tasajo prepared with lamb for a different take on the Cuban dish
of shredded meat in criollo sauce. ✉ *Calle 39, esquina de Calle 22,* ☎
61/2400. No credit cards.

$$-$$$ ✕ **El Cochinito.** This simple restaurant serves prime pork specialties such
as *chicharrónes de cerdo* (pork crisp), *masas* (pork loin), and *cochinillo
asado* (roast suckling pig). ✉ *Calle 39, esquina de Calle 24,* ☎ *61/2809.
No credit cards.*

$$-$$$ ▦ **Villa Gaviota.** The Gaviota swimming pool, a cool spot above the
Río Las Casas, is where all the island inhabitants want to be on weekends. The rooms here are surprisingly elegant, with marble floors and
a full complement of appliances that includes TVs, refrigerators, and
phones. South 2 km (1 mi) from Nueva Gerona, this is a handy base
from which to explore the town. ✉ *Autopista Nueva Gerona–La Fé,
Km 2,* ☎ *61/23290,* FAX *61/24486. 20 rooms. Restaurant, bar, air-conditioning, pool, free parking. MC, V.*

Ciénaga de Lanier and Environs

⑬ *30 km (19 mi) south of Nueva Gerona.*

Outside of Nueva Gerona, the Isla de la Juventud's other major attraction
is its swampland. But a visit is a long and somewhat costly undertaking, involving guides ($15–$20, not including tips), permits ($10),
entry fees ($1 for the crocodile farm), a rental car or taxi ($70), and a
full-day round trip from Nueva Gerona. (Permits can be acquired at
the Colony Puerto Sol or the Villa Gaviota.) The crocodile farm, 30
km (19 mi) south of Nueva Gerona, is of moderate interest.

★ The **Cueva Punta del Este,** 55 km (34 mi) southeast of Nueva Gerona,
is actually a series of caves famous for their paintings. As the year pro-
ceeds, the sunlight that beams into the caves illuminates different parts
of the aboriginal paintings, which date from around 800 BC. The
Colony Puerto Sol and Villa Gaviota arrange guides and all details of
visits to the site. These guided trips cost $25 per person, in groups of
at least 10 people.

$$$ ✕▦ **Colony Puerto Sol.** This remote spot 42 km (26 mi) southwest of
Nueva Gerona on the Bahía de Siguanea takes full advantage of its cap-
tive audience in every way, from the *pineritos* (the classic Isla de la Ju-
ventud cocktail of white rum, grapefruit juice, and ice) to the room
rates. Even so, the expense is moderate compared to hotels outside Cuba.
Known as the uncontested best hotel on the island, the Colony is a haven
for divers and snorkelers, privy to some of the best underwater scenery
in the world. The Mojito Bar at the end of the dock is spectacular in
the evening. ✉ *Carretera de Siguanea, Km 42,* ☎ *61/98181,* FAX *61/
76120. 68 rooms, 9 suites. Restaurant, bar, pool, dive shop, dock, boat-
ing, fishing, free parking. MC, V.*

On the Isla de la Juventud's south shore is the seemingly endless **Playa
Larga** (Long Beach), well worth a stop for its natural splendor. You
may even want to spend a day hiking west to Cocodrilo and Caleta
Grande, where descendants of the Cayman Islands still speak a melodic
Caribbeanized English. At **Punta Francés,** no fewer than 56 dive sites—
with such evocative names as The Tunnel of Love and Secret Passage—
let you explore the coral reefs, varied fauna, and sunken galleons
around the western tip of the Isla de la Juventud's southern claw. The
best way to access Punta Francés is via boat from the Colony Puerto
Sol (☞ Dining and Lodging, *above*).

Cayo Largo

⓮ *177 km (110 mi) southeast of Havana, 120 km (74 mi) east of the Isla de la Juventud.*

Popular with Canadian and Italian tour groups that often fly in directly, Cayo Largo is an ideal spot for a carefree vacation that could be anywhere on the globe. Contact with Cuban life and culture is very limited. The island is considerably more expensive than the Cuban mainland; expect to pay double normal Cuban prices for everything from diving excursions to windsurfing rentals to dinner. On the other hand, the pristine beaches and seductive aquamarine waters are boon and balm to the weary soul. This get-away-from-it-all island really gets away from it *all*.

From Combinado on the island's northwestern tip, around the small elbow called Cocodrilo that juts out from the island's southwest shore, and up the 20-km (12-mi) northeast-oriented straightaway from which Cayo Largo derives its name, there are eight hotels, all well equipped and offering tourist activities of every kind, around the clock. **Playa Sirena** is justly considered the best beach in Cuba for its superb 3-km (2-mi) white-sand strand. A 10-minute ferry (no charge) from Combinado goes out to the sliver of a peninsula off Cayo Largo's western tip in the morning and returns in the evening. Boat trips from Playa Sirena to nearby keys such as Cayo Rico and Cayo Iguana are available, along with a full range of water sports including diving and windsurfing. Ferries to Playa Sirena leave the pier at Isla del Sol at 8:30 and 10:30 AM and at 2:30 PM, returning at 1:30, 3, and 5 PM. The one-way fare is $3 per person. Day trips from Havana and Varadero offer packages including the 40-minute flight, half a day and lunch on Playa Sirena, snorkeling the offshore reef, and a visit to Cayo Iguana. For a taste of the best of Cayo Largo without fully renouncing the experience of Cuba, such a package may be the best of all worlds.

Dining and Lodging

$$$–$$$$ ✕ **Taberna del Pirata.** Lobster is the standard specialty here, along with
     ★ other criollo recipes featuring fresh fish. The thatched-roof bohío decor aside, this is more than the beach shack it may seem at first sight, with respectable fare and a good wine list. ✉ *Playa Sirena,*☎ 61/6786. *MC, V.*

$$$–$$$$ ✕⌸ **Villa Capricho.** This is a well-equipped spot with bungalows that try hard to seem rustic and South Sea-like, but, in the end, don't succeed. The Marlín Azul (Blue Marlin) restaurant, which specializes in seafood and paella, is one of the better dining facilities on Cayo Largo. ✉ *Playa Lindamar,* ☎ 61/2100, FAX 61/0110. *60 bungalows. Restaurant, bar, pool, dock, free parking. MC, V.*

$$$ ⌸ **Isla del Sur.** Along the strip of resorts and hotels in Cocodrilo, this is one of the better choices. All rooms have patios facing the sea, and the circular swimming pool in the center of the complex gives it a Venice-like, swim-home-for-cocktails feel. Evening entertainment is varied and constant here. ✉ *Playa Lindamar,* ☎ 5/48111, FAX 5/48201. *59 rooms. Restaurant, bar, air-conditioning, pool, beauty salon, travel services, free parking. MC, V.*

$$$ ⌸ **Pelícano Hotel.** This rambling complex of Mexican-style buildings, bungalows, and outbuildings in some ways epitomizes all that's wrong with Cayo Largo's tourism program, though the beach facing this spot is a cut above those farther east. Relentlessly modern, the Pelícano offers everything from basketball to diving to windsurfing. ✉ *Playa Lindamar,* ☎ 5/48165, FAX 5/48166. *212 rooms, 110 bungalows, 2 suites. 4 restaurants, café, piano bar, air-conditioning, pool, health club, dry cleaning, free parking. MC, V.*

MATANZAS PROVINCE

Once the sugarcane-producing heartland of Cuba, Matanzas Province offers attractions from its once splendid and culturally prominent provincial capital to its booming tourist beach destination at Varadero, to the quaint city of Cárdenas and the natural and historical riches of the Península de Zapata.

The city of Matanzas was a sugar and slave-trading port of great importance during colonial times. Alternately dubbed "The Athens of Cuba" for its cultural vigor and "The Cuban Venice" for its two rivers and many bridges, Matanzas is worthy of more attention than it usually gets from visitors headed for Varadero. On the other hand, Varadero—with more than four dozen hotels, most of them immense, stretching along the slender Península de Hicacos between the Atlantic Ocean and the Bahía de Cárdenas—is an overdeveloped resort. The city of Cárdenas, which is important to have a look at (a coffee break or lunch is plenty), has a character and charm all its own, while the Península de Zapata, beginning with the crocodile farm at Guamá and ending at the Bahía de Cochinos (Bay of Pigs) and the fascinating Museo Playa Girón, is an engaging combination of flora, fauna, and history.

Matanzas

15 *100 km (62 mi) east of Havana.*

Matanzas has a charm well worth investigating and far more interesting than its famous neighbor, Varadero, with all its high-rise glitz. Matanzas, which means "killings" or "slaughters," was so called as Cuba's early livestock abattoir and exporter of meat to Spain. An alternate story recounts the ambush and murder of Spanish shipwreck victims by local natives.

The San Juan and Yumurí rivers cut through the center of town and empty into the vast Bahía de Matanzas, still an important sugar port. The typical provincial faded pastel facades of elegant town houses with fluted columns are found scattered throughout the town center and along its two rivers.

To get to Matanzas, consider the wide and quick Vía Blanca, which runs 100 km (62 mi) from Havana and then another 40 km (25 mi) on to Varadero. It is one of Cuba's finest and most spectacular highways, with views of the coast and the Valle de Yumurí. The *Hershey Train*—a four-hour run from the Casablanca district across Havana harbor—is the other classic way to visit Matanzas.

Including lunch at La Viña, a quick tour of central Matanzas could take two to four hours, plenty of time to get the feel of this once-opulent 19th-century town.

The sky-blue **Hershey railway station** (✉ Calle 67/San Blas y Calle 155/ San Alejandro, ☎ 52/24–7254; ☞ Arriving and Departing *in* Western Cuba A to Z, *below*) is considered by many to be Cuba's most beautiful depot. Once the property of Pennsylvania-based chocolate barons, the railway was built to haul sugarcane but eventually added passenger service. Now its quaint little electric engine pulls two passenger cars with wooden benches into the railway's Matanzas station, in the Reparto Versalles (Versailles district), which was settled by French-Haitian refugees during the 19th century.

The **Iglesia de San Pedro Apóstol** (✉ Calle 57 y Calle 270) was built in 1870 by architect Daniel Delaglio, who also designed Matanzas' emblematic Teatro Sauto. The church's neoclassical symmetry and seriousness is relieved only by the tower's playful dormer windows.

Over the Yumurí estuary is the ornate **Puente Concordia,** which was built in 1878. The bridge is known for the intricately decorated columns at both ends.

The powder-blue building that previously was the Palacio Junco is now the **Museo Histórico Provincial.** It houses artifacts, photographs, and memorabilia chronicling the sugar and slave industries. ✉ *Calle 272 y Calle 79,* ☎ *52/24–3195.* ✆ *$2.* ☉ *Tues.–Sun. 10–noon, 1–6.*

A marble statue of a War of Independence fighter sits at the center of the **Plaza de la Vigía,** just south of the intersection of Calle 272 and Calle 83. Across from the plaza, the **Teatro Sauto** (☎ 52/24–2721) is one of Cuba's finest and best-preserved neoclassical structures. Also known as the Teatro Antillano, or Theater of the Antilles, it was built in 1863 at the peak of the city's power and prosperity. Tours of the triple-tiered interior, with its carved wood and frescoes, can be arranged at the theater for $2 a person. The **Galería de Arte Provincial** (✉ Calle 272, ☎ 52/24–9142) shows local painters, sculptors, and *orisha* (Santería deity) artisans. It's open Monday–Saturday 9–5 and charges $2 admission.

Some of the brightest sights in Matanzas are the restored frescoes at the **Catedral de San Carlos.** ✉ *Calle Milanés y Calle 282,* ☎ *52/24–8342.* ☉ *Weekdays 9–noon, 3–5; Sun. 9–noon.*

The **Plaza de la Libertad,** a leafy, shaded square (bordered by Calles 79, 83, 290, and 288), is centered by a bronze of José Martí and of a dramatic, bare-breasted woman that represents Cuba breaking out of her chains. The **Museo Farmacéutico** (✉ Calle Milanés, esquina de Calle Santa Teresa, ☎ 52/24–3179), the main sight on the Plaza de la Libertad, is a carefully restored, wood-paneled building. Built in 1882, it was a working pharmacy until it was closed in the mid-1960s and preserved as a museum. Porcelain pharmacists' jars and pharmaceutical instruments are displayed on the oak shelves. The museum, which charges $2, is open Monday–Saturday 10–6 and Sunday 9–1.

Dining and Lodging

$$ ✕ **Café Atenas.** On the Plaza de la Vigía, this friendly little café is near the major cultural treasures for which Matanzas became known as "The Athens of Cuba." The shady patio under a lush jungle of bougainvillea, grapevine, and ceiba trees may be less than a full-fledged restaurant, but the sandwiches and tapas are good, and the place is magic. ✉ *Calle 272, esquina de Calle 83,* ☎ *52/24–2702. No credit cards.*

$$ ✕ **La Viña.** This rustic and timeworn colonial charmer is the best known dining spot in Matanzas. This is, however, no guarantee as far as the fare is concerned. Stick with the guajiro specialties, such as *yuca con mojo* (manioc with criollo sauce), *arroz y moro* (rice with black beans), or *boniato* (sweet potato) in any of its many forms. ✉ *Calle 290 y Calle 83,* ☎ *52/24–2408. No credit cards.*

$ ⌂ **Hotel Louvre.** This cold-water (as of this writing, anyway) spot is a risky recommendation, not least because its policy on accepting foreigners has fluctuated in recent years. However, it's such an original and classic place in its decaying splendor that it's worth a try and may well have been restored and rehabilitated by the time you arrive. With antique-appointed bedrooms over the town's central square, the Louvre is the very essence of old Matanzas. ✉ *Plaza de la Libertad,* ☎ *52/24–4074,* ℻ *52/24–1040. 15 rooms. Restaurant, bar, free parking. No credit cards.*

SANTERÍA: A BLEND OF BELIEFS

IT SEEMS ANOTHER of Cuba's many ironies that a colony of the Spain that expelled its Jewish and Islamic communities in 1492 should prove such fertile ground for Santería, the marriage of West African animism and Spanish Catholicism. Throw in official Soviet-style atheism after 1959 and Pope John Paul II's moving visit in 1998, and the results are characterized by an extraordinary and exemplary degree of tolerance and spiritual eclecticism.

Santería is a fusion of Catholicism with, principally, the religion of the West African Yoruba tribe. Prohibited from practicing their religion in Cuba by their Spanish colonial masters, slaves superposed their pantheon of gods and goddesses over Christian saints. Any detail, be it a color or a characteristic, sufficed to identify an *orisha*, or Santería deity, with a Christian saint. Thus, for example, Ochún, the Venus-like goddess of fresh water, is associated with Cuba's patron saint La Virgen de la Caridad del Cobre (The Virgin of Charity of Copper). A beautiful mulatto, she's a symbol of sensuality, femininity, and love; wife of Orula; lover of Chango; and identified with the color yellow or gold. Chango—god of war, thunder, and fire—is associated with Santa Barbara. He is identified with the color red, and is avid for wealth and women. Yemayá is the black goddess of the sea who symbolizes life; she is also the patron saint of sailors, associated with the Virgen de Regla, and identified by the color blue. Obatalá is Zeus, associated with the Virgen de la Merced

and white, and respected by all the other orishas. The Yoruba religion has more than 400 orishas, of which some 40 have become part of Cuban Santería.

Throughout Cuban history, the Catholic church's presence has been discreet. During the Wars of Independence, the church sided with the Spanish, thus losing the little influence it had acquired. In 1959, most of the clergy fled with the wealthy Cubans to whom they had primarily administered, and the spiritual life of the island was left in the hands of Soviet-style dialectical materialism and Santería. Today in Cuba there are an estimated 10,000 *babalaos* (Santería priests), compared with some 300 Catholic priests.

Santería ceremonies build to sensorial crescendos of color, music (especially percussion), and a mixture of tobacco and incense. Devotees go into trancelike states of ecstasy, during which they're considered to be possessed by orishas and endowed with their powers. Even Fidel Castro, despite early efforts to suppress Santería, received the King of the Yorubas in 1986 and became a devotee of Obatalá on a trip to West Africa in the '70s. Castro may even owe his long tenure in power to the strength of Santería; the white dove that perched on his shoulder during his January 8, 1959, nationally televised victory speech is considered by *santeros* (believers of Santería) to be a symbol of prosperity, a sign sent to announce the chosen leader.

Nightlife and the Arts

With two locations, the **Casa de la Trova** is the main musical venue in Matanzas (which is known for the Afro-Cuban music of Santería). If you're lucky, you might catch Los Muñequitos, considered Cuba's top rumba combo. Performances are held Saturday afternoon and every evening. ⊠ *Calle 83 y Calle 304,* ☎ *52/24–2891;* ⊠ *Calle 272 y Calle 121,* ☎ *52/24–4129.*

The **Centro Nocturno** (⊠ Calle 83 y Calle 268, ☎ 52/24–2969) features musicians and a dance troupe, as well as stand-up comics. **Teatro Sal José White** (⊠ Plaza de la Libertad, ☎ 52/24–2911) stages jazz, dance, and classical music. The famous and ornate **Teatro Sauto** (⊠ Plaza de la Vigía, ☎ 52/24–8390) has folkloric performances, theater, and eclectic cultural opportunities.

Outdoor Activities and Sports

Matanzas is a big baseball town, with a first-division team that's usually a contender for the championship. The Matanzas team is nicknamed Los Henequeros for workers of the henequen fiber used in making rope, a local specialty. The 30,000-seat stadium (⊠ Av. Martín Dihigo s/n, ☎ 52/8813)—named **Victoria a Girón** in memory of the Bay of Pigs Invasion—occupies the site of Cuba's first baseball field, built in 1874. Check with the local tourist office for game times. Admission is just one peso.

Varadero

16 *140 km (87 mi) east of Havana.*

Varadero has suffered comparison with every place from Mexico's Cancún to Spain's Costa del Sol to Florida's Miami Beach. Even "Bangkok of the Caribbean" was tossed around before a government crackdown swept out thousands of *jineteras* (roughly translated as hustlers, often prostitutes) and the entire, corrupt police force en masse. Indeed, any resemblance to anything Cuban here is slight and fading fast. The narrow peninsula, really an elongated island separated from the mainland by the Laguna Paso Malo, is 18½ km (11 mi) long and is edged by nearly all white-sand beach and clear waters in mesmerizing blues, greens, and aquamarines. At an average width of 700 m (770 yards), Varadero extends northeast to Punta Hicacos, Cuba's northernmost point—just 211 km (131 mi) from Florida's Key West.

Depending on your tastes and ambitions, Varadero is either a paradigmatic tropical paradise or a tourist inferno, but the fact remains: the beaches are excellent and the tourist infrastructure, from cuisine to sailing and fishing to the disco-driven social scene, is as comprehensive and complete as anywhere in the world.

Laid out in three longitudinal avenues intersected by 69 cross streets, Varadero offers navigational ease. The town itself, a modest village of some 15,000 inhabitants, is now nearly lost among the maze of hotels. Originally inhabited by Taíno aboriginals, Varadero was settled by the Spanish in the late 16th century. It wasn't until the late 19th century that families from Cárdenas began to build summer houses here. In 1883, the first town council of families established a plan for building baths and recreational facilities. The Varadero Hotel opened in 1915, and in 1926, the Du Pont de Nemours family—powerful American industrialists whose early fortune was made in gunpowder—bought most of the peninsula and built a large estate complete with a golf course. Other wealthy Norteamericanos followed, including Al Capone. By the 1950s, numerous hotels were under construction, following the example of the Hotel Internacional, known as a quintessential den of iniquity complete with casino, mobsters, and abundant available women. After 1959, the Revolution declared the elitist enclave public property and rank-and-file Cubans were allowed on the beach; the U.S. embargo shut down the hotel boom, at least as far as Americans were concerned, though Varadero then became a favorite Russian resort where Eastern European tourists frolicked in the sun and guzzled mojitos right under Uncle Sam's nose.

Things to do and see in Varadero, aside from the obvious range of beach activities and water sports, begin with the Du Pont mansion, **Las Américas,** originally christened Xanadu after a verse from the Samuel Taylor Coleridge poem *Kubla Khan* (In Xanadu did Kubla Khan / A stately pleasure dome decree . . .). With six rooms for rent, this is by far the top lodging choice in Varadero, though reservations need to be secured many months in advance. The restaurant and top-floor terrace and bar offer a nonpareil place for an evening mojito overlooking both sides of the wind-whipped peninsula. Even if you're not staying at Las Américas, a guided tour of the house will help you to understand the level of luxury the Du Ponts established here. Such is the legend of the Du Pont villa that Cubanas celebrating their 15th birthdays—the age considered the beginning of young womanhood in Cuba—still come, sometimes from Havana or even farther away, to pose for photographs on the marble stairway dressed in antique ball gowns.

Parque Josone (⊠ Av. 1 y Calle 56, ☎ 5/66–2740), a municipal park that once was the home of a wealthy sugar-mill owner, is a tranquil spot with swans and flamingos, rowboats for rent, three restaurants, and various open-air bars. Admission is $5.

The **Museo Municipal** is housed in Varadero's prettiest early 20th-century summer house, built entirely of wood and painted sky-blue with white trim. Photographs of early Varadero and the de rigueur shots of Che and Fidel "taking" the Hotel Internacional after the Revolution are among the memorabilia. ⊠ *Calle 57, esquina de Av. Playa,* ☎ *5/61–3189.* 🖭 *$2.* ⊙ *Tues.–Sat. 9–6, Sun. 9–noon.*

The **Delfinarium** has a troupe of acrobatic dolphins to admire (and, for an extra fee, to swim with) at Punta Rincón Francés, near the eastern end of the peninsula. ⊠ *Punta Rincón Francés,* ☎ *5/66–8031.* 🖭 *$5.* ⊙ *Performances daily at 11, 2:30, and 4.*

The **Cueva de Ambrosio** contains some 72 aboriginal drawings thought to be more than 3,000 years old. Entering the cave, which is lit by sunlight that comes in through an opening in the ceiling, requires a 300-m (990-ft) walk through dense jungle. ⊠ *Punta Rincón Francés.* 🖭 *$2.* ⊙ *Mon.–Sat. 9–5.*

Dining and Lodging

$$$–$$$$ ✕ **La Fondue.** Fondues with Cuban cheeses are the specialty here; lobster, chicken, and beef in different cheese dressings are also standard fare. Its location makes La Fondue an easy stroll from many of the mid-range hotels in central Varadero. ⊠ *Av. 1, esquina de Calle 62,* ☎ *5/66–7747. Reservations essential. MC, V.*

$$$ ✕ **Albacora.** This excellent seafood restaurant is named for the albacore, or long-finned, tuna, which has darker meat than the bonito and—as served here with a lemon-based sauce—is exquisite. But Albacora is more than a one-trick pony; it serves other seafood and fish specialties, from lobster to crab to calamari. ⊠ *Calle 60, esquina de Mar,* ☎ *5/66–3650. MC, V.*

$$$ ✕ **Antigüedades.** Next to the entrance of the Parque Josone, this ro-
★ mantic spot is a jumble of antique artifacts and furniture, with tables set into through-the-looking-glass corners that seem like miniature

movie sets nestled amid the paraphernalia. The fare features fresh seafood, including lobster and shrimp. There's no menu: the waiter will recite what the last fishing boat brought in and what he recommends. ⊠ *Av. 1 y Calle 59, Parque Josone,* ☎ *5/66–7329. Reservations essential. MC, V.*

$$$ ✕ **El Bodegón Criollo.** First-rate Cuban cooking is served in this Varadero takeoff on Havana's Bodeguita del Medio—the famous Hemingway haunt—graffiti included. The food is carefully prepared, the prices are more than reasonable, and the musical trio is one of the reasons diners linger late into the evening. ⊠ *Av. de la Playa y Calle 40,* ☎ *5/66–7784. MC, V.*

$$$ ✕ **El Mesón del Quijote.** Cuban and international specialties are pre-
★ pared here, including everything from *moros y cristianos* (black beans and rice) to fresh fish dishes. The beamed ceiling and simple Castilian decor are perfect for a tavern named for the great Cervantes hero, and the setting atop a hill overlooking Avenida de las Américas serves up panoramic views. The fare offers no cause for disappointment. ⊠ *Av. de las Américas,* ☎ *5/66–7796. MC, V.*

$$$$ ✕▥ **Club Varadero.** Three kilometers (two miles) east of Varadero vil-
★ lage, this comprehensive complex offers everything from water sports to cabaret. There's no need to ever leave the hotel grounds. A Cuban–Jamaican joint venture, the hotel has some of the prettiest rooms in Varadero as well as one of the better buffets. The scuba and dive program and training course are considered among the most competent on the peninsula. ⊠ *Av. de las Américas, Km 3,* ☎ *5/66–7030,* ℻ *5/66–7005. 270 rooms and suites. 3 restaurants, bar, pool, beach, dive shop, dock, snorkeling, surfing, windsurfing, boating, jet skiing, parasailing, waterskiing, free parking. MC, V.*

$$$$ ✕▥ **Meliá Varadero.** This was the first five-star hotel to go up in Va-
★ radero and it remains at the top of the rapidly growing heap. The six wings that fan out from the dizzying circular atrium are impressive, and the quality of the rooms and restaurants doesn't disappoint. Each room has a balcony, the best with sweeping ocean views, while the swimming pools are bordered by thick tropical vines and trees. ⊠ *Playa de las Américas, Carretera de las Morlas,* ☎ *5/66–7013,* ℻ *5/66–7012. 490 rooms, 7 suites. 3 restaurants, bar, 2 pools, beach, dive shop, dock, snorkeling, surfing, windsurfing, boating, jet skiing, waterskiing, free parking. MC, V.*

$$$–$$$$ ✕▥ **Las Américas.** The old Du Pont mansion offers only half a dozen
★ rooms. If you can't get a reservation, it's worth stopping by to ask whether perhaps someone hasn't shown up. Unlike most of the vast tourist complexes in Varadero, this noble villa, product of a million-aire's fancy, has the most old-fashioned, oak- and mahogany-beamed rooms in Varadero. The upper story is one of the prettiest places to dine on the peninsula (reservations are essential), even if it is a bit over-priced and the food below par. So don't expect too much; just enjoy the views and the experience of living it up like a Du Pont. ⊠ *Av. de las Américas,* ☎ *5/66–7750,* ℻ *5/66–8481. 6 rooms. Restaurant, bar, free parking. MC, V.*

$$$ ✕▥ **Cuatro Palmas.** The pool and bar at this sprawling complex, which was built around former dictator Batista's summer house, are attractively arranged, and the atmosphere here is refreshingly relaxed. Rooms vary radically, from the somewhat substandard "standards" to the ones with upgraded facilities and double beds. Ask for one of those with views of the ocean. ⊠ *Av. 1, e/Calle 61 y Calle 62,* ☎ *5/66–7040,* ℻ *5/66–7028. 309 rooms, 7 suites. Restaurant, bar, pool, beach, free parking. MC, V.*

$$$ ✕▥ **Hotel Tuxpan.** This German-run resort is built around a kidney-shape pool and has a lobby designed to resemble a Mayan temple.

Still, the hotel is tastefully furnished, and everything is relentlessly punctual and well prepared. ⊠ *Av. de las Américas, Km 3.5,* ☎ *5/66–7560,* FAX *5/66–7561. 235 rooms. Restaurant, bar, pool, beach, free parking. MC, V.*

$$$ ✕⊞ **Sol Palmeras.** You'll find everything you might need at this well-equipped, well-organized complex run by Spain's Grupo Sol. The lobby is like a spectacularly lush jungle, with a racket of birdsong to add to the ambience. Most of the well-furnished rooms have views of the Atlantic, and the bougainvillea-covered bungalows have pretty terraces. (Bring mosquito repellent.) ⊠ *Autopista del Sur,* ☎ *5/66–7009,* FAX *5/66–7008. 375 rooms, 32 suites, 200 bungalows. Restaurant, bar, pool, free parking. MC, V.*

$$–$$$ ⊞ **Hotel Riu Las Morlas.** Rooms at this mid-price hotel have all the modern conveniences and ocean views. The Riu Las Morlas is smaller and has a more down-to-earth feel than many of the peninsula's hotels. ⊠ *Av. de las Américas,* ☎ *5/66–7230,* FAX *5/66–7007. 148 rooms, 9 suites. Restaurant, bar, minibars, pool, free parking. MC, V.*

Nightlife and the Arts

NIGHTLIFE

Many hotels in Varadero have dance clubs, but there are a few standouts. The $10 cover charge at the torrid disco **La Bamba** (⊠ Av. de las Américas, ☎ 5/66–6200) gets you access to an open bar. At the **Cabaret Continental** (⊠ Av. de las Américas, ☎ 5/66–7038), in the Hotel Varadero International, you pay $15 or $40 (with dinner) to see Varadero's best Tropicana-style cabaret show at 10 PM; afterward you can dance till dawn.

A Canadian favorite, **La Cancha (Disco Azúcar)** (⊠ Av. 1 y Calle 25, ☎ 5/66–1341) is the bargain disco (there's only a $5 cover), where you can learn salsa moves and even bring your own bottle of rum. The **Cueva del Pirata** (⊠ Autopista del Sur, Km 11, ☎ 5/66–7751) is an underground cave where, for $5, you can see an Afro-Cuban review and then dance afterward. **Havana Club** (⊠ Av. de las Américas, ☎ 5/66–4100) is another standby; the cover is $10. **Disco Kastillito** (⊠ Av. de la Playa y Calle 49, ☎ 5/66–3888) is a favorite, offering fashion shows with drop-dead models and feverish dancing until sunrise—for $5.

THE ARTS

The **Casa de la Cultura** (⊠ Av. 1 y Calle 49, ☎ 5/66–3311) hosts concerts and Afro-Cuban dance performances; admission is $3. The various restaurants of **Parque Josone** (⊠ Av. 1 y Calle 56, ☎ 5/66–2740), which charges $5 admission, have concerts. Also in the park is the **Rincón de los Enamorados** (Lovers' Corner), where choral or classical music is performed every night.

Outdoor Activities and Sports

For the most part, you make arrangements for water sports through hotels, with everything from windsurfers to catamarans available, along with jet skiing, waterskiing, parasailing, and nearly every imaginable kind of diving and snorkeling trip. Nonguests can use many of the hotel tennis courts for a $2–$3 fee.

FISHING

Marina Chapelin (⊠ Autopista del Sur, Km 13, ☎ 5/66–7093) can arrange fishing trips. A six-hour, four-person excursion costs $250.

GOLF

At the 18-hole **Golf Club Las Américas** (⊠ Av. de las Américas, ☎ 5/66–8180) the greens fee is $60; for a round of twilight golf (after 5:30), the fee is $20. Carts, clubs, and caddies are available for $10 each.

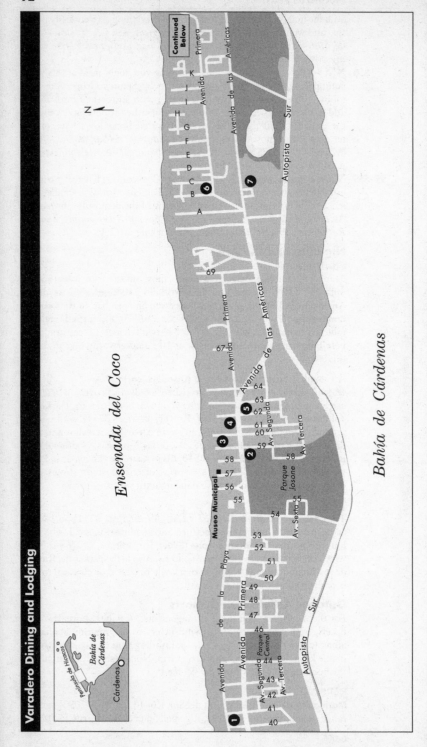

Ensenada del Coco

Bahía de Cárdenas

Continued Below

Museo Municipal

Varadero Dining and Lodging

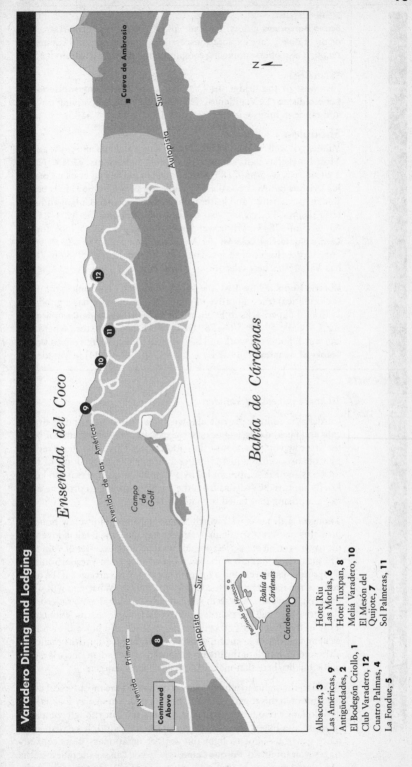

Ensenada del Coco

Bahía de Cárdenas

Cueva de Ambrosio

N

Continued Above

Albacora, **3**
Las Américas, **9**
Antigüedades, **2**
El Bodegón Criollo, **1**
Club Varadero, **12**
Cuatro Palmas, **4**
La Fondue, **5**

Hotel Riu
Las Morlas, **6**
Hotel Tuxpan, **8**
Meliá Varadero, **10**
El Mesón del
Quijote, **7**
Sol Palmeras, **11**

Scuba Barracuda (⊠ Av. 1 y Calle 58, ☎ 5/66–3481) can arrange day
or night dives, cave explorations, certification courses, and equipment
rental. It also offers snorkeling equipment and guided excursions for $25.

Just west of the bridge into Varadero, the **Centro Internacional de
Paracaidismo** (⊠ Via Blanca, ☎ 5/66–7265) offers skydiving training
and tandem jumps with a professional instructor for $135.

Shopping

Varadero is well endowed with souvenir shops and arts and crafts goods.
Most hotels have gift shops and souvenir emporiums. **ARTEX** (⊠ Av.
1 y Calle 61, ☎ 5/66–7189) sells a range of music and books. **Casa de
las Orishas** (⊠ Av. 1 e/Calle 33 y Calle 34, ☎ 5/61–3663) sells beads,
weavings, carvings, and leather goods based on Afro-Cuban and Santería themes. For cigars, visit the **Casa del Habano** (⊠ Av. 1 y Calle
61, ☎ 5/66–7843). While wandering through Varadero, look for the
Centro Comercial Caimán (⊠ Av. 1, e/Calle 61 y Calle 62, ☎ 5/66–
7692) for a cluster of shops. The center's **Max Music** (☎ 5/66–7692)
has Varadero's best selection of Cuban music.

Librería Hanoi (⊠ Av. 1 y Calle 44, ☎ 5/66–8917) is strong in the usual
sociopolitical tracts approved by the regime, and also has a good collection of paperbacks in English. The **Taller y Tienda de Cerámica** (⊠
Av. 1 y Calle 59, ☎ 5/66–7691) is a workshop and store where you
can watch potters at work and buy original pieces. There's even a **United
Colors of Benetton** (⊠ Av. 1 y Calle 39, ☎ 5/66–5334) in Varadero.

Cárdenas

⑰ *10 km (6 mi) east of Varadero.*

Cárdenas is a simple provincial town known for its many horse-drawn
cabs and buckboards, its flocks of bicycles, its crab fishery, and for being
the first town in Cuba to raise the national flag. This event, much revered
by Cubans, occurred in 1850 after a motley mercenary force of Ken-
tuckians and Mississippians led by a Venezuelan named Narciso López
briefly captured Cárdenas from the Spanish, hoping to provoke a national uprising that failed to materialize.

Though Cárdenas is well worth browsing through for a few hours, it
probably doesn't warrant an overnight stay unless you fall in love with
the town as an all but perfect antidote to the tourist excesses of Varadero.
The gigantic stone crab at the town line coming from Varadero and the
sculptures of a bicycle and a *caleta* (a horse-drawn carriage) at the other
end are the most emblematic Cárdenas symbols. What you will see in
between, however, may seem screechingly squalid after Varadero. But
the patient eye will be rewarded with an undeniable charm. With barely
a car in the streets (it's all pedestrians, cyclists, and horse-drawn buggies) and flocks of beautiful young women headed for the beaches of
Varadero in search of the dream European or Canadian, there is a dramatic quality here that makes Cárdenas hard to forget.

A ride to the sights in a horse-drawn carriage is the most typical event
to engineer in this town. The standard fare of one peso may soar as high
as a dollar or two for foreigners, but that's still fair enough compared
to horse and buggy rides anywhere else in the world. It's easier—and
more generous—not to fight this sort of inflationary practice. Carriages wait for hire in **Parque Colón,** where you can see the oldest statue
of Columbus in the New World (erected in 1858). On the park, at the
center of Cárdenas, the mid-19th-century **Catedral de la Inmaculada
Concepción** is known for the design of its stained-glass windows.

Other sights to seek out include the neoclassical **Casa Natal de José Antonio Echeverría,** now the municipal museum. Built in 1873, the two-story town house has a wooden spiral staircase, hand-carved and intricately decorated. Named for a student revolutionary murdered by Batista forces in 1957, the museum's top floor is filled with Echeverría memorabilia along with photographs and documents of other local Revolutionary martyrs and heroes. ⊠ *Calle Genes 240,* ☎ *5/52–4919.* ▦ *$2.* ☉ *Tues.–Sat. 9–6, Sun. 9–1.*

For a change of pace from sociology and politics to biology, the **Museo Oscar María de Rojas** is an eclectic potpourri of bugs, butterflies, *polymitas* (snails with multicolored shells), and even two fleas in nuptial dress. In addition, there are the usual photographs of Cárdenas heroes of the Wars of Independence and the Revolution as well as a lavish black baroque 19th-century horse-drawn hearse. ⊠ *Calle Calzada 4,* ☎ *5/52–4126.* ▦ *$1.* ☉ *Tues.–Sat. 9–6, Sun. 9–1.*

Dining and Lodging

$ ✕ **Café la Cubanita.** This simple café, an open-air restaurant that serves criollo specialties such as yuca con mojo and *tachino* (fried plantain), is popular with the locals. Don't expect greatness here, but it's a good way to get a look at what life in Cárdenas is all about. ⊠ *Av. 5 y Calle Concha,* ☎ *5/52–3678. No credit cards.*

$ ✕ **Restaurante Las Palmas.** One of the most impressive buildings in Cárdenas, this grandiose mansion is a hub of activity with its cabaret and disco. Fresh seafood is the best bet here, especially the crabmeat Cárdenas is known for. ⊠ *Av. Céspedes y Calle 16,* ☎ *5/52–4762. No credit cards.*

$ ▥ **Hotel La Dominica.** This traditional Cárdenas hotel is famous as the place where the Cuban flag was first raised. The ancient colonial architecture is charming, though the condition of the rooms leaves much to be desired. Still, if you find ancient places and decaying splendor romantic, you may prefer this to the luxuries of Varadero. ⊠ *Parque Colón,* ☎ *5/52–1502. 25 rooms. Restaurant, bar, free parking. No credit cards.*

Nightlife and the Arts

The Hotel La Dominica and the Restaurante Las Palmas have cabaret shows, both interesting in comparison to the extravaganzas at Varadero or at Havana's Tropicana. The cabaret performance is followed by disco.

Península de Zapata

⑱ *100 km (62 mi) southwest of Cárdenas, 190 km (118 mi) southeast of Havana.*

The Península de Zapata, so called for its slipper-shaped outline, is also known as La Ciénaga de Zapata (the Swamp of Zapata). It's Cuba's largest wetland and wildlife sanctuary, officially the Gran Parque Natural Montemar. On the peninsula's southern shore is the Bahía de los Cochinos, known around the world for the 1961 Bay of Pigs Invasion mounted by Cuban exiles with the backing and training of the U.S. Central Intelligence Agency. The invasion itself is known simply as "La Victoria" after Castro proclaimed it the first New World victory over American imperialism.

Places to visit on the Península de Zapata begin with the village of **Australia.** During the Bay of Pigs Invasion, Castro had his headquarters near the village in a sugar mill, part of which is now a museum housing photographs and memorabilia from "La Victoria." Turn-of-the-century locomotives still haul sugarcane in and out of the giant mill. The museum is open Mon.–Sat. 8–5, Sun. 8–1; admission is $2.

The **Finca Fiesta Campesina** (Km 142 off the Autopista Nacional) is an entertaining farm and museum showcasing most of Cuba's autochthonous flora and fauna, and a palm-tree climber who can, with lightning speed, scale a 30-m (99-ft) palm using a system of spike-free loops and stir-rups. There is also a *manjuarí*, Cuba's most primitive form of fish life, and a *jutía*, a weasel-like tree rat much prized for guajiro stews.

Some 3,000 crocodiles can be observed at **La Boca de Guamá** (a crocodile farm), many of them from the wooden walkways through the pools. Custodian Emilio Hernandez explains how Celia Sánchez, a Castro companion and adviser, was determined to restore the fail-ing crocodile population. He also explains that crocodiles are naturally aggressive, able to jump a meter (3 ft) and run as fast as a horse for 80 m (264 ft), reaching speeds of up to 60 kph (37 mph). There's even a restaurant on the premises (☞ Dining and Lodging, *below*). ⊠ *Car-retera 3-1-16, Km 19 south of Australia,* ☎ *59/2458.* ☜ *$3.*

La Laguna del Tesoro (Treasure Lagoon) is where, according to legend, Taíno aboriginals dumped gold and other priceless loot to hide it from the Spanish. No treasure has been found, although Taíno relics have been recovered from the lake and contributed to the **Museo Guamá**, a replica of a Taíno village. It includes sculpted figures, by the famous Cuban sculptor Rita Longa, of Taínos going about their daily business.

Dining and Lodging

$$ ✕ **La Boca.** The country criollo cooking is quite acceptable here, de-spite the concurrence of busloads of travelers on package tours. Roast crocodile tail is the house specialty, a famous Cuban favorite believed to be an aphrodisiac. The chicken in criollo sauce is standard fare, as are fish dishes, especially the *pargo* (red snapper). ⊠ *Carretera 3-1-16, Km 19 south of Australia,* ☎ *59/2458. No credit cards.*

$–$$ ✕🏠 **Bohío de Don Pedro.** This typical farm is a rustic refuge from the cane fields. A dozen bohíos, well-equipped thatched-roofed wooden cabins, are surrounded by a full complement of farm animals and the hospitality of Don Pedro and his wife. With the excellent Cuban home cooking thrown in, this authentic place is a boon and bargain for these or any parts. ⊠ *Finca Fiesta Campesina–Australia,* ☎ *59/2535. 12 cabins. Restaurant. No credit cards.*

$$$ 🏠 **Villa Guamá.** Once a Castro bass-fishing refuge (Bohío 33 was his), this odd hideaway spread over 12 little islands in the Zapata swamp-lands' Laguna del Tesoro has thatch-roofed bohíos with good screens and adequate comfort—though the mosquitoes can be fierce, and the 24-hour public-address music system goes a long way toward de-stroying the peace and quiet the place is supposedly known for. A 15-minute boat ride to the headquarters, which sits on stilts, is followed by a five-minute canoe ride to guest cabins. Visitors boat to the main lodge for meals. This is an interesting place to have a look at, but un-less you long to try the bass fishing, steer clear. ⊠ *Laguna del Tesoro,* ☎ *59/5551,* ☎ *59/5551. 50 cabins. Restaurant, 3 bars, dance club. MC, V.*

Bahía de Cochinos

⑲   *125 km (78 mi) south of Varadero.*

The bay gets its name from the *cochinos cimarrones* (free-range pigs) that Spanish colonists either lost or deliberately stocked in the Zapata swamps during the 16th century. The counterrevolutionary invasion that took place here April 17, 1961, and forever immortalized this inlet, was actually an alternate to the scrapped "Trinidad Plan." The inva-sion—bungled in every imaginable way by a combination of bureau-

WITHOUT KODAK MAX
photos taken on 100 speed film

Ever see someone

waiting for the sun to come out

while trying to photograph

a charging rhino?

New!
Kodak Max film:

Now with better color,
Kodak's maximum
versatility film gives
you great pictures in
sunlight, low light,
action or still.

WITH KODAK MAX
photos taken on Kodak Max 400 film

It's all you need
to know about film.

www.kodak.com

Distinctive guides packed with up-to-date expert advice
and smart choices for every type of traveler.

Fodor's. For the world of ways you travel.

cratic confusion and, fundamentally, by a lack of commitment on the part of everyone but the Cuban exiles accounting for nearly all of the 1,300-man landing force—resulted in a resounding defeat for the invaders. More than 1,100 brigade members were captured, with more than 110 killed. In December 1962, most of the prisoners were returned to the United States in exchange for a ransom of $53 million in medical supplies. Even today, "La Victoria" is one of Cuba's great rallying points and sources of pride. Along the road between La Boca de Guamá and Playa Girón, you will see menhirlike concrete slabs commemorating Cuban defenders who fell in the invasion.

At the head of the bay is **Playa Larga** (Long Beach). The Salinas Wildlife Refuge on the Laguna de las Salinas, 15 km (9 mi) south of here, and the Gran Parque Natural Montemar are accessed via Playa Larga, where a checkpoint allows cars through only with a guide and permit (both obtainable at the Villa Playa Larga hotel; ☞ Dining and Lodging, *below*).

Several attractions are not to be missed as you drive from Playa Larga to Playa Girón, on the far east side of the bay. **Caleta del Rosario,** 4 km (2½ mi) south of Playa Larga, is a lovely, small beach with crystalline waters, a café, and a few cabins to rent. The road is lined with karst or limestone sinkholes called cenotes. La Casa del Pescador (☞ Dining and Lodging, *below*) is a sweet little restaurant overlooking **El Cenote,** a 210-m-deep (693-ft-deep) sinkhole filled with unbelievably clear blue, green, and turquoise water. **La Cueva de los Peces** (Cave of the Fish), 15 km (9 mi) south of Playa Larga, is a 61-m-deep (201-ft-deep) cenote filled with multicolored fish surrounded by lush subaquatic tropical vegetation. The fish come from the Caribbean through a subterranean passage. Diving here through the banks of fish is superb.

Playa Girón is a sleepy village of some 400 inhabitants, in the middle of which stands a billboard that says: *PLAYA GIRÓN—LA PRIMERA DERROTA DEL IMPERIALISMO NORTEAMERICANO EN AMÉRICA LATINA* (Playa Girón—the first defeat of U.S. imperialism in Latin America). Now a mediocre tourist destination, with an ugly breakwater just off the beach, this is where most of the Bahía de Cochinos battle took place. The **Museo Playa Girón** (⊠ Playa Girón, Carretera 3-1-16, ☎ 59/4122) is one of Cuba's most interesting museums, featuring a photographic history of the social conditions that provoked the Revolution, the counterrevolutionary events after 1959 leading up to the Bay of Pigs Invasion, and the story of the invasion itself. The museum is open 9–noon and 1–5 daily; admission is $3.

★ **Caleta Buena,** 9 km (5½ mi) east of Playa Girón, is one of the region's prettiest spots to visit. At Caleta Buena, which means "good cove," the sea has formed a series of natural pools by entering through underwater caves. The bottom of sponge and coral is a polychromatic marvel, as are the many tropical fish. A 25-m (83-ft) tunnel through the limestone leads out to the sea, for well-prepared and -equipped divers. The restaurant is open until 5 and serves shrimp and lobster as the house specialty. (If you're having lunch here, the $2 admission is waived.) In springtime, be prepared for the dead land crabs and accompanying vultures that will cover the roads. ⊠ *Carretera 3-1-16, Km 9 east of Playa Girón,* ☎ *59/5589.* ☜ *$2; equipment rental for snorkeling, $3; diving, $20.* ☉ *Daily 10–5.*

Dining and Lodging

$–$$ ✕ **La Casa del Pescador.** This pretty restaurant next to the sinkhole known as El Cenote has it all: scenery; superb diving opportunities; and fresh shrimp, pargo, and lobster. Open only for lunch, this is a spot worth timing your appetite for. ⊠ *Carretera Playa Larga–Playa Girón, Km 8,* ☎ *no phone. No credit cards.*

$$–$$$ 🏨 **Villa Playa Larga.** With cabins spread around bougainvillea-filled gardens and lawns and water sports from windsurfing to diving, this comprehensive operation makes a good base for bird-watching in the Zapata wetlands, fishing in the Laguna de las Salinas, or just exploring the surrounding karstic landscape. And the beach here is excellent. ⊠ *Playa Larga, Ciénaga de Zapata,* ☎ *59/7225,* FAX *59/7219. 57 rooms. Restaurant, bar, cafeteria, air-conditioning, kitchenettes, pool, beach, dive shop, nightclub, free parking. No credit cards.*

$$ 🏨 **Villa Playa Girón.** The grim decor of these concrete cabins seems appropriate for defending against the invasion of capitalism in more than the military sense. Despite the kidney-shape pool and the acceptable buffet meals, this is a place to use only in case your itinerary can't be arranged to spend the night elsewhere (or for getting a good look at the Museo Playa Girón, which is very much worth the visit). The excursions the hotel organizes are its best feature. ⊠ *Playa Girón,* ☎ *59/4110,* FAX *59/4117. 292 rooms. Restaurant, bar, air-conditioning, pool, beach, dive shop, dance club, shop, free parking. MC, V.*

WESTERN CUBA A TO Z

Arriving and Departing

By Airplane

International flights fly directly to Varadero and Cayo Largo from Canada, Mexico, and Europe, though most flights connect in Havana or Varadero.

Cubana de Aviación flights to Nueva Gerona depart from Havana at 7:15 AM and 7:55 PM daily, and at 9:30 AM Monday and Friday. From the Nueva Gerona airport, return flights leave at 8:15 AM and 8:55 PM. **Aerocaribbean** (☎ 61/22690) operates charter flights from Havana and Varadero to Nueva Gerona and Cayo Largo. **Aerotaxi** (☎ 7/66–7540) operates flights from Havana to Cayo Largo, Pinar del Río, and Trinidad. Cayo Largo is connected by domestic flights to Havana, Cienfuegos, and Santiago de Cuba via Aerocaribbean, Aerotaxi, and Cubana de Aviación.

AIRPORTS

Nueva Gerona's **Aeropuerto Rafael Cabrera** (☎ 61/22690) is 15 km (9 mi) south of town. The Pinar del Río airport, **Aeropuerto Álvaro Barba** (☎ 82/2448), is 2 km (1 mi) north of town. The airport serving Varadero—**Aeropuerto Juan Gualberto Gomez** (☎ 56/63016)—is 16 km (10 mi) west of the peninsula.

By Bus

Bus service to western Cuba from other parts of the mainland is available, but generally not recommended. Buses between the Varadero station (⊠ Autopista Sur y Calle 36) and Havana's Terminal Ómnibus, however, are quick and frequent.

By Car

Automobile is the only reliable and convenient means of transportation in Cuba. The Autopista Nacional, a six-lane central artery designated A-1, connects all points in western Cuba and continues east as far as the center of Ciego de Ávila Province. For speed and safety, this is undoubtedly the best route to take, although the Carretera Central (Central Highway)—a standard two-lane highway that traverses the Cuban mainland from one end to the other—is more scenic, winding through little towns and villages. The road to take between Havana,

Matanzas, and Varadero is the Vía Blanca, a four-lane freeway in even better condition than the A-1.

High-speed travel should be approached cautiously as potholes tend to turn up in even the best surfaces. In addition, railroad tracks cross the A-1 in several places. Loose animals, farmers in horse-drawn carts, and, in May, crabs leaving the swamps to lay their eggs in the sand also add to the region's driving hazards.

By Taxi

A taxi between Havana and Matanzas takes an hour and costs $75, or whatever you can negotiate. Try for $25; it's only 100 km (62 mi). Taxis around western Cuba are generally available between major points, though rates can be extortionate.

By Train

Train service around western Cuba connects—albeit somewhat erratically—Pinar del Río, Matanzas, and Varadero with Havana. Train passage must be purchased in dollars at the **Ladis** office (⊠ Calle Arsenal y Calle Cienfuegos, ☎ 7/62–1770) outside Havana's railroad station. For railroad information, call the offices located at Av. de Bélgica and Calle Arsenal (☎ 7/62–1920).

A trip on the famous electric *Hershey Train* from Havana's Casablanca district to Matanzas is a four-hour rattle through the scenic Valle de Yumurí. Trains depart Havana at 4:35 and 9:25 AM and at 3:45 and 8:55 PM; they leave Matanzas at 3:55 and 10:20 AM and at 2:55 and 9:19 PM. The 9:25 AM train from Havana is the suggested trip, though this means your only viable train back leaves Matanzas at 9:19 PM and gets into Havana after 1 AM.

Getting Around

By Airplane

Outside of Havana, Varadero is the point best connected to the rest of Cuba by air. Cayo Largo is connected by domestic flights to Varadero and the Isla de la Juventud, and other points on the mainland.

Aerotaxi (☎ 7/66–7540) offers flights between Pinar del Río and Nueva Gerona Monday, Wednesday, Friday, and Saturday for $20 one way. (For more information on air travel, *see* Arriving and Departing, *above*.)

By Boat

Boats to Isla de la Juventud depart from Surgidero de Batabanó, 70 km (43 mi) south of Havana, at 7:30 AM, arriving in Nueva Gerona's ferry terminal at 1:30 PM. Hydrofoil connections aboard the Russian-built *Kometa* are far faster, leaving Surgidero de Batabanó at 10 AM and 4 PM for the two-hour trip. The regular ferry costs $10 one way; the hydrofoil costs $15.

By Bus

Bus travel is slow and hot, though rock-bottom cheap. Connections are so sporadic to remote areas such as the Zapata wetlands or the Península de Guanahacabibes that you'll spend more time waiting and riding than being anywhere.

By Car

Provincial roads in western Cuba are usually in fair-to-good condition. Even the Autopista Nacional, the island's greatest freeway, has occasional holes and heaves and shouldn't be trusted at high speeds. Stray animals, horse-drawn carts, hitchhikers, and (on the Península de Zapata) migratory crabs are the worst driving hazards. There are no toll roads, and gasoline availability is generally good at the Servi-Cupet stations. Payment is in U.S. dollars only.

Outside Varadero and Nueva Gerona, car rentals are difficult to arrange in provincial Cuba. They're available in Pinar del Río at the Hotel Pinar del Río and in the Varadero and Nueva Gerona areas through **Havanautos** (⊠ Hotel Pinar del Río, Calle Martí, Pinar del Río, ☎ 82/5071; ⊠ Av. 1, e/Calle 55 y Calle 56, Varadero, ☎ 5/66-7094; ⊠ Aeropuerto Juan Gualberto Gomez, ☎ 5/66-7300; ⊠ Servi-Cupet, Calle 39 y Calle 32, Nueva Gerona, ☎ 61/2300; ⊠ Villa Gaviota, Autopista Nueva Gerona–La Fé, Km 2, ☎ 61/3256). In Playa Girón, **Transauto** (⊠ Carretera 3–1–16, ☎ 59/4144) has an office across from Villa Playa Girón.

By Taxi

Rates are variable, but most drivers will ask for about a dollar a kilometer for travel within a city or town or small area. In Pinar del Río, tourist taxis can be arranged at the Hotel Pinar del Río. In Varadero, taxis wait outside the Hotel Cuatro Palmas; the fare from one end of the peninsula to the other shouldn't exceed $5. In Matanzas, taxis are available at the Plaza de la Vigía.

In Nueva Gerona, taxis gather at the corner of Calles 32 and 39, while horse-drawn buggies wait at the ferry terminal; the fare for a buggy to a hotel should be about $2. In Cárdenas, which has few cars, a horse-drawn carriage is the way to go.

Contacts and Resources

Emergencies

CÁRDENAS

Hospital Julio María Aristegui Villamil: (⊠ Carretera Varadero, Km 7, ☎ 5/52–4011). **Scuba Diving Emergencies:** a decompression chamber is available at the hospital's Centro Médico Sub Acuática. **Police:** (☎ 116).

MATANZAS

Hospital Juan Ramón Tabranis: (⊠ Calle Santa Rita s/n, ☎ 52/24-7011). **Pharmacy:** (⊠ Calle 81 esquina de Calle 284). **Police:** (☎ 116).

NUEVA GERONA

Hospital Heroes de Baire: (⊠ Calle 18 esquina de Calle 41, ☎ 61/2-3012). **Pharmacy:** (⊠ Calle 39 esquina de Calle 24, ☎ 61/2-1532). **Police:** (☎ 116).

PENÍNSULA DE ZAPATA

Hospital Playa Girón (⊠ Gran Parque Montemar, ☎ 59/4196); **Hospital Playa Larga** (⊠ Gran Parque Montemar, ☎ 59/7116). **Pharmacy:** (⊠ Carretera 3-1-16, Playa Girón). **Police:** (☎ 59/5107).

PINAR DEL RÍO

Hospital Quirúrgico: (⊠ Calle Isabel Rubio, or Carretera de Viñales, s/n, ☎ 82/4443). **Scuba Diving Emergencies:** the María la Gorda International Dive Center (⊠ Bahía de Corrientes, ☎ 84/3121) is fully equipped with decompression and hyperbaric chambers. **Police:** (☎ 82/2525). **Pharmacy:** (⊠ Calle Isabel Rubio esquina de Calle Martí).

VARADERO

Clínica Internacional: (⊠ Av. Primera esquina de Calle 61, ☎ 5/66–2122) for immediate medical attention. **Pharmacy:** (⊠ Av. Primera esquina de Calle 28, ☎ 5/66–2772). **Police:** (☎ 115). **Scuba Diving Emergencies:** the Cárdenas hospital (☞ *above*) has a decompression chamber.

VIÑALES
Hospital Policlínico: (✉ Calle Salvador Cisnero s/n, ☎ 8/38107). **Pharmacy:** (✉ Calle Salvador Cisnero, ☎ 8/93169). **Police:** (☎ 8/93124).

Health and Safety
Cuba's tap water is probably safe to drink, but bottled mineral water is even safer. Avoid unpeeled, unwashed fruit and uncooked vegetables, fish, and shellfish. Otherwise, mosquitoes and the tropical sun are the main threats; bring repellents and lotions. There are no poisonous snakes; scorpion bites cause nausea and fever but are not fatal. Crocodiles are aggressive; don't go wading in swampy areas, most of which are off-limits to foreigners anyway.

Street crime in Cuba is far less of a problem than in most parts of the world. Cubans are amazingly honest and friendly people and the regime is hard on crime. You're more likely to be hit by a falling cornice than a mugger.

Most reports claim that, as a result of the Castro regime's authoritarian stance on health, drug addiction, and sexual mores, the risk of contracting AIDS in Cuba is minor, though the increase in tourism and sexual liaisons between Cubans and foreigners is bound to change this situation rapidly. Other sexually transmitted diseases are fairly common. Extreme caution is advised in this area.

Gay and lesbian travelers would be wise to be discreet, as Cuban attitudes toward same-sex lovers—though difficult to predict—tend to be informed by a combination of machismo and early postrevolutionary puritanism about gays.

Telephones and Mail
To call Cuba from abroad, dial the international access number, then 53 (Cuba's country code), then the local code—63 for Artemisa and Mariel, 86 for Bahía Honda, 5 for Cárdenas and Cayo Largo, 7 for Havana, 61 for Isla de la Juventud, 84 for María la Gorda, 52 for Matanzas, 82 for Pinar del Río, 59 for Playa Girón and Playa Larga, 85 for Soroa and Las Terrazas, 5 for Varadero, and 8 for Viñales, Cayo Levisa, San Diego de los Baños, and San Juan y Martínez—then the local number. In addition, for all Matanzas numbers, you must dial 24 after the 52 local code.

Rates for calls on direct-dial hotel phones are very expensive ($7–$10 a minute for calls abroad); your best bet is to buy a phone card and use a public phone. For calls within Cuba, these cards will hold up well; a $10 card could last for weeks if used carefully. For calls to Europe or the United States, a $10 card appears to be worth about 6 minutes of communication. ETECSA (Empresa de Telecomunicaciones de Cuba) booths and hotel receptions sell cards, though they're often out of them. Cellular phones can be rented in Varadero for a daily charge of $7 plus an enormous deposit.

For local calls, dial the four-to-six-digit number. For long-distance calls within Cuba, dial 0 and then the provincial code and local number. For international calls from Cuba, dial 119 and then the country code, city code, and local number you want. For the international operator, dial 0, wait for the higher tone, and then dial 9. For operator-assisted calls to the United States, dial 66/1212.

Although Cubans deeply distrust their postal system—and entrust letters to anyone they meet who may be leaving the country—mail service is fairly reliable, especially if you post letters from hotels. Stamps, however, are much less expensive in state post offices than in hotels. It takes three or four weeks for mail to reach North America or Europe. (Note that mail to the United States may be opened and read by security police.)

In Pinar del Río, the main post office is at the corner of avenidas Martí and Isabel Rubio. There's another post office in the Hotel Pinar del Río. In Viñales, the post office is 100 m (330 ft) west of Hotel San Vicente (Carretera de Puerta Esperanza, Km 32). In Matanzas, it's 50 m (165 ft) north of Palacio Junco, on Calle 272 at Calle 79. Varadero has two post offices, one at the gate house at the junction of Avenida 1 and Avenida de las Américas, the other on Avenida Playa between Calles 39 and 40. Nueva Gerona's post office is at the corner of Calles 39 and 18.

Tour Operators and Travel Agencies

Havanatur, which has several locations in Havana and elsewhere in Cuba, can provide guides (☞ Havana A to Z *in* Chapter 2). **Tour & Travel** (✉ Av. de la Playa 3606, e/Calle 36 y Calle 37, Varadero, ☎ 5/66-3713, FAX 5/66-7036) organizes day excursions to Soroa, Viñales, Pinar del Río, Cárdenas, and Matanzas from either Varadero or Havana (☞ Havana A to Z *in* Chapter 2).

Visitor Information

Look for Cubatur and Havanatur offices in the main hotels of the major towns and cities in western Cuba. **Cubatur** (✉ Calle 33, Varadero, ☎ 5/66-7269) has offices throughout Cuba and serves as a de facto tourist-information office. **Publicitur** (✉ Calle 19, No. 60, e/M y N, Vedado, Havana, ☎ 7/55-2835) publishes and distributes tourist literature. **Asistur** (✉ Calle 23, No. 101, e/Av. Primera y Av. Tercera, ☎ 7/33-7277) offers services from legal advice to medical assistance to banking.

4 CENTRAL CUBA

Cuba's geographic heart pounds with the timeless rhythms of Afro-Cuban music, of life unfolding in splendid colonial cities, and of turquoise waves crashing on white-sand beaches. Its coral reefs are awash in color, its mangrove swamps attract flamingos by the thousands, and its lush mountain valleys are filled with birdsong of all types.

By David
Dudenhoefer

BORDERED TO THE NORTH AND SOUTH by inviting beaches, Central Cuba offers a varied panorama of landscapes—from mountains to mangroves—that are dotted with historic cities. Unlike many Caribbean islands, Cuba's early history centered on life in cities, and scattered across this region are three of the nation's seven original "villas"—Trinidad, Sancti Spíritus, and Camagüey—as well as the colonial town of Remedios. In each, time-worn churches and mansions line cobbled streets and tidy parks; in the verdant countryside beyond, old farmhouses overlook sugar plantations, royal palms tower over pastures populated by the people's cattle, and children in red-and-white uniforms play outside one-room schoolhouses.

Central Cuba's rich history contains many a tale of conquest. Its earliest inhabitants were the Taíno Indians, who island-hopped their way through the Caribbean from South America, arriving on Cuba about 200 years before the Spanish and overrunning the earlier Ciboney Indians, who had settled farther west. The Taíno developed rather sophisticated agricultural techniques, introducing such mainstays as *yuca* (manioc or cassava), potatoes, corn, tobacco, and cotton. Archaeological evidence suggests that they were also potters, weavers, hunters, and fishermen who plied the waters in powerful canoes. By the time Columbus arrived on the island in 1492, however, the Taínos were being challenged by the Caribs, a warlike South American Indian group. The Caribs never actually settled on Cuba, and although they began the conquest of the Taíno, they left its eventual completion—and the island's settlement—to the Spanish.

Another type of conquest—that of goods—led to central Cuba's first period of prosperity. Spanish law mandated that all commerce be conducted with colonial authorities. Such a monopoly drove prices up, and left many *criollos* (Cuban-born Spaniards) at odds with Spain. In the mid 16th century, buccaneers (loyal to European nations other than Spain) and pirates (loyal to no one but themselves) attacked ships and sold their plunder on black markets. For many central Cuban residents, smuggling became a highly lucrative profession.

Even after the liberalization of trade, many central Cuban families retained a philosophical distance from Spain. During the wars for independence that wracked the country in the second half of the 19th century, Camagüey was a hotbed of rebellion; the Spanish army even built a coast-to-coast barrier, La Trocha (consisting of fences, embankments, and watchtowers) through the middle of Ciego de Ávila to keep eastern rebels out of western Cuba. Much later, central Cuba's topography made it key in the Revolution. The Sierra de Escambray (Escambray Mountain range) was the haunt of Castro's guerrillas; indeed, rebel leader Che Guevara dealt a decisive blow to Fulgencio Batista's troops in Santa Clara, where his remains rest today.

The Sierra de Escambray, which rises from the provinces of Villa Clara, Cienfuegos, and Sancti Spíritus, has played an economic as well as a political role in the region. In addition to luxuriant forests and waterfalls, its upper slopes are covered with coffee farms; the rolling lowlands surrounding it are fertile grounds for sugar and tobacco. To the east, the land flattens in the provinces of Ciego de Ávila and Camagüey, which are almost completely covered with pasture.

Central Cuba's northern and southern coasts have many beautiful stretches of sand. The beach count leaps dramatically when you include the hundreds of *cayos* (keys) and islets that flank the shores. More and

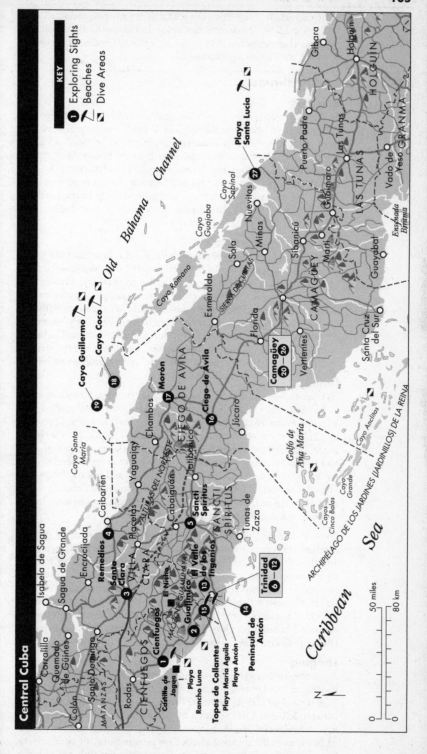

more visitors are discovering the northern cayos, collectively called the
Jardines del Rey (Gardens of the King). In the south, the less accessible archipelago known as the Jardines de la Reina (Gardens of the Queen)
is visited only by diving excursions.

Pleasures and Pastimes

Beaches

Each of the central provinces has a bit of sea and sand. Cienfuegos has
two small stretches just to the south of it. You'll find several more scattered along the road that connects Cienfuegos to Trinidad, 15 km (9
mi) to the south of which are the strands of the Península de Ancón.
Central Cuba's best beaches, however, are on its northern cayos—Villa
Clara's tranquil Cayo las Brujas and Ciego de Ávila's more developed
Cayo Coco and Cayo Guillermo—and around Santa Lucía, northeast
of Camagüey. Most of these beaches offer excellent (and affordable)
sportfishing and diving opportunities.

Colonial Architecture

Several cities of central Cuba have histories that date from the arrival
of the Spanish. Trinidad, the best preserved of these communities, has
block upon block of cobbled streets lined with 18th- and 19th-century
structures. Remedios is a similar time capsule, though on a smaller scale
and with a fraction of the tourists. Sancti Spíritus also has a small, though
nicely restored, colonial center, and though Cienfuegos is a younger city,
it has some splendid 19th- and early 20th-century architecture. The biggest
of the region's colonial cities is Camagüey, which has an extensive historical center, an eclectic mix of buildings, and a European ambience.

Dining

As is true all over Cuba, pork figures big on the region's menus, either
as *bistéc de puerco* (grilled pork), *bistéc de cerdo grillé* (grilled pork
loin), or *asado* (roasted pork); *carne de res* (beef) is scarce. Specialties
include *arroz congrí* (fried rice with beans and pork), often served as
a side dish, and the harder to find *ajiaco* (a thick stew made with pork
and tropical tubers). *Pollo* (chicken) is another mainstay and is often
served *frito* (fried). Restaurants in coastal cities and resorts always have
plenty of seafood on their menus, especially *langosta* (lobster), which
abound in the nearby reefs. Though some places claim to serve Italian
or Chinese food, it's best to avoid such fare here.

Outside Trinidad there are few restaurants, and *paladares* (private
eateries) are even harder to come by. Reservations are rarely necessary,
and though there's no tipping policy per se, you'll probably feel better if you tip as many people as you can—in and out of restaurants—
as Cubans earn starvation wages. For the moment, consider the U.S.
dollar the most reliable form of payment. Credit cards *not* affiliated
with U.S. banks or companies are accepted in all government restaurants and hotels, though never in paladares. For price categories, *see*
Dining *in* Smart Travel Tips A to Z.

Lodging

Accommodations range from massive, modern beach resorts to small,
historic, in-town hotels, and most are on the lower end of the price scale.
Rare is the double that costs more than $100; in fact, many hotels charge
between $30 and $50 for such a room, and lodging in private homes—
in Cienfuegos and Trinidad—costs even less. The facilities vary accord-
ingly, but even the cheapest places have private baths, air-conditioning,
hot water, TV, and phones in rooms. Credit cards *not* affiliated with U.S.
banks or companies are accepted in all government restaurants and hotels. For price categories, *see* Lodging *in* Smart Travel Tips A to Z.

WHERE CUBA'S WILD THINGS ARE

CUBA MAY NOT BE FAMOUS for its flora and fauna, but it actually has an impressive array of wildlife: from massive kapok trees to delicate orchids; from dinosaurian crocodiles to elegant flamingos. Flowering trees light up verdant landscapes, mornings are animated by bird choruses, and abundant gardens are frequented by countless colorful butterflies and the flitting, iridescent Cuban emerald hummingbird. Just offshore, the waters contain a living kaleidoscope of the coral reef—Cuba's richest and most extensive ecosystem.

The country's biological diversity is a result of its tropical location, varied environments—savannas, swamps, mountains, mangrove estuaries—its proximity to two continents, and the role islands play in the development of new species. Cuba may lack many of the animals found on the tropical mainland (no monkeys, no toucans, and thankfully, no poisonous snakes), but it has creatures that exist nowhere else. The local living spectrum ranges from albino salamanders that are found only in a few caves, to the pan-tropical coconut palm, which is as common in the Indian Ocean as it is in the Caribbean.

Among the island's rarer creatures are the world's smallest bird (bee hummingbird), frog (Cuban pygmy frog), and mammal (a tiny species of shrew called the *almiquí*). The only one of these animals you're likely to see is the bee hummingbird, known locally as the *zunzuncito*, the male of which weighs a mere 2 grams (0.12 ounce) and stands only 4 centimeters (1½ inches) tall. Head for the Península de Zapata for a glimpse of this diminutive bird. The island's more conspicuous species include the elegant royal palm, Cuba's national tree, and the greater-Antillean grackle—a black bird that makes a lot of noise.

The biggest draw for most nature lovers are Cuba's 388 bird species, 74 of which are indigenous. Some of the more striking are the Cuban parrot; Cuban parakeet; Cuban red-bellied woodpecker; and the mountain-dwelling Cuban trogon, or *tocorro*, named the national bird because its colors—red, white, and blue—match those of the flag. Cuba is also home to species with a wider distribution, such as the crested caracara, the great lizard cuckoo, and the flamingos that nest here by the thousands. Other autochthonous animals include the Cuban crocodile, various colorful lizard species, and the *jutía*: a cat-size rodent that's related to the guinea pig.

Nowhere on the Cuban mainland will you see as much wildlife as in the coral reefs, which hold hundreds of fish and invertebrate species: dark green moray eels, yellow staghorn coral, purple sea fans, multicolored parrot fish, eagle rays, spiny lobsters, sea stars on sponges, and bright red squirrel fish in caves—the diversity boggles the mind. Whether you slip into the Caribbean Sea, hike into the mountains, or navigate a coastal estuary, you can't help but be impressed by Cuba's varied wild things.

Exploring Central Cuba

The region is easy to reach and explore, thanks to the central, mostly flat highway that traverses the island from Havana to eastern Cuba. The road becomes only slightly hilly east of Santa Clara, where it passes near the northern extreme of the Sierra de Escambray, the verdant mountain range that dominates the southern corner of Villa Clara and about half of Cienfuegos and Sancti Spíritus provinces. Various roads wind into the mountains from Trinidad and Cienfuegos. One connects the two cities via Topes de Collantes; another, more direct route runs along the coast. The more easterly provincial capitals of Ciego de Ávila and Camagüey are surrounded by flat ranch land, with roads running north and northeast to the coast.

Numbers in the text correspond to numbers in the margin and on the Central Cuba, Trinidad, and Camagüey maps.

Great Itineraries

IF YOU HAVE 3 DAYS

Fly from Havana to the colonial city of 🏠 **Trinidad** ⑥–⑫ for a day of exploring. On day two, hit the beaches of the 🏠 **Península de Ancón** ⑭ or head into the mountains at 🏠 **Topes de Collantes** ⑮. Spend the third morning in the **Valle de los Ingenios** ⑬ before returning to Havana. Alternatively, you could drive to 🏠 **Santa Clara** ③, exploring that city by day and continuing to 🏠 **Remedios** ④ for the night. The next day, after touring Remedios, head to the reefs and beaches of Cayo las Brujas for the second night and third morning.

IF YOU HAVE 5 DAYS

Drive from Havana to the 19th-century city of 🏠 **Cienfuegos** ① and explore its historic center and/or the Castillo de Jagua across the bay. On day two, drive along the coast to the 18th-century city of 🏠 **Trinidad** ⑥–⑫. Spend day three in the city and the nearby **Valle de los Ingenios** ⑬. Head to 🏠 **Sancti Spíritus** ⑤ early on day four, explore its historic center, and drive west to either 🏠 **Remedios** ④ or 🏠 **Santa Clara** ③ for the last night. Spend the fifth morning seeing in-town sights before driving back to Havana.

IF YOU HAVE 7 DAYS

Fly from Havana to 🏠 **Camagüey** ⑳–㉖ and explore its historic center. On the afternoon of the second day, rent a car, and drive to the coastal resort of 🏠 **Playa Santa Lucía** ㉗, dedicating day three to sea, sand, and sun. On the fourth day, drive back through Camagüey to 🏠 **Sancti Spíritus** ⑤ or 🏠 **Trinidad** ⑥–⑫. If you spent the night in Sancti Spíritus, drive to Trinidad on day five, stopping at the **Valle de los Ingenios** ⑬. Spend the sixth morning exploring Trinidad or the 🏠 **Península de Ancón** ⑭, and then drive to the lively, 19th-century city of 🏠 **Cienfuegos** ①. On day seven, cross the bay to the Castillo de Jagua, enjoy a good lunch, then make the three- to four-hour drive back to Havana.

When to Tour

The rainy season runs roughly from May to October, the dry season from November to April. The fact that more tourists head here in January and February has more to do with Canadian cold fronts than Santa Lucía sunshine. The rainy season is actually a great time to visit because all is green and there are fewer tourists. The busiest months are July–August and January–March, with the last week of December and Easter week being peak. Rates during these times rise and yet rooms book up, making reservations essential.

CIENFUEGOS, VILLA CLARA, AND SANCTI SPÍRITUS PROVINCES

These three provinces contain several historic cities, half a dozen beaches, and natural attractions that range from the highland forests to coral reefs. The wonderfully preserved, 18th-century city of Trinidad may be the most spectacular of the colonial towns, but Cienfuegos, Sancti Spíritus, and Remedios all have enough colonial architecture to transport you back in time—and they have fewer visitors. Beaches line the coast near Trinidad and Cienfuegos, and the waters here have dozens of dive spots and offer excellent angling opportunities. In the exuberant valleys of the Sierra de Escambray, the crashing of crystalline waterfalls mixes with the songs of brightly colored birds.

Cienfuegos

❶ *232 km (144 mi) southeast of Havana; 61 km (38 mi) southwest of Santa Clara; 80 km (48 mi) northwest of Trinidad.*

Cienfuegos is an attractive, laid-back port city of 110,000 people that overlooks a deep bay of the same name. Its small historic core is surrounded by a gray ring of cement block housing and industrial buildings, beyond which lie fields of sugarcane and the dark green mass of the Sierra de Escambray.

A relatively young provincial capital, Cienfuegos was founded in 1819 by immigrants from Bordeaux as part of a Spanish scheme to establish a city in a region that had long been the haunt of pirates. Originally dubbed Fernandina de Jagua ("Fernandina" honors Spain's King Ferdinand and "Jagua" was the indigenous name for the region), the city was later named after General José Cienfuegos (a colonial governor of the province). It quickly became an important port and commercial center; sugar plantations came to cover its hinterlands, and slaves were imported to work on them. Families who made fortunes from cane and human bondage built elaborate mansions (known locally as *palacios* or palaces), many of which still stand.

Cienfuegos's French roots are reflected in some of its architecture and celebrated every April with a Francophile festival. Nevertheless it's a very Cuban city where the breeze often carries the melodies of local hero Benny Moré, one of the giants of the Cuban music *son*.

The city's main artery, Calle 37, is called El Prado in the old part of town, where it's flanked by late-19th-century colonnades and divided by a wide, landscaped median. To the south, Calle 37 runs roughly parallel to the waterfront **Malecón** where locals stroll at night. Note the illuminated billboard near the Malecón; it has an image of Moré and a line from one of his songs: *"Cienfuegos es la ciudad que más me gusta a mi"* ("Cienfuegos is the city I like most.") The palm-lined promenade stretches south to Punta Gorda, a point dominated by the former mansions of sugar barons and ending in a small seaside park.

Most of the important buildings of Cienfuegos surround the central **Parque José Martí,** which contains a statue of the Cuban revolutionary and intellectual for whom it was named. On the park's western end is a tiny **replica of the Arc de Triomphe,** a nod to the city's French heritage. Just south of the Martí statue stands a **domed kiosk** where the municipal band often gives weekend concerts. Across the street from it is a low building with fat columns, **El Palatino,** which is the park's oldest structure and which now houses a tavern. The stately building southeast of the band shell used to be the Casino Español, an elite club built in the late 19th century. It now houses the **Museo Provincial,** a museum dedicated to local history and furnished with antiques that once belonged to some of the casino's most respected members. ✉ *Av. 54 y Calle 27,* ☎ *432/9722.* 🎫 *$1.* ☉ *Daily 8–4:30.*

Avenida 54, which runs westward from El Prado, becomes the pedestrian-only **El Boulevard**—lined with shops and restaurants—as it travels alongside the park. You can follow El Boulevard along to the park's southwest corner and the Palacio Ferrer, an elaborate mansion built in 1917 by Spanish businessman José Ferrer and now the **Casa de Cultura.** The corner room on the second floor was once used by Enrico Caruso, and a spiral staircase leads from here up to a tower that offers a great view of the plaza. The cultural center is often the site of concerts by local musicians. ✉ *Av. 54 y Calle 25,* ☎ *432/6584.* 🎫 *50¢.* ☉ *Mon.–Sat. 9–7, Sun. 9–noon.*

The **Catedral de la Purísima Concepción,** the city's cathedral, has a high central bell tower reminiscent of a minaret. Inaugurated in 1869, its interior was recently restored and features a statue of the Virgin Mary and stained-glass windows (depicting the 12 apostles) that were made in France. ✉ *Av. 56 y Calle 29, east of Parque Martí,* ☎ *no phone.* 🎫 *Free.* ☉ *Daily 7–noon.*

The **Teatro Tomás Terry,** the city's principal theater, was built in 1889, and named for the millionaire whose fortune funded its construction. Even if you can't come for a concert or dance performance, try to pop inside to admire the painted ceilings, statues, and carved hardwoods. ✉ *Av. 56, No. 2703, north of Parque Martí,* ☎ *432/3361.* 🎫 *Free.* ☉ *Daily 9–6.*

★ Of Punta Gorda's palacios, the most impressive is the **Palacio de Valle,** built in 1917 by the sugar baron Asisclo del Valle. A sumptuous structure full of ornate relief work, crystal chandeliers, hand-painted tiles, Italian-marble columns, French windows, and Cuban hardwoods, the building is of eclectic design, but its foremost inspiration was the Alhambra—the Moorish palace in southern Spain. It now houses a gourmet restaurant on the ground floor and a rooftop bar that's the perfect spot from which to watch the sun set. ✉ *Av. 0 y Calle 37,* ☎ *432/45–1226.* 🎫 *Free.* ☉ *Daily 11–10.*

Perched above a fishing village overlooking the narrow entrance to the Bay of Cienfuegos (35 km/21 mi south of the historical center) is the ★ ☾ **Castillo de Jagua,** a Spanish fortress built in 1745 to keep out pirates who had grown accustomed to trading with locals. It has been completely refurbished (even the drawbridge works) and has an historical museum with weapons and other antiques. The dungeons now house a bar and restaurant. On your way down, note the small chamber beneath the steps; prisoners were chained here while being tortured. Considering the existence of this chamber, and the fact that the drawbridge still works, it's not advisable to sneak out without paying your bar bill. ✉ *Jagua,* ☎ *439/6402.* 🎫 *$1.* ☉ *Tue.–Sat. 9–5, Sun. 9–1.*

Cienfuegos' **Jardín Botánico** (Botanical Garden) covers 94 hectares (232 acres) and contains more than 2,000 plant species, most of which are from other countries. Created at the turn of the century by U.S. sugar farmer Edwin Atkins, the garden was administered by Harvard University until 1962, when it was taken over by the Cuban Academy of Science. It includes palms, bamboos, and other tropical trees as well as medicinal plants and a forest reserve that's home to many native animals. Guides are available (only one speaks English), and tips are greatly appreciated. ✉ *16 km (10 mi) east of Cienfuegos,* ☎ *432/45115.* 🎫 *$2.50.* ☉ *Daily 8–5.*

OFF THE
BEATEN PATH

EL NICHO – This cool, luxuriant valley full of idyllic swimming holes makes an excellent day trip from Cienfuegos. The entrance to the region is marked by a rustic restaurant. From here, footpaths (order your lunch before you go hiking) lead to a series of natural pools, filled with emerald waters, and two crystalline waterfalls surrounded by tropical greenery. Bird-watchers should be on the lookout for the great lizard cuckoo, the emerald hummingbird, and the Cuban trogon—the national bird. The tour company Rumbos (☞ Tour Operators and Travel Agencies *in* Central Cuba A to Z, *below*) offers cheap excursions here. If you drive yourself, head east to Cumanayagua, then take the next two rights. ☒ *55 km (34 mi) east of Cienfuegos,* ☎ *no phone.* ☲ *$2.* ☉ *Daily 8–6.*

Beach

The coast southeast of Cienfuegos has several nice beaches, the nearest of which is **Playa Rancho Luna,** a long, pale crescent lined with coconut palms 16 km (10 mi) southeast of town. A public beach popular with Cubans, Rancho Luna has tourist hotels directly to the west and east of it, and coral reefs aren't far from its shore.

Dining and Lodging

The best accommodations are just outside Cienfuegos, along the coast, though at press time, a Cuban company was converting one of the old downtown mansions into a boutique hotel (for more information, contact Cubanacan; ☞ Tour Operators and Travel Agents *in* Central Cuba A to Z, *below*). There are also plenty of rooms for rent in private homes on Punta Gorda, especially along the stretch of Calle 37 just before the Hotel Jagua.

$$–$$$ ★ ✕ **Palacio de Valle.** Elegance abounds on the ground floor of Cienfuego's most gracious mansion, with its ornately carved arches, marble columns, and crystal chandeliers. And there's usually someone playing the restaurant's grand piano. The food may play second fiddle to ambience, but it's still some of the best in town; the prices are definitely the highest. The specialty is langosta, which can be prepared five different ways, but the extensive menu also offers everything from filet mignon to *camarones al pincho* (shrimp shish kebab). ☒ *Av. 0 y Calle 37, Cienfuegos,* ☎ *432/45–1226. MC, V.*

$–$$ ✕ **La Cueva del Camarón.** In any other neighborhood, this mansion would be impressive, but since it practically sits in the shadow of the Palacio de Valle (☞ *above*), it looks like an attempt at keeping up with the Joneses. Nevertheless its bright interior—full of shiny marble, colorful tiles, and carved hardwoods—makes it an elegant place to dine. The varied menu is strong on such seafood dishes as *enchilado de camarones* (shrimp in a tomato sauce), paella, and langosta grillé. ☒ *Av. 2 y Calle 37, Cienfuegos,* ☎ *432/45–1128. MC, V.*

$ ✕ **Paladar Aché.** The plastic chairs and tables and pink walls of this tiny private eatery don't hold a candle to the brilliance of the city's mansion restaurants, but your meal here will be prepared by the owner instead of by underpaid government employees. The state only lets the owners serve chicken and pork, which are, consequently, prepared several ways and come with lots of arroz congrí and other Cuban side dishes. The paladar is in a yellow house 2½ blocks east of the Malecón and a block south of the Bahía Service Station; don't let locals lead you here as they may charge the owners for their services. ☒ *Av. 38, e/Calle 41 y Calle 43, Cienfuegos,* ☎ *no phone. No credit cards. Closed Mon.*

$$ ★ ✕▥ **Faro Luna.** Most of the rooms at this hotel—which sits on a rocky point just west of Playa Rancho Luna—have ocean views, especially those in the two-story bungalows. Rooms are bright and spacious, with beige-tile floors, wicker furniture, colorful floral bedspreads, large balconies, and lots of windows. The main building has a small restau-

rant-bar, next to which is a tile pool surrounded by coconut palms. Though it's a bit of a walk to the beach, the hotel has its own dive center, which arranges trips to dozens of offshore reefs and wrecks. ⊠ *Playa Rancho Luna, 16 km (10 mi) southeast of Cienfuegos,* ☎ *432/45–1389,* FAX *432/45–1162. 40 rooms. Restaurant, bar, pool, dive shop. MC, V.*

$$ ✕🔟 **Hotel Jagua.** This six-story cement structure dating from the 1950s towers over the palacios and wooden houses of Punta Gorda (it stands in what was once the Palacio de Valle's garden). Its designers, however, made poor use of a great location: rooms face the city, instead of the scenic point. At press time, rooms were dilapidated, but the hotel was about to be completely renovated. The large rectangular pool is surrounded by trees and overlooks the bay. The restaurant, which is just off the lobby, is a good bet. ⊠ *Punta Gorda, Cienfuegos,* ☎ *432/45–1003,* FAX *432/45–1245. 145 rooms. Restaurant, bar, pool. MC, V.*

$–$$ 🔟 **Rancho Luna.** What this complex of two-story cement buildings lacks in charm it makes up for in a terrific location behind a lovely beach of pale sand dotted with sea grape trees. Rooms are slightly cramped—with low ceilings and picture windows that don't afford much of a view—and somewhat dog-eared, but at press time plans for renovation were afoot. An open-air bar overlooks the large pool, the main restaurant serves buffets, and the rustic beachfront grill is open for lunch. ⊠ *16 km (10 mi) southeast of Cienfuegos, just east of Playa Rancho Luna,* ☎ *432/45–1389,* FAX *432/45–1162. 225 rooms. 2 restaurants, 2 bars, pool, aerobics, horseback riding, beach, snorkeling, boating, cabaret. MC, V. BP.*

Nightlife and the Arts

The **Casa de la Cultura** (Palacio Ferrer, Av. 54 y Calle 25, ☎ 432/6584) is often the site of performances by local bands or dance troupes; shows usually start at 9 PM. The stately **Teatro Tomás Terry** (Av. 56, No. 2703, ☎ 432/3361) occasionally hosts concerts and dance performances.

After the sun has set, several sidewalk cafés along El Boulevard get busy. Local musicians perform nightly at the **Café Cantante Benny Moré** (Av. 54 y El Prado, ☎ no phone). The **Disco Club Benny Moré** (Av. 54, e/Calle 29 y Calle 31, ☎ 432/45–1105) rocks till the wee hours every night but Monday. The bar atop the **Palacio de Valle** (⊠ Av. 0 y Calle 37, ☎ 432/45–1226) is the perfect spot for a sunset cocktail.

Outdoor Activities and Sports

FISHING

The fishing in the waters off Cienfuegos is good. The **Marina Puerto Sol Cienfuegos** (⊠ Punta Gorda, ☎ 432/45–1241) rents boat and basic gear at amazingly low rates.

HORSEBACK RIDING

Hacienda La Vega (⊠ 50 km/30 mi southeast of Cienfuegos on road to Trinidad, ☎ no phone), a working cattle ranch, runs a 3-hour, horseback tour through pastures and forest; it includes a swim on a secluded beach and a dairy tour. You can hire horses and a guide at the ranch, or you can go on a half-day tour run by Rumbos (☞ Tour Operators and Travel Agencies *in* Central Cuba A to Z, *below*).

SCUBA DIVING

The ocean around Cienfuegos has dozens of dive sites, from shallow reefs to deep shipwrecks. The coral here is healthy and well developed—one column stands 7 m (23 ft) high—and visibility varies from 15 to 40 m (45 to 120 ft). The **Faro Luna Diving Center** (☎ 432/45–1340), next to the hotel of the same name, is Cienfuegos's dive center.

Shopping

You'll find Cuban music, T-shirts, postcards, and other souvenirs at **Casa Arco** (✉ Av. 54, No. 3301, ☎ no phone) and other shops on El Boulevard. **El Embajador** (✉ Av. 54 y Calle 33, ☎ 432/45–1108) is *the* place for rum, coffee, and cigars. Local art and handicrafts are available at **Galería Moroya** (✉ Av. 54, No. 2506, ☎ 432/45–1208; ✉ Av. 54, No. 3517, ☎ no phone).

Guajimico

❷ *42 km (25 mi) southeast of Cienfuegos; 43 km (26 mi) northwest of Trinidad.*

The tiny agricultural community of Guajimico has little to offer in and of itself, but it sits in a wild area halfway between Cienfuegos and Trinidad, where the natural attractions range from patches of tropical forests to coral reefs. The nearby cattle ranch of **Hacienda La Vega** (☞ Outdoor Activities and Sports *in* Cienfuegos, *above*) runs horseback tours that include a stop at an isolated beach. **Yaguanabo,** another enclave a few miles farther east, is the starting point for horseback trips into the mountains to a swimming hole and the Cueva Martín Infierno. To arrange a trip contact Rumbos (☞ Tour Operators and Travel Agencies *in* Central Cuba A to Z, *below*). Tranquil **Playa Inglés,** between La Vega and Yaguanabo, is a pale, steep beach lined with sea grape trees and is visited almost exclusively by Cubans.

Dining and Lodging

$ ✕🏨 **Villa Guajimico.** It may be a long way from Cienfuegos, but this
★   dive resort and nature lodge offers the region's nicest accommodations. Overlooking the emerald waters of the Río Jutia estuary, the complex consists of comfortable bungalows scattered through the forest or behind the tiny, man-made beach. Each has a barrel-tile roof, a small porch, tile floors, and hardwood furniture. The swimming pool, open-air bar, and air-conditioned restaurant all have ocean views. Birds sing in the surrounding forest, and there are coral formations submerged a shell's toss from shore. ✉ *42 km (25 mi) southeast of Cienfuegos, Guajimico,* ☎ *432/45–1204,* 🖷 *432/45–1206. 51 bungalows. Restaurant, bar, pool, beach, dive shop, snorkeling, boating. MC, V.*

Santa Clara

❸ *61 km (38 mi) northeast of Cienfuegos; 88 km (26 mi) north of Trinidad; 92 km (55 mi) northwest of Sancti Spíritus.*

The capital of Villa Clara Province is a pleasant city of 200,000 with a busy center where cobbled streets are lined with historic buildings and a periphery of factories and modern apartment buildings. Santa Clara was the site of a decisive battle during the last days of 1958, and the remains of the quintessential revolutionary, Che Guevara, rest in a monument at the edge of town. But you need merely visit the central plaza of this provincial capital to discover that its history stretches back centuries and that it has a good bit going on today.

Founded in 1689 by a group of wealthy landowners from nearby Remedios, Santa Clara's rich agricultural land and fortuitous location between Havana and eastern Cuba have made it a relatively affluent provincial center. Santa Clara has Cuba's third largest university, and the student presence may have contributed to the city's reputation for being liberal.

Most of the museums and monuments are on **Parque Vidal.** The streets that border it are closed to traffic, and locals gather here at night and on weekends, when concerts are often held in its kiosk or on the street in front of the Casa de la Cultura. On the park's northeast end stands the stately **Palacio Provincial,** built in 1912 to house the provincial government, but now the city's library. Across the park from the library is the **Palacio Municipal,** or town hall, a structure dating from 1922. The neoclassical building next to the Palacio Municipal was originally an elite social club but is now a government cultural center, the **Casa de la Cultura;** climb its marble staircase to the old ballroom, which is still lovely despite decades of neglect.

Near the southern end of Parque Vidal stands a statue of Marta Abreu, a 19th-century philanthropist who financed, among other things, the construction of the city's main theater, the **Teatro la Caridad** (☎ 422/5548). Set on the park's northwest corner, it was completed in 1885. The oldest building on Parque Vidal is the **Museo de Artes Decorativos,** a former home built in the 1820s that is now open to the public. The house itself is half the attraction, with its marble floors, fluted columns, and hand-painted tiles. Its rooms hold an array of antiques—including crystal, china, statues, and furniture—that date from several centuries. ⊠ *Northwest corner of Parque Vidal,* ☎ *422/5368.* ☑ *$2.* ☉ *Mon. and Wed.–Thurs. 9–noon and 1–6; Fri.–Sat. 1 PM–10 PM; Sun. 6 PM–10 PM.*

★ Santa Clara's most popular attraction is the **Monumento Che Guevara,** a massive bronze sculpture of revolutionary Ernesto "Che" Guevara. The museum here chronicles Che's eventful existence, from his happy childhood in Argentina to his 1967 assassination in Bolivia, concentrating on his involvement in the Cuban Revolution. The mausoleum next door holds the remains of Che and 16 others who fought and died with him in the mountains of Bolivia—they weren't discovered and identified by forensic anthropologists until 1997 and didn't arrive in Cuba until 1998. ⊠ *Plaza de la Revolución, southwest end of Rafael Trista,* ☎ *no phone.* ☑ *Free.* ☉ *Tue.–Sat. 9–9, Sun. 9–noon.*

☾ On the north side of town, just across the Río Cubanicay, is the **Tren Blindado,** a military train that was carrying soldiers and weapons when it was derailed by Che and a group of rebels on the morning of December 28, 1958—a decisive moment in the Cuban Revolution. Guevara's troops went on to take the city, cutting Havana off from the eastern half of the country, which prompted Batista's flight from Cuba and Castro's victory—all in a matter of days. Several train cars, some containing displays, lie in the grass next to the tracks in memory of that battle; the bulldozer used to destroy the tracks stands on a nearby cement slab. ⊠ *Northern end of Independencia,* ☎ *no phone.* ☑ *Free.* ☉ *Mon.–Sat. 8–6, Sun. 9–noon.*

Dining and Lodging

$ ✕ **Restaurant 1878.** This popular restaurant just north of Parque Vidal accepts only Cuban pesos. The building itself is first rate: a 19th-century residence with wood-beam ceilings, high arches, red drapes and a few old paintings hung on whitewashed walls. Although pork dishes dominate the menu, you'll find a couple chicken and beef options. Though neither the food nor service will win awards, the prices are amazing. ⊠ *Calle Máximo Gómez,* ☎ *422/22428. No credit cards.*

$$ ☷ **Hotel La Granite.** Set on a 5-hectare (12-acre) farm near the airport, this tranquil resort specializes in fresh air and birdsong. Rooms are in two-story octagonal duplexes, with bright tile floors, hardwood furniture, and plenty of windows overlooking shady lawns. A kidney-shape pool sits next to the reception area, and a large restaurant nearby serves mostly buffets. You can follow trails through forests, orchards, and pastures on foot or on horseback. ⊠ *Carretera la Maleza, 3 km (2 mi) northwest of Santa Clara,* ☎ *422/28190,* ℻ *422/28192. 75 rooms. Restaurant, 2 bars, pool, horseback riding. MC, V.*

CHE GUEVARA: REVOLUTIONARY ICON

EVERYWHERE IN CUBA, you encounter the legendary visage of Che Guevara in beard and beret—an image captured by the Cuban photographer Korda in the early days of the Revolution—on billboards, walls, posters, T-shirts, key chains, watches, and buttons. That same face also often adorns walls in universities, bars, and coffeehouses throughout Latin America and Europe. For students and leftists, Che represents idealism, rebellion, and dedication to a higher cause. He was a renaissance revolutionary—doctor, writer, soldier, photographer, statesman—who continues to be studied and mythicized. Jean-Paul Sartre called him "the most complete human being of our age," but for those who have suffered the wrath of Communism, he's just a pretty face on a heartless system, and for millions, he has become a mere fashion statement. In Cuba, however, Che is the communist equivalent of a saint.

Ernesto Guevara was born into a middle-class family in El Rosario, Argentina, on June 14, 1928; che, the Argentine term for "buddy," became his nickname in Cuba years later. A precocious child who suffered from asthma at an early age, he learned to read when he was five and was devouring the works of Karl Marx and Cuban intellectual José Martí at the age of 15; by age 20, he was studying medicine at the University of Buenos Aires. In 1952, Guevara took a break from med school to travel around South America on a motorbike, and upon graduating, he hit the road again, heading north to Central America. He was in Guatemala when the democratically elected Arbenz government was overthrown by a CIA orchestrated coup, and he fled to Mexico a sworn enemy of U.S. imperialism.

In Mexico, he joined Fidel Castro's small revolutionary army as a doctor, and sailed to Cuba aboard the Granma in 1956. Though an asthmatic and intellectual, Che displayed an innate talent for guerrilla warfare (he later wrote two books on the subject) and was soon promoted to field commander. He led troops in the Sierra de Escambray, and in a battle that ensured dictator Fulgencio Batista's defeat, he and his rebels derailed a military train in Santa Clara. Following his victorious entrance in Havana, the eloquent and charismatic Argentine captured the hearts of the Cuban masses and became Castro's confidant (Castro even declared him a Cuban citizen). Not only did Che serve as the country's Minister of Finance and Minister of Industry, he represented Cuba abroad, speaking at the United Nations and forging ties with the Soviet Union. He became one of the socialist government's main architects, expounding a theory of the "new man," who would create a society based on equality and solidarity.

Perhaps driven by a desire to spread revolution, Guevara renounced his government positions in 1965, and left to fight with rebel forces in the Congo. From Africa, he traveled to Bolivia, where he joined yet another rebel army. He and his band of guerrillas were captured—with help from the CIA—and executed by the Bolivian army on October 9, 1967. Their mass grave was a secret for three decades, and Che's remains weren't found and identified till 1997, when they were flown to Cuba, and placed with pageantry in the mausoleum of the monument to him in Santa Clara.

$ ▣ **Santa Clara Libre.** This large, ugly hotel on Parque Vidal has two room sizes: tiny and not quite so tiny. They may not have been redecorated since the Revolution, but they're clean and have the basic amenities—in fact, those in front have nice views of the plaza and city beyond. For the best vistas, however, head for the rooftop bar; the basement disco is a popular nightspot. ⊠ *Parque Vidal 6,* ☎ *422/27548. 75 rooms. Restaurant, bar, dance club. MC, V.*

Nightlife and the Arts

The **Casa de la Cultura** (⊠ Parque Vidal 5, ☎ 422/27181) hosts several concerts a week at 9 PM and a street concert every Sunday at 4 PM. Occasional music and dance performances provide the perfect excuses to visit the lovely **Teatro la Caridad** (⊠ Parque Vidal 3, ☎ 422/5548). **El Boulevard,** the pedestrian mall on Independencia, just north of Parque Vidal, has several bars and sidewalk cafés that are popular watering holes.

Shopping

Stop by **ARTEX** (⊠ Parque Vidal 6, ☎ 422/26278) for Cuban music, T-shirts, and other souvenirs. The **Fondo de Bienes Culturales** (⊠ Estebez, just north of Parque Vidal, ☎ 422/4195) sells such local handicrafts as straw hats, leather bags, and knickknacks.

Remedios

❹ *45 km (27 mi) northeast of Santa Clara.*

San Juan de Remedios is one of Cuba's oldest towns. Founded in 1515 on the northern coast, it was moved inland to its current location in 1524 following harassment by pirates. Toward the end of the 17th century, a group of wealthy citizens tried to move Remedios still farther inland, but most of the townspeople resisted; those who wanted to move went on to found Santa Clara, which became the province's principal city. Remedios slipped into its shadow and has retained a sleepy, unspoiled atmosphere.

Though small (20,000 inhabitants), Remedios is culturally rich and remarkably well preserved. It's actually amazing that the city has survived at all, considering that its most famous tradition is Las Parrandas: an incendiary festival celebrated on Christmas Eve that practically leaves the entire town in ashes year after year. Legend has it that the festival began in the 1820s when a parish priest, who worried that not enough people where attending Christmas mass, sent a group of boys through the streets banging drums and making noise to wake people up and get them into the pews. The tradition has developed into an all-night festival lit by homemade lanterns and fireworks and animated by brass bands; its participants are cheered still more by copious food and drink.

Remedios's geographic heart is **Plaza Martí,** a tidy park shaded by royal palms and tropical trees and surrounded by 18th- and 19th-century architecture. **La Iglesia de San Juan Bautista** (Church of St. John the Baptist) is a squat colonial structure with a massive bell tower on the plaza's eastern end. Its splendidly restored 18th-century interior (head for the back door as the main doors are usually shut) includes high arches, an elaborate beamed cedar ceiling, and gilded-wood altars. Although its stone floor dates from 1550, most of the chapel was rebuilt in 1752; it underwent extensive renovation in the 1940s, including the construction of a new main altar using parts of the original baroque altar. The smaller altar to the right is dedicated to the Virgin de la Caridad, Cuba's patron saint. The gilded shrines along the walls are dedicated to various saints; note the pregnant Virgin, brought from Seville in the 1700s, to the left of the main door. ☎ *No phone.* 🎫 *Donations suggested.* ◯ *Mon–Sat. 8–noon and 3–6, Sun. 4–6.*

To the northwest of the plaza is the stout **Iglesia del Buen Viaje** (Church of the Good Voyage), which was built by mariners to protect an image of the Virgin Mary found floating in the ocean. The original structure, constructed in 1770, burned down in the 19th century and was replaced by today's version. In front of it stands a monument that bears some likeness to the Statue of Liberty; it's dedicated to local martyrs of Cuba's wars of independence. ☎ *No phone.* 🎫 *Free.* ◯ *Sun. morning masses (8–10).*

On the northern side of Plaza Martí, you'll find one of the city's preserved colonial buildings. The former home of composer Alejandro García Caturla is now the **Museo de la Música**, a museum dedicated to his life. Built in 1875, the house has a small central patio planted with palms and surrounded by rooms that contain antique furnishings or exhibits on the composer's works. ✉ *Camilo Cienfuegos 5,* ☎ *no phone.* 🎫 *1 Peso (5¢).* ◯ *Tue–Sat. 9–noon and 1–5, Sun. 9–noon.*

☞ If you can't be in Remedios on December 24, visit the **Museo de las Parrandas.** The city is divided into two neighborhoods—El Carmen and El Salvador—each of which creates its own floats, costumes, lanterns, and fireworks as part of an informal competition during the festival. Though no winner is ever declared, townspeople will tell you that not only does their neighborhood win every year, but the other half of Remedios isn't even good competition. The museum has faded photos and paraphernalia from past Parrandas. ✉ *Máximo Gómez 71, 1½ blocks west of Plaza Martí,* ☎ *42/39–5400.* 🎫 *$1.* ◯ *Tue.–Sat. 9–noon and 1–5, Sun. 9–1.*

Beaches

Thus far, few visitors have discovered the pale beaches and turquoise shallows of **Cayo las Brujas,** an island 30 km (18 mi) northeast of Remedios and connected to the mainland by a causeway; come quickly before things change. At press time, the island had only one beachside restaurant, but a hotel was under construction nearby. There's also the 10-room San Pasqual, which is set in an old cargo ship on a sandbar offshore. It's managed by the Rumbos tour company in Santa Clara (☞ Tour Operators and Travel Agencies *in* Central Cuba A to Z, *below*). If you want to visit just for a day, stop by the Rumbos office in Caibarién and pay your $5 for a permit to use the causeway.

Dining and Lodging

$ ✕ **El Louvre.** This small café with a hardwood bar, brass lamps, and an arched wooden ceiling has been in business since 1866. The view, overlooking Plaza Martí, probably isn't much different than when it opened, and they still serve *ponche de la parroquia,* a rum-and-milk cocktail that wily young men once gave to chaperones. (Once drunk, the chaperones would be less likely to interfere should the young men try to steal kisses from their girlfriends.) Though the menu has a wide array of beverages, dishes are limited to sandwiches, pollo frito, and bistéc de puerco. ✉ *Máximo Gómez 122,* ☎ *no phone. No credit cards.*

$ ✕🏨 **Hotel Mascotte.** Although such recent alterations as gleaming
★ white-tile floors detract from the historic atmosphere of this late-19th-century inn, it's still extremely charming. The thick square columns, high arches, and abundant potted plants in the public areas will enchant you. Guest rooms have tile floors and modern wooden furniture. The five in front have high ceilings and small balconies overlooking Plaza Martí; those in the back have no windows and are cramped. The restaurant enjoys a lovely view and serves a good selection of meat and

seafood dishes. ✉ *Máximo Gómez 112,* ☎ *42/39–5144. 10 rooms. Restaurant, bar. MC, V.*

Shopping

A small selection of wood sculptures and other local handicrafts are available at the **Fondo de Bienes Culturales** (☎ 42/39–5617), across Máximo Gómez from the Hotel Mascotte.

Sancti Spíritus

⑤ *360 km (224 mi) southeast of Havana; 92 km (55 mi) southeast of Santa Clara; 70 km (42 mi) northeast of Trinidad.*

The tranquil capital of Sancti Spíritus Province has an historic center that receives only a tiny fraction of the visitors who flock to Trinidad. It's a quiet, traditional Cuban city, where bicycles and horse-drawn taxis make up most of the traffic and locals hang out in the central plaza at night. Though not as impressive as Trinidad, Sancti Spíritus has some lovely colonial architecture, which the government is restoring and painting, and two small museums in former homes.

The oldest part of the city extends from the muddy Río Yayabo in the northeast to the **Plaza Serafín Sánchez,** a shady central plaza surrounded by such late-19th-century buildings as the Teatro Principal (Principal Theater) and the neoclassical Biblioteca (Library). For several blocks south of the plaza, **Calle Independencia** becomes a cobbled pedestrian mall lined with shops and restaurants; it ends in front of the 19th-century Colonia Español building.

The city's cathedral, the **Iglesia Parroquial Mayor del Espíritu Santo** (✉ Jesús Méndez y Rodríguez, ☎ 41/24855), is a sky-blue, colonial church dominated by a massive bell tower. Its interior is sparsely decorated—with a carved wooden ceiling and a blue-and-gold wooden arch framing a simple altar—but considering that it was built in 1680, it's amazingly well preserved. Down the hill behind the church is **Calle el Llano,** a cobbled street lined with some of the city's oldest houses, most of which are still private homes. Quinta Santa Elena, a garden café at the end of the street, has a good view of the 19th-century stone bridge over the Río Yayabo.

The small **Museo Provincial** is in a 19th-century mansion one block east of Calle Independencia. Its exhibits are devoted primarily to the wars of independence and the Revolution, but there's also a small room dedicated to slavery. ✉ *Céspedes 11 Sur,* ☎ *41/27435.* ✚ *$1.* ◷ *Tues.– Sat. 9–5, Sun. 9–noon.*

★ **El Museo de Arte Colonial** (Museum of Colonial Art) is a nicely restored colonial mansion furnished with antiques from several centuries. One block south of the Iglesia Parroquial Mayor del Espíritu Santo, the mansion was built in 1744 by the Valle Iznaga family, who owned sugar plantations, processing plants, a railroad, and a port, among other things. ✉ *Plácido 74,* ☎ *41/25455.* ✚ *$2; $1 fee for photos.* ◷ *Tues.–Sat. 8:30–5, Sun. 8:30–noon*

Dining and Lodging

$ ✕ **Restaurante El Conquistador.** Just down the street from the Iglesia Parroquial is a colonial house containing this simple restaurant with terra-cotta floors, whitewashed walls, and a small garden patio. Its sturdy wooden tables are draped with white cloths, and fresh flowers provide splashes of color. There's no menu, just a few nightly specials, and the food is always typical Cuban fare. They accept only Cuban pesos, so a meal here costs almost nothing. ✉ *Máximo Gómez 122,* ☎ *no phone. No credit cards.*

$$ ✕🖼 **Villa Rancho Hatuey.** The city's most comfortable accommoda-
★ tions are in the countryside just north of downtown. Dozens of two-
story, cement bungalows spread around verdant grounds have spacious
rooms with white-tile floors, queen-size beds, lots of windows, and large
bathrooms with tubs. The main building houses the reception, bar, and
one of the area's best restaurants. Light sleepers may want to request
a room at the back of the property since the on-site discotheque (it's
right next to the reception area) is popular. ⊠ *Carretera Central, 5 km
(3 mi) north of town,* ☎ *41/28315,* 𝔽𝔸𝕏 *41/28350. 76 rooms. Restau-
rant, bar, pool, dance club. MC, V.*

$ 🖼 **Hotel Plaza.** The historic Hotel Plaza, which overlooks the Parque
Sarafín Sánchez, has undergone an extensive renovation with mixed
results. The airy lobby (with its arches and wicker furniture) and the
central patio bar (full of cast-iron tables and potted plants) are charm-
ing, but guest rooms on the second and third floors are somewhat tacky.
Those in the old wing have high ceilings, but newer rooms in back are
small and dark; opt for one in front as they have small balconies and
park views. ⊠ *Independencia 1 Norte,* ☎ *41/27102. 28 rooms. Restau-
rant, bar. MC, V.*

Nightlife and the Arts

The **Casa de la Trova** (Máximo Gómez 26 Sur, ☎ 41/26802), across
from the Iglesia Parroquial, has live music starting at 9 PM Thursday
through Saturday and on Sunday afternoons. The city's main art
gallery, **Galería Oscar Fernandez** (⊠ Céspedes 26 Sur, ☎ 41/23117),
closes for lunch and on Monday. If you want to dance, head for the
discotheque at the **Villa Rancho Hatuey** (⊠ Carretera Central, 5 km/3
mi north of town, ☎ 41/28315).

Outdoor Activities and Sports

The Zaza Reservoir, 10 km (6 mi) southeast of town, is reputed to have
world-class bass fishing. The **Hotel Horizontes Zaza** (☎ 41/28512), on
the reservoir, can arrange excursions. The best place for bird-watch-
ing is the Reserva Ecológica El Naranjal, a protected, mountainous area
20 km (12 mi) south of Sancti Spíritus and near the town of Banao.
Tours can be arranged through **Lázaro Rodríguez** (☎ 41/25868), the
local representative of Ecoturs.

Shopping

Galería Arcada (⊠ Calle Independencia 55 Sur, ☎ 41/27106), a colo-
nial house on the pedestrian mall, sells an array of local handicrafts.
The **Tienda el Manje** (⊠ Cervantes 11 ☎ 41/23772) in the Casa de la
Cultura, also sells local handicrafts.

Trinidad

❻–⓬ *70 km (42 mi) southwest of Sancti Spíritus; 407 km (244 mi) south-
east of Havana; 85 km (51 mi) southeast of Cienfuegos.*

Trinidad seems to have weathered three centuries with hardly a wrin-
kle. Its enchanting cobblestone streets are lined with houses that have
brightly painted adobe walls and wooden shutters. Its historic center,
which covers more than 50 blocks, is like a vast, meticulously main-
tained museum full of restored mansions and manicured plazas. It's a
lively, friendly town, where many of the 60,000 locals frequently pull
their chairs out onto the street to gossip. The air rings with the sounds
of birds singing from wicker cages and the irresistible rhythms of
Cuban music.

The city was founded in 1514 by the conquistador Diego Velázquez and
named for the Holy Trinity. It grew little until the 17th century, when
its inhabitants began trading with pirates. Between 1750 and 1825, the

population rose from 6,000 to 12,000, and thousands of slaves were brought in to work on the sugar plantations in the nearby Valle de los Ingenios. Wealthy families built mansions here, filled them with imported treasures, and sent their children to European schools. By the second half of the 19th century, however, Trinidad's star began to fade as sugar prices fell, the struggles for independence began, and slavery ended. By the early 1900s, Trinidad was impoverished and isolated. But the neglect that prevailed during the first half of the 20th century has helped the city retain its colonial ambience. In 1988, the United Nations declared the historic center a World Heritage Site, and during the past decade, the government has worked hard to restore the colonial architecture. (Note that like many Cuban cities, Trinidad's streets go by pre- and postrevolutionary names; both are cited in addresses below.)

Exploring Trinidad

A GOOD WALK

An appropriate place to begin your tour of this historic city is the **Museo Histórico** ⑥. One block northeast along Calle Simón Bolívar (Desengaño) is the **Museo de Arqueología** ⑦, on the northwest corner of **Plaza Mayor** ⑧, the city's splendidly restored central square. From the Museo de Arqueología, walk north a block to the thick columns of the **Museo Romántico** ⑨ on the plaza's northeastern edge. From here follow Simón Bolívar north a block to Fernando Hernández (Cristo) and the Antiguo Convento de San Francisco, Trinidad's most famous landmark, which now houses the **Museo de la Lucha Contra Bandidos** ⑩. Return to the Plaza Mayor along Fernando Hernández. Just beyond the Museo Romántico is the city's cathedral, **La Santísima Trinidad** ⑪. On the plaza's southwestern side and across from the Museo de Arqueología is the **Museo de Arquitectura** ⑫.

TIMING

You can follow this tour in 20 minutes without stopping. If you visit all the museums and monuments, plan on spending the better part of a day.

SIGHTS TO SEE

⑦ **Museo de Arqueología.** The Archaeology Museum is in a lovely mansion built by local merchant Andrés Padrón in 1734. Within its restored rooms you'll find unremarkable exhibits on the region's original inhabitants, and the flora and fauna on which they depended for survival. There's also a small display on slavery. ⊠ *Calle Simón Bolívar (Desengaño) y Ruben Martínez Villena (Real del Jigüe)*, ☎ *419/3420.* ☞ *$1.* ⊘ *Mon.–Sat. 9–5.*

⑫ **Museo de Arquitectura.** This museum is dedicated to Trinidad's 18th- and 19th-century architecture. Exhibits on the city's development and its most important buildings fill the rooms of a sky-blue 18th-century house, once the home of the Sánchez Iznaga family. Don't miss the lovely garden patio. ⊠ *Fernando Hernández (Cristo)*, ☎ *419/3208.* ☞ *$1.* ⊘ *Sat.–Thurs. 9–5.*

★ ⑥ **Museo Histórico.** Set in the impressive Palacio Cantero, which was built by a sugar baron in 1830, the History Museum's displays trace the development of Trinidad from its founding by Diego Velázquez to the early years of the Revolutionary government. Two rooms are furnished with antiques, and elaborate murals cover some of the walls. A lookout platform atop the building's large tower affords a wonderful view. ⊠ *Calle Simón Bolívar (Desengaño) y Peña*, ☎ *419/4460.* ☞ *$2; $1 fee for photos.* ⊘ *Sun.–Fri. 9–5.*

⑩ **Museo de la Lucha Contra Bandidos.** The tall, yellow bell tower—all that remains of the original 18th-century church and Franciscan monastery—is Trinidad's most famous landmark, adorning postcards,

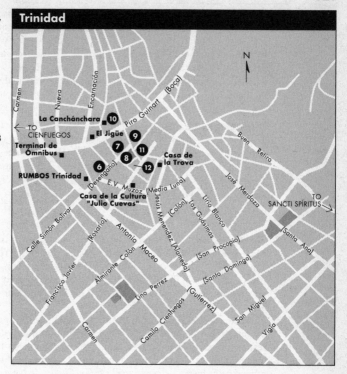

brochures, and T-shirts. You can climb the tower for a sweeping view of the city. The museum's displays explain the suppression of "bandits," who waged guerrilla warfare—with a little help from their friends at the CIA—from the Sierra de Escambray for the first six years of Castro's Revolutionary government. ⊠ *Fernando Hernández (Cristo) y Piro Guinart (Boca),* ☏ *419/4121.* ⊡ *$1.* ⊙ *Tues.–Sun. 9–5.*

NEED A BREAK?   Want to quench your thirst? Pop into **La Canchánchara,** a lively bar in an 18th-century building near the Museo de la Lucha Contra los Bandidos. There's usually a live band playing in the shady patio, and they always have plenty of soft drinks, cold beer, and such Cuban cocktails as the *mojito* (rum, lime juice, and mint) and the *canchánchara* (rum, lime juice, and honey).

★ **⑨** **Museo Romántico.** Rather than the stuff of Cupid's arrows, the romance in this museum's name refers to the one that Trinidad's prominent families had with their precious things. A great variety of antiques—most imported from Europe—fill the 14 rooms of this imposing mansion. Built in 1808, the house belonged to Count Burnet, though nearly all the antiques in it came from the homes of other families. Don't miss the view from the second-floor balcony. ⊠ *Ferando Hernádez (Cristo) y Simón Bolívar (Desengaño),* ☏ *419/4363.* ⊡ *$2.* ⊙ *Tues.–Sun. 9–5.*

★ **⑧** **Plaza Mayor.** The heart of the historic center, this charming little park is dominated by royal palms and has cast-iron benches, ceramic urns, the marble statue of a pale lady, and two brass greyhounds that were probably once cannons. It's surrounded by the restored homes of sugar barons and merchants, many of which now contain museums. ⊠ *Calle Simón Bolívar (Desengaño), e/Fernando Hernández (Cristo) y Ruben Martínez Villena (Real de Jigüe).*

⓫ **La Santísima Trinidad.** Although the city's cathedral was inaugurated in 1892, the building took the better part of the 19th century to complete (it was built to replace the 17th-century church that was destroyed by a hurricane). Don't let the rather bleak exterior (or limited hours) deter you from stepping inside; its interesting interior is replete with hardwood altars that date from the early 20th century and various colonial icons. ✉ *Fernando Hernández (Cristo),* ☎ *no phone.* ☉ *Mon.–Sat. 11:30–1.*

Dining and Lodging

There's practically a restaurant on every block of the historic center, and most occupy 18th-century mansions. The cheapest accommodations are the rooms for rent in *hostals* (private homes)—many of which are in lovely colonial buildings near the main sights—such as those belonging to **Osvaldo Saroza** (✉ Gustavo Izquierdo/Gloria 124, ☎ 419/3025), **Concepción Télles** (✉ Piro Guinart/Boca 159, ☎ 419/2562), and **María Pomares** (✉ Zerquera 361, ☎ 419/2164).

$ ✕ **Paladar Estela.** This popular paladar, 1½ blocks northeast of the Plaza Mayor, serves generous portions of typical Cuban fare. Your choice of a meat or fish entrée comes with several salads, arroz congrí, potatoes, fruit, and coffee—all for a very palatable price. Tables sit on or beside an attractive interior garden patio. ✉ *Calle Simón Bolívar (Desengaño) 557,* ☎ *419/4329. No credit cards.*

$ ✕ **Restaurante El Jigüe.** Set in the Plazuela de Jigüe, a tiny plaza shaded by one tree, this colorful, historic (the building dates from 1720) restaurant seems to say "come on in." Its bright interior has high ceilings, chandeliers, and landscapes hung on white walls. The menu ranges from bistec de cerdo grillé to *enchilado de* langosta (in a red sauce). ✉ *Ruben Martínez Villena (Real de Jigüe) 69,* ☎ *419/4136. No credit cards.*

$ ✕ **Sol y Son.** The best of this city's many paladares is just a few blocks
★ southwest of Plaza Mayor in an elegant, 19th-century home. It looks like an antiques shop, but in back, overlooking an attractive courtyard, is a small restaurant. Start with an *ensalada de temporada* (seasonal salad), then sink your teeth into a pollo *estofado* (chicken in a tomato sauce). ✉ *Calle Simón Bolívar (Desengaño) 283,* ☎ *no phone. No credit cards.*

$$ ▥ **Hotel Las Cuevas.** Spread over a grassy hill on the northern edge of
★ town, this collection of cement duplexes features wonderful views of Trinidad's red tile roofs, the Península de Ancón, and the blue Caribbean. The name means "The Caves," and caverns riddle the ground beneath the hotel; one of them is a museum, another holds the discotheque. A giant thatched roof covers the reception area and the main restaurant and bar; a smaller, air-conditioned restaurant sits next to the pool atop the hill. Most rooms are small, with low ceilings, stone walls, wicker furniture, and porches; those behind the pool are more spacious, but those in the lower H and F groups have the best views. ✉ *Lino Pérez (San Procopio),* ☎ *419/6133,* ℻ *419/6161. 112 rooms. 2 restaurants, bar, pool, dance club. MC, V.*

$ ▥ **Hotel la Ronda.** Though it caters mostly to Cubans, some of the rooms in this older, downtown hotel have been fixed up for visitors from abroad, which means such amenities as satellite TV and minirefrigerators. Though rooms are stuffy, public areas are pleasant, especially the rooftop bar and the central patio, which is shaded by a vine-covered trellis and filled with cast-iron furniture. The hotel is conveniently located next to Plaza Carrillo, just a few blocks south of the historic center. ✉ *Calle José Martí (Jesús María) 238,* ☎ *419/2248. 17 rooms. Restaurant, bar, refrigerators. No credit cards.*

Nightlife and the Arts

The **Casa de la Música** (☎ 419/3414), behind the cathedral, has nightly concerts at 9 PM with complete bar service. The **Casa de la Trova** (☎ 419/4135), two blocks east of the Plaza Mayor, has live music during the afternoon and nightly concerts at 10 PM for $1. Trinidad's most popular dance spot is the subterranean **Cueva Ayala** (✉ Lino Pérez (San Procopio), ☎ 419/4013) discotheque at the Hotel las Cuevas. The open-air theater in the **Ruinas del Teatro Brunel** (✉ Antonio Maceo/Gutiérrez, entre Calle Simón Bolívar/Desengaño y Francisco Javier/Rosario, ☎ 419/3994) has a nightly show at 10 that features several different kinds of folk dancing and costs just $3.

Shopping

Bazar Trinidad (✉ Antonio Maceo/Gutiérrez y Francisco Javier/Rosario, ☎ no phone) sells paintings by local artists and other souvenirs. The shop inside the **Casa de la Música** (☎ 419/3414, behind the cathedral, has an extensive selection of Cuban music. The **Casa del Tabaco** (✉ Antonio Maceo/Gutiérrez y Francisco Javier/Rosario, ☎ 419/6256) is the place for cigars, rum, and coffee.

El Valle de los Ingenios

⑬ *3 km (2 mi) to 12 km (7 mi) east of Trinidad.*

Just east of Trinidad, the road winds its way through the verdant Valley of the Sugar Mills, where Trinidad's colonial fortunes were made. Just 3 km (2 mi) outside of town on the left is a simple *mirador* (scenic overlook), with an open-air restaurant and a rustic wooden tower that affords an excellent view of the pale-green cane fields and darker Sierra de Escambray beyond—a panorama best photographed in the morning. Twelve kilometers (7 miles) beyond the lookout on the left is **Manaca-Iznaga,** where an 18th-century farmhouse that once belonged to one of the region's wealthiest families stands next to the Torre de Iznaga, a 43-m (141-ft) tower built in the early 1800s. Legend has it that the two Iznaga sons were in love with a beautiful slave girl, and their father told one to build a tower and the other to dig a well, with the promise that whomever built higher or dug deeper could have her. But when they were done, both the tower and well were 43 m, so the old man got the girl. The tower actually had a much more practical purpose: it was a place from which to keep an eye on the thousands of slaves who worked the surrounding plantations. The large bell that was rung when slaves tried to escape lies on the ground near the farmhouse.

Dining

$ ✕ **Restaurante Manaca.** The Iznaga family's former manor house is now occupied by a restaurant. The building's ochre walls, square columns, wood-beam ceiling, and terra-cotta floors provide an authentic colonial ambience. There's an old sugar mill out back, and scattered on the lawn in front are the cauldrons used to boil down molasses. Lunches are usually accompanied by the music of an excellent little band. The house specialty is *puntas de cerdo a la Iznaga* (strips of pork loin in a tomato-vegetable sauce), but the menu includes everything from fresh seafood to grilled chicken. ✉ *Manaca-Iznaga,* ☎ *419/7241. No credit cards. No dinner.*

Península de Ancón

⑭ *12 km (7 mi) south of Trinidad.*

The beaches that line the southern edge of this narrow peninsula, which curves eastward into the Caribbean, are the best in the province. Most people who visit Trinidad actually stay here; it lies conveniently close to the historic city, and the area's largest hotels overlook its pale sands. The first beach you'll come to as you head south from Trinidad is the attractive **Playa Maria Aguilar. Playa Ancón,** just to the east of Playa Maria Aguilar, is the peninsula's most appealing stretch. Coral reefs lie submerged just off Península de Ancón's shore and around the tiny island of **Cayo Blanco,** which is a popular day trip; many local hotels and tour operators offer excursions here.

Lodging

$$ ☒ **Hotel Ancón.** This vast, beachfront complex is practically two hotels. Rooms in the massive main building are unattractive little boxes, the best of which have tiny balconies overlooking the sea. Those in the Modulo Nuevo—the newer, two-story buildings next door—are spacious, tastefully furnished, and have large balconies. The crazy thing is that all the rooms cost the same, so request one (with an ocean view) in the Modulo Nuevo. The beach is a long, narrow strip of white sand shaded by thatched parasols. The restaurants are on the ground floor of the main building, next to which are a large pool, tennis courts, and other facilities. ☒ *Playa Ancón,* ☎ *419/6120,* ℻ *419/6147. 279 rooms. 4 restaurants, 3 bars, pool, 2 tennis courts, beach, boating, bicycles. MC, V.*

$$ ☒ **Hotel Costa Sur.** Deluxe rooms here—in the newer cement bunga-
★   lows close to the beach—have lots of windows, small porches, wicker furniture, and large baths. Superior rooms in the main building are considerably smaller, but they're less expensive and have sea-view balconies. Standard rooms—smaller still and farther from the beach—cost slightly less. All rooms have bright tile floors, cable TV, air-conditioning, and other modern amenities. ☒ *Playa Maria Aguilar,* ☎ *419/6174,* ℻ *419/ 6173. 131 rooms. 2 restaurants, bar, pool, volleyball, beach, boating, bicycles. MC, V. BP.*

Outdoor Activities and Sports

The ocean around the Península de Ancón holds plenty of coral, the most accessible of which lies a mere 300 m (985 ft) off the shore from the Hotel Costa Sur. The **Puerto Sol Marina** (☎ 419/6205), near the end of the peninsula, has a dive center and boats equipped for deep-sea fishing; you can make arrangements to fish or dive through the beach hotels or through Cubatur (☞ Tour Operators and Travel Agents *in* Central Cuba A to Z, *below*).

Topes de Collantes

⑮ *21 km (12 mi) north of Trinidad.*

Nestled high in the Sierra de Escambray at the end of a road that winds its way north from Trinidad, this sylvan enclave has long been a health resort. It's also the perfect base for a hike. At an altitude of 800 m (2,600 ft) above sea level, the climate is very refreshing (the average temperature is 21°C/70°F), and regular precipitation keeps everything green. Because the area receives mostly Cuban tourism, the accommodations and restaurants aren't as good as those in Trinidad, but the rates are quite reasonable. If you don't want to spend the night, the tour operator Rumbos (☞ Tour Operators and Travel Agents *in* Central Cuba A to Z, *below*) offers day trips from Trinidad.

The mountains around Topes de Collantes are covered with a mosaic of coffee farms and patches of forest that are protected within the **Parque Natural Escambray.** This nature preserve has several deep, lush valleys that are home to such birds as the Cuban parrot, the emerald hummingbird, and the trogon. Several trails lead to waterfalls; the most accessible is the **Salto de Caburní,** just a 2 km (1 mi) hike along a trail that starts at the Villa Caburní hotel, 2 km (1 mi) north of Topes de

Collantes. The spectacular **Salto de Rocío** cascades down a rock face about 17 km (10 mi) north of Topes. Tours (the only way to visit) truck you to a point just 2 km (1 mi) from the falls. The grotto of **La Batata,** several kilometers west of Topes, has a river running out of it with a swimming hole; you can visit on a 7-km (4 mi) guided hike that passes a lookout point.

Dining and Lodging

$ ✕🏠 **Los Helechos.** The name means "The Ferns," a nod to the tree ferns that abound in the surrounding forest. Although you'd think that rooms here would offer views of all the greenery, few do; alas, this place was originally a boarding school. The best and brightest quarters are in the main building, a three-story, cement structure with a frightful paint job; still, even those on the top floor have mediocre vistas. They also have balconies, tile floors, wicker furniture, and tacky Chinese curtains. A simple restaurant serves a decent selection of Cuban dishes, and just down the hill is a large, indoor pool. ✉ *Topes de Collantes,* ☎ *42/40330,* ℻ *42/40228. 58 rooms. Restaurant, bar, pool, sauna, bowling, exercise room, dance club. No credit cards.*

Outdoor Activities and Sports

Enjoying the great outdoors is about the only thing to do in Topes de Collantes, and hiking is the way to do it. **Gaviota Tours** (☎ 42/40228) offers inexpensive excursions to the waterfalls; La Batata; and Hacienda Codina, a nearby farm.

CIEGO DE ÁVILA AND CAMAGÜEY PROVINCES

These two provinces are known for their white-sand beaches, which are lapped by waters rich in marine life. But there's more to the region than sun, sand, and deep-blue sea. On the mainland of Ciego de Ávila Province you'll find bass-laden lakes; off its northern shore, the mangrove shallows of Cayo Coco and Cayo Guillermo are often filled with flamingos. In Camagüey Province, between the northern cays and the coastal resort of Santa Lucía, there are enough coral reefs and wrecks to keep a scuba diver submerged for weeks. The sportfishing here is legendary (it was Hemingway's favorite angling area), and the eponymous provincial capital city is steeped in Cuban history and rich in Cuban culture.

Ciego de Ávila

16 *430 km (258 mi) southeast of Havana; 74 km (44 mi) east of Sancti Spíritus; 90 km (54 mi) south of Cayo Coco; 100 km (60 mi) northwest of Camagüey.*

Most people simply pass through the provincial capital—a quiet, unattractive city of 100,000 people—en route to Cayo Coco and Cayo Guillermo to the north, Camagüey to the east, or the port of Júcaro to the south. Founded in the 16th century, Ciego de Ávila didn't grow much till the early part of 20th century. Most of the principal buildings, such as the Biblioteca (Library) in the old town hall and the more modern Catedral (Cathedral) next door, and are near the central **Parque Martí.** One block west of the park on Independencia is the **Casa de la Cultura,** a cultural center housed in what was once the Colonia Español, an elite social club. One block south of Parque Martí is the **Teatro Principal,** a large, recently renovated theater that was built in 1923.

The simple **Museo Provincial** (✉ Jose Antonio Echeverria 25, ☎ 33/8431), housed in a former high school four blocks west of Parque Martí, has exhibits on local history, including a model of La Trocha, the barrier across the length of the country built by the Spanish during the first War of Independence. The museum is open Tuesday–Saturday 8–noon and 1–5. Two blocks northwest of the Museo Provincial is **El Fortín** (✉ Calle 1 y Máximo Gómez), one of the small forts that dotted La Trocha's length.

Dining and Lodging

$ ✕ **Restaurant Colonial.** The setting couldn't be more attractive: you're seated in rustic leather chairs, at wooden tables and beneath a painted wooden ceiling, with views through the arches of an interior garden patio. A guitar trio usually accompanies dinner with soft Latin music. The Spanish-influenced menu has such dishes as *fabada austuriana* (a white bean, ham, and potato soup) and *cachelo madrileño* (pork ribs in a red sauce). ✉ *Independencia 110,* ☎ *332/3595. No credit cards.*

$ ▦ **Hotel Ciego de Ávila.** It may not be much to look at, but this six-story cement hotel northwest of town is the best around. It's a fairly large place, with a big pool, a modern restaurant that serves a limited menu, and a popular discotheque. Standard rooms are plain, rect-angular boxes with satellite TV, small desks, and picture windows with a view of the pool, a small marsh, and the city beyond. The *cabañas* (suites) behind the pool are twice as big, with kitchenettes and lounges, but they're dangerously close to the disco. ✉ *Carretera Ceballos,* ☎ *332/8013. 136 rooms. Restaurant, bar, pool, dance club. MC, V.*

$ ▦ **Hotel Sevilla.** A half block from Parque Martí, this hotel was com-pleted in 1920, which makes it one of the town's oldest buildings. Re-cently renovated, its lobby now shines, with high arches, stained glass, and potted plants; most of it is occupied by the restaurant. Rooms are small, but authentic, with high ceilings and colorful tile floors. Although those on the street have small balconies, they don't have hot water; second-floor rooms are your best bet. ✉ *Independencia 57,* ☎ *332/5603. 24 rooms. Restaurant, dance club. No credit cards.*

The Arts

Weekend nights often see concerts or dance performances in the **Casa de la Cultura** (✉ Independencia 76, ☎ 332/3974).

The **Casa de la Trova** (✉ Libertad y Simón Reyes, ☎ no phone) has live music every night but Tuesday. The **Galería Raúl Martínez** (✉ In-dependencia 65, ☎ 33/23900) has monthly exhibitions by local artists. They're open Tuesday–Sunday, 8–noon and 2–5; admission is free.

Outdoor Activities and Sports

The vast, uninhabited keys of the Jardines de la Reina archipelago to the south of Ciego de Ávila and Camagüey provinces was once the haunt of pirates (five colonial shipwrecks are submerged here) and is now a fabulous place for diving. There are no hotels on the islands, but a **live-on dive boat** (☎ 339/1309, ℻ 339–8104) offers access to them out of Júcaro, a small port south of Ciego de Ávila.

Shopping

The **Fondo de Bienes Culturales** (✉ Simón Reyes 17, ☎ 332/5616), two blocks west of Parque Martí, sells handicrafts and paintings by local artists.

Morón

⑰ *35 km (21 mi) north of Ciego de Ávila; 55 km (33 mi) south of Cayo Coco.*

Though dilapidated, Morón is a more pleasant town than Ciego de Ávila, as it has half the population and twice the historic architecture. It's also the nearest city to the distinctly un-Cuban hotels of Cayo Coco and Cayo Guillermo. Its main road is lined with the colonnades of neo-classic buildings (in poor repair) and is usually full of bicycles and horse-drawn taxis.

The town was the operations center for a private railroad, and its hand-some **train station,** built in 1923, is a structure worth admiring; nearby stand the stately homes of the railway's administrators. Morón is also known as the "City of the Rooster" (after a cocky public official in the Spanish town for which it was named), and thus has a large steel sculp-ture of a cockerel, **El Gallo de Morón,** that crows (thanks to a recorded broadcast) twice daily, at 6 AM and 6 PM. It's on the main road near the south end of town. The **Museo Municipal** (⊠ Castillo 164, ☎ 33/54510) has an extensive collection of pre-Columbian artifacts. It's open Tuesday–Sunday 8–noon and 2–5; admission is 1 peso (5¢).

Most people use Morón as a base for bass fishing. Oddly though, bass are called *trucha* in Cuba, though it's the Spanish term for "trout." **La-guna la Redonda,** a shallow lake 14 km (8 mi) north of Morón, is a renowned fishing spot, and its narrow canals that wind between the silt roots of giant mangroves make an interesting boat ride. A small marina offers 45-minute boat trips (for one to four people) and half-day fish-ing excursions complete with tackle. Cubanacan (☞ Tour Operators and Travel Agents *in* Central Cuba A to Z, *below*) also arranges fishing trips. The **Laguna de la Leche,** 5 km (3 mi) north of Morón, is much larger than La Redonda. Named for its milky water (*leche* means "milk") it doesn't have great fishing, but it does offer decent bird-watching.

Dining and Lodging

$ ✕ **Restaurant Las Fuentes.** This charming restaurant is in an old resi-dence near the north end of Morón's main drag. Cow-skin chairs and wooden tables surround a small courtyard full of potted plants and *fuentes* (fountains), for which the restaurant is named. Paintings lit-erally cover the walls, and set in the back corner is a small bar. The menu ranges from *bistec de rinorada* (steak) to *camarón enchilado* (shrimp in a red sauce). ⊠ *Calle Martí, e/Libertad y Agramonte,* ☎ *no phone. No credit cards.*

$ 🏨 **Club de Caza y Pesca.** Set in an elegant, restored mansion near the
★ train station, this small hotel specializes in fishing packages and pro-vides guests with guides, licenses, and gear. The building was originally the home of the railroad administrator, which seems to have been a lucrative job given the structure's marble floors and gracious staircase and columns. The restaurant and bar are on the ground floor; the up-stairs guest rooms have large windows, high ceilings, blue-tile baths and such amenities as minibars and satellite TV. There's a small pool and another bar in the garden out back. ⊠ *Cristóbal Colón 41,* ☎ *335/4562,* 🖷 *335/6268. 7 rooms. Restaurant, bar, pool, fishing. MC, V.*

Nightlife

The **Casa de la Trova** (⊠ Libertad 74, ☎ 335/4158) has live music every night but Monday. Shows start around 9.

Cayo Coco and Cayo Guillermo

⑱–⑲ *55 km (33 mi) and 88 km (53 mi) north of Morón.*

These two green islands, set in the turquoise sea some 27 km (16 mi) north of the mainland, have more than a dozen white-sand beaches, twice that many coral reefs, and mangrove shallows that attract great flocks of flamingos. Ernest Hemingway made frequent fishing trips to these keys and described them in *Islands in the Stream.* (Sportfishing charters are available out of the marinas on both keys; you can arrange them at any hotel.) Long uninhabited, and visited only by local fishermen and the occasional millionaire, the islands now have half a dozen modern beach resorts, with several more under construction.

A causeway traverses the shallow Bahía de Perros (Bay of Dogs) south of Cayo Coco; from this key, shorter causeways stretch west to Cayo Guillermo and east to the undeveloped Cayo Romano. All three islands are covered with a thick scrub vegetation; mangrove swamps line their southern shores, and bleached-sand beaches scallop their northern edges. The fishing is excellent; in addition to the marlin that so fascinated Papa, you'll find hundreds of other species—from the delicate butterfly fish to the menacing barracuda—as well as a dizzying array of invertebrates. The diving (particularly off Cayo Guillermo) is also incredible, with dozens of healthy black-coral reefs just offshore from major hotels and visibility that averages 20–35 m (66–115 ft).

Cayo Coco was named for the white ibis, a pale wader called the "coco" in Cuba, but its mangroves and sandy shallows attract dozens of species, including flamingos (which gather by the thousands in the shallow bay to the south), roseate spoonbills, tricolored herons, and reddish egrets. The island's roughly 90 indigenous species are joined by another 120 varieties between November and April, and its forests are also home to everything from wild pigs to anole lizards.

Despite its varied wildlife, most people visit Cayo Coco for its swaths of sugary sand shaded by coconut palms and washed by blue-green waters—the stuff of travel posters in Toronto storefronts or the daydreams of snowbound accountants. Nine beaches run for a total of 21 km (12 mi) along the northern coast, and only two of them have hotels. The most spectacular beaches are Playa Flamingo and nearby Playa Prohibida (Forbidden Beach)—a protected area with high dunes and scrubby native palms.

NEED A BREAK?	About 10 km (6 mi) south of Cayo Coco, on a tiny islet along which the the causeway passes, is **Paradero La Silla**—a rustic snack bar that's as good a place to bird-watch as it is to wet your whistle. The wooden tower next to it overlooks shallows where flamingos, herons, and other leggy waders regularly hunt for their dinner. Cold drinks and light meals are served under a thatched roof.

Cayo Guillermo's beaches are narrow, but still captivating. The ocean in front of them is so shallow that you can wade out more than 90 m (290 ft). The most spectacular beach is Playa Pilar, which was named after Hemingway's old fishing boat. On the key's northwest end, it's backed by 20-m (66-ft) dunes and overlooks Cayo Media Luna, an islet where Fulgencio Batista once had a vacation home. Cayo Guillermo has some of the best diving in the country, with 37 dive spots nearby.

Dining and Lodging

The hotels on Cayo Coco and Cayo Guillermo are generic, Caribbean megaresorts. A stay here will put you in full vacation mode, with meals, snacks, drinks, and everything from beach chairs to sea kayaks included in the rates. In addition, all the hotels have amphitheaters—where nightly shows range from Cuban folk dancing to fashion shows—and discos.

$$$$ ✕🏨 **Sol Club Cayo Guillermo.** The colonial days meet the new millennium here. The spacious lobby has a high, beamed ceiling and thick square columns, but at its center is a modern fountain with a brass sculpture. Beyond glass doors lies a pool (with the obligatory sunken bar) surrounded by coconut palms and tropical gardens. The spacious rooms—in one- and two-story buildings scattered about the sparsely planted

Finally, a travel companion that doesn't snore on the plane or eat all your peanuts.

MCI WORLDCOM WorldPhone®

123 456 7891 2345
J.D. SMITH

When traveling, your MCI WorldCom Card is the best way to keep in touch. Our operators speak your language, so they'll be able to connect you back home—no matter where your travels take you. Plus, your MCI WorldCom Card is easy to use, and even earns you frequent flyer miles every time you use it. When you add in our great rates, you get something even more valuable: peace-of-mind. So go ahead. Travel the world. MCI WorldCom just brought it a whole lot closer.

You can even sign up today at www.mci.com/worldphone or ask your operator to make a collect call to 1-410-314-2938.

EASY TO CALL WORLDWIDE

1 Just dial the WorldPhone access number of the country you're calling from.
2 Dial or give the operator your MCI WorldCom Card number.
3 Dial or give the number you're calling.

Argentina	
To call using Telefonica	0-800-222-6249
To call using Telecom	0-800-555-1002
Brazil	**000-8012**
Mexico	
Avantel	01-800-021-8000
Telmex ▲	001-800-674-7000
Collect access in Spanish	980-9-16-1000
Morocco	**00-211-0012**

For your complete WorldPhone calling guide, dial the WorldPhone access number for the country you're in and ask the operator for Customer Service. In the U.S. call 1-800-431-5402.

▲ When calling from public phones, use phones marked LADATEL.

EARN FREQUENT FLYER MILES

AmericanAirlines®
AAdvantage®

Continental Airlines
OnePass®

▲Delta Air Lines
SkyMiles®

MILEAGE PLUS®
United Airlines

U·S AIRWAYS
DIVIDEND MILES

MCI WorldCom, its logo and the names of the products referred to herein are proprietary marks of MCI WorldCom, Inc. All airline names and logos are proprietary marks of the respective airlines. All airline program rules and conditions apply.

MCI WORLDCOM

The first thing you need overseas is the one thing you forget to pack.

FOREIGN CURRENCY DELIVERED OVERNIGHT

Chase Currency To Go® delivers foreign currency to your home by the next business day*

It's easy—before you travel, call 1-888-CHASE84 for delivery of any of 75 currencies

Delivery is free with orders of $500 or more

Competitive rates— without exchange fees

You don't have to be a Chase customer—you can pay by Visa® or MasterCard®

 CHASE

THE RIGHT RELATIONSHIP IS EVERYTHING.®

1•888•CHASE84
www.chase.com

grounds—have tile floors, Caribbean-style furniture, small baths, and sliding doors that open onto covered porches or balconies facing the ocean. This is the best destination for divers, since it has a modern dive center and plenty of reefs nearby. ⌧ *Cayo Guillermo,* ☎ *33/30–1760,* FAX *33/30–1748. 276 rooms. 3 restaurants, 3 bars, snack bar, pool, sauna, 2 tennis courts, aerobics, exercise room, horseback riding, volleyball, beach, dive shop, snorkeling, boating, fishing, bicycles, motorbikes, shops, cabaret, nightclub, children's programs (5–13), travel services, car rental. MC, V. All-inclusive.*

$$$–$$$$ ✕⊞ **Hotel Tryp.** Cayo Coco's original hotel, the Tryp is a miniature resort city, with several pools, some 20 bars and restaurants, and nearly a thousand rooms spread along a mile of pale beach. The hotel consists of two compounds, each with its own reception: the original complex, to the west, has a lot of charm, with large rooms in Spanish-style structures surrounded by lush gardens; the snazzy new wing has a modern, open-air lobby that overlooks a vast pool area with sculptures, fountains, and a sunken bar. Rooms throughout are done in earth tones and have tile floors, balconies, and large baths with tubs. ⌧ *Cayo Coco, due north of causeway,* ☎ *33/30–1300,* FAX *33/30–1386. 972 rooms. 8 restaurants, 11 bars, 2 cafés, 4 pools, beauty salon, massage, sauna, 6 tennis courts, aerobics, exercise room, horseback riding, Ping-Pong, volleyball, beach, dive shop, snorkeling, windsurfing, boating, jet skiing, fishing, motorbikes, shops, billiards, cabaret, nightclub, children's programs (4–12), travel services, car rental. MC, V. All-inclusive, BP.*

$$$ ✕⊞ **Iberostar Daiquirí.** Second only to its white beach, which extends
★ into blue-green shallows, is this hotel's airy lobby set beneath a soaring wooden roof and complete with shiny marble floors; painted columns; colorful, tinted glass; and a small bar surrounded by tropical greenery. Restaurants and three-story buildings with guest quarters surround the circular pool, which has a sunken bar beneath a thatched roof. Rooms have beige-tile floors, wood and wicker furniture, original art, and small balconies; about half have ocean views. ⌧ *Cayo Guillermo,* ☎ *33/30–1650,* FAX *33/30–1645. 312 rooms. 3 restaurants, 2 bars, pool, massage, sauna, 2 tennis courts, aerobics, exercise room, horseback riding, volleyball, beach, snorkeling, windsurfing, boating, fishing, bicycles, motorbikes, shops, cabaret, children's programs (4–12), travel services, car rental. MC, V. All-inclusive.*

Camagüey

 535 km (321 mi) southeast of Havana; 174 km (104 mi) southeast of Ciego de Ávila; and 255 km (153 mi) northwest of Holguín.

Cuba's third largest city (population 315,000) and the capital of the country's most extensive province, busy, rambling Camagüey has an old quarter that's bigger than Havana Vieja (though not quite as impressive). Its narrow, cobbled streets—lined with an eclectic mix of architecture—converge on plazas dominated by colonial churches. The Camagüeyanos, as its citizens are known, are proud of their city, its nearly five centuries of history, and its rich cultural heritage. They're very accommodating to the few visitors that pass this way, which makes the town a pleasant place to visit, indeed.

Camagüey was one of the seven villas founded by Diego de Velázquez at the beginning of the 16th century. Originally called Puerto del Principe (Prince's Port), it started out on the northern coast and was moved twice, reaching its current location in 1528. It wasn't until the early 1900s that it took the name Camagüey, after a tree common to the region. As the vast plain surrounding it was converted to ranchland, the city became a prosperous commercial center. During the 17th and 18th centuries, buccaneers and pirates, led by the likes of Henry Morgan, marched inland and sacked the city several times. As protection against such invasions, Camagüey was transformed into a maze of narrow streets, few of which are parallel, which made ambushes harder in the old days and makes it easier for visitors to get lost today.

As sugar exports came to complement ranching profits, Camagüey developed a criollo upper class that was supportive of the independence movements that swept the country in the second half of the 19th century. Some of its most fortunate sons took up arms against the Spanish, and many paid dearly for their treason. The most famous of these rebels was Ignacio Agramonte, who was not only killed by the Spanish, but whose body was burned in public. Agramonte consequently became the town hero, whose name figures big in local landmarks.

Set in a fairly dry, flat region, for centuries the camagüeyanos drank rainwater collected in giant ceramic vessels called *tinajones*. In the early 20th century, when a water system was finally built, it is estimated that there were 1,900 such containers, more than enough to give Camagüey its moniker of the "City of the Tinajones." Those giant jugs are now displayed all over town, and their industry gave birth to a ceramic-making tradition. One popular legend has it that if a local maiden gives a visitor water from a tinajón, he'll fall in love with her and never leave.

Exploring Camagüey

A GOOD WALK

Start out at the central **Plaza de los Trabajadores** ⑳, dominated to the east by the **Catedral Nuestra Señora de la Merced** ㉑ and to the south by the **Casa Natal de Ignacio Agramonte** ㉒. From here, walk three blocks northeast on Ignacio Agramonte to the **Iglesia de la Nuestra Señora de la Soledad** ㉓. From this church, head south down the quiet Calle Maceo, crossing the tiny Plaza Maceo to Independencia, and continuing one block south to **Parque Ignacio Agramonte** ㉔. After visiting the **Santa Iglesia de la Catedral** ㉕, and other sights around the park, walk south from the Casa de la Trova along Cisneros, veering right just after crossing Raúl Lamar, and taking the next left onto Hurtado to the **Plaza de San Juan de Dios** ㉖.

TIMING

This route should take 40 minutes to walk, without stops; with stops you can just about visit everything in half a day. If you dally, perhaps stopping for a meal and listening to a few songs in the Casa de la Trova, you can stretch the tour into a full day.

SIGHTS TO SEE

㉒ **Casa Natal de Ignacio Agramonte.** This yellow, colonial building with a high, wooden balcony was probably one of the tallest structures in town when Ignacio Agramonte was born to a wealthy ranching family here in 1841. Agramonte grew to become a general in the Ten Years War, Cuba's first war for independence from Spain. When he was killed in battle in 1873, he ascended to the rank of hero. Though only half the original house remains, it has been nicely restored and converted to a museum. Its courtyard, planted with palms and heliconias, has one of Camagüey's famous tinajones. Rooms upstairs are furnished with period pieces or filled with displays about the wars for independence. ⊠ *Agramonte 59,* ☎ *322/97116.* 🎫 *$2.* ☉ *Tues.–Sat. 10–6, Sun. 8–noon.*

★ ㉑ **Catedral Nuestra Señora de la Merced.** Originally erected in 1748, this church was reconstructed in 1848, repaired after a fire in 1906, and renovated yet again in 1998. The clock on its facade was the city's first public timepiece, made in Barcelona in 1773; its current machinery was

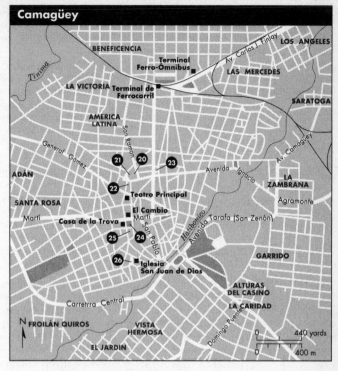

imported from the United States in 1901. The church's interior has massive square columns and a vaulted ceiling decorated with faded art-nouveau frescoes dating from 1915. The painted wooden altar was made in 1909, to replace one destroyed by the fire, but the paintings on the walls around it date from the 18th and 19th centuries. To the right of the altar is the Santo Sepulcro: a Christ figure in a glass casket that was made in 1762 using the silver from 22,000 Mexican coins. It is carried to the cathedral and back every Good Friday in a religious procession that was prohibited for nearly four decades. The crypts beneath the altar have been partially excavated and converted into a tiny museum of tombs, icons, and other antiquities; it is not for the claustrophobic. If the church is closed, enter through the convent next door. ⊠ *Independencia y Agramonte,* ☎ *no phone.* 🎫 *Free.* ⊙ *Mon.–Sat. 9:30–11:30 and 2:30–6.*

23 **Iglesia de la Nuestra Señora de la Soledad.** The weathered exterior of this 18th-century temple dedicated to Our Lady of Solitude belies its well-preserved interior. Thick, square columns rise into high arches decorated with lovely floral frescoes, above which is a *mudejar* wooden ceiling with ornate carved beams. According to legend, a statue of the Virgin fell from a wagon at this spot in the late 1600s; seeing it as a sign from heaven, the locals built a hermitage for it, which was later replaced by this church, completed in 1776. ⊠ *República y Agramonte,* ☎ *322/92392.* ⊙ *Mon.–Sat. 6–11 and 4–6, Sun. 6–noon.*

24 **Parque Ignacio Agramonte.** Originally the city's central square, or Plaza de las Armas, this didn't become a proper park until 1912. Note the bronze statue of Agramonte on his steed at its center. In the park's southwestern corner is a 19th-century house that is now the Casa de la Trova, whose courtyard hosts performances by local musicians every day but Monday. The neoclassic building to the north is the Biblioteca (Library); a few doors farther north is the Palacio Municipal (Town Hall), which was originally erected in 1730, but almost completely rebuilt in 1906; local artists often exhibit in its foyer. ⊠ *Martí, e/Cisneros y Independencia.*

The historic bar **El Cambio** (⊠ Martí y Independencia, ☎ 322/95888), across from the Parque Agramonte's northeast corner, is a convenient stop for a little liquid refreshment. Dating from 1909, this proletariat watering hole has ceramic work by local artists on its walls and ceiling fans revolving slowly over its simple wooden bar and tables.

★ ㉖ **Plaza de San Juan de Dios.** This splendid cobbled square, surrounded by meticulously restored 18th- and 19th-century buildings (most still private homes), has been declared a national monument. On its eastern edge, the old **Hospital de San Juan de Dios** now holds the offices of several cultural organizations. In the portico of its large garden you'll find a simple museum with exhibits on the building's history, some old photos, and surgical instruments from days of yore—thank goodness for modern medicine. More interesting is the view from the roof. ☎ *322/91388.* ⊠ *$1.* ⊙ *Weekdays 9–5.*

Also on the plaza is Camagüey's oldest church, the **Iglesia de San Juan de Dios,** which was built in 1728 to replace the original (1686) St. John's. It underwent some structural changes in 1847 and an extensive restoration in 1986. Its simple, traditional interior has a terra-cotta floor, white-stucco walls, and a sloped wooden ceiling. Four ancient hardwood altars stand along the walls, each of them dedicated to a different saint—St. John's is the second on the left. The main altar is dedicated to the Holy Trinity, and is unique in that the Holy Spirit is represented as a man, instead of as the usual dove. ☎ *No phone.* ⊠ *Free.* ⊙ *Mon.–Sat. 7–11 and 3–6.*

㉔ **Plaza de los Trabajadores.** Before the Revolution, the Workers Plaza was known as the Plaza de La Merced, after the church and convent that define its eastern edge. It's a distinctly Cuban spot, with a large mural of Che Guevara, whose eternally youthful visage stares past the ancient facade of La Merced. A kapok tree towers over the plaza's center, and in the southwest corner stands the stately La Popular, built in 1928, and the seat of a local cultural society. ⊠ *Fernando Hernández y Simón Bolívar.*

㉕ **Santa Iglesia de la Catedral.** Built in 1864, this cathedral replaced one built in 1617 and has seen several renovations. The most recent renovation took 15 years, and wasn't completed till 1998; it included replacing the wood-beam ceiling, which is identical to the original. The most striking part of its spacious interior is the large wood-and-marble altar, behind which shine stained glass and a statue of the Virgin Mary. ⊠ *Parque Ignacio Agramonte,* ☎ *no phone.* ⊠ *Free.* ⊙ *Weekdays 8–11 and 4–6, Sun. 10–noon.*

Dining and Lodging

$ ✕ **La Campana de Toledo.** Set in a restored 18th-century house over-
★ looking the timeless Plaza de San Juan de Dios, this charming restaurant was named for the *campana* (bell) that hangs in its courtyard, which was apparently brought to Camagüey from Toledo, Spain, by a merchant who lived here. Seating is either in the courtyard, which is shaded by trees and decorated with tinajones, or in the front of the house, with a view of the plaza. The traditional Cuban dishes include bistéc de puerco grillé and *boliche mechado* (roast tenderloin stuffed with bacon and served in a light sauce), a specialty here; all come with arroz congrí. ⊠ *Plaza San Juan de Dios 18,* ☎ *322/95888. No credit cards.*

$$ ✕⊡ **Villa Maraguan.** Located in the countryside 10 km (6 mi) east of
★   the town, this quiet collection of brick duplex bungalows surrounded
by lawns and fruit trees offers Camagüey's best accommodations. Rooms
have small desks, refrigerators, white bathrooms decorated with hand-
painted tiles, and big porches with rocking chairs overlooking the gar-
dens. Cement paths lead past trees and benches to the pool and the spacious
restaurant, with its colorful tile floor, stained glass, and ceramic art. The
food is some of the city's best, with specialties such as pollo *pampero*
(breaded and fried) and *ternero maraguan* (baby beef in a red sauce). ⊠
Circunvalación Este, near Carretera Central, ☎ *322/72017,* ℻ *322/71854.
34 rooms. Restaurant, bar, refrigerators, pool. MC, V.*

$ ⊡ **Gran Hotel.** This stately, five-story building in Camagüey's historic
★   heart has been a hotel since 1938. Its bright, elegant lobby has chan-
deliers hung from high ceilings and various other antiques, the eleva-
tor being one of them. Rooms also have high ceilings and old tile floors;
those facing the street are the biggest, but they can be noisy at night.
Although the fifth-floor restaurant is lovely (it's furnished with antiques
and surrounded by windows and glass doors that open onto a
wraparound balcony), the food disappoints. Even if you stay else-
where, stop in for a sunset drink at the rooftop bar. The small pool,
recently added in back, is the venue for one of Cuba's two water bal-
lets. ⊠ *Maceo 67,* ☎ *322/92094. 72 rooms. Restaurant, 3 bars, cof-
fee shop, pool. MC, V.*

$ ⊡ **Hotel Colón.** The historic Colón was inaugurated in 1927 and has
been well cared for ever since. The well-preserved lobby has ornate
columns and ceiling, marble staircase, and dark wooden bar and re-
ception area. The garden patio in back—surrounded by painted
columns, lit by antique street lamps, and furnished with cast iron ta-
bles—is flanked by the main bar and an open-air restaurant. Rooms
are on the second floor, and though they have an historic feel, they're
a bit stuffy. The two that face the street have small balconies and
would be the best if it weren't for their tacky decor. ⊠ *República 472,*
☎ *322/83368. 48 rooms. Restaurant, 2 bars. MC, V.*

Nightlife and the Arts

At the **Casa de la Trova** (⊠ Cisneros 174, ☎ 322/91357), on Parque
Agramonte, local musicians perform Cuban son in an 18th-century court-
yard every day but Monday from 10:30 to 3 and from 8:30 to mid-
night. The city's most popular dance club is the open-air discotheque
at the **Hotel Camagüey** (⊠ Carretera Central, 4 km/2 mi southeast of
town, ☎ 322/87267). The impressive **Teatro Principal** (⊠ Padre Vale-
cia 64, ☎ 322/93048), two blocks northwest of the Plaza de los Tra-
bajadores, hosts monthly performances by the city's renowned ballet,
regular concerts by the symphony orchestra, and occasional shows by
the *ballet folclórico* (folkloric ballet).

Outdoor Activities and Sports

You can hike the forests and explore the caves (including the Cueva
del Indio with its pre-Columbian drawings) of the **Sierra de Cubitas,**
a protected area 45 km (27 mi) northwest of the city. Make arrange-
ments through the tour operator **Rumbos** (☞ Tour Operators and
Travel Agents *in* Central Cuba A to Z, *below)* or the **Asociación de Es-
peliologia** (☎ 322/98269).

The **Marlin Dive Center** (⊠ Playa Santa Lucía, ☎ 323/6335) offers day
trips to a rustic restaurant on Cayo Gaguanas in the Jardines de la Reina
archipelago. The trips include a morning dive, lunch, and snorkeling,
and low-altitude flights across the country.

Shopping

The large store run by the artists' association, **ACAA** (⊠ Padre Valencia 2, ☎ no phone), on the northern end of the Plaza de los Trabajadores, has an extensive selection of ceramics and other handicrafts. The **Fondo de Bienes Culturales** (⊠ Av. de la Libertad y Vega, ☎ no phone) sells ceramics, straw work, and other handicrafts.

En Route Halfway between Camagüey and Santa Lucía, next to the Saramajuacan River, stand the ruins of **Santa Isabel,** a 19th-century sugar mill that was destroyed by the Spanish when its owner—a cousin of Ignacio Agramonte—joined the rebel army. An open-air restaurant next to the ruins serves light food, varied refreshments, and *guarapo* (fresh sugarcane juice).

Playa Santa Lucía

★ ㉗ *128 km (77 mi) northeast of Camagüey.*

Once a simple fishing and salt-collecting village east of the Bahía de Nuevitas, the beach resort of Santa Lucía has long been popular with camagüeyanos, some of whom have vacation homes here. Its 20 km (12 mi) swath of white sand is shaded by coconut palms and lapped by calm, blue-green waters. About a mile offshore is a barrier reef that beckons both divers and snorkelers. The tourist area consists of five hotels and other facilities that run along a 2-km (1-mi) stretch of beach just west of town.

If you desire a wider, and perhaps even whiter beach, you can drive 4 km (2 mi) west to **Playa los Cocos,** an idyllic stretch shaded by both coconut palms and thatched parasols. It overlooks the entrance to Bahía de Nuevitas, near the fishing village of La Boca. **Cayo Sabinal,** just west of the bay, has deserted beaches, a working lighthouse, a rustic hotel and restaurant, the ruins of a Spanish fortress, and a lagoon that's home to flamingos. The drive around the bay and out onto this key is about 100 km (60 mi).

Dining and Lodging

$-$$ ✕ **Pumarola Mambo.** The ambience here is all beach: basic wooden tables beneath a thatched roof or out on the sand, ocean breezes, and occasional live music. The menu is varied, though almost exclusively marine in origin: *fritura de calamar* (fried squid), *pescado al horno* (baked fish), and langosta *a la mediterránea* (in a tomato wine sauce) are just a few of the dishes on offer. ⊠ *Marina, Playa Santa Lucía,* ☎ *32/36404. No credit cards.*

$$$ ▥ **Hotel Cuatro Vientos.** The architecture here is a mix of Cuban and
★   Spanish, with arches, marble floors, barrel-tile and thatched roofs, and murals by Camagüey artists. Rooms are in two-story buildings scattered around the ample, luxuriant grounds. They have white-tile floors; hardwood furniture; large baths with tubs; and either sliding glass doors that open onto balconies or porches with views of the gardens, pool, or sea. The buffet is excellent, and meals are included in rates, as are drinks at the main bar; you have to pay at the beach grill and at the disco. ⊠ *Playa Santa Lucía,* ☎ *32/36317,* ℻ *32/36–5142. 402 rooms. 2 restaurants, 3 bars, snack bar, pool, massage, sauna, 2 tennis courts, aerobics, exercise room, horseback riding, volleyball, dive shop, snorkeling, boating, jet skiing, fishing, motorbikes, shops, billiards, cabaret, nightclub, children's programs (3–15), travel services, car rental. MC, V. All-inclusive.*

$-$$ ▥ **Villa Tararaco.** Built in 1956, this small beach hotel is Santa Lucía's oldest, but it is well maintained. The lobby, restaurant, and bar are in a spacious cement building, in the middle of which grows a stand of bamboo. Guest rooms are in a low, cross-shape building nearby, and only half—those with numbers beginning with 2 or 3—have ocean views. They're small but attractive, with wicker furniture, tiny porches, and such amenities as air-conditioning and satellite TV. A thatched bar and grill overlooks the beach nearby. ✉ *Marina, Playa Santa Lucía,* ☎ *32/36136,* ℻ *32/36–5166. 31 rooms. 2 restaurants, 2 bars. MC, V. MAP.*

Nightlife and the Arts

The **Centro Cultural** (✉ On main road, between Villa Caracol and Club Santa Lucía, ☎ 32/36205) has courtyard concerts by musicians from Camagüey during the high season, and an air-conditioned piano bar. The most popular dance club is **Feria Flamingo** (✉ On main road, between Cuatro Vientos and Club Santa Lucía, ☎ no phone), an open-air disco with a covered dance floor surrounded by a bar, snack bar, pool table, and palm trees decorated with Christmas lights. **100% Cubano** (☎ no phone), a small bar in the Centro Comercial, often has live music at night.

Outdoor Activities and Sports

FISHING

The ocean off Playa Santa Lucía has good fishing, with everything from marlin and sailfish to snapper and grouper. The **Marlin Marina** (☎ 32/35294) offers both sport- and bottom-fishing charters.

SCUBA DIVING

With a barrier reef 2 km (1 mi) offshore, two dozen shipwrecks nearby, and average visibility (best between April and November) of about 25 m (66 ft), Santa Lucía is a world-class dive destination. The **Shark's Friends Diving Center** (☎ 32/36–5182), just west of the hotels, runs trips to about 35 different spots, including 24 shipwrecks, the oldest of which dates from the 1800s. Their most famous dive is a shark-feeding show, but it costs twice what the others do. They also offer a day trip to Cayo Caguamas, in the Jardines de la Reina.

Shopping

The **Centro Cultural Mar Verde** (☎ 32/36205) on the main road, has two excellent shops: one sells a good selection of Cuban music as well as some books, and musical instruments; the other, paintings, sculptures, and ceramics by Camagüey artists. The **Centro Comercial,** a small shopping center just behind the Centro Cultural, has a number of tiny shops that sell souvenirs, tobacco, rum, coffee, and film.

CENTRAL CUBA A TO Z

Arriving and Departing

By Airplane

Havana is the main international hub, though there are some charter flights from Canadian cities to Camagüey and Ciego de Ávila. Domestic flight schedules change frequently, but at press time, **Cubana** (☎ 7/33–4949 in Havana, 419/2296 in Trinidad, 33/25316 in Ciego de Ávila, and 322/91328 in Camagüey) flew from Havana to Ciego de Ávila (Tues. and Thurs. at 1:30, returning at 3:30) and Camagüey (Mon., Tues., Thurs., and Sat. at 2:30 and Wed., Fri., and Sun at 8:30 PM; returning 2 hours later). Though there were no scheduled flights to Trinidad at press time, there may be when you read this; call Cubana.

At press time, **Trinidad's airport** (☎ 419/2547), 1 km south of town on the road to Casilda, was closed but scheduled to reopen soon. Ciego de Ávila's international airport, **Aeropuerto Máximo Gómez** (☎ 332/5303) is 24 km (13 mi) north of town, near Ceballos. Camagüey's international airport, **Aeropuerto Ignacio Agramonte** (☎ 322/61010), is 7 km (4 mi) northeast of town on the road to Nuevitas and Alta-gracia. Taxis and car rental representatives meet every flight.

By Boat

Thousands of people visit Cuba on private boats every year, and there are a number of marinas in the central provinces with mooring space, electricity, water, diesel, and other services. The largest operation is **Marina Puerto Sol** (☎ 432/45–1241 in Cienfuegos, 419/6205 in Playa Ancón, 33/30–1737 on Cayo Guillermo). **Marina Marlin** (☎ 33/30–1322 on Cayo Coco, 32/36404 in Playa Santa Lucía) is another good bet.

By Bus

Air-conditioned **Viazul** (⊠ Av. 26 y Zoológico, Havana, ☎ 7/81–1413) buses depart Havana for Trinidad daily at 8:15, and for Santiago, stopping in Ciego de Ávila and Camagüey, at 3 PM. There's also a bus from Varadero (⊠ Calle 36 y Autopista, ☎ 5/61–4886) to Trinidad departing every other day at 7:30, returning at 2:30.

Less comfortable public buses leave from Havana's **Terminal de Omnibuses** (⊠ Av. Rancho Boyeros, ☎ 7/70–3397). Because of vehicle and gas shortages, schedules change regularly, which makes calling ahead essential. At press time, there were departures for Cienfuegos at noon (returning at 6 AM); Santa Clara at 8 PM (returning at 12:30 PM); and Sancti Spíritus, Ciego de Ávila, and Camagüey at 9:20 AM and 7:45 PM (returning at 9:30 PM, 8:25 PM, and 7 AM respectively). From Havana buses take 4½ hours to reach Cienfuegos, 5 hours to Santa Clara, 6 hours to Sancti Spíritus, 5½ hours to Trinidad, 7½ hours to Ciego de Ávila, and 9 hours to Camagüey.

By Car

Central Cuba's roads are generally in very good repair. It's a 3½-hour drive from Havana to either Cienfuegos or Santa Clara, and another hour to Remedios. The four-lane highway that heads from the nation's capital to Santa Clara and Jatibonico and the two-lane road that connects it to Ciego de Ávila and Camagüey form an east–west aorta through which little traffic flows. Peripheral arteries head south to Cienfuegos and north from Ciego de Ávila to cayos Coco and Guillermo and from Camagüey to Santa Lucía. The old road loops south from the highway to Sancti Spíritus at Cabaiguan, continuing east toward Ciego de Ávila; another good road heads southwest from Sancti Spíritus to Trinidad. Cienfuegos and Trinidad are connected via Topes de Collantes by a rough mountain road and a smoother, more direct coastal route.

By Train

Trains are cheap, so they're very popular with Cuba's impoverished masses. If time isn't an issue (trains sometimes arrive more than a day behind schedule, so pack plenty of food and water) a rail trip can be a wonderful way to mix with the Cuban people. Schedules change frequently, but at press time *El Especial* departed from Havana's **Estación Central** (⊠ Av. Egido) for Santa Clara, Ciego de Ávila, and Camagüey at 4:20 PM. The train for Cienfuegos leaves from Santa Clara, where you'll have to spend a night.

Getting Around

By Boat

A rusty **ferry** (☎ 423/96402) crosses the bay from Cienfuegos to the Castillo de Jagua daily at 5, 6, 8, 11, 1, 3, and 5:30.

By Bus

Bus schedules change frequently, making it imperative to check ahead of time. From **Cienfuegos** (⊠ Calle 49 y Av. 56, ☎ 432/8114) buses depart daily for Santa Clara at 5:30 and 9 AM, Trinidad at 6:30 and 11:30

AM, and Cumanayagua at 6:30 AM. From **Santa Clara** (✉ Carretera Central, ☎ 422/92115) there are daily departures for Cienfuegos at 7:20 and 11:20 AM, Sancti Spíritus at 8 AM and 5 PM, Tinidad at 1:20, and Ciego de Ávila and Camagüey at 7 PM. Daily buses to Remedios depart at 6:40 and 9 AM and 3:30 and 7 PM from the **Santa Clara Terminal Intermunicipal** (✉ Carretera Central at Amparo, ☎ 422/3470).

From **Sancti Spiritus** (✉ Masso, 3 km/2 mi south of town, ☎ 41/24142) departures for Santa Clara are daily at 6 AM, for Trinidad every other day at noon, and Ciego de Ávila and Camagüey every other day at 7 AM. Buses leave **Trinidad** (✉ Prio Guinart, e/Izquierdo y Maceo, ☎ 419/2460), for Sancti Spíritus daily at 7 AM and Cienfuegos daily at 9 and 2:15. **Ciego de Ávila** (✉ Carretera Central, ☎ 33/25109) has daily departures for Camagüey at 5 AM and 4:40 PM and Sancti Spíritus and Cienfuegos at 8 AM. From **Camagüey** (✉ Carretera Central y Peru, ☎ 322/71602), departures for Cienfuegos are at 4:30 PM on odd days and 6 AM on even days, for Sancti Spíritus every other day at noon, and for Santa Clara every other day at 7 AM.

By Car
Driving within central Cuba's towns can be confusing. There are many one-way streets, and intersections aren't always well marked. If you have any doubts about where you're going, just ask someone; people are happy to help strangers. Traffic is invariably light—mostly bicycles and horse-drawn taxis—and parking spaces are abundant and free.

Rental-car rates range from $40 to $60 a day (though sometimes they're as high as $70 a day). You can rent cars from **Havanautos** (✉ Punta Gorda, Cienfuegos, ☎ 432/45–1211; ✉ Hotel Caneyes, Av. Eucaliptos y Circunvalación, Santa Clara, ☎ 422/5895; ✉ Carretera Casilda, Trinidad, ☎ 419/6301; ✉ Aeropuerto Máximo Gómez, Ciego de Ávila, ☎ 33/26–6345; ✉ Carretera Central, Camagüey, ☎ 32/27–2239).

By Taxi
Transtur (☎ 432/45–1172 in Cienfuegos, 422/6856 in Santa Clara, 419/5314 in Trinidad, 33/26–6229 in Ciego de Ávila, 322/71015 in Camagüey) runs taxis that have dollar meters, are relatively expensive, and are often waiting right outside major hotels. Cubans have considerably cheaper taxis, which aren't supposed to pick up tourists, but will. Your choices also include horse-drawn, communal taxis that charge 1 peso, and rickshaws, whose prices are negotiable but should never cost more than $1.

By Train
Trains leave the **Cienfuegos Terminal** (✉ Calle 49 y Av. 58, ☎ 432/5495) for Santa Clara every other day at 10:30 AM. From the **Santa Clara Terminal** (✉ Pedro Estévez, north of town, ☎ 422/22895), trains head east to Ciego de Ávila and Camagüey at 8:40 PM and west to Havana at 8:40 AM. From the **Camagüey Terminal** (✉ Quioñes at Padre Olalla, ☎ 322/83214), trains depart for Ciego de Ávila, Santa Clara, and Havana at 6:20 PM. Because train schedules change regularly, these departures should be confirmed; and don't expect trains to leave on time.

Contacts and Resources

Emergencies
Diving accidents: Cuba has several decompression chambers. In case of a diving accident, the dive center will make arrangements for use of a chamber if necessary. **Fire:** ☎ 115. **Medical Emergencies: Ambulance** (☎ 432/5019 in Cienfuegos, 422/3965 in Santa Clara, 41/24462 in Sancti Spíritus, 419/2362 in Trinidad, 185 in Ciego de Ávila, 322/

92860 in Camagüey), **Asistur** (☎ 432/45–1624 in Cienfuegos), **Servimed** (☎ 432/45–1623 in Cienfuegos, 419/6240 in Trinidad). **Pharmacies:** Servimed, which provides medical services for tourists, often has access to medicines you won't find in the pharmacies. **Police:** ☎ 116.

Health and Safety

Tap water is generally safe (many of the big hotels have additional filter systems) but most travelers take advantage of widely available bottled water. The most common health risks are heat stroke and sunburn; drink plenty of fluids and use plenty of sunscreen. If you get sick during your stay, you'll receive prompt treatment—most hotels have resident nurses, and a doctor can usually be at the hotel within a half hour.

Although central Cuba is quite safe on the whole, you should always keep an eye on your things. Gay and lesbian travelers should be cautious about public displays of affection, even in the liberal university town of Santa Clara, which seems to have a rather large and visible gay population. For years it was considered criminal to be anything other than a happy heterosexual; old ways die hard.

Telephones and Mail

Although you can make local and international calls from most hotels, it's considerably cheaper to call from a public phone using the cards that are sold at many hotels, shops, *correos* (post offices) and ETECSA phone company offices. There should be a rate chart posted next to phones that accept these cards.

You can mail letters and make international calls from the following correo branches, which are open weekdays 8 AM–6 PM: **Cienfuegos** (⊠ Boulevard No. 3514, ☎ 432/6102), **Santa Clara** (⊠ Colón, e/Parque Vidal y Machado, ☎ 422/3298); **Sancti Spíritus** (⊠ Independencia Sur 8), **Trinidad** (⊠ Maceo 418, ☎ 419/4328); **Ciego de Ávila** (⊠ República y Calle 4, ☎ 33/27510); **Camagüey** (⊠ Cisneros, e/Agramonte y Gómez, ☎ 322/95312).

Tour Operators and Travel Agencies

The tour operators Cubanácan and Rumbos (and, to some extent, Cubatur) provide a variety of services in addition to their tours. They have representatives in large hotels (as is the case in all hotels on cayos Coco and Guillermo) as well as in regional offices.

Cubanácan (⊠ Av. 20, No. 3905, Cienfuegos, ☎ 432/45–1133; ⊠ Maceo 453, Santa Clara, ☎ 422/5189; ⊠ Colón 49, Morón, ☎ 335/3168; ⊠ Av. Finlay, Camagüey, ☎ 322/61403), **Cubatur** (⊠ Playa Santa Lucía, ☎ 32/36291; ⊠ Península de Ancón, ☎ 419/6180), **Rumbos** (⊠ Independencia 167, Santa Clara, ☎ 422/7292; ⊠ Caibarién ☎ 42/03–3305; ⊠ Izquierdo 103, Trinidad, ☎ 419/3210; ⊠ Independencia 32, Sancti Spíritus, ☎ 41/28388; ⊠ Carretera Central, Ciego de Ávila, ☎ 33/28738; ⊠ Edificio Girón 1, Camagüey, ☎ 322/95888; ⊠ Playa Santa Lucía, ☎ 32/36106).

Visitor Information

You can pick up maps and other printed materials at the provincial offices of the Ministry of Tourism, **MINTUR** (⊠ El Prado y Av. 20, Cienfuegos, ☎ 423/45–1627; ⊠ Sullama 13, Trinidad, ☎ 419/3813; ⊠ Máximo Gómez 82, Ciego de Ávila, ☎ 33/23335; ⊠ Carretera Central y Céspedes, Camagüey, ☎ 322/71712).

5 EASTERN CUBA

Rife with cultural treasures, sublimely beautiful eastern Cuba is a stage with a variety of sets—from the sun-drenched, palm-lined beaches to the lush, majestic Sierra Maestra. The sagas that unfolded in this region, often called El Oriente, add great drama to Cuba's history.

E
ASTERN CUBA IS FULL OF TALES about rebellion and revolution. The stories go back all the way to the 16th century, when Hatuey, a Taíno Indian chief, rose up

By John Marino   against the Spaniards and was captured and burned at the stake near Baracoa in 1523. On October 10, 1868, Carlos Manuel de Céspedes freed the slaves on his plantation near Bayamo and proclaimed Cuba's independence from Spain, launching the Ten Years War. In 1895, Cuban patriot and poet José Martí landed on the south coast of the Bahía de Guantánamo; he was killed shortly thereafter in a battle against the Spanish at Dos Ríos in Granma Province. The region is the birthplace of Fidel Castro (who was born in Holguín) and his Revolution (with the attack of the Moncada army barracks in Santiago on July 26, 1953). Granma Province itself takes its name from the boat that carried Fidel Castro and 81 revolutionaries from exile in Mexico back to Cuba in 1956. Although their landing—at Playa las Coloradas in the province's southwestern corner—was disastrous, the survivors fled to the Sierra Maestra, the rugged eastern mountain range, and continued fighting for their cause.

In this region you'll find Cuba's "second city," Santiago de Cuba, which is the nation's most Caribbean community in terms of both climate and spirit. It has always been open to foreign influences and has been touched as much by French, African, and Caribbean creole cultures as it has by that of Havana. The city explodes during its July carnival, a four-day festival of music, dancing, and merrymaking. One of the country's great pleasures may be enjoying a *mojíto* (light rum, sugar, mint, and soda) on the balcony of Santiago's Hotel Casa Granda. From here, you can watch the goings-on in the Parque Céspedes, the city's historic heart and the central meeting point for *Santiagueros* (as the citizens of this community are called). The city also sizzles at night, when local musicians share a microphone at the Casa de la Trova.

Cuba's oldest Spanish settlement, quirky Baracoa on Guantánamo's isolated northern coast, is another eastern attraction. El Yunque, an anvil-shape mountain, rises into the clouds from the lush forests surrounding the city. Resort areas—full of hotels with all the modern amenities—line eastern Cuba's coasts; Guardalavarca on Holguín's northern coast and Granma's southern coast draw Canadian and European tourists looking for sun and fun. Water sports—from fishing to scuba diving to white-water rafting—are options throughout the region, and hikers can follow mountain trails to Castro's old rebel headquarters in the Sierra Maestra, now a national park.

Pleasures and Pastimes

Arts and Culture

After the 18th-century slave rebellions on Haiti, a wave of French planters settled in eastern Cuba, and you can see their imprint in the region's architecture. Music seems to be always in the air in Santiago, the birthplace of *son,* a forerunner of salsa. You can catch evening live-music performances at hotels, theaters, and clubs, and local musicians seem to jam day and night at the city's Casa del la Trova. Santiago is also home to all types of *teatro*—from children's theater to modern dramas—as well as to poets and painters. It's chock-full of art galleries and crafts shops. Works by artisans in Baracoa, an isolated town that still seems influenced by its Taíno predecessors, are also noteworthy.

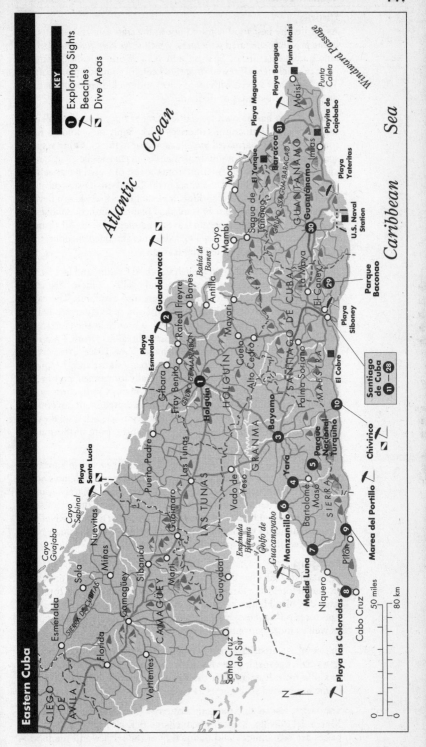

Eastern Cuba

KEY
1 Exploring Sights
Beaches
Dive Areas

Dining

As a rule, the best food is found not in the state-run restaurants, but in the privately operated *paladares,* which serve *comida criolla* (the island's own mixture of Spanish and New World cuisines). Roasted pork or chicken and stewed or spiced beef are common main courses. They're usually served with *arroz* (rice) and red kidney or black beans or fried sweet bananas or plantains.

Eastern Cuba has its own specialties. One is *fufú,* a mashed plantain side dish laced with crumbs of crispy pork. Santiago is known for its roast pig and its marinated *yuca* (cassava or manioc). Other regional specialities include *prú,* a soft drink made from pine needles, sugar, roots, and herbs. Owing to its isolation from the rest of Cuba, Baracoa's cuisine is closer to that found elsewhere in the Caribbean. Dishes rely heavily on the coconut. Fish and shellfish, for example, are served in a flavorful orange coconut sauce. *Bacán* is mashed plantain and coconut stuffed with pork, wrapped in plantain leaves, and then cooked. All along the roadsides, children sell *cucurucho,* a desert of shredded coconut, fruits, nuts, and sugar wrapped in palm leaves.

Hotel restaurants tend to serve such standard Continental fare as roast beef and potatoes, creamy casseroles, and paella. Chinese cuisine and Italian food (mostly pizza and pastas) are also available. The closest thing to a Western-style chain restaurant you're likely to see is Pizza Nova, a Canadian pizzeria chain (there's a branch at the Hotel Santiago in Guardalavarca). Most hotels serve breakfast from 7 AM to 10 AM and, coincidentally, also keep those hours (7 PM–10 PM) in the evening for dinner. Cuban meals are relaxed; reservations are rarely required, although slightly conservative attire, especially for women, may be. The U.S. dollar is the most reliable form of payment. Credit cards *not* affiliated with U.S. banks or companies are accepted in all government restaurants, though never in paladares. For price categories, *see* the chart *under* Dining *in* Smart Travel Tips A to Z at the front of this guide.

The Great Outdoors

El Oriente is blessed with appealing dark-sand beaches in southwest Granma Province; stunning white-sand stretches along Holguín's northern coast; and isolated coastal enclaves surrounding Baracoa, in the far reaches of Guantánamo Province. Water-sports outfitters stand ready to help you fish, dive, windsurf, or set sail in a yacht. River rafting and hiking in the Sierra Maestra or, perhaps, the Baconao Natural Reserve are also possibilities.

Lodging

Santiago de Cuba has extraordinary lodgings, from the historic, well-situated Hotel Casa Granda to the flamboyant, modernist Hotel Santiago de Cuba. Hidden in the decaying elegance of Vista Alegre are some fine *casas particulares* (private homes that rent out rooms to guests) as well as more conventional lodgings.

In sleepy, isolated Baracoa your options range from a hotel in a fort to a small, oceanside guest house, whose former owner ironically fled to Cuba from Russian after the Russian Communist revolution. Her home has hosted such guests as Erroll Flynn and Che Guevara.

Top-notch resorts line the southern coast from Santiago de Cuba to Marea del Portillo. Most of them charge flat, all-inclusive rates. The prices are economical, and the quality of the service and the food is better than average. Guardalavarca is becoming a haven for Europeans and Canadians. It has a handful of mostly all-inclusive resorts and a few free-standing restaurants and discos along a fine, wide, white-sand beach. This area offers the perfect beach vacation, *and* it's a convenient hub from which to explore Santiago and Baracoa. Credit cards *not* affiliated with U.S. banks or companies are accepted in most major hotels. For price categories, *see* the chart *under* Lodging *in* Smart Travel Tips A to Z at the front of this guide.

Exploring Eastern Cuba

The spirit of eastern Cuba, the birthplace of rum and revolution, is intoxicating. The region includes the provinces of Granma, Holguín, Santiago, and Guantánamo. Together with Las Tunas, they once composed the single province of El Oriente, a moniker still used for the region today.

Although sleepy, the provincial capital of Holguín is a good regional hub—one that's quite close to the beautiful beaches of Guardalavarca. South of it lies Bayamo, the capital of Granma Province and the gateway to the Sierra Maestra. Directly west is the colorful port town of Manzanillo, with a wide *malecón* and a beautiful historic center. An hour's drive south brings you to Playa las Coloradas, where Castro landed in 1956. About 40 minutes east of here is Marea del Portillo, with two lovely resorts on Mediterranean-like beaches. From here the road hugs the southern coast while snaking along in the shadow of the Sierra Maestra to Santiago de Cuba, one of Cuba's most gracious cities. The Baconao Nature Reserve—which has several beaches, restaurants, hotels, and other attractions—is just 45 minutes east of the city.

Santiago is the gateway to Guantánamo Province. Although famous for its U.S. military base, its most outstanding attraction is the isolated, colonial town of Baracoa near Cuba's easternmost point. The town is a 260 km (161 mi) drive from Santiago along the awesome La Farola Highway, which brought Baracoa in contact with the rest of Cuba when it was constructed during the 1970s. Pine-covered highlands, jungle-covered foothills, miles of beaches, and surging rivers fill the area around Baracoa. El Yunque looms over the city. The mountain was a sacred place for the indigenous Taínos, and their imprint is still strongly felt in Baracoa. Locals still boast of their Taíno blood, evident in their features.

Great Itineraries

IF YOU HAVE 3 DAYS

Spend two days touring ▦ **Santiago de Cuba** ⑪–㉘, taking in its many historical sights, shopping in its many stores and galleries, and seeing live-music shows in its many venues. On the third day visit **Parque Baconao** ㉙, a nature preserve just east of the city.

IF YOU HAVE 5 DAYS

Spend two days exploring ▦ **Santiago de Cuba** ⑪–㉘. On the third day, head east for a day trip to **Parque Baconao** ㉙. Rise early on the fourth day and take the gorgeous south coast road west for an overnight trip to the beach town of **Marea del Portillo** ⑨, where the Sierra Maestra crashes into the Caribbean Sea.

IF YOU HAVE 7 DAYS

Spend three days exploring ▦ **Santiago de Cuba** ⑪–㉘ On the fourth day, head east, visiting **Parque Baconao** ㉙ and stopping in ▦ **Guantánamo** ㉚ for the night. The next day continue your journey east along the famous La Farola Highway to **Baracoa** ㉛. Spend the fifth and sixth days exploring the town and El Yunque or the Playa Maguana before returning to Santiago on the seventh day.

When to Tour

Although peak season is technically December through April, July is a hectic month in eastern Cuba owing to Santiago's Carnaval (Carnival) and the Festival del Caribe. Reservations should be made well in advance during these peak times. The spring and fall off-seasons see prices drop by as much as 25% in places, though hotels may offer fewer amenities (some may even close entirely). Discounts during these times may not be as great in Guardalavarca—one of the driest spots in the off-season—and Santiago, which tends to draw visitors year round.

HOLGUÍN AND GRANMA PROVINCES

These two provinces northeast of Santiago have acres of sugar and banana plantations, rice paddies, and cattle fields. The eponymous provincial capital of Holguín Province affords a look at a typical Cuban city. But the province is best known for Guardalavaca, a north coast town on a white-sand beach. Although small, it has top-notch resorts, watersports outfitters, and tour operators; nearby, you'll find several other beaches as well as marinas and other attractions.

Granma Province has the most varied landscapes—from the forbidding peaks of the Sierra Maestra to the dry south coast—and was also the sight of events that were important not only to the Revolution, but also to Cuba's earlier struggles for independence. Both its capital, Bayamo, and the port town of Manzanillo are interesting stops filled with historic structures. The coastal road south leads to beaches and natural reserves at Playa las Coloradas, where Castro's rebels landed in the yacht *Granma*. The province is also a gateway to the Sierra Maestra via the Bayamo–Manzanillo roadway. These mountains crash down along the south coast and rise from a jungle interior. The road winds along an awesome turquoise coast in the shadow of steep, muscular rock.

Holguín

● *734 km (456 mi) southeast of Havana; 134 km (83 mi) northwest of Santiago de Cuba.*

For most visitors, Holguín is a gateway to the beach resorts at Guardalavaca, just 50 km (31 mi) north. But an hour or two wandering through this pleasant, easygoing provincial capital will provide you with insight not only into Cuban history but also into Cuban life.

Holguín's small historic district hugs the **Plaza Calixto García,** a square graced by large shade trees and a marble bust of Calixto García, a local general in the Ten Years War (1868–78) for independence from Spain. It's lined with colonial buildings—some containing residences, others with small shops—as well as the Casa de la Trova (where music is often performed), the Teatro Comandante Eddy Sunoi, and the Casa de Arte. The **Museo Historia Provincial,** in the former Casino Español, contains an exhibit of pre-Columbian artifacts and displays on the Revolution and the province's role in it. Locally, the building is known as La Panquera (The Parrot Cage) owing to the fact that brightly dressed Spanish officers peered through its caged windows while the city was under siege by General García's troops in 1868. ⊠ *198 Calle Frexes,* ☎ *no phone.* ⊡ *$1.* ⊙ *Mon.–Sat. noon to 7.*

You can learn more about the Ten Years War and its local patriot at the **Casa Natal Calixto García,** which contains some of his belongings. ⊠ *147 Calle Miro, just off Plaza Calixto García,* ☎ *no phone.* ⊡ *$1.* ⊙ *Tues.–Sun. 9–4.*

The **Museo de la Historia Natural Carlos de la Torre** (Carlos de la Torre Natural History Museum), a Moorish-style structure with beautiful ceramic tile work, contains preserved specimens of Cuban wildlife; be sure to check out the snail-shell collection. ⊠ *Calle Maceo, ½ block* *south of Plaza Calixto García,* ☎ *no phone.* 🎫 *$1.* ⊙ *Tues.–Sat. 8–6, Sun. 8–noon.*

Plaza Julio Graves de Peralta, bounded by Luz Caballero, Aricios, Maceo, and Manduley streets, has murals of Cuban patriots of the Revolution and previous wars of independence. Look for the portrait of a youthful Fidel Castro; it may be the only one you'll see in Cuba. The Catedral de San Isidorio, on Calle Maceo, dates from 1720.

Exactly 450 steps lead up to **La Loma de La Cruz,** a hill named for the large white cross that has been here since 1790. From here you have a lovely view of Holguín and the surrounding limestone hills. There are also artisan shops and a snack bar. ⊠ *Staircase is on Calle Maceo, 10 blocks north of Plaza San José.*

The **Plaza de la Revolución,** northeast of central Holguín, has a marble bust of local hero General Calixto García and his marble mausoleum. This wide, open park is used for political rallies and other events. Look for the white colonial building containing the Communist Party headquarters.

OFF THE BEATEN PATH

FINCA MAYABE – Just southeast of Holguín, a rural road takes you to the hilly Mayabe sector. Here you'll find Finca Mayabe, a recreation of a farm with fruit trees, animals (horseback riding is a possibility), and a hotel, Mirador de Mayabe (☞ Dining and Lodging, *below*) with a bar-restaurant.

FINCA MANACAS – Fidel Castro was born at Finca Manacas in the town of Biran, 60 km (37 mi) southeast of Holguín. Although the two-story house isn't open to visitors, you can get a special pass (free) to enter the premises from the Communist Party headquarters in Holguín. Castro's father leased land here from the United Fruit Company and raised sugarcane. The property eventually encompassed 26,000 acres and included a cattle farm, a repair shop, a store, and other facilities.

Dining and Lodging

$ ✕🏨 **Hotel Pernik.** Partially paid for by the Bulgarian government (and named for a town in Bulgaria), this Soviet-inspired hotel has more than 200 rooms and plenty of amenities, including transportation to and from the airport, a tourist desk, and a car-rental agency. The restaurant serves better-than-average Cuban specialties and often has live-music performances. ⊠ *Av. Dimitrov y Av. XX Aniversario,* ☎ *24/48–1011,* 🖷 *24/48–1140. 202 rooms. Restaurant, bar, air-conditioning, pool, beauty salon, shop, nightclub, car rental, travel services. MC, V.*

$ ✕🏨 **Mirador de Mayabe.** At this charming spot, you can stay in one
★ of the hillside cabins or in the gracious Casa del Pancho, whose beautifully appointed rooms have balconies. Either way, chances are you'll have a good view of Holguín Valley. The on-site bar-restaurant, Taberna Pancho, serves decent fare, although its biggest draw may be its mascot: a beer-drinking donkey named Poncho. (Note that in the rainy season, mosquitoes are a problem here; bring plenty of bug spray). ⊠ *Loma del Mayabe, La Cuaba,* ☎ *24/42–2160,* 🖷 *24/42–5347, 4 rooms, 20 cabins. Restaurant, bar, pool, beauty salon, shop, travel services. MC, V.*

En Route The road to Guardalavaca passes through the Plaza de la Revolución and rolling farmland as it runs out of town. Near Gibara, a dusty port town 28 km (17 mi) north of Holguín, the **Silla de Gibara** (Saddle of Gibara) rises from the flat lands. (Locals believe that this is the land mass first sighted by Columbus when he discovered Cuba; Baracoans, however, hotly dispute this, claiming that he saw El Yunque near Cuba's eastern tip.)

As you continue north to Guardalavaca, you'll pass through sugar country. If you go through the town of Rafael Freye, take the road that runs by the large sugar mill to Bahía Barley, which is where Columbus supposedly landed. Two **monuments** commemorate the event: one at Playa Blanca, a white-sand stretch with an all-inclusive resort, and another at Fray Benito.

Farther along the road to Guardalavaca is **Bahía de Naranjo,** a national park, with mangroves, fish hatcheries, and an aquarium (there are dolphin shows daily at 10:30 and 2; $10 lets you swim with Flipper). East of the bay is **Playa Esmeralda,** a beautiful white-sand beach with two hotels and a marina.

Guardalavaca

❷ *70 km (43 mi) northeast of Holguín.*

Guardalavaca's biggest draws are its opportunities for sunning, swimming, sailing, and scuba diving. You'll find a handful of hotels, restaurants, and discos as well as a beautiful white-sand beach. You can make arrangements to participate in water sports, go horseback riding, or visit the Bahía de Naranjo and its aquarium (☞ *above*) through your hotel.

Guardalavaca is part of the town of **Banes,** whose urban center is 20 km (12 mi) southeast of the beach resort. Castro married his first wife at the Iglesia de Nuestra Senora de la Caridad on the town's Plaza Martí. Fulgencio Batista, the dictator Castro eventually toppled, lived here in 1901. But Banes is best known for its archaeological treasures. The **Museo Indocuban** has one of Cuba's largest collections of such indigenous artifacts as pottery, jewelry, and tools. There are also murals depicting Indian life. ⊠ *Calle General Marrero 305, esquina de Av. José Martí,* ☎ *no phone.* ☜ *$1.* ☉ *Tues.–Sat. 9–5, Sun. 8–noon.*

Dining and Lodging

$$ ✕ **El Ancla.** The specialty here is seafood, prepared according to local recipes. The restaurant is set above a charming stretch of beach on the western end of town. ⊠ *Playa Guardalavaca, Banes,* ☎ *no phone. MC, V.*

$$ ✕ **El Cayuelo** On your way to Banes, consider stopping at this beachfront restaurant. You can't go wrong by ordering one of the local seafood specialties. ⊠ *Playa Guardalavaca,* ☎ *no phone. No credit cards.*

$ ✕ **Pizza Nova.** This Canadian chain restaurant serves high-quality pasta dishes, salads, and pizza in a café setting. It's not far from a park that hosts an artisans fair by day. ⊠ *Guardalavaca,* ☎ *no phone. MC, V.*

$$$$ 🏨 **Las Brisas Club Resort.** One of Cuba's better all-inclusives, Las
★ Brisas has an upscale feel, wide-open public spaces, and many amenities, including a private beach and a large, elegant pool. Guest rooms have satellite TV and balconies. Nonguests can pay a day charge to use the facilities. ⊠ *Playa Guardalavaca,* ☎ *24/30218,* 🖷 *24/30018. 230 rooms. 4 restaurants, 3 bars, air-conditioning, in-room safes, pool, 4 tennis courts, beach, horseback riding, snorkeling, windsurfing, boating, jet skiing, waterskiing, fishing, shops, nightclub, children's programs, travel services, car rental. MC, V. All-inclusive.*

$$$$ 🏨 **Sol Rio del Luna.** This resort sits on the verdant Playa Esmeralda, 3 km (2 mi) west of Guardalavaca and near the Bahía de Naranjo national park. The grounds are beautifully landscaped, and the rooms are large and well kept. Nearby is the Sol Rio del Luna's sister property, the Sol Rio Mar (☞ *below*). ⊠ *Playa Esmeralda, Holguín–Guardalavaca Hwy.,* ☎ *24/30030,* 🖷 *24/30035. 222 rooms. Restau-*

rant, bar, air-conditioning, in-room safes, pool, beauty salon, 2 tennis courts, health club, beach, dive shop, dock, snorkeling, windsurfing, boating, jet skiing, waterskiing, fishing, shop, nightclub, travel services, car rental. MC, V. All-inclusive.

$$$ ★ 🏨 **Cubanacán Atlántico.** Among the upscale Atlántico's draws are its gorgeous pool (edged by a terrace that runs along a bluff over the beach) and its fine restaurant. Accommodations include guest rooms (which operate on EP) or all-inclusive bungalows. Views are of the beach or a lagoon with mountains in the distance—both vistas are equally appealing. Along the walkway to the beach, be sure to stop in the "friendship garden," where guests have left rocks painted with scenes and/or sayings. ✉ *Playa Guardalavaca,* ☎ *24/30180 or 24/30280,* FAX *24/30200. 233 rooms. Restaurant, bar, air-conditioning, pool, beach, dive shop, snorkeling, windsurfing, boating, jet skiing, waterskiing, fishing, shop, nightclub, car rental, travel services. MC, V. All-inclusive, EP.*

$$$ 🏨 **Sol Rio Mar.** Although this hotel is virtually identical to its sister property, the Sol Rio del Luna (☞ *above*), it's slightly more affordable. Rooms have satellite TVs, and the on-site Mongo Vina restaurant is quite good. A stay here gets you access to the tennis courts at the Sol Rio del Luna. ✉ *Holguín–Guardalavaca Hwy., Playa Estero Ciego,* ☎ *24/30102 or 24/30062,* FAX *24/30065 244 rooms. Restaurant, bar, air-conditioning, refrigerators, pool, beauty salon, health club, dive shop, dock, snorkeling, windsurfing, boating, jet skiing, waterskiing, fishing, shop, nightclub, car rental, travel services. MC, V. All-inclusive.*

$$ 🏨 **Hotel Club Amigo Guardalavaca.** Built in the early 1990s and thoroughly spruced up in 1999, this hotel offers clean, affordable rooms (with cable TV) only 100 yards from Guardalavaca's main beach. Although its restaurant isn't the best, its pool is huge and has a water slide. ✉ *Playa Guardalavaca,* ☎ *24/30–1212 or 24/30–1224,* FAX *23/30221. 225 rooms. Restaurant, bar, air-conditioning, pool, horseback riding, dive shop, snorkeling, shop, nightclub, car rental, travel services. MC, V.*

$ 🏨 **Villas Cabañas.** There are few frills here. But the air-conditioned rooms (set in bungalows) are the cheapest you'll find near both the beach and town. ✉ *Playa Guardalavaca,* ☎ *24/30144. 35 rooms. Restaurant, bar, café, air-conditioning. No credit cards.*

Nightlife and the Arts

Cabaret Nocturno (☎ no phone) is a hot nightspot that offers transportation to and from the major hotels. You can dance at the disco **Ecos Nocturno Nightclub** (☎ no phone). **La Roca Disco** (☎ no phone), at the west end of town, has a dance floor that's open to the breezes and an outdoor terrace with ocean views; after the disco's flashing lights, the twinkling stars are soothing.

Outdoor Activities and Sports

Base Nautica Marlin Guardalavaca (✉ Carretera Guardalavaca, Rafael Freire, Playa Guardalavaca, ☎ 24/30060 or 24/30064) offers boat rides, waterskiing, snorkeling, scuba diving, and deep-sea fishing. They also rent catamarans and windsurfers. **Marina Bahía de Naranjo** (✉ Carretera Guardalavaca, Rafael Freire, Playa Guardalavaca, ☎ 24/30185) has boat rentals, services for boaters, and some accommodations.

Shopping

Artisans hawk their wares in a plaza near the Pizza Nova restaurant at the center of town (it's after the turnoff for Cubanacán Atlantico and near the Havanautos car rental booth). The fair is held daily from dawn to dusk. The **Centro Commercial** (☎ no phone), fronting the beach near the town's western end, may be in an ugly building, but it sells plenty of consumer goods (to anyone with dollars) and has a crafts shop that's worth a look.

Bayamo

 71 km (44 mi) south of Holguín; 127 km (79 mi) northwest of Santiago.

Bayamo, the capital of Granma Province, is descended from one of Spain's first seven villas: the 1513 settlement of Villa de San Salvador de Bayamo, situated near present-day Yara and later moved to its current location. There's little evidence left of its colonial beginnings. In 1869, the townspeople burned Bayamo to the ground rather than let it fall into Spanish hands during the Ten Years War.

Parque Céspedes is a charming square containing large shade trees and long marble benches and surrounded by historic buildings, shops, and museums. It's still a center of local life, and a good place to drink in the rhythms of a quiet Cuban town. Horse-drawn carriage rides are available from here.

At the square's center is the granite-and-bronze **statue of Carlos Manuel de Céspedes,** the hero of the Ten Years War. He wrote the famous Grito de Yara (Shout of Yara)—a declaration of independence from Spain—which he read aloud on October 10, 1868, after freeing his slaves. Look also for the **statue of Perucho Figueredo,** who wrote Cuba's national anthem; its words describe the valor of the local townspeople: *Run to the battle, Bayamenses / Let the motherland proudly watch you / Don't fear death / To die for the motherland is to live.* On the east side of the square is the **Poder Popular,** the old town hall where Céspedes abolished slavery after founding an independent republic briefly in 1868.

The **Casa de Carlos Manuel de Céspedes,** a beautiful two-story house on the plaza's north side, is the birthplace of Céspedes. It has been a museum since 1968, the centennial anniversary of the signing of the Cuban Declaration of Independence, and is filled with period furniture and the personal effects of this Cuban patriot. Also on display is the printing press where Céspedes published Cuba's first independent newspaper. ⊠ *Calle Maceo,* ☎ *no phone.* 🎫 *$1.* ☉ *Tues.–Sat. 9–5, Sun. 9–1.*

On the north side of the plaza is the **Museo Provincial,** which is housed in the birthplace of composer Manuel Muñoz Cedeño. He wrote "La Bayamesa," a tribute to the beauty of the town's women, who are, tradition holds, among Cuba's most lovely. There are exhibits on the region's colonial history and its geography. ⊠ *Calle Maceo 58,* ☎ *no phone.* 🎫 *$1* ☉ *Tues.–Sat. 9–5, Sun. 9–1.*

NEED A BREAK?   After seeing Bayamo's historic sights, duck into the **Islazul Café** (⊠ North side of Parque Céspedes, ☎ no phone) or **La Casona** (⊠ Plaza de Himno, ☎ no phone) for a drink and snack or **La Bodega** (⊠ Plaza de Himno, ☎ no phone) for some wine.

One of Bayamo's most peaceful spots is the **Plaza de Himno** (Anthem Square) northwest of Parque Céspedes. The plaza is dominated by the **Iglesia de San Salvador.** First built in 1613 and rebuilt several times starting in 1740, the church is famous as the first place "La Bayamesa" was sung in 1868. Its stone and wood interior is gloriously restored, and it's open to visitors late in the afternoon, before the 5 PM mass. The plaza is also the home of **Casa de la Nacionalidad Cubana,** the town's archives. It is not officially open to the public, but you can ask questions of the staff and maybe have a peek at the antique furniture and interior courtyard. A list of cultural events happening around town is usually posted here. Southeast of the plaza is the **Iglesia de San Juan Evangelista,** a church that was partially destroyed in the 1869 fire, but whose tower remains intact. The **Retablo de los Heroes** is a monument to Cuban independence fighters, from Céspedes to Celia Sánchez (who, in addition to being a revolutionary, was also Castro's lover and confidante).

Dining and Lodging

$ ✕🏨 **Villa Bayamo.** This attractive complex is 6 km (4 mi) outside the city on the road to Manzanillo. The restaurant, El Tamarindo, is famous for its roast pork. ✉ *Carretera via Manzanillo, Calle Mabay,* ☎ *24/42–3102. 12 rooms, 12 cabins. Restaurant, bar, air-conditioning, pool, nightclub. MC, V.*

$ 🏨 **Hotel Sierra Maestra.** Although it looks unkempt and institutional from the outside, inside this hotel is well maintained. The lobby is a little noisy (music blasts from speakers here), but the rooms are comfortable and have satellite TVs. The restaurant serves meals that are filling, if uninspired. ✉ *Carretera Central, Km 7.5,* ☎ *24/48–1013. 204 rooms. Restaurant, bar, air-conditioning, pool, shop, nightclub, travel services. MC, V.*

Nightlife and the Arts

Adjacent to the Hotel Sierra Maestra is the **Cabaret Bayamo** (✉ Carretera Central, ☎ 23/48–1013), whose lively dinner shows (nightly) feature high-stepping, costumed dancers. Another cabaret is inside the hotel, but it isn't as high-charged as the Bayamo.

Shopping

Stop by the **Casa de Bien Fonda Cultura** (✉ Plaza de Himno, ☎ no phone) for beautiful ceramics, paintings, and leatherwork.

Yara

4 *46 km (29 mi) west of Bayamo, 23 km (14 mi) east of Manzanillo.*

West of Bayamo, the road to Manzanillo passes through banana and cane fields. The biggest settlement between the two cities is Yara, a striking sugar town in the shadow of the Sierra Maestra. The road into it is lined with palm and mango trees; it takes you past worn wooden plantation houses—made brittle by the tropical heat and sun—a sugar mill, and a train station. The town was first settled by Diego Velázquez in 1513, but it is most famous for being *the* Yara in Céspedes' Grito de Yara and as the place where Céspedes fought his first battle against the Spanish in 1868.

The **Museo Municipal,** just off the main square, has displays on the town's history. ✉ *Calle Grito de Yara 107,* ☎ *no phone.* 💳 *50¢.* ◷ *Tues.– Sat. 9–5, Sun. 9–1.*

En Route   The few people who live in the isolated Sierra Maestra region seem as rugged as the terrain that surrounds them. Along the road out of Yara, you'll see thatch-roof huts, farmers guiding ox-drawn plows through fields; men pulling small, crop-filled carts up steep hills; and boys struggling on bicycles with an armful of farm tools. There's a frontier feeling here, accentuated, perhaps, by the popularity of cowboy hats in the area. From Yara, it's 15 km (9 mi) to Bartolomé Masó, where the road then climbs to Providencia. At an intersection here, turn left and continue on to Santo Domingo, the base for exploring the Sierra Maestra, especially the Parque Nacional Turquino.

Parque Nacional Turquino

★ **5** *Entrance at Santo Domingo, roughly 30 km (19 mi) south of Yara.*

The Sierra Maestra was the legendary home of Castro's rebel army, and a visit through its dramatic terrain makes it clear why the revolutionaries chose it as a place to hide from—and launch clandestine strikes against—Batista's forces. Its massive spine, averaging 1,372 m (4,500 ft) in height, cuts 130 km (81 mi) across El Oriente, throwing a shadow over the southern coast from southwest Granma Province to Santiago de Cuba. The range is covered by moist, tropical forests with huge ferns and towering bamboos. It's cut by steep ravines, rocky valleys, and rushing rivers, and its peaks are often covered with clouds. Its history and majesty are preserved in the Parque Nacional Turquino.

Santo Domingo, on the banks of the Río Yara and in a valley between two steep mountainsides, is usually the hub for visits to the park. The village has restaurants, accommodations, and shops with provisions. You can hire a guide (they're obligatory, but only charge about $5 a day) and buy a $10 permit to enter the park at the Villa Santo Domingo hotel (☞ Dining and Lodging, *below*). Note: there have been reports that you need the $10 permit to enter the park, but the manager at the Villa Santo Domingo says that, with a guide, such a permit isn't necessary. It's best to call ahead to find out what you need and to make sure that the park is open; if the Cuban National Institute of Science or another agency is conducting research, the park may be closed to visitors.

It's a steep 5 km (3 mi) ascent from Santo Domingo village to the **Alto del Naranjo**—a parking lot with beautiful views—which marks the park entrance. If you haven't hired a guide in Santo Domingo, you can do so at the visitors center here.

★ The **Comandancia de la Plata,** the Revolutionary headquarters, is just 3 km (2 mi) west of the park's entrance. A relaxing, one-hour walk on a clearly marked trail along a ridge brings you to a remote forest clearing. Here, you'll find Castro's command post, hospital, and residence—built with an escape route into an adjacent creek. This is the perfect trek if you have limited time: you can get a taste of the region in the morning, and return to the lowlands by early afternoon.

If you want to see more of the park, the summit of **Pico Turquino**—Cuba's highest peak at 1,974 m (6,476 ft)—is 13 km (8 mi) from the Comandancia de la Plata. A journey here involves a night of camping, typically at a tent camp at the mountain's base. Cooks are sometimes available, but you have to bring your own food. Showers and fog alternate with sun and daytime heat, and humidity alternates with chilly windy nights, so, in addition to good hiking boots, you need clothing that you can layer and a lightweight rain jacket.

Dining and Lodging

$ ✕🏨 **Villa Balcón de la Sierra.** This complex in the town of Providencia rents rooms in 10 cabins with wonderful views. The restaurant serves basic fare. ⊠ *Municipio Bartolomé Masó, Providencia,* ☎ *23/59–5180. 20 rooms. Restaurant, bar, air-conditioning, pool, hiking. No credit cards.*

$ ✕🏨 **Villa Santo Domingo.** Its rooms may be rustic (a little on the
★ musty side with furnishings that have seen better days) but this is *the* hub for trips into the Sierra Maestra. Further, the modest cabins have a lovely setting along the banks of the Río Yara, and the friendly ambience and cool, fresh mountain air make for a pleasant enough stay. The basic bar-restaurant serves hearty meals: breakfast is likely to be fried eggs served with rice and beans, dinner may well be barbecued chicken—again, with rice and beans. You can hire guides here for trips to the Parque Nacional Turquino or go for a horseback ride along the river and on mountain trails. *Municipio Bartolomé Masó, Santo Domingo,* ☎ *23/42–5321. 20 cabins. Restaurant, bar, air-conditioning, hiking, horseback riding, games room. No credit cards.*

Manzanillo

⑥ *70 km (43 mi) west of Bayamo.*

The charming, cheerful port town of Manzanillo stretches 3 km (2 mi) along the Bahía de Guacanayabo. It has a beautiful historic district whose pastel-painted structures have elements of Moorish architecture. And, while you're here, you'll undoubtedly hear some street-organ music; the instruments were first imported to Cuba through this city, which is still full of them.

The main plaza, **Parque Céspedes,** is the best place to experience Manzanillo's unique sense of style. It's dominated by a central bandstand, with colorful, intricately painted tiles and a domed top. Many of the buildings surrounding the plaza are fine Moorish inspirations. You'll also find a café; an art gallery; shops; and the Casa de la Cultura, which has art exhibits, live-music shows, and other cultural events. The **Museo Histórico Municipal** has displays on local history and popular culture. One exhibit is dedicated to Taty Labernia, who was so famous for her renditions of *boleros* (traditional Cuban songs that are descendents of troubadour ballads) that they called her La Reina del Bolero (The Queen of the Bolero). ⊠ *Calle Bartolomé Masó,* ☎ *no phone.* ⌨ *$1.* ⊘ *Tues.–Sat. 9–5.*

To reach the **Monumento Celia,** a monument to revolutionary hero Celia Sánchez, a longtime confidante of Fidel Castro, you climb a beautiful staircase lined by Moorish-style residences. ⊠ *Calle Caridad y Calle Martí.*

☺ Wandering the bay-side boulevard known as the *malecón* and exploring its adjacent **Parque de Recreación Bartolomé Masó** is a great way to spend an afternoon. This small park features rides and snack vendors in a shady clearing on the shore. It's lit up at night and is particularly lively on weekends.

In the sugar country just 13 km (8 mi) south of Manzanillo is **La Demajagua,** the farm where poet, patriot, and cane farmer Carlos Manuel de Céspedes freed his slaves and called for rebellion against Spain. There's a large monument at the entrance to the estate, and you can see the bell used by Céspedes to summon his slaves to freedom. The **Museo Histórico La Demajagua,** in Céspedes' former home, displays documents, photos, and other items. ☎ *No phone.* ⌨ *$1.* ⊘ *Daily 9–5.*

Lodging

$ 🏨 **Hotel Guacanaybo.** On a bluff overlooking the bay, this modest, Soviet-inspired hotel offers the best accommodations, amenities (including satellite TV), and food you're likely to find in the area. All the rooms have bay views and small balconies. ⊠ *Av. Camilio Cienfuegos,* ☎ *23/ 54012, 104 rooms, 4 suites. Restaurant, bar, air-conditioning, pool, health club, shop, nightclub, travel services. MC, V.*

Media Luna

⑦ *40 km (25 mi) southwest of Manzanillo.*

The road south from Manzanillo passes through cane fields and smoking sugar mills to the town where Celia Sánchez was born. Eight km (5 mi) south of this town lies the turnoff to Pilón, the beach resort Marea del Portillo, and the beautiful south-coast road to Santiago de Cuba.

On the road to Pilón you'll find the **Casa Natal de Celia Sánchez,** the simple white-and-green house where Sánchez was born in 1920. The patio at the back is beautiful; you can rest here after seeing the exhibits of her eclectic clothing as well as photos, documents, and other items chronicling her life as a rebel. *Carretera de Pilón,* ☏ *no phone.* ▦ *$1.* ☉ *Tues.–Sat. 9–5, Sun. 9–1.*

Playa las Coloradas

❽ *30 km (19 mi) southwest of Media Luna.*

Throughout Granma Province, signs marking municipal limits bear the names of the towns and images of the *Granma,* the boat that carried Castro and his rebels to Cuba in their 1956 "invasion" of the island. Playa las Coloradas is the beach where it all began.

Even in its decline **Niquero,** the area hub, is beautiful. The local Communist Party headquarters is in a lovely stone mansion, seemingly immune to the decay affecting the French-style plantation houses, playful Victorian homes, and Spanish colonial buildings that surround it. The road to Playa las Coloradas heads straight through town, passing some of these structures. (Although there's a restaurant and small bungalows for rent here, operating hours are sporadic, especially in the off-season. Your best bet is to spend the night in Manzanillo or at one of the fine resorts in Marea del Portillo.)

★ Playa las Coloradas is at the start of the **Parque Nacional Desembarco del Granma,** the national park honoring the *Granma* landing. It sprawls across Cuba's southwestern end and is covered by woodlands (home to rare plants and birds), by a unique dry region of cacti and steep terraces, and by lagoons filled with marine life. The **Monumento de Desembarcadero,** near the park's entrance, is a huge replica of the *Granma* built on the exact spot where Castro and his rebels ran aground. You'll find a map showing the rebels' escape route, some revolutionary slogans, and a stage used for political events. The main road through the park runs from the monument to El Oriente's southwestern tip. There are well-marked hiking trails off it including the Morlotte-Fustete Trail, which leads to caves and sinkholes, and the Sendero Arqueologico Natural El Guage, which takes about two hours to hike and which passes mangroves, coastline, and areas purported to have Taíno remains.

Down a road exploding with bougainvillea, you eventually get to El Oriente's southwest corner, which is marked by the 33-m-high (108-ft-high) **Faro de Santa Cruz** (Santa Cruz Lighthouse) built in 1877. Cabo Cruz is the pretty, but poor, fishing town that surrounds it. The rocky coast is flanked by exceptionally blue water. Fishermen work over nets in wooden boats along the shore. It's a beautiful picture, and the last stop on this coastal road.

Marea del Portillo

❾ *110 km (68 mi) east of Manzanillo; 19 km (12 mi) east of Pilón.*

The road to Pilón moves into the southern shadow of the Sierra Maesta near Marea del Portillo; here, sugar country gives way to a dry, craggy coastline, punctuated by green pastures, palm trees, and surging rivers. Marea del Portillo is a great place from which to explore this beautiful region. You'll be well attended at the two resorts, whose all-inclusive rates are a bargain by Caribbean standards. (Note that only one of them is open in the off-season.) Water-sports activities abound, nightlife is supplied on site, and there are plenty of stunning beaches.

Dining and Lodging

$$–$$$ 🏨 **Hotel Farallon del Caribe.** The nicest of the town's two resorts is
★   filled with airy terraces, and each room has satellite TV as well as a balcony overlooking the beach or the lagoon and mountains. You'll

Close-Up

FROM THE *GRANMA* TO HAVANA

O N NOVEMBER 25, 1956, Castro and 81 other heavily armed men set sail from Mexico in a boat designed for 25 unarmed passengers. The idea was to "invade" Cuba and drive Batista from power, but it was a rough trip—filled with food shortages and seasickness. Mechanical problems delayed the landing two days beyond schedule. The rebels missed an important rendezvous with sympathizers who were organized by Celia Sánchez and who were to take them deep into the interior of the Sierra Maestra.

Batista's troops got word of the plan and attacked as soon as the rebels landed, killing or capturing most of them. (Only Castro, his brother Raúl, Che Guevara, and 15 others escaped.) After the attack, Batista's flacks announced Castro's death, which made international news. But Batista, who knew the truth, dispatched troops to the area to hunt Castro down.

From his base camp in the Sierra Maestra, Castro sent patrols of as few as eight men to attack rural outposts, targets that were relatively easy, but greatly symbolic (such rural guards had harassed locals since the the days of Spanish rule). Throughout 1957, Castro and his forces were increasingly successful; he garnered more local support (and knowledge of the rugged terrains) and mounted attacks on larger installations. As the rebellion in the countryside gained momentum, resistance and acts of terrorism in urban areas increased as well. When the regime shut down universities in response to student activism, students channeled their anger into riots. Batista retaliated with a vengeance, but this only isolated him further. In addition, there were several conspiracies to overthrow the dictator on the part of his own military leaders. The U.S. government, which had long been a Batista ally, began withdrawing its support. The regime was crumbling—a fact that seemed clear to everyone but Batista.

In July 1958, leaders of several insurgent groups met in Caracas, Venezuela, to discuss uniting their efforts. Under the Pact of Caracas Castro emerged as the leader of the Revolution. Later that summer Batista sent more than 10,000 troops to the Sierra Maestra; despite heavy attacks by air, land, and sea, his large offensive failed. By fall, military desertions had greatly increased (in several cases, soldiers surrendered without one shot being fired), and forces loyal to Batista were frantically trying to return to western Cuba. With the desertions, arms and equipment fell into the hands of an increasingly bold citizenry. Uprisings throughout the island became more common.

In December of 1958, Che Guevara and a band of rebels (locals among them) successfully derailed a military train carrying soldiers and weapons in Santa Clara, capital of Villa Clara Province. The rebels marched through central Cuba just as a military coup seized control of the government. Batista fled to the Dominican Republic on January 1, 1959. Upon hearing of his flight, the army simply stopped fighting. Rebel forces advanced unchallenged, the 26 of July Movement leaders denounced the leadership instituted by the coup, and Fidel Castro arrived victoriously in Havana one week after Batista's flight.

find many on-site amenities, including a pool set on a terrace above the beach. The food served at the breakfast and dinner buffets is a cut above that offered by other hotels in the region. ⊠ *Carretera de Pilón, Km 14,* ☎ *23/59–7081, 23/59–7082, or 23/59–7083,* FAX *23/59–7080. 140 rooms. Restaurant, bar, air-conditioning, pool, health club, beach, dive shop, snorkeling, windsurfing, boating, jet skiing, waterskiing, fishing, shop, nightclub, travel services. MC, V. All-inclusive.*

$$–$$$ 🏨 **Villa Marea del Portillo.** This hotel is quite close to the beach and is jam-packed with amenities. Open public spaces look out to the sea or the green mountains. You'll find rooms and suites in a main hotel building as well as villas scattered throughout the grounds. All accommodations are spacious and have contemporary furnishings, air-conditioning, and satellite TV. ⊠ *Carretera de Pilón, Km 14,* ☎ *23/ 59–4421. 70 rooms, 4 suites, 56 villas. Restaurant, bar, air-conditioning, pool, 2 tennis courts, exercise room, hiking, beach, dive shop, dock, snorkeling, windsurfing, boating, jet skiing, waterskiing, fishing, shop, nightclub, travel services, car rental. MC, V. All-inclusive.*

En Route Beyond Marea del Portillo, the road swings along the coast, with the green cliffs and ravines of the Sierra Maestra to one side, and the sparkling blue Caribbean and dark-sand coast to the other. The route passes through small coves, coastal villages, and budding resorts. Hawks circle overhead, and your biggest traffic concern is the occasional stray herd of sheep or cattle. Thirty kilometers beyond Marea del Portillo is the Río de la Plata, the site of the rebels' first attack on Batista's troops. The small **Museo de la Plata** (☎ no phone), just off the road, tells the story. It's open Tuesday–Saturday 9–4; admission is $1.

Chivirico

❿ *70 km (43 mi) east of Marea del Portillo; 60 km (37 mi) west of Santiago de Cuba.*

A little more than halfway to Santiago lies Chivirico, a beach town with two fine all-inclusive resorts run by the international chain, SuperClubs. The beaches here offer all kinds of water-sports activities; the diving is particularly noteworthy owing to several area wrecks and the deep Cayman Trench.

$$$–$$$$ 🏨 **SuperClubs Sierra Mar.** High-quality food and service are among
★ this resort's hallmarks. It's perched on a bluff overlooking a pretty beach 10 km (6 mi) east of town. Rooms have top-flight amenities, including air-conditioning and satellite TV. Open terraces and the pool deck overlook the beach and the mountains. In the off-season discounts are as much as 50%. ⊠ *Playa Sevilla, Guamá,* ☎ *22/29110,* FAX *22/29007. 200 rooms. Restaurant, bar, air-conditioning, in-room safes, pool, barbershop, beauty salon, hot tub, massage, sauna, spa, aerobics, archery, exercise room, hiking, horseback riding, Ping-Pong, volleyball, beach, dive shop, dock, snorkeling, windsurfing, boating, jet skiing, waterskiing, fishing, bicycles, shop, nightclub, travel services, car rental. MC, V. All-inclusive.*

$$–$$$ 🏨 **SuperClubs Los Gallones.** At this intimate resort set on a coastal hill-
★ top the large rooms count king-size beds, air-conditioning, satellite TVs, and fine views among their features. A lovely pool and sundeck and a charming restaurant also make this one of the nicer properties around. Note that a stay here enables you to use the facilities at the Sierra Mar, and there are discounts of up to 50% in the off-season. ⊠ *Playa Sevilla, Guamá,* ☎ *22/26160,* FAX *22/29110. 200 rooms. Restaurant, bar, air-conditioning, pool, barbershop, beauty salon, hot tub, massage, sauna, spa, aerobics, exercise room, Ping-Pong, volleyball, beach, dive shop, dock, snorkeling, windsurfing, boating, jet skiing, waterskiing, fishing, bicycles, shop, nightclub, travel services. MC, V. All-inclusive.*

SANTIAGO DE CUBA AND GUANTÁNAMO PROVINCES

Santiago Province is home to the Sierra Maestra, to the west; the Cordillera de la Gran Piedra, to the east; and the Sierra de Cristal, to the north. Although rugged and sparsely populated, the province is El Oriente's geographic and cultural center. The region's most important city, Santiago de Cuba, sits on a wide, south-coast bay, smack in the middle of the province. Founded in 1514, it was Cuba's first capital and still rivals Havana in terms of art, culture, music (the nightlife here is the region's liveliest), and historical sights. Nearby beaches line the coast off the Baconao Nature Reserve.

Most famous for being the site of the U.S. Naval Base—one of the few remaining outposts of the Cold War—Guantánamo Province embodies El Oriente's untamed spirit. Much of the region is within the protected biosphere reserve known as the Cuchilla del Toa, and its topography varies from a flat arid coastal zone (almost desert dry), to lush rain forest to pine-covered mountains. The main destination for visitors, Baracoa was only reachable by water until the 1970s, when Castro had the Farola Highway built over a formidable mountain range. Much of the east coast is still remote, served only by a string of country roads.

Santiago de Cuba

★ ⑪–㉘ *860 km (534 mi) southeast of Havana; 86 km (53 mi) southwest of Guantánamo.*

The birthplace of rum, revolution, and son, Santiago has played an important enough role in island history—from the beginnings of the wars for independence to Castro—to earn it the title of Hero City. Yet Santiago also has an independent spirit, bred through its isolation from Havana and its tradition of trading with and welcoming settlers from neighboring Caribbean islands.

The city's unique architecture reflects a blend of Caribbean, Spanish and other European influences. The African roots of its people are among the most pronounced in Cuba, and this adds considerable flavor to the food as well as a lyrical lilt to Spanish that's spoken here. There's often music in the air here, from hypnotizing Cuban salsa to the folksy *nueva trova* to the latest Latin ballads. (As in many Cuban cities, Santiago's streets often go by pre- and postrevolutionary names; both are provided in addresses below.)

Exploring Centro Histórico

At the center of the city's historical district you'll find Parque Céspedes. The plaza and the streets just off it form the city's cultural heart. They're filled with museums, historical sights, art galleries, bookstores, and spots where the music never seems to stop.

A GOOD TOUR (OR TWO)

Start your tour at **Parque Céspedes** ⑪, a large, busy plaza. Shop- and vendor-lined Calle Heredia runs along the plaza's southern edge, which is dominated by the **Santa Ifigenia Basilica Metropolitana** ⑫. On the park's north side is the beautiful colonial **Poder Popular** ⑬. From here follow Calle Aguilera (Marino) east, crossing Calle Félix Peña (Santo Tomás) to the **Casa de Don Diego Velázquez** ⑭. From here, take Félix Peña south to the intersection of Calle Bartolomé Masó (San Basilio). Turn right and walk 2½ blocks to the **Balcón de Velázquez** ⑮. After taking in the stunning city and bay views, you can visit two sights slightly off the path or continue on the walking tour. If you head west on Bartolomé Masó to Avenida Jesús Menédez, you'll come to the **Fábrica de Tabaco César Escalante.** This is a good jumping-off point for a cab trip 14 km (9 mi) southeast to the **Castillo del Morro.**

Alternatively, you could continue walking south from the Balcón de Velázquez along **Calle Padre Pico** ⑯. Follow Padre Pico still farther south to Calle Diego Palacios and the revolutionary **Museo Lucha Clandestina** ⑰. After touring the museum, retrace your steps to Parque Céspedes and Calle Heredia. Walk east roughly 2½ blocks beyond the park to reach the **Casa Natal de José María Heredia** ⑱. From here, art and history lovers can head one block north to the **Museo Bacardí** ⑲, between Calle Hartman (San Félix) and Calle Pío Rosado (Comisaria), rum lovers can go one block south to the **Museo del Ron** ⑳, and culture mavens can walk 1½ blocks west to the **Museo de Carnaval** ㉑. From the Museo de Carnaval, walk one block east along Calle Heredia; at Calle Maya Rodriguez (Reloj) turn left and continue to the intersection of Calle Aguilera and the charming **Plaza Dolores** ㉒—the perfect place to rest your feet.

TIMING

If you wear your most comfortable shoes, get an early start, and are selective about which museums you explore (or visit each only briefly), you can just about squeeze the walking portions of this tour into a 7-hour day. If you have the time, break this tour up into two days—seeing the sights just west of Parque Céspedes and visiting the Castillo San Juan on one day and then following the walk to the many museums east of Parque Céspedes on another. Be sure to paint the historical center red at least one night during your visit—perhaps taking in a show at the Casa de la Trova or the Casa del Estudiante.

SIGHTS TO SEE

⑮ **Balcón de Velázquez.** Once used by local authorities to monitor boat traffic, today this ceramic-tiled terrace is simply a great place to linger while taking in views of both the city and the bay. Music shows and other events are often held here, particularly on weekend evenings. ⊠ *Calle Bartolomé Masó (San Basilio) y Calle Corona.*

⑯ **Calle Padre Pico.** The climb up the stone steps to this street will reward you with more than just dramatic views. The street is part of the beautiful Tivoloi neighborhood, where 18th-century French colonial mansions sit side by side with 16th-century structures. Locals gather on its shady edges to gossip, play dominoes, or watch visitors like you make their ascent.

⑭ **Casa de Don Diego Velázquez.** Constructed in 1516, this may well be Cuba's oldest house. Diego Velázquez, the Spanish conquistador who founded this city and was the island's first governor, lived upstairs. The bottom floor housed a gold foundry. Today the residence, with its intricate woodwork and smashing views, and an adjacent 19th-century house form part of the **Museo de Ambiente Histórico Cubano** (Cuban Lifestyle Museum) and are filled with antiques from the 16th through 19th centuries, and other exhibits. ⊠ *Calle Félix Peña (Santo Tomás) 612,* ☎ *no phone.* 🎟 *$1. Mon.–Sat. 9–4, Sun. 9–noon.*

⑱ **Casa Natal de José María Heredia.** The birthplace of pro-independence poet José María Heredia (who, in 1839, died at age 36 while exiled in Mexico) is a Spanish colonial mansion with displays of period furniture and the poet's works and belongings. Literary readings and other events are often held here. ⊠ *Calle Heredia 262,* ☎ *no phone.* 🎟 *$1.* 🕙 *Tues.–Sun. 9–5.*

OFF THE
BEATEN PATH

CASTILLO DEL MORRO – Sixteen kilometers (10 miles) south of the city is the Spanish fortress known as El Morro. It dates from 1640 and was designed by Giovanni Antonelli, the Italian architect and engineer responsible for fortresses bearing the same name in both Havana and San Juan, Puerto Rico. Dominating a bluff at the entrance to the Bahía de Santiago de Cuba, El Morro was built to ward off pirates (and rebuilt after a 1662 attack by the English pirate Henry Morgan). Inside you'll find a museum with exhibits on, appropriately enough, pirates. There are wonderful views from interior rooms, which have wooden floors and stone walls, as well as from various terraces. From the lowest terrace, the view of the fortress itself, formed from the sheer face of the bluff, is powerful. The way into the structure takes you down and then back up a 207-step staircase; a drawbridge over a moat leads to the entrance. ⊠ *Ruta Turristica (Carretera del Morro),* ☎ *no phone.* 🎫 *$1,* ⊙ *Daily 9–4.*

FÁBRICA DE TABACO CÉSAR ESCALANTE – If Cubanos are your passion, a visit to this small cigar factory, where locals roll stogies in the traditional way, is a must. To visit, you must hire a guide ($3) through the Rumbos travel agency in Parque Céspedes. A plaza, Parque Alameda, is nearby and across the street is the stately Aduana (Customs House). ⊠ *Av. Jesús Menéndez 703, esquina de Calle Bartolomé Masó (San Basilio),* ☎ *no phone.* 🎫 *Free (but only with guide).* ⊙ *Mon.–Sat. 7–4.*

★ ⑲ **Museo Bacardí.** Cuba's oldest (and Santiago's finest) museum was founded in 1899 by Emilio Bacardí Moreau, a member of the rum-making family who also served as Santiago's mayor. Beyond its jarring neoclassical facade, you'll find strikingly varied collections. The basement contains artifacts—including mummies and a shrunken head—from indigenous cultures throughout the Americas. The first floor houses colonial items (the antique weapons and the brutal relics of the slave trade are especially thought provoking). The second floor is home to an art gallery with works from the 19th and early 20th centuries. The beautiful building across the street from the museum is the seat of the municipal government. ⊠ *Calle Pío Rosado (Comisaria) y Calle Aguilera,* ☎ *226/28402.* 🎫 *$2.* ⊙ *Weekdays 10–8.*

↻ ㉑ **Museo de Carnaval.** The spirit of one of the Caribbean's most vibrant street parties, Santiago's annual July Carnaval, is alive here every day. You'll find historic photos and newspaper clippings, floats, costumes, and musical instruments. Music and dance troupes often perform here; when they do, shows usually take place at 4 PM during the week or on Saturday evenings. ⊠ *Calle Heredia 303,* ☎ *no phone,* 🎫 *$1.* ⊙ *Tues.–Sun. 9–5.*

⑰ **Museo Lucha Clandestina.** This museum is in a 19th-century building that was once the city's police headquarters. It was attacked by Frank País and a band of rebels on November 30, 1958. Displays give you a complete overview of Castro's Revolution, and the architecture and bay views are as compelling as the exhibits. ⊠ *Calle General Jesús Rabí 1,* ☎ *226/24689.* 🎫 *$1.* ⊙ *Tues.–Sat. 9–5, Sun. 9–noon.*

⑳ **Museo del Ron.** Exhibits here take you through the rum-making process. You'll also find displays of antique rum paraphernalia and bottles. In the same building (but accessible only through an entrance around the corner) is the **Taberna del Ron,** which sells rum products and gifts. ⊠ *Calle Bartolomé Masó (San Basilio) 358,* ☎ *no phone.* 🎫 *$1.* ⊙ *Tues.–Sun. 9–6.*

★ ⑪ **Parque Céspedes.** The central meeting place for Santiagueros, this large plaza is always abuzz with sound and movement, whether it's the municipal band playing or children riding bicycles or being pulled

158

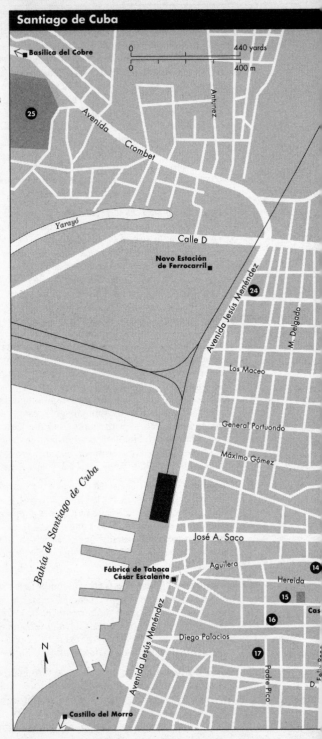

Santiago de Cuba

Basilica del Cobre

0   440 yards
0   400 m

Antunez

Avenida Crombet

Yarayó

Calle D

Novo Estación
de Ferrocarril

Avenida Jesús Menéndez

M. Delgado

Los Maceo

General Portuondo

Máximo Gómez

Bahía de Santiago de Cuba

José A. Saco

Aguilera

Fábrica de Tabaca
César Escalante

Hereida

Cas

N

Diego Palacios

Avenida Jesús Menéndez

Padre Pico

D. Félix Peña

Castillo del Morro

Calle 4

26

Pinar del Río

Avenida   Juan   G.   Gomez

Latour

René   Ramos

Avenida Mariana Grajales

Patricio Lumumba

Calle 6

Rufino Chávez

Calle E

Av. de los Libertadores

Calle 4

Avenida de Céspedes

Paseo de Martí

Narciso López (San Antonio)

Félix Peña

Hartman

Moncada

Calle 3

Calle 2

Calle 1

Los Maceo

Mayía Rodríguez

Saturnino Lora

Avenida de los Libertadores

23

General   Portuondo

Máximo Gómez

27

Sanchez Hechavarría

28

Barnada

Avenida   Garzón

José A. Saco

B. Betancourt

Félix   Varela

P. Martínez

Aguilera

19

21

22

General Carlos Roloff

18

Bartolomé Maso

20

12   de   Agosto

Diego Palacios

Mayía Rodríguez

P. Valiente

Hartman

General   Julio   Sanguily

Valeriano   Hierrezuelo

Comandante   Borrero

Calle 6

in small animal-drawn carnival carts. The plaza's shady benches are full from early in the morning to late in the evening. At the center of the park is a large bronze statue of the plaza's namesake Carlos Manuel de Céspedes, whose Grito de Yara declared Cuba's independence from Spain in 1868 and began the Ten Years War. Have a mojíto at Hotel Casa Granda's (☞ Lodging, *below*) café, which overlooks this beehive of activity.

㉒ **Plaza Dolores.** This long, shady plaza—the city's former marketplace— is ringed by outdoor cafés and open-air restaurants. It takes its name from the church overlooking its eastern end, the **Iglesia de Nuestra Señora de los Dolores,** which was recently renovated and turned into a concert hall.

⑬ **Poder Popular.** On the north side of Parque Céspedes, this beautiful colonial structure was where Castro gave his victory speech on January 2, 1959. Occasionally it hosts exhibits and special performances. ✉ *Calle Aguilera.*

⑫ **Santa Ifigenia Basilica Metropolitana.** The twin towers and striking dome of this Moorish-style cathedral loom over the southern edge of Parque Céspedes. Although a church was first built on this site in 1523, the current building dates primarily from 1922. Reports have it that the remains of Diego Velázquez are buried within the cathedral, but church officials deny this. (Exhaustive searches have turned up nothing; Don Diego's bones were no doubt returned to Spain long ago.) The cathedral is elevated above the plaza and a row of ground-floor shops. Inside, you'll find a painted ceiling that has been beautifully restored and such works of religious art as a sculpture of Cuba's patron saint, La Virgen de la Caridad. Residents who congregate here are extremely friendly; they may try to engage you in conversation if mass isn't being conducted. ✉ *Calle Heredia, e/Calle Félix Peña (Santo Tomás) y Calle General Lacret (San Pedro),* ☎ *no phone.* 💳 *Small donation suggested.* ⊙ *Daily 8–10 and 5–7.*

Exploring Metropolitan Santiago de Cuba

If you have an extra day, try to take in some of metropolitan Santiago's sights. There are several places of interest on and near the bay just to the north of the Centro Histórico. Avenida de las Américas edges modern Santiago's northern perimeter before arcing sharply southeast. Along and just off this boulevard are several noteworthy contemporary and historical sights.

A GOOD DRIVE

Start at the **Antiguo Cuartel Moncada** ㉓ for a taste of revolution. Next head northwest for a taste of rum: take Paseo de Martí to Avenida Jesús Menéndez and follow it south two blocks to the **Fábrica de Ron Caney** ㉔, opposite the modernist Santiago train station. From here take Menéndez north to Avenida Crombet; veer left and follow Crombet to the **Cementerio Santa Ifigenia** ㉕ and the wondrous José Martí memorial. The cemetery is a good jumping-off point for the 20 km (12 mi) trip northwest of Santiago, to the **Basilica del Cobre.** Alternatively, you could cut north from the cemetery through the Centro Urbano José Martí, a housing project that captures the spirit of socialist life, to Avenida Las Américas. This wide boulevard arcs past the large Universidad de Oriente (Eastern Cuba University) just before passing through the **Plaza de la Revolución** ㉖. Follow Las Américas to the traffic circle formed by it, Avenida Victoriano Garzón, Avenida Raúl Pujol, and Avenida Manduley. Travel around to Avenida Manduley and the elegant neighborhood of **Reparto Vista Alegre** ㉗. Just south of here is the famous **Loma de San Juan** ㉘.

In case you want to see the world.

At American Express, we're here to make your journey
a smooth one. So we have over 1,700 travel service locations in over 130 countries ready to help. What else
would you expect from the world's largest travel agency?

do more

Travel

Call 1 800 AXP-3429 or visit
www.americanexpress.com/travel

In case you want to be welcomed there.

We're here to see that you're always welcomed at establishments everywhere. That's why millions of people carry the American Express® Card – for peace of mind, confidence, and security, around the world or just around the corner.

do more

Cards

And in case you'd rather be safe than sorry.

We're here with American Express® Travelers Cheques. They're the safe way to carry money on your vacation, because if they're ever lost or stolen you can get a refund, practically anywhere or anytime. To find the nearest place to buy Travelers Cheques, call 1 800 495-1153. Another way we help you do more.

do more

Travelers Cheques

TIMING

Excluding the trip to El Cobre, you can follow this tour in a day. You'll save money and your sanity by hiring a car and driver rather than renting a car and driving yourself. A *taxi particular* will charge roughly $30 for this tour. In addition, many hotels offer half-day Havanatur excursions that hit many of these sights.

SIGHTS TO SEE

★ ㉓ **Antiguo Cuartel Moncada.** On July 26, 1953, Castro and 100 men attempted to storm this former army barracks. It was Carnaval time in Santiago; the streets were full of revelers, and Castro had hoped that security would be lax. Unfortunately, his hopes were dashed, and the rebels were either killed or captured. Castro, who fled to the mountains, was eventually caught, tried, and imprisoned on the Isla de la Juventud off western Cuba's south coast. Although unsuccessful, the attack ignited the sparks of Castro's revolution. He wrote his famous speech *La Historia me Absolverá* (*History Will Absolve Me*), which was smuggled out of prison, printed, and distributed throughout the island. Although luck had not been on his side in 1953, it certainly was in 1955, when Batista granted many political prisoners their freedom. Castro left for the United States, where he began soliciting support for his 26 of July Movement (named in honor of the ill-fated barracks attack) to rid Cuba of Batista's regime. From there, he took his cause to Mexico. In 1956, just a year after being released from prison, Castro made his historic journey from Mexico to Cuba aboard the *Granma* (☞ box "From the *Granma* to Havana," *above*).

Today the former stronghold of Batista's troops contains a grammar school and the **Museo de 26 de Julío.** The bullet holes surrounding the doorway to the museum are re-creations of those left after the original attack, which were quickly patched over by Batista's men. The exhibits here tell the entire story of the attack and the events that followed. They're among the nation's most comprehensive of those dedicated to Revolutionary history. Take the guided tour (it's customary to tip docents $1 or $2). ⊠ *Av. General Portuondo y Av. Moncada,* ☎ 226/ 52710. ☝ *$2.* ☉ *Mon.–Sat. 9–6, Sun. 9–noon.*

OFF THE
BEATEN PATH

BASILICA DEL COBRE – After a 20 km (12 mi) drive through the countryside northwest of Santiago, you'll see the red-tile tower of La Basilica de Nuestra Senora de la Caridad del Cobre—which was dedicated to Cuba's patron saint in 1916—before the turn-off to the copper mining town in which it is set. The story of the Virgin dates from the early 1600s, when three men in a boat first saw her floating on water; several other area sightings were followed by tales of the Virgin's miraculous powers. (Her image has also been blended with that of Óchún, the *orisha*, or goddess, of love in the Santería religion.) Each September, pilgrims journey here—sometimes crawling uphill for miles on their knees—on the Virgin's feast day (September 12). Her shrine is filled with gifts from the faithful, including Ernest Hemingway's Nobel Prize, which he left here in 1952. A staircase at the back of the cathedral leads to the chapel containing the Virgin's wooden image. In front of the cathedral, you'll find a plaque commemorating Pope John Paul's visit here during his historic 1998 trip to Cuba. ⊠ *Carretera Central,* ☎ *no phone.* ☝ *$1 suggested donation.* ☉ *Daily 6:30–6.*

㉕ **Cementerio Santa Ifigenia.** This cemetery is home to the majestic mausoleum of the great poet-patriot in the wars of independence, José Martí. The structure is true to Martí's wishes (expressed in one of his poems) that he be buried below the flag of Cuba and surrounded by roses. Marble steps lead to the tomb, above which is a domed tower. Other highlights include a memorial to Cuban soldiers who have fallen in battle and the tombs of Carlos Manuel de Céspedes and those who died in the Moncada Barracks attack. You need a guide ($1) to enter. ⊠ *Av. Crombet,* ☎ *no phone.* ⛬ *Free(but only with guide).* ☉ *Daily dawn–dusk.*

㉔ Fábrica de Ron Caney. Cuba's oldest rum distillery, a former Bacardí family enterprise, now makes Havana Club. The on-site shop—which has a bar, live music, and free samples—is the central attraction. ⊠ *Av. Jesús Menéndez y Calle Gonzalo de Quesada,* ☎ *no phone.* ⛬ *Free.* ☉ *Mon.–Sat. 9–6.*

☝ ㉘ Loma de San Juan. Made famous by Teddy Roosevelt and his Rough Riders, San Juan Hill lies just south of Vista Alegre. Today it's a park covered by monuments, left by U.S. and Cuban militaries, to the battle fought here during the Spanish-American War. It's a lovely passive spot, with amusements for small children in the Parque de Diversiones 26 de Julio at the base of the hill. It also marks the official start of the Baconao Nature Reserve, which covers the mountain and coastal regions east of Santiago. Nearby you'll find the **Parque Zoológico** (⊠ Av. Raúl Pujol, near San Juan Hill, ☎ no phone), which has animals from around the world. It's open Tuesday–Sunday 1–5, and admission is $1.

㉖ Plaza de la Revolución. Just about every city on the island has a Revolution Square, perhaps the most prominent marker of Cuban socialism. This one was the site of Pope John Paul's address to Santiago during his historic visit. Towering beside the plaza is the dramatic **monument to Major General Antonio Maceo,** one of the heroes of the wars of independence. It shows the general on his horse, going down in a battlefield of machetes that rise from the ground around him. Nearby the square is the **Teatro Heredia,** a music hall and theater that hosts some of the city's most significant performances.

㉗ Reparto Vista Alegre. This elegant neighborhood of mansions (some of them casas particulares) is a place of historical splendor. French-inspired plantation homes, stately Spanish colonial mansions, even art deco gems are beautifully decaying amid riotous vegetation and clear Caribbean sun. Russian moto-side cars, 1958 Chevy Bel Airs, and 1959 Cadillacs roll down the wide, quiet streets where time seems to have frozen four decades ago, just before the Revolution. Look for the **Palacio de Pioneros** (⊠ Av. Manduley y Calle 11), a three-story mansion that once belonged to rum baron Pepe Bosch, but now is a school for Young Pioneers. The building is easy to find owing to the Soviet MIG fighter jet in the front yard.

Dining

Vista Alegre is full of outstanding restaurants and paladares. Recommended, privately operated establishments in this neighborhood include **Paladar El Amanecer** (⊠ Calle 10, No. 224, ☎ 226/43627) and **Paladar El Morro** (⊠ Av. Victoriano Garzón, ☎ no phone).

$$–$$$ ★ ✕ La Maison. This elegant, white-marble, colonial mansion contains a boutique; a café; and a restaurant with a stage for the nightly fashion, comedy, and music show (show entrance and a glass of champagne cost $5; dinner-show packages run $20). The café, which is on the lovely back patio and is open 10–6, serves mediocre pizza and pasta dishes, but it's a great place for a drink either before or after browsing in the boutique. The restaurant, open for dinner 6–midnight, offers seafood (paella is a specialty) as well as steaks. ⊠ *Av. Manduley y Calle 1, Vista Alegre,* ☎ *226/41117. MC, V.*

$$ ★ ✕ Restaurant Zun Zún. Formerly the Tocororo, this restaurant has won all sorts of culinary awards, and, indeed, its well-prepared dishes and extensive wine list befit its elegant Vista Alegre setting. You can dine outdoors or inside amid the decor of the house's former owner, an Arab merchant. The grilled seafood, including lobster and shrimp, is prepared according to several different recipes. ⊠ *Av. Manduley 159, Vista Alegre,* ☎ *226/41528. MC, V.*

$ ✕ **1900 Santiago.** Housed in the former mansion of the rum-making Bacardí family (who fled to Puerto Rico after the Revolution), this is an old Santiago standard. Although the quality of the food has declined recently, and the menu has lost its sense of adventure, you can't beat the ambience. The formal dining room, with its antique furnishings, is particularly striking; the informal back patio, whose offerings vary only slightly from those inside, is a good spot for a drink. Although the restaurant only accepts pesos, they'll change dollars on the spot. ⊠ *Calle Bartolomé Masó (San Basilio) 354, e/Calle Pío Rosado (Comisaria) y Calle Hartman (San Félix),* ☎ *226/23507. No credit cards.*

$ ✕ **Restaurant Don Antonio.** Although this Rumbos-run spot serves much of the same food as its many Rumbos-run neighbors, its setting in a restored colonial mansion on Plaza Dolores is terrific. Ceiling fans spin slowly overhead and large windows open up to the plaza's northwest corner. ⊠ *Calle Aguilera y Calle Porfiro Valiente, Plaza Dolores,* ☎ *226/23913. MC, V.*

$ ✕ **La Restaurant Terracina.** Here you can feast on Italian fare in a white-tile, European-café setting overlooking the plaza. The pizza, pastas, and seafood dishes are good by local standards, and the service is friendly. ⊠ *Calle Aguilera, Plaza de Dolores.,* ☎ *226/52307. No credit cards.*

$ ✕ **Taberna de Dolores.** The most colorful of the restaurants in colonial buildings on Plaza de Dolores has a bar, an interior dining area, and a back patio. Although the atmosphere here isn't fancy, it's old fashioned (you can't wear shorts inside). You'll find good local food at affordable prices (this is a peso-only place that will, nonetheless, change dollars). ⊠ *Calle Aguilera y Calle Maya Rodriguez (Reloj), Plaza de Dolores,* ☎ *226/23913. No credit cards.*

Lodging

Santiago has some fine casas particulares, particularly in the Vista Alegre neighborhood. The owners of each will gladly point you to neighborhood paladares. **Guadalupe o José** (⊠ Calle 6, No. 307, Vista Alegre, ☎ 226/43118) has two air-conditioned rooms with bath. Rates are $20 per room (no credit cards) per night. **Mireya Guerra López** (⊠ Calle 6, No. 252, Vista Alegre, ☎ 226/41904) has two nice rooms with air-conditioning and private bath; the nightly rate is $20 per person (no credit cards).

$$$ 🏨 **Hotel Santiago** With the look of a tropical erector set, this colorful, postmodern hotel has a playful appeal. Although at press time it was suffering from a lack of maintenance, the Spanish Sol Meliá chain had just assumed management, which bodes well for its future. And you can't beat the amenities: three pools, a huge front lobby with a piano bar, a rooftop nightclub, a gym, a handful of restaurants, and rooms with satellite TV. The buffet breakfasts and dinners at the main restaurant are usually quite good. The house band, Aldo y Su Grupo, which plays a happy hour set at the terrace lounge, is hot. ⊠ *Av. de las Américas, e/Av. Manduley y Av. Cuarto,* ☎ *226/42634,* FAX *226/41756 270 rooms, 30 junior suites. 3 restaurants, 3 bars, air-conditioning, 3 pools, barbershop, beauty salon, sauna, 4 tennis courts, basketball, health club, shops, nightclub, travel services. MC, V*

$$–$$$ 🏨 **Hotel Casa Granda.** Run by the French Alcor chain, this hotel is one ★ of the nicest in the city, if not in all of Cuba. Its marble porch—trimmed with plants, crimson awnings, and a black-and-white tile floor—is perched above the east side of Parque Céspedes and has a large wooden bar. Even if you don't stay here, be sure to stop by for a mo-

jíto or a light meal (they make terrific *cubanos,* roast pork and ham sandwiches served with pickles and a salad). The formal dining room offers delectable seafood and steak dishes. Guest rooms are large, full of beautiful antiques, and have satellite TV. At press time, the hotel was taking over the adjacent Hotel Venus; the expansion was slated to add rooms and such amenities as a health club, a pool, and a disco. ⊠ *Calle Heredia 201, Parque Céspedes,* ☎ *226/86600,* 🖷 *226/86035. 56 rooms, 3 suites. Restaurant, bar, air-conditioning, room service, shop, travel services. MC, V.*

$$ 🏨 **Hotel Horizontes Las Américas** Bright, modern, and well maintained, this hotel offers low-key charms: a friendly staff, rooms with satellite TV and radios, and live music every night by the pool. One of its restaurants is known for its comida criolla. ⊠ *Av. de las Américas y Av. General Cebreco,* ☎ *226/42011,* 🖷 *226/86075. 68 rooms. 2 restaurants, bar, air-conditioning, pool, shop, nightclub, travel service, car rental. MC, V.*

$$ 🏨 **Hotel San Juan.** The former Motel Leningrad has a bucolic setting at the foot of San Juan Hill and is surrounded by large shade trees and rolling, green fields. Rooms in the villa-style accommodations are equally appealing; all have satellite TV. You can spend time by the rectangular pool; on the pleasant terrace; or in the bar, which is open 24 hours and has live music in the evening. ⊠ *Carretera a Siboney y Calle 13,* ☎ *226/87200,* 🖷 *226/87–1376. 112 rooms. Restaurant, bar, air-conditioning, pool, barbershop, beauty salon, sauna, health club, travel services. MC, V.*

$$ 🏨 **Hotel Versalles.** The Versalles is set on a pretty hilltop 2 km (1 mi) from the airport just south of Santiago on the road to El Morro. There are nice views of the city from here, and it's quiet at night. All accommodations have satellite TVs; rooms are slightly cheaper than the cabins. ⊠ *Ruta Turristica (Carretera del Morro) Km 1, Alturas del Versalles,* ☎ *226/90–1016. 46 rooms, 14 cabins. Restaurant, bar, air-conditioning, pool, health club, shop, nightclub, travel service, car rental. MC, V.*

$$ 🏨 **Villa Gaviota.** The attractive Vista Alegre setting of this marble for-
★ mer residence is matched by comfortable rooms (with satellite TV), well-maintained facilities, reliable service, and good food. It's run by Gaviota, a public corporation dedicated to tourism and created by the Cuban military. You can arrange special trips from here to see the U.S. Navy base at Guantánamo Bay. ⊠ *Av. Manduley 502, Vista Alegre,* ☎ *226/41368,* 🖷 *226/87066. 36 rooms. Restaurant, bar, air-conditioning, pool, shop, travel services. MC, V.*

$ 🏨 **Hotel Balcón del Caribe.** Set on cliffs over the coast near El Morro, this hotel affords spectacular views. The staff is friendly, and the San Pedro del Mar Cabaret next door has nightly spectaculars. All guest quarters have satellite TV; cabins can accommodate three people. ⊠ *Ruta Turristica (Carretera del Morro), Km 7,* ☎ *226/90–1011. 76 rooms, 24 cabins. Restaurant, bar, air-conditioning, pool, shop, travel services. MC, V.*

Nightlife and the Arts

CARNAVAL

Carnaval began as a celebration by slaves who were given respite from their labors at Easter time. Despite its initial link with a Christian holiday, the rhythms and rituals of this festival (now celebrated in July here) have their roots in pagan Africa. Neighborhood associations called *carabalís* compete to build the most colorful floats, create the most inspired costumes, and stage the most spectacular processions. Men dress in colorful outfits and wear papier-mâché masks; women don skimpy bikinis and wraps of see-through silk and feathers. The primal rumba beat—accentuated by maracas, Chinese coronets, and wooden flutes—drives the processions. Although the main one runs along the bay-side Avenida Jesús Menéndez, the entire city gets lively.

The **Balle Folklórico Cutumba** (✉ Av. José A. Sacó 170, ☎ 226/25860) practices in the morning and late afternoon Tuesday–Saturday. There's also a show every Sunday at 10:30 AM; admission is $3. **Carabalí Izuama** (✉ Calle Pío Rosado/Comisaria, e/Calle los Maceo y Calle San Antonio, ☎ no phone) welcomes visitors to its practice sessions. If you miss Carnival, you can get a taste of it at **Museo de Carnaval** (☞ Exploring, *above*). Sometimes the museum stays open late on Saturday to host performances of Carnaval dance and music; admission to these shows is $1. You can watch members of **La Tumba Francesca** (✉ Calle los Maceo, No. 501, esquina de San Bartolomé, ☎ no phone) carabalí rehearse.

FILM

When's the last time you paid $1 to see a movie? That's what Santiago's main movie theater, the **Cine Rialto** (✉ Calle Félix Peña/Santo Tomás, just off Parque Céspedes, ☎ no phone) charges. It plays dated foreign films and U.S. action flicks.

MUSIC

Street musicians often perform (just follow your ears) for tips along Calle Heredia and in Parque Céspedes. This central plaza is also the best place to see the excellent Santiago Municipal Band (their rendition of "La Virgen Guerrera" is haunting); try to catch a performance early Sunday evening.

Near El Morro, **Cabaret San Pedro del Mar** (✉ Ruta Turristica/Carretera del Morro, ☎ 226/91486) has shows every night but Tuesday for $10. Although they aren't as extravagant as others in the city, they're well-orchestrated and take place on a terrace overlooking the ocean. **Casa del Estudiante** (✉ Calle Heredia 204, ☎ no phone) has live music on Saturday and Sunday evenings. The folksy *trova* combines African rhythms with Spanish guitar, and the lyrics explore themes of romance or social protest. The **Casa de la Trova** (✉ Calle Heredia 208, ☎ no phone) is open from noon until the wee hours. Groups perform here all the time, and they draw locals and visitors alike.

The **Claqueta Bar** (✉ Calle Félix Peña/Santo Tomás 654, ☎ no phone), just off Parque Céspedes, serves cheap drinks on its outdoor terrace; sometimes there's live music here weekend evenings. Early in the evening, a band plays at the bar-café on the porch of the **Hotel Casa Granda** (☞ Lodging, *above*). Its rooftop bar often hosts live-music shows and is also a nice spot for a drink. Aldo y Su Grupo, the outstanding (and friendly) house band at the **Hotel Santiago** (☞ Lodging, *above*) specializes in salsa. They perform their happy hour set from 6–9 at the terrace bar outside the main restaurant. At 10, they head up to the rooftop Salón Pico Real disco, where things really sizzle.

The **Teatro Heredia** (✉ Av. de las Américas y Av. de los Desfiles, ☎ no phone) hosts performances of classical and Cuban music, opera, and poetry readings. There are also children's shows here on weekend mornings. The **Tropicana Santiago** (Circunvalación, 4 km/2 mi north of Hotel Santiago, ☎ no phone) puts on a full cabaret, with dozens of dancers—men in Spandex, women in feathers and jeweled bikinis—floating through the colored lights and tropical decor. Most hotels offer cabaret packages for $30, (including transport, entrance, and one drink).

Outdoor Activities and Sports

You can arrange day trips to the area immediately east of Santiago, which encompasses the sprawling Baconao Natural Reserve. There are beaches and plenty of hiking opportunities here. The beach zone west of Santiago, along the coastal road into Granma Province, is also just a day trip away.

Nonguests can use the sports facilities at the **Hotel Santiago** (☞ Lodging, *above*)—including pools and tennis and basketball courts—for a $10 fee; equipment rentals are also available. **Marina Marlin** (⊠ Punta Gorda, ☎ 226/91446) can arrange water-sports equipment rentals and boat trips. They offer bay tours, day-long excursions (including lunch) to area beaches, and full-day fishing charters.

Despite the continued chill in official United States–Cuba relations, all of Cuba is crazy about the American pastime of baseball. You can catch the madness at **Estadio Guillermón Moncada** (Av. de las Américas, ☎ no phone), the stadium of the hometown team, the Santiago Orientales. The season runs from November through March, and games are played Tuesday through Thursday 7:30 PM and weekends at 1:30.

Shopping

Santiago and its environs have some of the best arts and crafts in the region—from surrealist oil paintings to stuffed dolls to wood carvings. The city's painters are particularly good; if you buy an artwork, just remember to purchase a $10 export permit from the artist.

Art galleries and shops ring **Parque Céspedes,** the heart of the historic district. Two galleries worth a look here are the Galería Santiago and Galería del Oriente. **Calle Heredia,** which runs along the south side of Parque Céspedes, is lined with bookstores, galleries, and shops (including those in the Casa de la Trova and the Casa del Estudiante) that purvey crafts and music. Artisans also sell their creations from stands set up along this street. The road to and the area around **El Morro** has its share of artisans hawking their wares.

Arte Universal (⊠ Calle 1, e/Calle M y Calle Terraza, ☎ no phone), has art exhibits (and works for sale) Monday–Saturday 9–7 and Sunday 9–5. Admission is $1. At **Casa del Caribe** (⊠ Calle 13, No. 154, esquina de Calle 5, Vista Alegre, ☎ 226/42285) you can buy books or take a course on Cuban or Caribbean culture. **Cubartesania** (⊠ Calle Bartolomé Masó/San Basilio y Calle Félix Peña/Santo Tomás, ☎ no phone), just off Parque Céspedes, is a state-run store that sells high-quality paintings, prints, and a wide selection of crafts. For upscale fashions check out the boutique at the restaurant **La Maison** (☞ Dining, *above*). **Tienda Cubalse** (⊠ Av. General Cebreco y Calle 15, ☎ no phone) sells imported goods.

Parque Baconao

🟤 *10 km (5 mi) east of Parque Céspedes to San Juan Hill and beginning of Parque Baconao.*

The Baconao Biosphere Reserve starts at San Juan Hill in Santiago and covers some 800 sq km (309 sq mi) east of the city. It's packed full of an amazing variety of attractions. In addition to beaches and mountain peaks, you'll find several museums, a flower farm, and an artists colony—among other things. From Santiago, take the Carretera de Siboney, and follow the signs to Playa Siboney, a Caribbean beach 19 km (12) southeast of town.

La Gran Piedra, a gigantic rock offshoot of the Sierra Maestra, rises 1,200 m (3,900 ft) and offers views of Haiti and Jamaica on clear days.

(Visibility is best first thing in the morning.) The cutoff from the Carretera de Siboney is right beyond the **Prado de las Escultas,** a contemporary sculpture garden. The road climbs about 15 km (9 mi), passing from lush jungle vegetation—with towering bamboo and palms that block out the sun—to scrub forest open to the rays and affording great views. The road ends at a hotel and restaurant; a large stairway leads to the rock peak from here. Nearby is the **Jardin Ave de Paraiso,** a colorful farm with gardens full of tropical flowers. Exhibits at the **Museo La Isabelica,** housed in a former plantation, depict the life of a French coffee farmer—one of many who settled in this region during the Haitian revolution in 1792. The museum is open daily 9–4, and admission is $1.

The **Museo Granita Siboney,** a few kilometers east of the cutoff to La Gran Piedra, is housed in the farmhouse where Castro and his cohorts met (having hid their weapons in a well here) before attacking the Moncada Barracks. The farmhouse is on a large, shady piece of land. The museum inside commemorates the event with photos, news articles, documents, blood-stained clothing, and weapons. Twenty-six memorials to the attack line the road from here to Santiago. ⊠ *Carretera de Siboney, Km 13.5,* ☎ *no phone.* ☑ *$1.* ⊙ *Tues.–Sun. 9–5.*

Playa Siboney is a town with charming wooden vacation homes and a clean, dark-sand Caribbean beach. There are a couple of nice casas particulares and paladares here as well as traditional lodging and dining options. It's a good spot for a lunch stop.

A few kilometers beyond Siboney, a turn-off route takes you to **El Oasis** (⊠ Carretera de Baconao), a cluster of stone cottages forming an artists community. Visitors are welcome at the cottages, which serve as studios and homes. The artwork here is quite good, and the prices are lower than shops and galleries in the city. Across the road is the Finca Guajira Rodeo (☞ Outdoor Activities and Sports, *below*), whose restaurant and bar are open when there's a rodeo on. **Playa Bucanero** is the site of a sprawling all-inclusive resort a few kilometers down the turn-off at El Oasis. Gray cliffs surround this white-sand beach, which is for the exclusive use of guests at the Coralia Club de Bucanero (☞ Lodging, *below*).

☾ The **Valle de la Prehistoria** (Prehistoric Valley) is a park of rolling green fields, filled with life-size replicas of dinosaurs, Cro-Magnon man, and other prehistoric creatures. The park, whose towering sculptures are made of cement poured over wood and metal frames, is divided into different eras: from Mesozoic to Cenozoic to Paleozoic. There's also a natural science museum. Some people have dismissed the place as "tacky," but it's hard not to have fun here. (Just watch the kids.) ⊠ *Carretera de Baconao, Km 22,* ☎ *no phone.* ☑ *$1 entrance fee; $1 fee for taking pictures.* ⊙ *Daily 8–7.*

☾ The **Museo Nacional de Transporte,** an antique car museum, has classic American vehicles from Model T Fords to 1958 Thunderbirds. The car in which Fidel Castro rode to attack the Moncada Barracks and a Cadillac belonging to Cuban singer Beny Moré are here. Across the street is a toy museum. ⊠ *Carretera de Baconao, Km 24,* ☎ *no phone.* ☑ *$1 (joint admission with toy museum).* ⊙ *Daily 8–5.*

There are several **beaches** in this area. **Playa Daiquiri,** which gave its name to the famous drink first made here in 1898, was the landing site of Teddy Roosevelt and his Rough Riders. The beach itself is unattractive and is reserved for military use during parts of the year. A kilometer beyond Daiquiri lies **Playa Bacajagua,** which you can visit for a nominal fee. **Playa Sigua,** the next beach town on the Carretera de Baconao, is

known for its two good restaurants: Casa del Pedro del Cojo, special-
izing in creole dishes, and Los Coraldes, whose forte is seafood.

☺ At the **Aquario Baconao,** about 15 km (9 mi) east of Playa Daiquiri,
you can see sharks, seals, ells, turtles, and other marine life. The highlight is the dolphin pool and show; you can also swim with the dolphins. ⊠ *Carretera de Baconao, Km 26, Playa Larga,* ☎ *no phone.*
🎫 *$3.* ☉ *Tues.–Sun. 9–4.*

The **Laguna Baconao,** a 4-sq-km (2-sq-mi) circular lagoon surrounded
by mountains, is the last stop along the Carretera de Baconao. There's
a crocodile farm here, and boat trips on the lagoon are possible.

Dining and Lodging

$ ✕ **La Reuda.** This eatery at the entrance to the town of Playa Siboney
is rustic. But you can't beat their barbecued meats and seafood prepared the Cuban way. There's also a bar here. ⊠ *Playa Siboney,* ☎
226/39352. MC, V.

$$$ 🏨 **Coralia Club de Bucanero.** The area's nicest resort is less than an
hour's drive from Santiago. The hotel is built around a pristine beach
surrounded by cliffs. Rooms, which have cable TV and other ameni-
ties, are in simple, one-story structures spread out along the shoreline;
interior and exterior color schemes match the terra-cotta bluffs that
rise from the sea. ⊠ *Carretera de Baconao, Km 4.5, Arroyo La Costa,*
☎ *226/86363,* 𝖥𝖠𝖷 *226/86070. 200 rooms. Restaurant, bar, air-condi-
tioning, pool, barbershop, beauty salon, hot tub, sauna, 4 tennis courts,
health club, volleyball, beach, dive shop, snorkeling, windsurfing,
boating, jet skiing, waterskiing, fishing, shops, nightclub, travel ser-
vices. MC, V. All-inclusive.*

$$$ 🏨 **Hotel Carisol Resort.** Rooms here (equipped with satellite TV and
other amenities) either face the sea or the mountains. The resort has a
nice beach and all the facilities you need. In addition the food and the
service are both good. ⊠ *Carretera Baconao Km 10, Playa Cazonal,*
☎ *226/28519,* 𝖥𝖠𝖷 *226/27191. 120 rooms. Restaurant, bar, air-conditioning, pool, 2 tennis courts, health club, hiking, beach, dive shop,
snorkeling, windsurfing, boating, jet skiing, waterskiing, fishing, shops,
nightclub, travel services. MC, V. All-inclusive.*

$$ 🏨 **Balneario del Sol.** Guest quarters are either in rooms or in four-room
cabins that dot the grounds; all have such amenities as satellite TV. Be
sure to check out the saltwater pool, which extends out to the coastal
cliffs that front the property. ⊠ *Carretera Baconao, Km 38.5, Playa
Larga,* ☎ *226/26005. 115 rooms, 24 cabins. Restaurant, bar, air-con-
ditioning, 2 pools, 2 tennis courts, health club, beach, dive shop,
snorkeling, windsurfing, boating, jet skiing, waterskiing, fishing, shops,
nightclub, recreation room, travel services. MC, V.*

$$ 🏨 **Villa La Gran Piedra.** Here 22 self-contained villas (with satellite TV)
are spread out along a cliff-side ridge of La Gran Piedra. The restau-
rant-bar is in a country lodge. ⊠ *Carretera de la Gran Piedra, Km.
14,* ☎ *226/5913. 22 cabins. Restaurant, bar, air-conditioning, kitch-
enettes, pool. MC, V.*

Outdoor Activities and Sports

For a cowboy rodeo Cuban style, stop by the **Finca Guajira Rodeo** (⊠
3 km/2 mi beyond the Playa Siboney turn-off onto Carretera de Baconao, opposite El Oasis, ☎ no phone). Competitions are held Tuesday, Thursday, Saturday, and Sunday at 2:30, and entrance costs $5.
Horseback rides are also available here.

Shopping

There are *artesanía* vendors nearly everywhere you look in Baconao.
Good-quality art is often sold (at good prices) beside roads. The artists

colony **El Oasis** (☞ *above*) is a logical shopping stop. Several artists keep their workshop/home/gallery open every day until around dusk. The artists are much more interesting than the professional gallery staffs in the city; prices are better than in the cities, too.

Guantánamo

30   *86 km (53 mi) northeast of Santiago.*

The eponymous provincial capital has been derided as a bore, and despite its scenic parks and aging plantation homes on wide palm-lined streets, the label seems to fit. The people here, however, are anything but boring. Much of the populace is descended from immigrants from Haiti, Jamaica, and other Caribbean nations, who came to cut cane in the late-18th and early 19th centuries. (Even today, some residents still speak English.) The town is the home base of the Orquestra Revé, and local musicians, who mix modern tropical music and traditional Afro-Cuban drumming known as *son-changuí,* play around town. The traditional lyrics to Cuba's most famous song, "Guantanamera," is about a beautiful woman from here.

The **Guantánamo Naval Base** rims the two entrances to Guantánamo Bay 25 km (16 mi) south of the capital. It's behind a virtual no-man's land of minefields and barbed wire. Your best chance of seeing it is from Alturas de Malone, high above the city. The United States has controlled the base since 1903, when it was granted an indefinite lease under the Platt Amendment. The terms were changed in 1939 but America remains in the role of an unwanted tenant, standing on extremely beneficial terms. It pays a bit more than $4,000 a year in rent, but the checks to the Cuban government remain uncashed (they're supposedly kept in one of Castro's desk drawers). Although closed to Cuba since Castro took power in 1959, the base has, in recent years, been used as a way station for Haitian and Cuban refugees. (A plan to house refugees from the Kosovo war here was scrapped as insensitive due to cultural and climatic differences between this tropical island and the refugees' Eastern European homeland.) Inside the base, the 7,000 military personnel and their families live with all the comforts of home, including a golf course, several pools, sports facilities, shopping malls, a McDonald's, an airport, and marina facilities.

Dining and Lodging

$ ✕▥ **Hotel Guantánamo** Although nondescript, this hotel is really the only game in town. The food and accommodations are adequate; rooms have satellite TV and other standard amenities. ✉ *Calle 13 y Calle Ahogado, Plaza Mariana Grajales,* ☎ *21/32–6015. 124 rooms. Restaurant, bar, air-conditioning, pool, shop, nightclub, travel services. MC, V.*

En Route   Beyond Guantánamo, the road to Baracoa skitters along a dry south-coast region with coves and small beaches cut into the rocky coastline. **Playa Yateritas** is one of the area's most popular beaches, with light sand and a protected coastline. **Cajobabo,** a town 45 km east of Guantánamo, was, on April 11, 1895, the landing site of José Martí and five other patriots who came to conquer Cuba after years of exile. A huge billboard points toward Playita Cajobabo, the beach where they landed. You'll find a museum with exhibits on the event as well as a restaurant here.

North of Cajobabo, the famous highway known as La Farola climbs the **Sierra del Purial** to Baracoa. It twists through deep valleys, slithers past cascading rivers, and winds over bare peaks. The many *miradores* (lookouts) along the way are good places for a picnic lunch. Near the

Close-Up

THE CUBAN AMERICANS

AFTER CASTRO'S REVOLUTION, thousands of Cubans fled the island. The first exiles were close associates of dictator Fulgencio Batista. But by late 1962, 250,000 Cubans—disenfranchised by Castro's austere reforms—had left their homeland. Most were white upper- and middle-class professionals. As Castro embraced communism, many of his fellow guerillas became disillusioned and also left; later, they were joined by gay Cubans, writers, and artists.

During the 1980 Mariel Boat Lift, the U.S. accepted thousands more Cubans; it was later discovered that many were convicts and other "undesirables" whom Castro had released from prisons and psychiatric wards. Since then, still more rank-and-file Cubans—including New York Yankees pitcher Orlando "El Duque" Hernández—have braved strong currents, bad weather, and sharks making the 90-mile journey to Florida on makeshift wooden rafts. Today, there are about 750,000 Cuban-born U.S. citizens, most of whom live in Miami, south Florida, New Jersey, and Puerto Rico.

Cuban-Americans have excelled at achieving the American dream while retaining their culture. Many frown on Castro and his regime, and such organizations as the Cuban American National Foundation have lobbied to keep the U.S. trade embargo in effect. Still, a growing number of Cuban-Americans believe that current U.S. policies are hurting Cuba more than those of Castro. Groups such as Cambio Cubano have called for an open dialogue with Castro to encourage democracy. To learn more about the current debates, contact the Center for Cuban Studies (124 W. 23rd St., New York, NY 10011, 212/242-0559), which publishes *Cuba Update*.

summit, the road passes through tall pine forests before dropping into tropical vegetation. At this point, you'll start to see roadside vendors selling fresh fruit, crafts, and cucurucho. As the road nears Baracoa, majestic El Yunque—a massive green mountain shelf—comes into view.

Baracoa

★ *164 km (102 mi) northeast of Guantánamo; 250 km (155 mi) northeast of Santiago.*

Cuba's first Spanish settlement was founded in 1512 by Diego Velázquez, who went on to settle six other cities. Today Baracoa is one of the island's most charming towns. Its historic center is bounded by three fortresses and El Malecón, a wide ocean-side roadway (La Farola runs into it) bordered by sea-grape trees and coral coastline on one side and buildings—some historic, some modern and sterile—on the other.

One of El Malecón's fortresses, **Fuerte Matachin,** was completed in 1802. Today it houses the **Museo Histórico Matachin,** whose displays discuss the history of the town, including its Taíno roots. There are examples of Taíno pottery, sculpture, and other artifacts; exhibits on Baracoa's famous citizens; and displays explaining the town's role in the wars of independence and the Revolution. ⊠ *Calle Martí y El Malecón,* ☎ *no phone.* 🎫 *$1.* ☯ *Daily 8–noon and 2–6.*

The **Plaza de Antonio Maceo Grajales** is a nice shady spot with a central monument to its namesake, a local general who fought in the Ten Years War. A block over, at another shady plaza on the malecón, is a striking monument to Columbus's landing. Cuba was Columbus's second stop on his first trip to the Americas, and Baracoans claim it was El Yunque that he described before landing. From here you can walk along the malecón, or hitch a ride on one of the horse-drawn carts—more utilitarian than charming—that ply the route.

NEED A BREAK?

While you're on the malecón, be sure to stop by the **Hotel La Rusa** (☞ Lodging, *below*), a charming guest house with a colorful history. In the lobby you can see some of the personal effects of the house's former owner, a Russian woman who fled the Bolshevik Revolution and wound up living in Baracoa, only to become a supporter of Castro's movement. There's a small bar-restaurant here with tables overlooking the water.

In Baracoa's historic heart, the **Plaza Independencia,** note the large bust of the Indian chief Hatuey—Cuba's first rebel—who fought against the Spanish and was burned at the stake for his audacity in 1512. The plaza is home to the **Catedral de Nuestra Señora de la Asunción** (✉ Calle Antonio Maceo 152). Built in 1833, the church is best known for possessing the Cruz de la Parra that Columbus supposedly used to name and claim Cuba for Spain. (Scientific tests have confirmed that it is, indeed, old enough to have been brought by the discoverer.) The cross is also said to have magical powers. Unfortunately, its magic doesn't extend to the church's opening hours; you can only visit during masses.

El Castillo de Seboruco, a fortress that now houses the Hotel El Castillo (☞ Dining and Lodging, *below*), dominates a hill overlooking the historic city. Although construction on it started in 1739, the fort wasn't finished until nearly 200 years later. Even if you don't stay here, stop by for the views of El Yunque and the city. Baracoa's third fortress, **Fuerte de la Punta,** was built in 1803 on a spit of land over the entrance to the bay. The fortress now contains the Restaurant La Punta (☞ Dining and Lodging, *below*).

Five kilometers (3 miles) west of town, where the Río Duaba empties into the sea, the **Duaba obelisk** marks the spot where Antonio Maceo landed with a group of rebels in 1885 during the Second War of Independence. The **Finca Duaba,** 7 km (4 mi) west of town, is a replica of a farm where you can get a taste of country life. It's full of tropical plants, trees, and crops such as coffee and bananas. You can also go horseback riding or take a swim in the Río Duaba here. A rustic restaurant serves a good comida criolla lunch for about $10 per person. ✉ *Ruta Duaba,* ☎ *no phone.* 🎟 *$1.* ✆ *Tues.–Sun. 9–4.*

About 40 km (65 mi) east of the city, the province narrows to its easternmost point, **Punta Maisí,** marked by a lighthouse and small village.

Dining and Lodging

$ ✕ **Restaurant La Punta.** At this restaurant in the Fuerte de la Punta you can dine on traditional food 24 hours a day. Tables are on a shady patio overlooking the harbor. You'll also find a crafts shop. ✉ *Av. Los Mártires,* ☎ *no phone.* MC, V.

$ ✕🏨 **Hotel Castillo.** El Castillo de Seboruco was renovated and trans-
★ formed into this charming hotel. Views are of Baracoa—from its quaint historic center to its malecón—El Yunque, and the sea. Even the pool and its terrace offer panoramic vistas. Rooms mix comfortable, classic antiques with modern conveniences, and the attentive staff provides top-notch service. The on-site Restaurant Duaba has an airy dining room and an outdoor patio overlooking the pool. This is *the* place to try Bara-

coa's famous (and flavorful) cuisine, more Caribbean than Cuban. Recommended dishes include *dorado a la Santa Barbara* (dolphinfish in a red coconut sauce) and *pollo en salsa caribeña* (chicken sautéed in a fruit and beer sauce). The full-course meal-of-the-day here costs a mere $8.95. ✉ *Calle Calixto García, Loma El Paraíso,* ☎ *21/214–2147,* FAX *21/214–2125. 34 rooms. Restaurant, 2 bars, pool, air-conditioning, shop, travel services, car rental. MC, V.*

$ 🏨 **Gaviota Villa Maguana.** For those seeking isolation this guest house is perfect. It sits on a beach rimmed with palm trees; the sands here are white, and the waters are protected by a cove. The house, which has a shady outdoor terrace and a TV lounge, has been spruced up under Gaviota management. Day-trippers can eat at the restaurant and enjoy the beach. As there are only four rooms, reservations should be made in advance through the Hotel Castillo or any Gaviota office. ✉ *Playa Maguana,* ☎ *no phone. 4 rooms. Restaurant, air-conditioning, refrigerators, beach. MC, V. BP.*

$ 🏨 **Hotel Port Santo.** Although this hotel is removed from the historic center, it's modern (rooms have satellite TV and other amenities), it's close to the airport, and it overlooks the bay. ✉ *Carretera del Aeropuerto,* ☎ *21/214–3578 or 21/214–3590. 63 rooms. Restaurant, bar, air-conditioning, pool, shop, travel services, car rental. MC, V.*

$ 🏨 **Hotel La Rusa.** The charming, rust-color La Rusa overlooks the oceanside malecón. It takes its name from its former owner, Mima Rebenskaya, a Russian immigrant who made it her home. The woman is the inspiration of Alejo Carpentiero's novel *The Rites of Spring.* Her guests included Errol Flynn and Che Guevara, not to mention El Comandante himself. The rooms have nice views. ✉ *Av. Máximo Gómez 161,* ☎ *21/43011. 13 rooms. Restaurant, bar, air-conditioning. MC, V.*

Nightlife and the Arts

The town band plays in Plaza Independencia every Sunday, and the adjacent Plaza Martí hosts weekend chess tournaments. You can often catch live-music shows at the **Casa de la Cultura** (✉ Calle Antonio Maceo 124, ☎ no phone). The **Casa de la Trova** (✉ Calle Antonio Maceo 149, ☎ no phone) is the best spot to hear live music. It's open nightly until about 2 AM, and admission costs $1. Listen for *el nengen* or *el kiribá,* two styles of music that predate the Cuban son. **Encanto Cine-Teatro** (✉ Calle Antonio Maceo 148, ☎ no phone) shows films nightly.

Outdoor Activities and Sports

BEACHES

About 20 km (12 mi) west of town, you'll find the lovely **Playa Maguana,** site of the Gaviota Villa Maguana hotel (☞ Dining and Lodging, *above*). A series of dark-sand beaches stretch east of Baracoa, and there's 30 km (19 mi) of good cement road along the coast. Right outside town you'll cross the Río Miel. Legend has it that after swimming in these waters, you'll fall in love in Baracoa and stay here forever. About 20 km (12 mi) east of town is **Playa Baragua,** one of the few light-sand beaches on this stretch. A few kilometers farther along, the road passes beneath a natural arc called the Túnel de los Alemanes (German's Tunnel) before ending 25 km (16 mi) east of Baracoa, at the Río Yumurí and the adjacent village by the same name. The river tumbles out of a steep canyon. Boats ferry passengers across the river and up into the canyon for nominal fees.

WHITE-WATER RAFTING

Baracoa has plenty to offer outdoor adventurers, including white-water rafting down the Río Toa. Gaviota runs a six-hour tour (minimum of four people) that costs about $16 per person.

HIKING

You can hike the mysterious El Yunque, an anvil-shape mountain covered in green jungle and mist. Gaviota offers an eight-hour trek (minimum of five people) for roughly $12 per person. If you don't want to break a sweat, you can take a half-hour plane tour of the area (also organized by Gaviota) for $22.

Shopping

The works of Baracoa's many fine artisans and painters are often influenced by their Taíno ancestry. They sell their creations along the malecón and in the city's plazas. **Galería Yara** (⊠ Calle Antonio Maceo 120, ☎ no phone) has an eclectic collection of paintings, jewelry, and crafts.

EASTERN CUBA A TO Z

Arriving and Departing

By Airplane

Holguín's **Aeropuerto Internacional Frank País** (☎ 24/46–2534) is just south of the city. A taxi into town costs $10, and transfers are available to both Holguín and Guardalavaca. The Cuban national airline, **Cubana** (⊠ Edificio Pico de Cristal, Parque Calixto García, Holguín, ☎ 24/42–5707), operates flights to Germany. The airport also sees a good deal of international charter-flight service.

Santiago's **Aeropuerto Internacional Antonio Maceo** (☎ 226/91–1014) is 8 km (5 mi) south of the city center; a taxi ride into town will cost about $10. **Havanatur** (⊠ Calle 8, No. 54, Vista Alegre, Santiago, ☎ 226/43603) operates an airport shuttle service, but you must make arrangements in advance; the costs are $15 round-trip, $10 one-way.

Canadian Airlines (☎ 416/207–3888 in Toronto) flies to Santiago from Toronto. **Cubana** (⊠ Calle Félix Peña/Santo Tomás 671, Santiago, ☎ 226/24156, or 226/20898; ⊠ Aeropuerto Antonio Maceo, ☎ 226/91014) provides direct service between Santiago and Madrid, Spain; Paris, France; and Frankfurt, Germany. **Sunholiday Tours** (☎ 809/952–5629 in Jamaica or 800/433–2920 in the United States) flies from Montego Bay, Jamaica to Santiago. **Taíno Air** (☎ 809/687–7114 in Santo Domingo) flies to Santiago from Santo Domingo, Dominican Republic, on Thursday and Sunday.

By Bus

Cuba's buses are crowded, poorly maintained, and slow—all this and tickets are still in great demand. Tourist buses, however, can take you on tours of all lengths. Most can be booked through your hotel or at local offices of Havanatur and other state travel agencies.

By Car

The main routes into and out of eastern Cuba are well maintained, and once you're out of the cities traffic is light (your biggest concern will be the occasional stray sheep or cow). Further, there are state-run Servi-Cupet gas stations spread out along major routes (many are open 24 hours and sell food and beverages; only dollars are accepted). Renting a car is the best way to cover vast distances, but you're better off hiring a car and driver for short journeys. Note that signage is poor, and it's easy to get mixed up when passing through a city. Ask directions: Cubans will gladly help you out of a mess.

The Autopista Nacional runs from Havana to Santiago (860 km/534 mi) as well as between Santiago and Camagüey, 325 km (202 mi) to the west. You're much more likely to take the northern highway to

Bayamo (127 km/79 mi) and then onward to Holguín (140 km/87 mi), the gateway to the north coast region. The stunning 200-km (124-mi) road that runs west from Santiago along the coast is squeezed between the Sierra Maestra mountain range and the Caribbean Sea. Equally impressive is the road east to Baracoa (250 km/155 mi), which runs along the arid coastline before turning north and becoming the famous La Farola highway, which winds through mountains.

By Train

There's an overnight *especial* train that runs between Havana and Santiago (once daily in both directions), with stops at major cities: Las Tunas, Camagüey, Ciego de Ávila, Santa Clara, and Matanzas. The trip takes about 15 hours. Taking the rail allows you to see a lot of the countryside, and on the fast trains, you'll find air-conditioning, reclining seats, and a food car.

Besides the daily overnight especial train to Havana there's rail service to Holguín, Bayamo, and Guantánamo. Most train stations are near a city's historic center. The one exception is Holguín, whose station is 15 km (9 mi) to the south in the town of Cacocum. Tickets can be bought at train stations.

Santiago's modern train station, the **Estación de Ferrocarriles** (⊠ Av. Jesús Menéndez) is on the harbor, six blocks west of Parque Céspedes.

Getting Around

By Airplane

Flying within Cuba is economical, and air routes connect most major cities in the country. Holguín and Santiago have international airports, and there are smaller airports in Bayamo, Guantánamo, and Baracoa. Cubana (☞ Arriving and Departing by Airplane, *above*) has several daily flights between Havana and Santiago and a daily flight between Havana and Holguín.

By Bus

In general, city buses aren't recommended. Shuttle and tour buses, however, are a good option (☞ Tour Operators and Travel Agents, *below*).

By Car

If you plan to rent a car, the two main agencies are **Havanautos** (☏ 266/86161 in Santiago, 24/33–5360 in Holguín, 21/43511 in Baracoa) and **Transautos** (☏ 266/33–5015 in Santiago, 24/48–1011 in Holguín).

By Taxi

Modern, well-maintained tourist taxis, which charge dollars, congregate in front of hotels, transportation hubs, and major sights. Private cabs with yellow plates are much cheaper, and you can hire them for a day of driving around town for about $25.

Contacts and Resources

Emergencies

Traveler's assistance for legal, financial, and medical problems is available through **Asistur** (⊠ Parque Céspedes, Santiago, ☏ 226/63–8284), which is open 24 hours a day.

Ambulance: (☏ 24/48–01640 in Holguín, 23/185 in Bayamo, 226/22848 in Santiago, 21/32–6013 in Guantánamo, 21/42472 in Baracoa). **Hospitals: Clínica Internacional** (⊠ Calle 13 y Calle 14, Vista Alegre, Santiago, ☏ 226/42589) is a medical clinic catering to foreigners, with an English-speaking staff on duty 24 hours a day. The clinic also has a fairly well-stocked pharmacy. In Guardalavaca, the **Clínica Internacional**

(☎ 24/30291) is at the entrance to town and is open 24 hours a day; consultations cost $20. In Holguín try **Hospital Lenin** (24/48–1640). **Pharmacies: Farmacia Las Américas** (✉ Av. Victoriano Garzón y Calle 10, Santiago) is open 24 hours a day. **Police:** ☎ 116.

Health and Safety
There's very little crime (tourists are particularly safe) in eastern Cuba. In Santiago you may be bothered by panhandlers, particularly around Parque Céspedes, or by young men wanting to serve as your guide or refer you to a casa particular or to a paladar. Ignore their advice, and try to remain polite. It's best to avoid tap water; bottled water is widely available.

Telephones and Mail
All major hotels have international phone service, and many have desks for international express mail. You can also make international calls at phone offices. Holguín's two **phone centers** (✉ Parque Calixto Garcí; ✉ Calle Martí y Calle Máximo Gómez) are open daily 8 AM–10 PM. Bayamo's **Centro Telefónico** (✉ Av. Miguel Enrico Capote y Calle Saco) is open daily 8 AM–11 PM. In Santiago, the **Centro de Llamadas Internacionales** (✉ Parque Céspedes) is open 24 hours a day. To make international calls in Guantánamo, your best bet is the **Hotel Guantánamo** (✉ Calle 13 y Calle Ahogado, Plaza Mariana Grajales, ☎ 21/32–6015). Baracoa's **post office/communications center** (✉ Calle Antonio Maceo 136, Plaza Independencia) is open daily 8 AM–10 PM.

Cuban mail, although affordable, is very slow; time-sensitive material should be sent by international mail services, such as **DHL** (✉ Hotel Pernik, Av. Dimitrov y Av. XX Aniversario, Holguín, ☎ 24/48–1984; ✉ Parque Céspedes, Santiago, ☎ 226/7795).

Tour Operators and Travel Agencies
Most major hotels throughout the region have tour desks where you can book everything from flights to rental cars to tours.

Santiago tour operators serve all the town's sights as well as such surrounding areas as Baconao and El Cobre. You can also arrange tours to Baracoa, Marea del Portillo, and Guardalavaca. Companies include **Fantástico Tours** (✉ Aeropuerto Internacional Antonio Maceo, ☎ 226/46–2534), **Havanatur** (✉ 54 Calle 8, Vista Alegre, ☎ 226/43603) and **Tour and Travel** (✉ Parque Céspedes, ☎ 266/86152).

Visitor Information
The tour desks (☞ Tour Operators and Travel Agencies, *above*) at major hotels throughout the region can provide you with travel information and assistance. Major state-run agencies include **Rumbos** (✉ Parque Céspedes, Santiago, ☎ 226/86973).

6 PORTRAITS OF CUBA

Cuba at a Glance: A Chronology

Cuban Music: Irresistible Rhythms

Ideas and Images

CUBA AT A GLANCE: A CHRONOLOGY

1000 B.C. Guanahatabey Indians (possibly from the southeastern United States) begin to populate Cuba.

A.D. 900 Ciboney Indians (a South American Arawak group) begin arriving, gradually pushing the Guanahatabeyes to the western third of the island.

1400s During the middle of the century, Taíno Indians (another, more advanced Arawak group) settle on the island; later in the century, Carib Indians (a warlike group believed to be from South America) challenge the Taíno, though they never actually settle on the island.

1492 Christopher Columbus, commissioned by King Ferdinand and Queen Isabella of Spain, "discovers" Cuba and claims it for the Spanish crown. Columbus believes he has discovered a shorter trade route to the Far East. At the time of his landing, the indigenous population is an estimated 112,000.

1508 Sebastian de Ocampo circumnavigates Cuba and determines that it is an island and not, as Columbus had suggested, part of the Asian mainland.

1511 Diego Velázquez arrives from Hispaniola with 300 soldiers and establishes the settlement of Baracoa. Velázquez becomes governor of Cuba; by some accounts, he was given the appointment by the Crown, by others, he simply took the title upon himself. By any account, Velázquez was responsible for the conquering of the island's native people, including the great chieftain Hatuey.

1514 Havana is founded.

1520 Three hundred slaves arrive from Africa.

1538 The seat of government is moved to Havana.

1555 The French pirate Jacques de Sores burns Havana. This attack is one of many—by pirates seeking loot for themselves or buccaneers seeking booty for other European nations—that will occur in Cuba over the next 100 years. The Spanish monopoly of the island's imports and exports encourages some islanders to become involved in smuggling. Cuba's indigenous population now numbers 5,000; its African population is roughly 800.

1728 A university is established in Havana.

1740 Government authorities create the Real Compañía de Comercio to handle all Cuban imports and exports. The monopoly buys Cuban goods at a fixed price and resells them elsewhere at a tidy profit. The seeds of discontent among Creole (Cuban-born Spaniards) farmers and manufacturers—sown earlier by such monopolies—begin to grow.

1762 England captures Havana after a three-month attack at the end of the Seven Years' War (French and Indian War), during which Spain has been France's ally against England. The most important legacy left by the English during their brief occupation of the city is the removal of Spain's crippling trade restrictions. The English relinquish Havana to Spain in exchange for the territory of Florida.

1762–1870 Roughly 700,000 African slaves are brought to Cuba (most between 1811 and 1870) as sugar supplants cattle and tobacco as the country's major commodity.

1763 The first Cuban newspaper is published.

1764 Cuba's postal service is initiated.

1848 U.S. President James Polk offers $100 million for Cuba. Spain declines the offer.

1854 U.S. President Franklin Pierce makes an unsuccessful $130 million bid for the island. By this time, Cuba accounts for a third of the world's sugar production.

1868 The Ten Years' War, the first Cuban attempt at revolution against Spanish rule, begins when Carlos Manuel de Céspedes issues the Grito de Yara (like the U.S. Declaration of Independence) on his plantation in eastern Cuba. It is largely a guerilla war—led on the political front by Céspedes and on the military front by the Dominican-born Máximo Gómez and the Cuban-born mulatto Antonio Maceo—and results in 200,000 deaths before the Treaty of El Zanjón is negotiated in 1878. The treaty guarantees a list of government reforms.

1886 Slavery is officially abolished.

1890–1895 American trade with and investment in Cuba increases significantly, particularly in relation to the sugar industry.

1892 The great poet, journalist, and lawyer José Martí founds the Partido Revolucionario Cubano (Cuban Revolutionary Party) and begins collaborating with Gómez and Maceo.

1893 Equal civil status of blacks and whites is proclaimed.

1895 Led by Martí, Gómez, and Maceo, Cuban rebels—angered by Spain's refusal to make reforms that had been promised at the end of the Ten Years' War—begin the Second War of Independence. Martí is killed in May, on his first day in battle.

1898 The U.S.S. *Maine* explodes in Havana Harbor, precipitating the Spanish-American War. This war lasts for less than four months, and Spain's loss marks the end of its holdings in the Caribbean.

1899 Cuba becomes an independent republic under U.S. protection.

1901 The U.S. congress approves the Platt Amendment. Among its provisions are that the United States may institute military intervention in Cuba and that the United States will buy or lease land for a military installation on Cuban soil. Cuba accepts the terms of this amendment, though not without controversy.

1902–17 Although the U.S. occupation ends in 1902, U.S. involvement in Cuban affairs does not. As the fledgling nation hits political rough spots that threaten its stability, the Platt Amendment is invoked in 1912 and again in 1917.

1920 Sugar prices plummet. With the Cuban economy in turmoil, U.S. investors capitalize on cheap property.

1920–30 Cuban students and other intellectuals begin calling for political, economic, and education reforms. A period of *cubanismo* (Cuban nationalism) begins as do calls for an end to the Platt Amendment and U.S. meddling. Student leader Julio Antonio Mella and others found the Cuban Communist Party in 1925.

1928 President Gerardo Machado, who had been in power for four years, has the constitution changed to allow a six- rather than four-year presidential term. As the only candidate in a bogus election in April of that year, he continues as Cuba's president (although his policies of persecuting critics—particularly students—make him seem more of a dictator to many islanders).

1929 While in exile in Mexico, Mella mysteriously dies (many point the finger at Machado) and becomes a martyr for the Cuban reform movement.

1933 President Machado is overthrown in a revolt led by Fulgencio Batista, then an army sergeant. The new government makes shocking changes. Among them are the establishment of a Department of Labor; the institution of women's suffrage; the opening of the university to all, regardless of income; and the nullification of the Platt Amendment (except for the lease of the naval base at Guantánamo).

1934 The Universidad de la Habana (University of Havana) is reopened after a three-year suspension of classes.

1940 After having ruled—since 1934—through a series of puppet presidents, Batista is elected president.

1945 Cuba becomes a member of the United Nations.

1950 Fidel Castro graduates from the University of Havana with a law degree after having, as both an undergraduate and graduate student, participated in revolutionary activities throughout Latin America. He is nominated to run as the Orthodox Party's candidate to Cuba's House of Representatives.

1952 Eight years after retiring, Fulgencio Batista takes over the government, cancels the upcoming elections, and institutes a police state. Castro's political career is put on hold, and his career as a Cuban revolutionary leader begins.

1953 Castro heads a failed attack on the Moncada Army Barracks in eastern Cuba on July 26. Most of the attackers are killed. Castro is arrested and sentenced to 15 years in jail on the Isla de la Juventud.

1955 Batista grants amnesty to all political prisoners in Cuba. Upon his release, Castro sets out for Mexico.

1956 Castro and 81 would-be rebels sail from Mexico to Cuba aboard the yacht *Granma*. Their boat is met in Oriente Province by Batista's men. Only a handful of rebels, including Ernesto "Che" Guevara and Castro's brother Raúl, survive the landing. The rebels proceed to the jungle of the Sierra Maestra, where they establish their headquarters.

1957 The rebels win a series of small skirmishes. Public sentiment sways their way as the brutality of Batista's regime is made known to the world.

1958 Guevara leads the rebel capture of the central Cuban provincial capital of Santa Clara.

1959 Batista flees to the Dominican Republic on New Year's Day. Castro and his followers march to Havana, where they take control of the Cuban government.

1960 A game of political and economic cat-and-mouse ensues among Cuba, the United States, and the Soviet Union. After Castro signs a trade agreement with the U.S.S.R., U.S. oil companies based in Cuba refuse to refine the crude oil that's part of that trade agreement. In response, Castro nationalizes the American oil companies; America cancels the balance of Cuba's sugar quota; Castro appropriates all U.S. businesses and landholdings; the Soviets agree to purchase the balance of the U.S. sugar quota.

1961 In January, the U.S. government breaks relations with Cuba. Castro allies himself with the Soviet Union. In April, U.S.-trained Cuban exiles are deployed in the Bahía de Cochinos (Bay of Pigs) Invasion. It is expected that the invasion will spur a revolt against Castro. It does not.

1962 In late October the Soviet intent to install mid-range missiles in Cuba leads to a U.S. naval blockade of the island. The so-called Cuban Missile Crisis is resolved when the sites are ordered dismantled and shipped back to the Soviet Union by Soviet premier Nikita Khruschev. In return, U.S. president John F. Kennedy promises not to attack Cuba. Trade embargoes are imposed.

1963 U.S. citizens are prohibited from traveling to Cuba, and conducting business with Cuba becomes illegal.

1965–67 Guevara leaves Cuba in 1965 to fight with rebel forces in the Congo. From Africa, he travels to Bolivia, where he joins another rebel army. He and his guerrillas are captured and executed by the Bolivian army on October 9, 1967.

1976 Castro is elected president, and a socialist constitution is approved. Castro turns his attention to the international stage, and especially to Africa. For the next several years, Cuban troops are sent abroad.

1980 The Mariel Boat Lift results in an influx of 125,000 Cuban refugees to the United States. It's later discovered that many of those permitted to leave Cuba during this exodus were criminals, residents of psychiatric hospitals, and other "undesirables."

1988 Cuba withdraws its troops from Angola and strikes a peace accord with South Africa.

1991 Following the collapse of the U.S.S.R., Soviet troops are withdrawn from Cuba. In the early 1990s, Castro declares a "Special Period in Time of Peace" and calls for Cubans to practice belt-tightening austerity as Soviet economic support disappears.

1994 Another refugee exodus results in a revision of U.S. immigration policy regarding Cuban asylum-seekers.

1996 Castro receives an audience with Pope John Paul II at the Vatican. Cuban fighter planes attack an aircraft flying for the humanitarian organization Hermanos al Rescate (Brothers to the Rescue). In angry response, the United States passes the Helms-Burton Act, stating that the United States will not trade with any other country doing business with Cuba.

1997 For the first time since the Revolution, Christmas is declared an official holiday in Cuba. Also in that year, Che Guevara's remains are found, identified, and transported to Cuba for burial at a monument in the central province of Santa Clara.

1998 Pope John Paul II visits Cuba. Discussion in the U.S. government continues about the possibility of lifting the ban on travel to and doing business with Cuba.

1999 Elian Gonzalez, a 5-year-old Cuban boy, is rescued off the coast of Florida in November. When it's discovered that his mother and stepfather died during their attempt to reach the United States, an international custody battle ensues. Castro stages protests calling for the boy's return to his biological father in Cuba, and the anti-Castro community in America lobbies loudly for him to stay with his mother's relatives in Florida.

CUBAN MUSIC: IRRESISTIBLE RHYTHMS

THE COURTYARD OF A nineteenth-century mansion-cum-restaurant rings with the music of an acoustic trio as they perform a spirited rendition of Compay Segundo's "Chan Chan" for a tour group. The percussionist's fluid hands work the taut skins of his drums, the guitarist rocks and strums with the quickening beat, and the *tres* player's fingers dance over the frets of his instrument—his right hand plucking a tinny melody on its double strings. As the tres solo winds down, the musicians belt out the song's refrain: "De Alto Cedro voy para Marcané, Luego a Ceto voy para Mayarí" ("From Alto Cedro I head to Marcané, Then to Ceto and on to Mayarí").

Their performance of that popular ode to itinerancy would be enough to pack a midsize nightclub in any northern metropolis, and the song's shuffling rhythm has the waiters swaying and tapping their feet, but the tourists hardly look up from their lunches. Perhaps they missed the album and film *Buena Vista Social Club,* both of which begin with that same song. Perhaps they missed breakfast. Whatever the reason for their indifference, they wouldn't be the first visitors to start taking Cuban music for granted—good music is so common on the island that some travelers simply come to expect it.

Wherever you go in Cuba, you're likely to encounter some tantalizing tropical sound, be it the mellifluous harmonies of a guitar trio, the brassy refrains of a salsa band, or the irresistible rhythms of an Afro-Caribbean drum-and-dance troupe. Music is Cuba's pulse, and though the crumbling buildings and bus lines may give the impression of a nation suffering from some geriatric ailment, you need only step into a dance club or enjoy an impromptu concert at a Casa de la Trova to confirm Cuba's eternal youth. The number of musicians on the island seems surpassed only by the number of cigars, and there's hardly a citizen who doesn't dance.

Cuban music may have gained unprecedented popularity in North America and Europe following the release of the *Buena Vista Social Club,* but within Latin America, the island has been synonymous with good music for nearly a century. Cuban styles, artists, and dance steps have dominated the airwaves and nightclubs of Latin American for decades, especially during the 1940s and '50s. As a music center, Havana stands shoulder to shoulder with Mexico City, Buenos Aires, and Rio de Janeiro—cities several times its size.

The group of veteran performers who collaborated on the Grammy-winning album *Buena Vista Social Club* drew on a vast and varied musical heritage. Subsequent solo albums by such Buena Vista luminaries as Compay Segundo, Ibrahim Ferrer, and Rubén González dug deeper into the island's rhythmic gold mine, but in musical terms, there's plenty more going on in Cuba. Such living legends as Segundo and González may be the deans of Cuban music, but theirs is a university with campuses in every town and alumni on every street.

At the heart of Cuban music is a marriage of African and European traditions, the roots of which stretch back to the days when Havana was one of Spain's principal New World ports and when one of the most important cargoes was human. African slaves brought with them the songs, dances, and rituals of their ancestors, which formed the basis for most of the island's musical styles. Cuba's two disparate musical traditions were originally kept separate—on Sunday, while the colonists danced the latest steps from France, the slave quarters pulsated with the drum beats of mother Africa—but it didn't take long for fusion to begin.

The Spanish taught the Africans to play European instruments and styles, creating slave bands to entertain them. Slaves with talent saw in music a chance to escape the drudgery of manual labor and an opportunity for upward mobility. (In fact, a colonial census of 1827 found that more than half of Havana's musicians were black.) Spain provided the language and most of the instruments, but Africa gave Cuban music its soul. Even today, when a salsa band performs at a popular Havana dance club, and the packed dance floor resembles a stormy sea of flesh, it is Africa who reigns over the moment; Europe is a mere footman.

The fact that slaves from the same ethnicities were allowed to live together in groups called *cabildos* helped to preserve distinctive African languages and cultures. These cabildos were allowed to take their music to the streets of Havana and other cities on Christmas Eve and the Epiphany (January 6). Such colorful celebrations were a popular subject of 19th-century engravings, which portray throngs of blacks in masks and elaborate costumes, drumming, dancing, and holding pagan idols on poles over crowds. Although these spectacles offended conservatives (they were banned on several occasions in the late 19th and early 20th centuries) the tradition survived in the *carnavales* (carnivals) of Havana and Santiago, the *parrandas* (Christmas Eve parades) of Remedios, and in the private rituals of Santería and the public *danzas afrocubanas* performed throughout the island.

The streets of Cuba's major cities have served as cradle and stage for many a musical form, such as the *guaracha,* a lively genre characterized by a shuffling rhythm and satirical, risqué lyrics. (The sexual innuendo common in guaracha lyrics is nothing new—back in 1801, an anonymous chronicler criticized the vulgarity of the guarachas he heard on the streets of Havana.) One of the 20th century's great guaracha composers was Ñico Saquito, whose humorous songs such as "Maria Cristina" and "Adios Compay Gato" are in the repertoires of most Cuban musicians, and whose protégé Compay Segundo has brought the genre to a wider audience in recent years.

Another genre born in the streets is the *pregón,* which was inspired by the melodic announcements of *pregoneros,* ambulant vendors who sang about their wares as they wandered the city. Among the most popular pregóns are "Frutas de Caney"; several 1950s hits of Celia Cruz and the Sonora Matancera, such as "Crocante Habanero"; and "El Manisero," a 1940s classic composed by Moisés Simmons and made famous by Rita Montaner.

The genre most closely associated with rural Cuba is the *guajira* (which is related to the style called *canción*), a rhythmic song with lyrics about country life (the words *guajiro/guajira* mean "man/woman from the country"). Ñico Saquito also composed many guajiras, but the most famous one, "Guantanamera," was the work of Joseíto Fernandez. When sung anywhere other than Cuba, its lyrics are taken from a poem by José Martí, but when Fernandez popularized this song on his weekly radio show, he always invented new words. It consequently has countless verses and is often used by Cuban musicians as a vehicle for poetic improvisation.

In the early part of the 20th century, the *bolero* (a descendent of the songs of the troubadours) was hot all over Latin America, popularized by such silver-voiced crooners as the Mexican Agustín Lara and the Puerto Rican Daniel Santos. Boleros remain quite popular in Cuba and are played by everything from guitar duos to dance bands. Their lyrics are largely romantic; some of the best provide melodramatic testimony to the ravages of unrequited love.

Lyrics may be sentimental or humorous, but a song's most important aspect is usually its rhythm; more than listening to music, Cubans like to dance to it. Most of the island's musical genres are danceable, and some, such as the *danzón,* were born in the dance hall. Created in the western city of Matanzas in the late 1800s, the rhythmic, sensual danzón was the craze of the early 20th century, with its smooth violin and flute melodies, syncopated bass, and piano improvisation. It, in turn, begot the *chachacha,* (a genre created by band leader Enrique Jorrín in response to the way people moved to danzón) and the *mambo* (a style that made greater use of syncopation, percussion, and horns).

Another of the 20th century's major genres was the *son,* a versatile dance rhythm that originated in the eastern cities, and eventually replaced danzón in Cuban dance halls. Like the danzón, the son had its roots in the 19th century, but reached its glory during the first half of the 20th century when the phonograph and radio helped Cuban artists reach audiences all over the world. During the 1920s and '30s, the island experienced a boom in musical acts and venues. American jazz began to influence Cuban composers, and the country exported such major stars as singer Rita Montaner, who performed on both stage and screen; vivacious pianist, singer, and composer Bola de Nieve (Snow Ball); and the Trio Matamoros, the most successful of the island's many guitar trios and duos.

As vibrant as the '20s and '30s were, Cuban music reached its acme during the '40s and '50s—the reign of the mambo and son. The American big-band sound began to influence Cuban music in the '40s, and the horn sections of the country's dance orchestras expanded. One composer who was profoundly influenced by jazz was Dámasco Pérez Prado, dubbed "El Rey del Mambo" (The Mambo King). Pérez Prado composed wild, distinctive instrumental pieces with unimaginative titles such as "Mambo No. 8," and was famous for the way he grunted and shouted to the music. A protégé of Pérez Prado named Benny Moré founded his own orchestra in 1950, and went on to become one of the country's most popular performers. A tall, thin man with a dark complexion and penchant for wearing large hats, Moré was the king of son, and like Prado, was influenced by American jazz. But Cuban performers also had an impact on the music scene to the north, especially the percussionist and composer Chano Pozo, who went to New York in 1946 and sowed the seeds of Latin jazz.

One of Cuba's greatest dance bands in the '40s and '50s was the Sonora Matancera, which worked with most of the island's best singers, though none better than Celia Cruz. Her musical career has endured more than half a century, and she remains a living legend of Latin music, but Cruz never topped her work with the Sonora Matancera in the '50s. Perhaps that was due to the energy of Havana during that decade, and the amazing quality of its musicians.

Like many Cuban musicians, Cruz and her band emigrated following the 1959 Revolution, when the nation's musical focus shifted from dance hits to political ballads. But even Cuban protest music is danceable,

such as that of Carlos Puebla, the revolutionary songster whose paean to Che Guevara, "Hasta Siempre," remains one of the country's most popular songs. The '60s and '70s marked the rise of *nueva trova,* a less rhythmic genre known for the quality and political consciousness of its lyrics. Cuba's two great *trovadores,* Silvio Rodríguez and Pablo Milanés, became immensely popular throughout Latin America, but they're as much poets as musicians, which makes it difficult for non-Spanish speakers to fully appreciate their genius.

In the past few decades the island's musicians have kept abreast of developments in Latin music. Cuba has plenty of excellent salsa bands, such as the legendary Los Van Van, which was founded in the '70s, and the younger-but-popular Charanga Habanera. The island has also remained on the forefront of Latin jazz, producing such outstanding musicians as Chucho Valdéz, Arturo Sandoval, and Paquito de Rivera, the three of whom played together in the group Irakere, and the latter two of whom emigrated years ago, as did the gifted pianist Gonzalo Rubalcaba.

Even after three centuries of musical evolution and an impressive selection of sounds, young Cuban artists continue to experiment with rock, reggae, and rap—blending them with older but no less vital styles—to create still more new genres. One band that does a provocative job of spanning the centuries is Síntesis, which melds, to great effect, ancient African rhythms with Latin rock and salsa. But then, the secret of Cuban music has always been its variations on traditional themes, which is why the island's musical future is bound to be a reflection of its remarkable past.

—by David Dudenhoefer

IDEAS AND IMAGES

The Written Word

Havana's literary life, despite the restrictions on freedom of expression set forth in 1961 by El Comandante himself ("Within the Revolution, everything. Against the Revolution, nothing!"), seems vibrant and vigorous. Cuba and Havana in particular have always been inspirational to such writers as Cirilo Villaverde, José Martí, Graham Greene, Ernest Hemingway, Alejo Carpentier, and Guillermo Cabrera Infante. Drama, conflict, and eros steam from every crack and crevice in this Caribbean pressure cooker, a place where revolution and romance seem to make it hard *not* to write.

Nonfiction

A Reader's Companion to Cuba, edited by Alan Ryan, is a collection of colorful travel essays by such visitors to Cuba as Anthony Trollope, Frederic Remington, Anaïs Nin, Langston Hughes, Tommy Lasorda, Thomas Merton, and James Michener. Kenneth Triester's *Habaneros: Photographs of the People of Havana* was intended to be a photographic journal of Havana's architecture, but Triester's fascination with the city's people became the subject of this visual essay. Andrei Codrescu, a National Public Radio commentator and author—himself an exile of post-Communist Romania—ventured to Cuba in 1998 on the eve of the Papal visit. He spent nearly two weeks interviewing farmers and scholars, prostitutes and politicians, to produce *Ay, Cuba: A Socio-Erotic Journey,* a very human, very informative picture of "pre-post-Communist" Cuba. In *Havana Dreams* Wendy Gimbel shows how the lives of four generations of women in one Cuban family are swept up in and transformed forever by the Revolution. Of the many books on Che, John Lee Anderson's *Che Guevara: A Revolutionary Life* is among the more recent, well-researched, and balanced.

For a comprehensive (though dry) overview of the island, pick up *Cuba: A Short History,* edited by Leslie Bethell as part of *The Cambridge History of Latin America* series. Not as dry but just as comprehensive is *Cuba: From Columbus to Castro and Beyond* by Jaime Suchlicki. The Cuban Missile Crisis was a turning point in the uneasy history between Cuba and America. Robert F. Kennedy's *Thirteen Days: A Memoir of the Cuban Missile Crisis* provides an insider's view of the standoff. *The Kennedy Tapes: Inside the White House During the Cuban Missile Crisis* offers that view in the words of still other men who were there. And for that dictator's-eye-view you just can't get anywhere else, Fidel Castro himself is the author of more than 30 publications—books, speeches, and pamphlets. Some of these are out of print but may be available through on-line booksellers such as Amazon.com or Barnesandnoble.com.

Baseball fans will want to read *The Pride of Havana: A History of Cuban Baseball,* a lively mixture of politics and sport by Cuban-born author Roberto Gonzalez Echevarria. William P. Mara's *Cubans: The Ultimate Cigars* delves into the history and near-mythical appeal of Cuban cigars. For those of an epicurean mind, *A Taste of Old Cuba: More than 150 Recipes for Delicious, Authentic, and Traditional Dishes Highlighted with Reflections and Reminiscences,* by Maria Josefa Lluria de O'Higgins, and *The Flavor of Cuba: Traditional Recipes from the Cuban Kitchen,* by Laura Milera, may whet your appetite.

Fiction

As many an Ernest Hemingway fan will tell you, Papa wrote the bulk of his lifework in Cuba over a period of 20 years, including *For Whom the Bell Tolls, To Have and Have Not, The Green Hills of Africa, Across the River and into the Trees, A Moveable Feast,* and *Islands in the Stream.* Zoe Valdés (*I Gave You All I Had, Cafe Nostalgia,* and *Yocandra in the Paradise of Nada: A Novel of Cuba*) and Guillermo Cabrera Infante (*Holy Smoke, Infante's Inferno, Mea Cuba,* and *Three Trapped Tigers*), exiled in, respectively, Paris and London, are among the most important, contemporary, anti-Castro novelists. Miguel Barnet (*Biography of a Runaway Slave* and *Rachel's Song*) may well be the most famous novelist living in Havana.

In *Havana Bay,* by Martin Cruz Smith (author of *Gorky Park*), a Russian detective is sent to contemporary Havana to investigate the death of a colleague. Cristina García's *Dreaming in Cuban* is a novel about revolution, separation, and, of course, dreams. *Cuba and the Night* is travel writer Pico Iyer's first attempt at fiction. The setting is Cuba, the theme is love. *Cubana: Contemporary Fiction by Cuban Women* is an anthology of 16 stories offering insight into the hearts of Cubanas and their contemporary world. Abilio Estevez's *Thine Is The Kingdom: A Novel* is a massive undertaking with a tremendous cast of colorful characters set in pre-revolutionary Havana.

John Blackthorn—a pseudonym for, as the book jackets state, "a political figure whose name is known in international capitals and intelligence circles"—has written two suspenseful novels on Cuba. An American historian finds himself caught between the Cold War past and a frightening future in *Sins of the Fathers*. In *I, Che Guevara* a novel of intrigue set in contemporary Cuba, Castro steps down, two rival political parties emerge, and a mysterious elderly man (who might possibly be Che) begins making speeches around the island.

Captured on Camera

Cuban Cinema

Cuba's cinema industry—spearheaded by the Instituto Cubano del Arte y la Industria Cinematografica (ICAIC; Cuban Institute of Art and Cinematography)—was originally established to create documentaries, newsreels, and feature films designed to spread Revolutionary ideology throughout Cuba and the Third World. But the ICAIC has accomplished so much more.

Two men, Colombian Nobel prize–winning novelist Gabriel García Marquez and Filmoteca director Alfredo Guevara have been key factors in the success story of Cuban film. Guevara (no relation to Che) is one of Havana's most important personalities, a dedicated Communist Party member and Castro crony who has miraculously managed to get films critical of the regime made and shown. García Marquez encouraged Castro to found the international film school in San Antonio de los Baños just south of Havana in 1986. With the sponsorship of Latin American filmmakers and the participation of García Marquez himself (who teaches screenwriting courses), the school has turned out a generation of fine filmmakers.

ICAIC production company chief Camilo Vives predicts that Cuba will continue to make three to five films annually as long as co-production with other, more solvent, countries remains possible. When asked about the degree of freedom of expression permitted in Cuban cinema, Vives responded with a question of his own: "Is there truly free cinema anywhere? In Hollywood, for example, there are commercial considerations that obviously establish limits on what can be made. As is easily confirmable, there is a reasonable level of social criticism in Cuban films, perhaps more than there might be in a so-called free (and free market) system. And in the ongoing daily debate over how best to allocate funds here, the arts—cinema included—don't do too badly in Cuba. I can think of a lot of places where, in hard times, support for the arts would be the first thing to go."

Must-See Movies

In *Fresa y Chocolate* (*Strawberry and Chocolate*), Cuban director Tomás Gutiérrez Alea (who died in 1996) tells the tale of Diego, a young Cuban homosexual who falls in love with David, a young Cuban heterosexual with all the prejudices associated with the Communist doctrine. Understanding and friendship eventually chip away at ideology. (An interesting follow-up to this drama would be the documentary, *Gay Cuba,* an in-depth exploration of the lives of gays and lesbians on the island through the century. It focuses on the negative changes wrought by the Revolution, and the positive ones brought by education and growing tolerance in recent times.) In Alea's satire *Guantanamera,* a former university professor travels westward across the country to Havana with the body of her aunt and her funeral-director/bureaucrat husband. On the way, she repeatedly encounters a former student (who has become a truck driver) and both of them uncover some interesting truths about life, love, and themselves.

On video, *Soy Cuba* (*I Am Cuba*), made its U.S. debut in 1995. Originally released in 1964, it was a Cuban-Soviet coproduction. Awe at the nearly impossibly sophisticated camera work of this anti-America propaganda film will be tempered by the clear view of hindsight (the propaganda seems naive and ineffective) and by the phonetically speaking "Americans."

Buena Vista Social Club, the biggest music and cinema phenomenon to come out of Cuba since *Fresa y Chocolate,* is Wim Wender's 1999 cinematic follow-up to Ry Cooder's tuneful collaboration with the Buena Vista Social Club, a legendary pre-Revolutionary Cuban musical group. Having discovered a group of brilliant semi-retired, out-of-work musicians in Havana in 1996, Cooder became interested in the quality of their music and recorded a compact disk he passed along to Wenders while they were working together on the 1997 film *The End of Violence.* Wenders became intrigued with this "very young music made by some very old people" and filmed, among others, Ibrahim Ferrer (81), Compay Segundo (91), Ruben Gonzalez (80), and Pío Levy (82) playing and discussing their music in Havana, Amsterdam, and New York. The result? More than 1.5 million albums sold and a runaway box office hit. Segundo, who gave a standing-room-only solo concert at Barcelona's Palau de la Musica in June of 1999, attributes his longevity to "a cigar at breakfast, rum with dinner, and being constantly in love." All in all, this musical documentary eloquently mixes music with impressionistic flashes of city life in contemporary Cuba. The concert scenes filmed in Amsterdam and New York portray a stage so full of irrepressible joy that it becomes impossible to miss the point: in Cuba making music is a powerful physical and spiritual tonic.

If you need more of a musical fix, *A Night in Havana: Dizzy Gillespie in Cuba* captures the trumpeter's 1985 appearance in the fifth annual International Jazz Festival of Havana. The documentary includes Gillespie's explication of the Afro-Cuban musical connection meshed with performance footage.

Cuba has given many European and American commercial filmmakers an idea or two in the past 50 years. If you haven't read Graham Greene's book be sure to rent the video: *Our Man in Havana* is a Cold War classic. The kiss from one brother to another in Havana on, literally, the eve of the Revolution is one of dozens of indelible images from *The Godfather, Part II.* In the 1979 action-adventure flick *Cuba,* Sean Connery plays a man hired to train the Batistas to fight against Castro's guerillas. Sydney Pollack's 1990 film *Havana* sees a professional gambler (Robert Redford) visit Cuba on the cusp of Batista's downfall. En route to the island, he meets and falls in love with a woman who is inextricably connected to the Revolution.

SPANISH VOCABULARY

Words and Phrases

English	Spanish	Pronunciation

Basics

English	Spanish	Pronunciation
Yes/no	Sí/no	see/no
Please	Por favor	pore fah-**vore**
May I?	¿Me permite?	may pair-**mee**-tay
Thank you (very much)	(Muchas) gracias	(**moo**-chas) **grah**-see-as
You're welcome	De nada	day **nah**-dah
Excuse me	Con permiso	con pair-**mee**-so
Pardon me	¿Perdón?	pair-**dohn**
Could you tell me?	¿Podría decirme?	po-dree-ah deh-**seer**-meh
I'm sorry	Lo siento	lo see-**en**-to
Good morning!	¡Buenos días!	**bway**-nohs **dee**-ahs
Good afternoon!	¡Buenas tardes!	**bway**-nahs **tar**-dess
Good evening!	¡Buenas noches!	**bway**-nahs **no**-chess
Goodbye!	¡Adiós!/¡Hasta luego!	ah-dee-**ohss/ah**-stah-**lwe**-go
Mr./Mrs.	Señor/Señora	sen-**yor**/sen-**yohr**-ah
Miss	Señorita	sen-yo-**ree**-tah
Pleased to meet you	Mucho gusto	**moo**-cho **goose**-to
How are you?	¿Cómo está usted?	**ko**-mo es-**tah** oo-**sted**
Very well, thank you.	Muy bien, gracias.	**moo**-ee bee-**en**, **grah**-see-as
And you?	¿Y usted?	ee oos-**ted**
Hello (on the telephone)	Diga	**dee**-gah

Numbers

1	un, uno	oon, **oo**-no
2	dos	dos
3	tres	tress
4	cuatro	**kwah**-tro
5	cinco	**sink**-oh
6	seis	saice
7	siete	see-**et**-eh
8	ocho	**o**-cho
9	nueve	new-**eh**-vey
10	diez	dee-**es**
11	once	**ohn**-seh
12	doce	**doh**-seh
13	trece	**treh**-seh
14	catorce	ka-**tohr**-seh

15	quince	**keen**-seh
16	dieciséis	dee-**es**-ee-**saice**
17	diecisiete	dee-**es**-ee-see-**et**-eh
18	dieciocho	dee-**es**-ee-**o**-cho
19	diecinueve	**dee-es**-ee-new-**ev**-ah
20	veinte	**vain**-teh
21	veinte y uno/veintiuno	**vain**-te-**oo**-noh
30	treinta	**train**-tah
32	treinta y dos	train-tay-**dohs**
40	cuarenta	kwah-**ren**-tah
43	cuarenta y tres	kwah-**ren**-tay-**tress**
50	cincuenta	seen-**kwen**-tah
54	cincuenta y cuatro	seen-**kwen**-tay **kwah**-tro
60	sesenta	sess-**en**-tah
65	sesenta y cinco	sess-**en**-tay **seen**-ko
70	setenta	set-**en**-tah
76	setenta y seis	set-**en**-tay **saice**
80	ochenta	oh-**chen**-tah
87	ochenta y siete	oh-**chen**-tay see-**yet**-eh
90	noventa	no-**ven**-tah
98	noventa y ocho	no-**ven**-tah-**o**-choh
100	cien	see-**en**
101	ciento uno	see-**en**-toh **oo**-noh
200	doscientos	doh-see-**en**-tohss
500	quinientos	keen-**yen**-tohss
700	setecientos	set-eh-see-**en**-tohss
900	novecientos	no-veh-see-**en**-tohss
1,000	mil	meel
2,000	dos mil	dohs meel
1,000,000	un millón	oon meel-**yohn**

Colors

black	negro	**neh**-groh
blue	azul	ah-**sool**
brown	café	kah-**feh**
green	verde	**ver**-deh
pink	rosa	**ro**-sah
purple	morado	mo-**rah**-doh
orange	naranja	na-**rahn**-hah
red	rojo	**roh**-hoh
white	blanco	**blahn**-koh
yellow	amarillo	ah-mah-**ree**-yoh

Days of the Week

Sunday	domingo	doe-**meen**-goh
Monday	lunes	**loo**-ness
Tuesday	martes	**mahr**-tess
Wednesday	miércoles	me-**air**-koh-less
Thursday	jueves	hoo-**ev**-ess

Friday	viernes	vee-**air**-ness
Saturday	sábado	**sah**-bah-doh

Months

January	enero	eh-**neh**-roh
February	febrero	feh-**breh**-roh
March	marzo	**mahr**-soh
April	abril	ah-**breel**
May	mayo	**my**-oh
June	junio	**hoo**-nee-oh
July	julio	**hoo**-lee-yoh
August	agosto	ah-**ghost**-toh
September	septiembre	sep-tee-**em**-breh
October	octubre	oak-**too**-breh
November	noviembre	no-vee-**em**-breh
December	diciembre	dee-see-**em**-breh

Useful phrases

Do you speak English?	¿Habla usted inglés?	**ah**-blah oos-**ted** in-**glehs**
I don't speak Spanish	No hablo español	no **ah**-bloh es-pahn-**yol**
I don't understand (you)	No entiendo	no en-tee-**en**-doh
I understand (you)	Entiendo	en-tee-**en**-doh
I don't know	No sé	no seh
I am American/British	Soy americano (americana)/ inglés(a)	soy ah-meh-ree-**kah**-no (ah-meh-ree-**kah**-nah)/ in-**glehs** (**ah**)
What's your name?	¿Cómo se llama usted?	koh-mo seh **yah**-mah oos-**ted**?
My name is . . .	Me llamo . . .	may **yah**-moh
What time is it?	¿Qué hora es?	keh **o**-rah es?
It is one, two, three . . . o'clock.	Es la una. . . . Son las dos, tres	es la **oo**-nah/sohn lahs dohs, tress
Yes, please/No, thank you	Sí, por favor/No, gracias	**see** pohr fah-**vor**/no **grah**-see-us
How?	¿Cómo?	**koh**-mo?
When?	¿Cuándo?	**kwahn**-doh?
This/Next week	Esta semana/ la semana que entra	**es**-teh seh-**mah**-nah/lah seh-**mah**-nah keh **en**-trah
This/Next month	Este mes/el próximo mes	**es**-teh mehs/el **proke**-see-mo mehs
This/Next year	Este año/el año que viene	**es**-teh **ahn**-yo/el **ahn**-yo keh vee-**yen**-ay
Yesterday/today/ tomorrow	Ayer/hoy/mañana	ah-**yehr**/oy/mahn-**yah**-nah
This morning/ afternoon	Esta mañana/ tarde	**es**-tah mahn-**yah**-nah/**tar**-deh

Tonight	Esta noche	**es**-tah **no**-cheh
What?	¿Qué?	keh?
What is it?	¿Qué es esto?	keh es **es**-toh
Why?	¿Por qué?	pore **keh**
Who?	¿Quién?	kee-**yen**
Where is . . . ?	¿Dónde está . . . ?	**dohn**-deh es-**tah**
the train station?	la estación del tren?	la es-tah-see-**on** del **train**
the subway station?	la estación del Tren subterráneo?	la es-ta-see-**on** del trehn soob-tair-**ron**-a-o
the bus stop?	la parada del autobus?	la pah-**rah**-dah del oh-toh-**boos**
the post office?	la oficina de correos?	la oh-fee-**see**-nah deh koh-**reh**-os
the bank?	el banco?	el **bahn**-koh
the . . . hotel?	el hotel . . . ?	el oh-**tel**
the store?	la tienda . . . ?	la tee-**en**-dah
the cashier?	la caja?	la **kah**-hah
the . . . museum?	el museo . . . ?	el moo-**seh**-oh
the hospital?	el hospital?	el ohss-pee-**tal**
the elevator?	el ascensor?	el ah-**sen**-sohr
the bathroom?	el baño?	el **bahn**-yoh
Here/there	Aquí/allá	ah-**key**/ah-**yah**
Open/closed	Abierto/cerrado	ah-bee-**er**-toh/ ser-**ah**-doh
Left/right	Izquierda/derecha	iss-key-**er**-dah/ dare-**eh**-chah
Straight ahead	Derecho	dare-**eh**-choh
Is it near/far?	¿Está cerca/lejos?	es-**tah sehr**-kah/ **leh**-hoss
I'd like . . . a room	Quisiera . . . un cuarto/una habitación	kee-see-ehr-ah oon **kwahr**-toh/ **oo**-nah ah-bee-tah-see-**on**
the key	la llave	lah **yah**-veh
a newspaper	un periódico	oon pehr-ee-**oh**-dee-koh
a stamp	un sello de correo	oon **seh**-yo deh koh-**reh**-oh
I'd like to buy . . .	Quisiera comprar . . .	kee-see-**ehr**-ah kohm-**prahr**
cigarette	cigarrillo	ce-ga-**ree**-yoh
matches	cerillos	ser-**ee**-ohs
a dictionary	un diccionario	oon deek-see-oh-**nah**-ree-oh
soap	jabón	hah-**bohn**
sunglasses	gafas de sol	**ga**-fahs deh sohl
suntan lotion	loción bronceadora	loh-see-**ohn** brohn-seh-ah-**do**-rah
a map	un mapa	oon **mah**-pah
a magazine	una revista	**oon**-ah reh-**veess**-tah

paper	papel	pah-**pel**
envelopes	sobres	**so**-brehs
a postcard	una tarjeta postal	**oon**-ah tar-**het**-ah post-**ahl**
How much is it?	¿Cuánto cuesta?	**kwahn**-toh **kwes**-tah
It's expensive/ cheap	Está caro/barato	es-**tah kah**-roh/ bah-**rah**-toh
A little/a lot	Un poquito/ mucho	oon poh-**kee**-toh/ **moo**-choh
More/less	Más/menos	mahss/**men**-ohss
Enough/too much/too little	Suficiente/ demasiado/ muy poco	soo-fee-see-**en**-teh/ deh-mah-see-**ah**-doh/**moo**-ee **poh**-koh
Telephone	Teléfono	tel-**ef**-oh-no
Telegram	Telegrama	teh-leh-**grah**-mah
I am ill	Estoy enfermo(a)	es-**toy** en-**fehr**-moh(mah)
Please call a doctor	Por favor llame a un medico	pohr fah-**vor ya**-meh ah oon **med**-ee-koh
Help!	¡Auxilio! ¡Ayuda! ¡Socorro!	owk-**see**-lee-oh/ ah-**yoo**-dah/ soh-**kohr**-roh
Fire!	¡Incendio!	en-**sen**-dee-oo
Caution!/Look out!	¡Cuidado!	kwee-**dah**-doh

On the Road

Avenue	Avenida	ah-ven-**ee**-dah
Broad, tree-lined boulevard	Bulevar	boo-leh-**var**
Fertile plain	Vega	**veh**-gah
Highway	Carretera	car-reh-**ter**-ah
Mountain pass, Street	Puerto Calle	poo-**ehr**-toh **cah**-yeh
Waterfront promenade	Rambla	**rahm**-blah
Wharf	Embarcadero	em-bar-cah-**deh**-ro

In Town

Cathedral	Catedral	cah-teh-**dral**
Church	Templo/Iglesia	**tem**-plo/ee-**glehs**-see-ah
City hall	Casa de gobierno	kah-sah deh go-bee-**ehr**-no
Door, gate	Puerta portón	poo-**ehr**-tah por-**ton**
Entrance/exit	Entrada/salida	en-**trah**-dah/sah-**lee**-dah
Inn, rustic bar, or restaurant	Taverna	tah-**vehr**-nah
Main square	Plaza principal	plah-thah prin-see-**pahl**

Market	Mercado	mer-**kah**-doh
Neighborhood	Barrio	**bahr**-ree-o
Traffic circle	Glorieta	glor-ee-**eh**-tah
Wine cellar, wine bar, or wine shop	Bodega	boh-**deh**-gah

Dining Out

A bottle of . . .	Una botella de . . .	**oo**-nah bo-**teh**-yah deh
A cup of . . .	Una taza de . . .	**oo**-nah **tah**-thah deh
A glass of . . .	Un vaso de . . .	oon **vah**-so deh
Ashtray	Un cenicero	oon sen-ee-**seh**-roh
Bill/check	La cuenta	lah **kwen**-tah
Bread	El pan	el pahn
Breakfast	El desayuno	el deh-sah-**yoon**-oh
Butter	La mantequilla	lah man-teh-**key**-yah
Cheers!	¡Salud!	sah-**lood**
Cocktail	Un aperitivo	oon ah-pehr-ee-**tee**-voh
Dinner	La cena	lah **seh**-nah
Dish	Un plato	oon **plah**-toh
Menu of the day	Menú del día	meh-**noo** del **dee**-ah
Enjoy!	¡Buen provecho!	bwehn pro-**veh**-cho
Fixed-price menu	Menú fijo o turistico	meh-**noo fee**-hoh oh too-**ree**-stee-coh
Fork	El tenedor	el ten-eh-**dor**
Is the tip included?	¿Está incluida la propina?	es-**tah** in-cloo-**ee**-dah lah pro-**pee**-nah
Knife	El cuchillo	el koo-**chee**-yo
Large portion of savory snacks	Raciónes	rah-see-**oh**-nehs
Lunch	La comida	lah koh-**mee**-dah
Menu	La carta, el menú	lah **cart**-ah, el meh-**noo**
Napkin	La servilleta	lah sehr-vee-**yet**-ah
Pepper	La pimienta	lah pee-me-**en**-tah
Please give me	Por favor déme	pore fah-**vor deh**-meh
Salt	La sal	lah sahl
Savory snacks	Tapas	**tah**-pahs
Spoon	Una cuchara	**oo**-nah koo-**chah**-rah
Sugar	El azúcar	el ah-**thu**-kar
Waiter!/Waitress!	¡Por favor Señor/Señorita!	pohr fah-**vor** sen-**yor**/sen-yor-**ee**-tah

INDEX

NOTES

NOTES

NOTES

NOTES

NOTES

NOTES

NOTES

NOTES

Fodor's

Looking for a different kind of vacation?

Fodor's makes it easy with a full line of specialty guidebooks to suit a variety of interests—from adventure to romance to language help.

Fodor's. For the world of ways you travel.